Programmed Writing

A Self-Administered Approach for Interventions with Individuals, Couples, and Families

Brooks/Cole Professional Books
Consulting Editor: C. Eugene Walker, University of Oklahoma

Family Therapy and Beyond: A Multisystemic Approach to Treating the Behavior Problems of Children and Adolescents
Scott W. Henggeler and Charles M. Borduin

Changing Expectations: A Key to Effective Psychotherapy
Irving Kirsch

Panic Disorder and Agoraphobia: A Comprehensive Guide for the Practitioner
Editors: John R. Walker, G. Ron Norton, and Colin A. Ross

The History of Clinical Psychology in Autobiography
Editor: C. Eugene Walker

Programmed Writing: A Self-Administered Approach for Interventions with Individuals, Couples, and Families
Luciano L'Abate, in collaboration with Janet Cox

Programmed Writing
A Self-Administered Approach for Interventions with Individuals, Couples, and Families

Luciano L'Abate

In collaboration with

Janet Cox

Brooks/Cole Publishing Company
Pacific Grove, California

Brooks/Cole Publishing Company
A Division of Wadsworth, Inc.

Printed in the United States of America
10 9 8 7 6 5 4 3 2 1

Library of Congress Cataloging in Publication Data
L'Abate, Luciano, [date]
   Programmed writing : a self-administered approach for interventions
with individuals, couples, and families / Luciano L'Abate and Janet
Cox.
       p.   cm.
   Includes bibliographical references and index.
   ISBN 0-534-14484-5
   1. Creative writing—Therapeutic use. I. Cox, Janet. II. Title.
RC489.W75L33 1991
616.89' 16—dc20   90-27793
                                                          CIP

Sponsoring Editor: *Claire Verduin*
Editorial Associate: *Gay C. Bond*
Production Editor: *Linda Loba*
Manuscript Editor: *Lorraine Anderson*
Permissions Editor: *Mary Kay Hancharick*
Interior and Cover Design: *Katherine Minerva*
Typesetting: *ExecuStaff*
Cover Printing: *Phoenix Color Corporation*
Printing and Binding: *Arcata Graphics/Fairfield*

This book is dedicated to the work of
Dan MacDougald, J. D.,
who started the whole process of using programmed
self-instructional materials with individuals more
than a generation ago.

PREFACE

For too long has talk—the verbal medium—dominated the psychotherapeutic enterprise, to the point that the two—talk and psychotherapy—have become synonymous. It is time for therapists to challenge this hegemonic equation and offer ourselves and our clients options and alternatives based on the written medium. The skyrocketing costs of health care and the inevitable increases in costs for professional time raise the question of whether we can find cost-effective alternatives to expensive face-to-face professional-client contacts. Is it possible to help people in need of our services with a minimum or modicum of personal contact, leaving up to them the major responsibility for change and progress in their lives? Can we combine synergistically both the verbal and the written media for a betterment of the human condition?

Writing has a distinguished history of being used for therapeutic or para-therapeutic purposes. In fact, it may be used by more therapists than we know or suspect. Yet, it has not received the professional interest and systematic use it deserves as an adjunct or even as an alternative to face-to-face, verbally based, professional-client contacts. If we stress the importance and useful-ness of the written medium, this emphasis in no way means a denial of the importance of the verbal medium. Yet we must not forget that many people drop out of the therapeutic enterprise or never come back after one or two sessions. Why is that? Could it be that we are not giving them choices and options? Can we offer them professional services at a cheaper rate than for face-to-face contacts, no matter how important those contacts may seem? Is face-to-face contact necessary for behavioral change? We would argue that some people profit by these contacts. However, for each person who stays and profits by these prolonged personal, verbal contacts, there are many other persons who do not. Could the latter profit from being exposed to alternative solutions, like working with a professional or semiprofessional in writing at a distance through the mail? We believe that writing offers this alternative. However, we of the professional mental health community have not yet fully exposed and explored writing. We need to find its limits just as we have found the limits of the verbal medium for therapeutic purposes. Who will benefit by writing? Who will benefit by talking? Who will benefit by a combination of both? Who will benefit by neither?

The use of writing for therapeutic or paratherapeutic purposes inevitably will be rejected by therapists who believe that the therapist-client relationship is the very basis, if not the only basis, for change. Therapists who stress the unique importance of the relationship at the expense of any other possibly helpful methodology usually also reject the importance of evaluation of the outcome of their interventions. The number of therapists who think this way may decrease. The community and those responsible for third-party payments, like insurance companies, without which the whole psychotherapeutic enterprise would not even exist, will start demanding cost-effective methods of intervention. These cost-effective methods involve more active involvement and responsibility from our clients, a burden that perhaps can be better documented in writing than through the spoken word.

Once the advantages of the written medium become known and established, it may become a method of intervention of choice for some individuals and an adjunct for others. Writing does furnish a decided advantage over speaking, and that is the possibility of directly linking evaluation to intervention. Hence, the use of writing offers a potential solution to the well-known nomothetic-idiographic and descriptive-prescriptive controversies. Once we link evaluation to intervention we can use a nomothetic method—programmed writing—that can be tailor-made and administered idiographically to our clients, as will be shown here. Writing enables us to do what speaking cannot. It permits us to link nomothetic and idiographic, descriptive and prescriptive, in a way that will combine synergistically the verbal and the written media. This combination is bound to offer more options to therapists as well as to our clients. That was and is our major goal. We hope we have succeeded.

The authors would like to thank the following reviewers for their helpful suggestions: Dr. Donald K. Freedheim, Case Western Reserve University, Cleveland, Ohio; Dr. Allan Hedberg, Fresno, California; and Dr. Arthur N. Wiens, Oregon Health Sciences Center, Portland, Oregon.

Luciano L'Abate
Janet Cox

CONTENTS

PART I

Understanding the Use of Programmed Writing

CHAPTER ONE

What Is Programmed Writing?

The purpose of this chapter and this text is to introduce the use of programmed writing as an additional or alternative way to help people at risk for possible breakdown, in need of preventive services, and in crisis. Programmed writing is a way of intervening with individuals, couples, and families by assigning structured, self-administered, self-instructional, systematically written lessons as regular homework. A sequence of questions concerning a topic or an issue makes up a lesson. A sequence of lessons linked by a topic constitutes a workbook. These lessons are completed by each individual, couple, or family, either alone or together, depending on the assignment. Individual answers are discussed first between partners or among family members and later reviewed with the help of a professional therapist, facilitator, counselor, or trainer.

Thus, programmed writing consists of lessons or series of lessons that are assigned to be completed at home. These written homework assignments are focused on specific topics relevant to the client's issues. Even though programmed writing is self-administered, completed assignments need scrutiny by the professional helper. The professional looks over the written answers and provides feedback either face to face or through written correspondence. The written assignments are used as a springboard for further discussion and exploration in the professional's office, and ideally, in the respondents' home, among themselves if they are a couple or a family. Generalizations, distortions, omissions, and other errors in thinking are pointed out by the helper and worked on face to face or through additional homework assignments. Consequently, programmed writing tends to extend the professional helper's influence outside of the office and into the home or workplace.

Although our experience with programmed writing has been thus far strictly personal (L'Abate, 1986b, 1987a, 1987b, 1987c, 1990a), we have been impressed by its usefulness in helping us deal with specific problems that usually require a great deal of the professional helper's time and energy, and consequently result in higher costs for psychotherapeutic or preventive mental health services. Still, its impact on the overall therapeutic and preventive outcome has yet to be fully recognized outside of the experience of a few clinicians, and its potential for improving the welfare of many people remains essentially untapped.

Writing as Secondary Prevention

Writing can be used either in conjunction with other forms of intervention or as the only form of intervention at a particular stage of treatment or in certain therapeutic or preventive contexts. Writing in general has the potential to increase the efficiency and effectiveness of therapy or preventive intervention. It can be used in addition or as an alternative to traditional verbal psychotherapies or preventive approaches.

Writing in general and programmed writing as defined here can be considered a type of secondary prevention. It can be used either preliminary to, preparatory to, in parallel with, or after either primary or tertiary prevention. It is *pre-, para-,* or *posttherapeutic* when it is administered *in addition or as an alternative* to tertiary prevention (that is, therapy) and *parapreventive* when it is used with or in place of primary prevention approaches (Johnson, Levis, & L'Abate, 1986; L'Abate, 1986b, 1990a).

Primary prevention consists of psychoeducational programs aimed at people who are at risk for a worsening of their conditions. Such programs vary in degree of structure, ranging from structured enrichment programs to various individual, premarital, marital, and family skill training programs (L'Abate, 1986a; L'Abate & Milan, 1985; Levant, 1986). Programmed writing is deemed *parapreventive* to the extent that it takes place alongside primary prevention approaches.

By definition, therapy (that is, tertiary prevention) is the face-to-face process that occurs between an individual, a couple, or a family and a professional helper based on a contract that the professional will help the client(s) with whatever psychological problems are brought to the professional's attention. Hence, writing is *paratherapeutic* to the extent that an experienced and knowledgeable professional assigns it and looks it over, using it to get more knowledge about the respondent(s) and to ask further questions, bringing up issues evoked by the answers, correcting and pointing out pitfalls in the inevitable omissions, distortions, and generalizations typical of answers from people in crisis, in need, or at risk.

Because programmed writing falls in between the process of psychoeducational skill training (primary prevention) and of therapy (tertiary prevention), it constitutes one type of secondary prevention (L'Abate, 1990a). Along the continuum of preventive approaches from primary to secondary and then to tertiary, writing can be used independently of other verbal and nonverbal interventions. Writing in general as a means of intervention consists of assigning self-paced, self-administered written homework varying in degree of structure and in content. Programmed writing is the most structured of all homework assignments relying on writing as a medium of communication between client(s) and professional helpers.

As noted in the preceding paragraphs, a real dichotomy has existed between assumedly preventive and so-called therapeutic activities (L'Abate, 1986a; Mace, 1983). The use of workbooks as paratherapeutic instruments of secondary prevention aims to blur this distinction. Instead of reinforcing the dichotomy of primary versus tertiary prevention, programmed materials make it easy to conceive of a whole continuum of interventional activities, ranging from nothing to hospitalization. As we discuss in greater detail in Chapter 5, a whole continuum of nonoverlapping interventions can take place between the preventive and the therapeutic extremes. Programmed materials, for example, can be administered as the sole form of intervention for preventive purposes, as in high schools with juveniles at risk for dropping out of school or with depressed adolescents at risk for suicide or drug dependency. In conjunction with various psychotherapies or medication, programmed materials can be administered to increase synergistically the chances for therapeutic change.

Programmed Writing and the Laboratory Method

Programmed writing is an application of the laboratory method in clinical psychology (L'Abate, 1968a, 1969, 1973, in preparation). This method seeks to evaluate and intervene with individuals, couples, and families through the help of semiprofessionals, like graduate students, and paraprofessional intermediaries, such as volunteers, former patients, part-time workers, students. These personnel use standard operating procedures for evaluation and intervention, with the support and supervision of a more experienced professional. This approach attempts to combine practice with research and to link theory with practice (L'Abate, 1986b, 1987, 1987b, 1987c, 1990a). Other applications of this method have dealt with the evaluation of individuals (children and adults), couples, and families (L'Abate, 1968b; L'Abate & Wagner, 1985, 1988), monitored play therapy for children (L'Abate, 1979), and structured enrichment for functional and semifunctional couples and families, one of the many approaches in primary prevention (L'Abate & Weinstein, 1987; L'Abate & Young, 1987).

Through the laboratory method, it is possible to operate idiographically with clients and at the same time collect nomothetically cumulative records that attest to the validity of a given viewpoint or approach. Instead of favoring one of two diametrically opposed conceptual positions—for instance, the aesthetic versus the pragmatic—one can help in ways that combine both positions. One can be a practitioner, using personal intervention styles in the therapy session, and at the same time be a "scientist," collecting repeatable data, without diminishing the importance of one position at the expense of the other. For example, the practice of programmed writing does not violate the practice of therapy as applied by each individual therapist. It is possible to create written homework assignments and workbooks that derive either from theory (L'Abate, 1986b, 1990a) or from practice, or, as we shall see, from existing self-help books. The personnel implications of this approach will be discussed in greater detail in Chapter 5 and in Part II.

When these written homework assignments and workbooks are also coupled with the help of subprofessional personnel and with psychoeducational programs, one can (or should) obtain verifiable results at a much lower cost than for traditional therapeutic practices. Instead of research and practice remaining two separate enterprises, as they are now, the use of the laboratory method makes it possible to combine research and practice without doing an injustice to either one (Calam & Elliott, 1987).

Programmed materials should be sharply differentiated from training manuals. The former are for the use of patients, clients, or offenders, and require a series of written answers to specific questions. The latter are used exclusively for the training of psychotherapists (Lambert, Shapiro, & Bergin, 1986; Matarazzo & Patterson, 1986). The purposes of both kinds of approaches are the same: to standardize procedures, thus making psychotherapy and behavior change more amenable to evaluation and empirical testing. Recently, Kazdin, Kratochwill, and VandenBos (1986) advocated the use of treatment manuals as one way of promoting "generality of research findings to clinical practice" (p. 393). Programmed writing goes one step further, enabling evaluation of the comparative outcome of specific therapeutic approaches that have been reduced to a question-answer format.

Toward a Classification of Writing

Writing assignments can be classified according to their structure, content, and specificity. Structure encompasses a range of at least four possibilities—open, focused, guided, and programmed—varying along a continuum from least to most structured. Content may range from a focus on symptomatic behaviors, such as anxiety or depression, to issues of identity and of intimacy. There is virtually no topic that cannot be dealt with in writing that is not already dealt with in speaking. In fact, some people reveal more in writing than they can disclose orally. Specificity usually goes hand in hand with structure—that is, the greater the structure, the greater the specificity and explicitness.

At the extreme of least structure and specificity is *open writing.* The instructions about content are general: "Write about anything that comes to your mind," as in a diary or journal (Baker, 1988). In this case the helper wants to see how this assignment is handled with a minimum of structure or demands. From the information received from this source, the helper can suggest continuation of writing in an open style ("to see what happens") or proceed to the next step in structure.

The next step in increasing the structure of writing is *focused writing:* "Write whatever comes to your mind when you make yourself depressed (anxious, fearful, tense) at a set time and for a set duration." By definition, writing an autobiography would be considered a focused activity. From reading this information, the professional may ask the client to narrow the focus. To deal with issues of identity, for example, it may be helpful to have clients write about their five major roles—as children, as single adults (personhood), as married adults (partnership), as parents, and as parents to one's parents, under three temporal conditions (past, present, and future).

Birren and Hedlund (1987), for instance, advocate the use of journals and autobiographies for students as well as for geriatric patients, and maintain that autobiography is most useful when it is guided. Their advocacy, however, is not paired with any kind of evidence. They review the history of and rationale for the use of biography, including methodological issues, but fail to acknowledge Progoff's contribution (1975, 1980), as well as that of many other pioneers who preceded them. For example, the use of autobiography and of other personal documents was advocated by Gordon Allport as early as 1942, and the autobiographical movement itself has historical roots as far back as the seventeenth century.

Wrightsman (1988) reviews the use of autobiography, and discusses many individual reasons for writing an autobiography: special pleading, exhibitionism, desire for order, literary delight, securing a personal perspective, relief from tension, redemption and social reincorporation, monetary gain, assignment, assisting in therapy, scientific interest, public service and example, and desire for immortality (pp. 257–263). An autobiography, like all verbal, nonverbal, or written expressions, is subject to various sources of possible distortion: self-deception or unintentional self-justification, blindness to one's own motives, oversimplification, effects of mood, unreliability of self-report, errors of memory, implicitness and arbitrariness of conceptualization, scarcity of available documents, and expense in producing and analyzing (Wrightsman, 1988, pp. 265–269).

The third step in increasing the structure of writing is what de Vries, Birren, and Deutchman (1990) call *guided writing*. At this step, the helper assigns specific topics, such as "Major Life Branching Points" or "History of Your Sexual Development." These topics may be based on what has been written in a focused vein, or on answers to questions asked beforehand ("Here are some questions about depression that you need to answer"). The articles by Birren and Hedlund (1987) and by Baker (1988) are recommended for therapists who want to start using open, focused, or guided writing as an additional or alternative paratherapeutic approach.

The last step in specificity and explicitness is *programmed writing* of the kind promoted here, consisting of a systematic series of various lessons on a particular topic to be completed at home over a period of time. While instructions for open, focused, or guided writing can be given verbally, those for programmed writing are written down. The number of lessons varies from a minimum of three to as many as are necessary to deal with whatever troublesome problem or symptom is presented to the professional (Johnson, Levis, & L'Abate, 1986; L'Abate, 1986b, 1987a, 1987b, 1987c, 1990a; L'Abate and Platzman, in press).

The topics about which one can write on a focused, guided, or programmed basis are as varied as the human condition. Nevertheless, certain topics seem to repeat themselves, relating to symptomatic behaviors—such as anxiety and depression, anger, arguing and fighting—and to issues of identity and of intimacy.

History of Writing as a Substitute for or an Adjunct to Psychotherapy

Writing as a form of therapeutic intervention does not have an especially long, rich, or varied history.

A review of the field of psychotherapy and of primary prevention shows that writing has not often been used as an adjuvant in the process of helping people in trouble. At best, writing has been used for single-shot, ad hoc purposes or to log behavior (Baucom & Epstein, 1990; Lange & van der Hart, 1983; McMullin, 1986; Norcross, 1986; Primakoff, Epstein, & Covi, 1986; Shelton & Levy, 1981). It is not mentioned at all in leading reviews of therapy (Garfield & Bergin, 1978, 1986; Gurman & Kniskern, 1981). As we shall see, its potential to help people at risk for trouble or already in trouble remains virtually untapped. The situation is not different now from what it was more than a quarter of a century ago, when Phillips and Wiener (1966) commented: "Writing has apparently seldom been used as the modality for psychotherapy; references are few and thin" (p. 160).

Freud was influenced by creative writing techniques in developing his method of free association (Monte, 1980, p. 63). In addition to the early suggestions of Allport (1942) about therapeutic use of autobiographical writing, cited at length by Wrightsman (1988, pp. 268–273), use of written autobiographies by college and high school students as a paratherapeutic or parapreventive modality is discussed by Ricci (1958) and Shaffer (1954). The earliest references to the clinical usefulness of writing can be found in Landsman (1951), Messinger (1952), Farber (1953), and Widroe and Davidson (1961). Ellis (1955, 1965) and Pearson (1965) devoted a whole American Psychological Association symposium to this topic (Raimy, 1965). In that symposium, Burton (1965) advocated written productions as adjuncts to therapy as a way of fostering therapeutic growth. On the other hand, Burton enumerated a number of potential disadvantages of psychotherapists' use of written communication, which will be mentioned in Chapter 2.

Self-instructional manuals were used extensively in the 1970s by behavioral therapists. More than a decade ago, in fact, Glasgow and Rosen (1978), who reviewed most of the literature on their use, noted that "the validation of available self-help behavior therapy manuals is extremely variable at the present time" (p. 11). Most of the self-instructional training (SIT) approaches used by cognitive and cognitive-behavioral therapists consists mostly of simple, specific, and short verbal instructions handed out to clients on an ad hoc basis, without reliance on writing or on the therapist's feedback.

Haley has reported a case of overcoming a writing block through the assignment of regular writing periods (1984, pp. 192–194). Gelcer and Schwartzbein (1989) comment from a Piagetian viewpoint on how the use of keeping notes on the part of parents receiving Selvini-Palazzoli's invariant prescription will help improve their cognitive skills (Selvini-Palazzoli, Cirillo, Selvini, & Sorrentino, 1989). Kelley and Williams (1988) recommend the use of "assigned writing" as adjunct to therapy, while Solly and Lloyd (1989) recommend it for "recovery and spiritual growth." All of these reports, unfortunately, are mostly impressionistic.

Because the use of writing in psychotherapy and prevention is relatively new, it has meager empirical support as yet. Support for it, outside of evidence gathered in the first author's laboratory (L'Abate, 1977, 1990a), can be found in a 1966 study by Phillips and Wiener and in a substantial body of work by Pennebaker (1989a, 1989b) and his associates (Pennebaker & Beall, 1986; Pennebaker, Colder, & Sharp, 1990; Pennebaker, Hughes, & O'Heron, 1987;

Pennebaker, Kiecolt-Glaser, & Glaser, 1988), which up to the present represents the best source of evidence supporting the use of writing as an alternative or additional source of help for people.

Pennebaker's research contribution highlighting the use of writing in primary prevention is crucially important for an advocacy of writing as a paratherapeutic adjunct. He found that undergraduates who wrote on painful topics for 20 minutes a day for four days showed lower white cell counts and fewer physical symptoms three months later than students who wrote about trivial topics.

The use of homework assignments has been discussed by L'Abate (1986b) and by L'Abate, Ganahl, and Hansen (1986). Written homework assignments were found by these researchers to be nearly as effective in helping clients in nonclinical samples as combinations of homework assignments and structured enrichment. Approximately two-thirds of various samples in different studies improved with homework assignments alone, while an even greater percentage improved with the combination of face-to-face structured enrichment and homework assignments (L'Abate, 1977, 1990a).

The most important and pioneering work on the paratherapeutic effectiveness of writing remains the study by Phillips and Wiener (1966, pp. 130–135, 159–185), who investigated writing under controlled conditions. They demonstrated that it was possible (and apparently therapeutic) to help students in a university counseling center using written notes between student and therapist without face-to-face contact. Referring to a master's thesis by Test (1964) and an abstract by Phillips, Test, and Adams (1964), they evaluated three groups, using the Minnesota Multiphasic Personality Inventory (MMPI), the Edwards Personal Preference Schedule (EPPS), the Butler-Haigh Q-Sort, the Otis Self-Administering Intelligence Test, and a personal data sheet, all of which were used before and after treatment. All the students were applicants to a university counseling service. One group ($N = 11$) received group therapy, a second group ($N = 8$) received individual therapy, and a third group ($N = 12$) received what the authors called "writing therapy." All communication between the student and the therapist in the third group took place in writing, without any visual or oral contact between the student and the therapist. The student communicated with the therapist only through written notes about his or her problems, and the therapist answered in writing. Students would leave their notebooks in a particular place, finding the therapist's comments when the notebook was returned to them from one week to the next. Subjects in each group received an equal number of sessions (ten), and a control (no-therapy) group was evaluated on a pre-post basis. The control group of 16 showed the greatest number of dropouts—eight, a 50% attrition rate. In the other three experimental groups, the attrition rate was 16%.

Those who received group therapy did not show any reliable changes on the MMPI or on the Butler-Haigh Q-Sort. On the EPPS, significant pre-post changes were found on Deference ($p < .05$) and Aggression ($p < .01$). Somewhat less reliable improvements ($p < .05$) were found on the Affiliation and the Endurance subscales. Grade point average also improved, from C– to B– ($p < .01$). Those who received individual therapy showed significant changes on the Depression, Psychasthenia, and Schizophrenia subscales of the

MMPI. On the Edwards there were changes on the Aggression, Endurance, Abasement, Dominance, Succorance, and Autonomy subscales at various levels of significance. The third group—those involved in writing therapy—showed the largest number of changes, and the most significant ones. On the MMPI, significant improvements were found on the Depression, Psychasthenia, Psychopathic Deviate, Schizophrenia, and Social Introversion subscales. On the EPPS, changes were obtained on the Heterosexuality and the Abasement subscales; on the Butler-Haigh Q-Sort, congruence increased, and the self-ideal discrepancy shifted. The control (no-therapy) group also showed significant changes on these paper-and-pencil tests, decreasing considerably the validity of the results. The authors rationalized these changes in terms of the fact that the eight dropouts were not included in the analysis and speculated that the remaining eight controls may have been psychologically healthier and thus may have improved without intervention.

On the basis of this admittedly exploratory study and their tentative, if not questionable, results, Phillips and Wiener (1966) considered writing therapy as "a new approach to treatment and training" (p. 159). They concluded: "Writing therapy has been used in several forms as an adjunct tool, or as a replacement for, more formal, oral therapy, especially where the latter was not possible or practicable. Like much of the reporting on short-term therapy, the existing literature on writing as a paratherapeutic modality consists mostly of clinical impressions" (pp. 151–162). After 25 years this conclusion stands unchallenged; in addition, therapeutic writing (in the form of diary keeping) as an adjuvant to meditation has received the endorsement of Progoff (1975, 1980) and of Reiner (1978).

The Link with Programmed Instruction

Once we conceive of writing becoming programmed, then we need to acknowledge its link with programmed instruction (PI), a highly structured technique popular among educators in the 1960s and 1970s. PI is the basic process by which information is furnished to the reader gradually and in small portions. The vehicle for PI can be a monitor screen, a teaching machine, or simply questions written on paper. Questions can be objective (that is, multiple choice or true-false) or open-ended, and responses can be checked for accuracy almost immediately. PI has given way in recent years to what is now called computer-assisted instruction (CAI). CAI presupposes that information has been already programmed, and a computer is used to administer the information with or without responses from the reader.

In this book, we use PI to follow the Socratic method of question and answer in increasingly complex steps, as illustrated in Part II. At this time, it remains to be seen whether and how PI can be applied to interpersonal relations before being extended to CAI. It remains to be seen whether CAI, or even PI for that matter, will be used extensively for paratherapeutic purposes. Programmed writing, however, leaves this possibility open. Written homework and self-administered assignments are one step away from adaptation to television and personal computer technologies, where the potential for mass delivery is immense and completely untapped.

PI applied to interpersonal relations can increase any behavior when practice and learning need to take place in an impersonal context, devoid as much as possible of personal and interpersonal distractions. There is no question that PI can be used to increase cognitive skills, perhaps even reflectivity and interpersonal effectiveness and competence (Clements, 1986; Clements & Gullo, 1984; Hausser, 1976; Parham, 1974; Scandura, 1984; Shaw, 1978; West, 1979; Wolf & Garett, 1978). However, very few applications of PI or of CAI have been discussed in the mental health and psychotherapy literature in the last few years. PI is the technological background for the application of programmed writing to dysfunctional personal and interpersonal behavior. When the technology of writing is coupled with the technology of PI, the positive benefits can be multiplied manyfold. More than twenty years ago, L'Abate and Brown (1969) stressed the potential of PI as applied to interpersonal relations. This technology has already been applied to psychoeducational structured enrichment programs with functional and semifunctional couples and families administered by professionals and paraprofessionals (L'Abate & Weinstein, 1987; L'Abate & Young, 1987).

The practice of PI and CAI (Atkinson & Wilson, 1969; Hartley, 1972; Kersh, 1964; Kinger & Worcester, 1965; O'Day, 1971; Richmond, 1965), as shown by the obsolescence of the references just cited, seems to have reached its peak in the late 1960s and early 1970s. Applications to interpersonal relationships, by the same token, seem to have been limited to a few in-patient psychiatric programs (Merley & Laying, 1976) and to assertion training (Muehlenhard & McFail, 1983).

PI has been applied successfully in mental health interventions and offender rehabilitation. Among the pioneers in the efforts with offenders were McKee and Seay (1968), who used PI for interpersonal grooming—that is, for teaching simple skills, progressing to more and more complex interpersonal skills, such as interviewing. Siegel (1978) described how computer-based instruction in prison schools, using a specific system, aids learning. Most PI and CAI programs (Diem & Knoll, 1981) in the United States have educational purposes, to teach students or inmates basic skills. For instance, Chaneles (1983) devoted a whole issue of a correctional education journal to reviewing current trends in PI theory and practice. Unfortunately, most of these efforts are directed strictly toward academic learning rather than toward personal, social, or interpersonal learning. There does not seem to be much information about the possible applications of PI to mental health in general and or the mental health of offenders in particular.

Hackley and Hagan (1975), in evaluating the Opportunities for Youth Program for juveniles, which is based on either work or teaching machines, concluded: "Those involved in the teaching machines program had lower delinquency rates at the end of the project than those who did not take part. . . . Our findings, however, encourage only faint optimism with regard to uncovering effective 'cures' for the ills of delinquency" (p. 105).

In spite of their negative conclusion, Hackley and Hagan believed that teaching machines were "confidence-building devices" for juveniles. There is room to be more optimistic about the potential of individualized instruction and programmed writing for prisoners. We need programs to prepare inmates for socially constructive roles in communities. As discussed in greater detail in the rest of these chapters, a PI approach can be used to create workbooks for acting out, internalizing, neurotic, anxious, or depressed persons. The issue now remains one of finding ways and means of decreasing costs (Roid, 1974), increasing personal and interpersonal effectiveness, and decreasing interpersonal conflict with highly resistant behavior patterns, either at intrapersonal or at intrafamily levels.

In conclusion, PI is an existing technology that is basic to the practice of programmed writing. It allows the construction of programmed, stepwise, written homework assignments. Its principles are basic to the practice of imparting information through the Socratic method. One of the most crucial issues of PI is the problem of feedback. How does the respondent know whether the answers are appropriate, or correct? Without feedback, even programmed writing would be futile. Corrective feedback—from self, from partner, from family members, and finally from a professional—is crucial to change. Until this issue is resolved, it will be impossible to apply programmed writing through existing video or computer technology.

Writing Research

Another line of inquiry that offers support for the paratherapeutic use of writing can be found in writing research (Nystrand, 1986). Instead of reviewing the literature, we think it sufficient to show how this area can furnish the theoretical and empirical support that paratherapeutic writing will need to achieve legitimacy in the therapeutic and prevention communities. Nystrand (1986) has this to say about written communication:

> Researchers see both writing and reading as constructive, interpretative activities in which both writer and reader test hypotheses about possible meanings. . . . Writers are said to represent and evaluate their intentions continuously in the conventions of written text. . . . What is not always recognized, however, is that writers and readers interact not only with the text but also with each other by way of the text. . . . Communications between writers and readers require that the text they share configure and mediate these respective interests and expectations. . . . More fundamentally, each [writer and reader] presupposes—indeed counts on—the sense-making capabilities of the other. There is a condition of reciprocity between conversants that undergirds and continuously regulates discourse at every turn. (p. ix)

This condition of reciprocity between the writer and the reader is elaborated further by Nystrand:

> The principle of reciprocity is an essential key to understanding the interactions and negotiations of writers and readers. Most research on writer-reader interaction

has focused on (a) the effects of reflection, for example, when writers reread what they have written . . . ; (b) concrete response . . . ; (c) projection. . . . Much of this research works from the premise that writers and readers ultimately collaborate via the internal representation of meaning created in the process of writing and reading. (p. 14)

Nystrand, then, considers writing a social interactional process based on the principle of reciprocity as a way to improve meaning transmission:

Writing is no less interactive than speech in either principle or practice. As discourse, writing is nonetheless an interactive medium even if the reader does not know the writer. . . . As long as writers and readers collaborate in their complementary and reciprocal tasks of composing and comprehending . . . the result is coherent communication. (pp. 40–41)*

Nystrand defines the reciprocity principle as "the function of all social acts, including discourse. *In any collaborative activity the participants orient their actions on certain standards which are taken for granted as rules of conduct by the social group to which they belong*" (Nystrand's emphasis) (p. 48). He cites some research suggesting that "expectation for reciprocity may be present from birth" (p. 49). For him, writing follows the norm or principle of reciprocity as much as talking does. Thus, Nystrand's position can be used as the basis for a theoretical understanding of writing as a paratherapeutic modality. Of course, further research on its clinical and paratherapeutic effectiveness is crucial.

Conclusion

Writing in general and programmed writing in particular, when used in the context of a caring and compassionate professional relationship, can enhance, even shorten, therapy or primary prevention. In some cases, it has provided real breakthroughs in dealing with difficult clinical problems, such as depression, anxiety, and obsessions. Clearly, its advantages have not been fully explored, and its disadvantages need to be considered. The opinions and impressions expressed here are only a first step toward finding external evidence under controlled conditions—that is, objective evaluation before and after intervention.

*From *The Structure of Written Communication: Studies in Reciprocity between Writers and Readers*, by M. Nystrand. Copyright © 1986 by Academic Press.

CHAPTER TWO

Writing as an Additional Way to Help

When speech fails, write!

The purpose of this chapter is to lay the groundwork for a systematic use of writing as an alternative to or as an additional form of communication between professional helpers and their clients. Its application in psychotherapy and primary prevention is based in part on the following rationale. If a topic is important enough to talk about, it is important enough to be written about. Writing is also a way of finding out whether a client's verbal claims of change are supported by a written record of performance. Writing forces clients to do more than just talk about change. It puts them on the spot, so to speak, to *produce* and to *perform*. If talk is therapeutic in and of itself, why not add another possibly helpful dimension to it?

The Functions of Writing and of Programmed Materials

Programmed materials can fulfill a variety of functions and can be administered at a number of different points in the therapeutic process. This multiplicity of purpose, in our opinion, stengthens the rationale for using these materials as an adjunct in all sorts of therapeutic and preventive endeavors.

First, programmed materials can aid in the process of therapy by serving as *preparation* for therapy. Requiring clients to work on change outside the therapist's office by completing lessons and behavioral tasks in between appointments allows the therapist to assess the client's motivation and competence to enter and remain in a close, prolonged, and committed relationship. For instance, persons with certain character disorders use language to impress and manipulate the helper. The helper can prescribe writing and behavioral tasks to check on whether clients are serious about changing or just say that they are.

Homework assignments enable helpers to make a more practical evaluation of clients' motivation for change. If clients are really interested in changing, will they work for it? Talk is cheap (and expensive when coming from a professional helper's mouth!) and just talking is not enough to see whether clients are motivated toward change. How hard, how well, how frequently clients work on assignments is a more direct way to assess whether they are motivated or not. Sometimes, completion of programmed written assignments and behavioral tasks may become a condition for acceptance into face-to-face, verbal psychotherapy. It also minimizes the probability of attrition. If a client does drop out, the therapist's emotional and material involvement will have been minimal.

Perhaps the most important requirement of the client in therapy is to assume responsibility for change. Commitment to complete programmed materials may make the client more responsible and less passive. As a result, clients may eventually become less and less reliant on professional expertise. Assignments increase clients' active involvement in the process of change, allowing them to take responsibility for change rather than relying solely on the help giver. Written homework assignments may expedite the initial therapeutic process of learning about an individual, couple, or family, with minimal investment of the therapist's time and effort. Eventually, all of the foregoing considerations may eventually decrease the possibility of failure in the process of therapy.

Second, programmed writing can serve as an *adjuvant* to verbal psychotherapy. It can become a supplementary and complementary form of experience and expression that overlaps little with conventional "talk" psychotherapy. It may allow the exploration and elaboration of areas that have not been touched upon during verbal sessions; it may be a more comfortable medium for people who cannot express themselves well orally.

This process may save time (and money) by shortening the length and costs of psychotherapy, making the process more effective and more cost-efficient. If we want to help people think in more positive ways, the written word may be more cost-effective than the spoken word. One of the most practical implications of writing—open, focused, guided, or programmed—is its cost. For instance, by requiring clients from the very onset of therapy to spend one hour writing for each hour of therapy as part of the initial therapeutic contract, the length of therapy can be shortened without diminishing its effectiveness. This assertion, of course, needs to be supported by hard data. Some recent evidence will be presented in Chapter 5. If one therapeutic, paratherapeutic, or pre-therapeutic approach is as effective as another, the cheapest approach becomes the treatment of choice. If we can demonstrate that writing, regardless of its structure or specificity, can shorten the process of therapy or of primary prevention without lowering effectiveness, a decided advance may take place. This advance would mean that professional helpers could help many more clients per unit of time than has been possible in the past. So writing, especially programmed writing, may be one way of increasing therapeutic effectiveness, decreasing costs, and expanding the number of people who can be helped (Gibbs, 1989, pp. 411–413).

Practically, writing instructions down or having the client write them down can save a professional helper's time and energy, and help avoid misunderstandings, selective forgetting, and downright distortions. When the same instructions for the same kind of resistant problem need to be repeated to different clients, these instructions can be printed and handed to clients. All the wisdom accumulated over years of clinical and preventive practice can be encapsulated in these detailed instructions.

From a help giver's viewpoint, then, use of writing avoids the need for verbal repetition of instructions from one case to another and from one session to another, thus rendering the time spent in the professional's office more efficient. The advantage for clients is that they gain a sense of self-mastery and control when they keep regular, routine appointments with themselves and with each other, concentrating on critical issues in their lives. In our experience, writing assignments help clients to feel that they are engaged and involved in doing something productive and worthwhile between sessions, gaining in self-knowledge and getting their deepest thoughts out in the open where they can be looked at by the therapist. The process of introspection is likewise aided by writing. Clients learn to think through and reflect on previously impulsive and repetitive patterns of behavior.

A related application of programmed writing deals with the issue of secondary diagnosis. With couples and families, for instance, it is possible to administer different workbooks for the use of individual family members while focusing on interaction issues in face-to-face therapy. In a couple with a character disorder in one partner and depression in the other, for instance, both partners may need to work on different workbooks that deal with their individual issues, while in therapy they are working on their relationship. It is possible to have very motivated couples and families work both on individual and on relationship issues at home, combining individual, marital, and family workbooks.

Use of programmed materials should increase generalization from the office to the home if as much time is spent weekly on each workbook lesson as is spent in the therapist's office. An added bonus in using programmed materials is that clients can be assigned lessons that will keep them busy and centered while the therapist is away on vacation. Furthermore, workbooks can be an alternative to psychotherapeutic practices. For example, populations that are resistant to face-to-face therapy (such as addicts, psychopaths, juveniles, schizophrenics, or acting-out individuals) may be less resistant to the workbook approach. Through the use of written forms, it is possible to deal with resistant patterns from the very beginning of any psychological intervention, according to theoretical notions of both linear and circular prescriptions (L'Abate, Baggett, & Anderson, 1984; L'Abate & Levis, 1987; Weeks & L'Abate, 1982). And finally, populations such as incarcerated individuals, missionary families, and military personnel may have easier access to programmed materials than to traditional psychotherapy.

A third and important function of workbooks is as a *research tool*. Programmed writing lends itself more to research possibilities than does verbal psychotherapy. Workbooks can verify theoretical and therapeutic approaches cost-effectively. Programmed materials have an advantage over traditional psychotherapies in that they enable us to control treatment and therapist variables that are otherwise too complex to control. They make it possible to verify a variety of therapeutic issues, like patient-treatment match and the comparative usefulness of different theoretical or clinical models (L'Abate, 1990a). For instance, at present the first author is working with various associates to evaluate the comparative therapeutic effectiveness of different workbooks. In one study, we are comparing four different workbooks dealing with depression (L'Abate, & Boyce, research in progress). Other associates are comparing the relative efficacy of three programs designed to decrease state versus trait anxiety in undergraduates (Russ, 1991), and the efficacy of programs derived from the content scales of the MMPI-2 to decrease peaks in the profiles of under-graduates (Fraizer, research in progress).

Programmed Writing as Complement to the Therapist's Role

Programmed writing, then, is a method that complements and supplements the professional's personal contribution. A written method can be reproduced ad infinitum. The personal, stylistic contributions of the therapist are not reproducible, even though they are a significant, and for some, the most signifi-cant determinant of the therapeutic outcome. An analogy may help clarify this point. In the mental health field, relying mainly or solely on the professional's intuitions and personal style is like trying to build skyscrapers with bare hands and primitive tools, somewhat like building the Egyptian pyramids. Relying on intuitions, without methodology, makes it difficult to distinguish between a serious professional and a charming charlatan or a glib quack, who may show many seductive qualities but who lacks the professional know-how and respon-sibility to help people in trouble. To build skyscrapers, we need a multitude of architects, engineers, designers, programmers, supervisors, and construction workers, along with a full complement of up-to-date machinery. By the same token, to deal with so many people at risk, in need, and in crisis, we need to use all the modern tools and instruments available to us. Programmed writing is a method that, in the hands of sensitive, experienced, responsible, and knowledgeable professionals and semiprofessionals, can improve the effec-tiveness and efficiency of therapy and prevention, much like building a sky-scraper with modern tools rather than primitive ones or bare hands.

Programmed writing, then, introduces the concept of *reproducible plans*. A reproducible plan can be verified. A verbal or nonverbal intuition, no matter how crucial to the process of change, cannot be verified because it is either not reproducible or it is very expensive to reproduce. Programmed writing offers reproducible plans that can, should, and must be tested, and changed if they need improvement. If these plans are found wanting and cannot be changed, they should be discarded. Very few therapists can be discarded, since no agreed-upon criteria yet exist to judge their professional competence. A reproducible plan, written down on paper, is cheap. It costs the paper it is printed on and the time and energy it took to create it. However, once this plan has been written down, it can be reproduced ad infinitum. The words of the therapist and the energy and talent behind those words are very expen-sive, because they are not reproducible.

The therapist's words can be directed toward the specific, *idiographic* charac-teristics, contents, and issues that are peculiar to specific clients (individuals, couples, or families). Above and beyond those specific verbal contents, however, there is a *nomothetic,* or general, process. This is the process that programmed writing attempts to deal with. The professional's words and actions in the office deal with the idiographic contents, which are always, or most of the time, specific to individuals, couples, or families. Programmed writing, on the other hand, attempts to deal with the nomothetic process when clients are away from the professional's office and need to learn new skills and novel ways of dealing with change-resistant conflicts and issues. These problems persist in spite of the professional's best words and well-intentioned actions. The idiographic-nomothetic controversy will be dealt with in greater detail in Chapter 3.

Advantages and Disadvantages of Programmed Writing

To summarize the foregoing considerations, the advantages of programmed materials are multiple. They avoid distortions, omissions, and generalizations (repressions, forgetting, misunderstandings) on the client's part, as well as useless repetitions on the therapist's, thus saving the therapist's time and energy. They tend to improve communication (one can be as explicit and specific as one wants to be), and they are cost-effective. As preparation for psychotherapy, they are a way of assessing motivation and thus may be used to decrease attrition, one of the most important issues in psychotherapy practice. Through workbooks, therapists can learn more about their clients, using a different modality from talking and getting information faster than clients can tell it. As research instruments, they are more explicit and specific than the spoken word. Because of their efficiency and cost-effectiveness, workbooks promise to bridge the gap that seems to exist between structured psychoeducational skills training (primary prevention) and relatively unstructured psychotherapy approaches (tertiary prevention).

Programmed materials now provide a cost-effective vehicle for therapeutic change if certain conditions can be met. Writing assignments help to structure the process of therapy, provided they do not control it. Depending on their structure, they can be linked to definite psychiatric diagnoses as measured by objective personality tests, thus linking the process of evaluation with intervention and making a diagnosis prescriptive as well as descriptive, as argued in the next chapter. These programs can also help in dealing with dual diagnosis, by having a written process that deals with one symptom take place alongside verbal face-to-face psychotherapy sessions that deal with another condition. In this parallel process, responsibility for change remains on the shoulders of the client and not solely on the therapist's.

If money is an issue, appointments can be spaced at longer intervals provided the client works on written assignments in between. When the therapist goes on vacation, a contract can be made to see that written assignments are completed during this absence. If people want to change and want to work for change, writing offers the potential of helping them achieve their goal, provided the assignments receive corrective feedback from a responsible professional.

Still, in spite of these advantages, writing in its different degrees of structure has its limitations. Obviously, it cannot be used with people who cannot read or write. But by the same token, how many people who cannot read and write are helped by verbal psychotherapies? These people can use tape recorders, which are also an option for those who become tired of writing and want another medium of expression in addition to writing. Volunteers or paraprofessionals can read the questions and write down the answers for people who cannot read or write.

Another disadvantage of workbooks is that they do not motivate poorly motivated or highly resistant individuals, even though a workbook program to motivate poorly motivated individuals can be written (for example, the program on negative treatment indicators from the MMPI-2 content scales). It takes considerable commitment and motivation to change while using workbooks. Persons who are unwilling or unable to make such a commitment should not waste their time or that of the therapist.

The use of programmed writing may not be applicable to all professionals or to all therapies, and certainly not to all clients. It would be a serious mistake to assume that these materials can be administered to everybody. One needs to consider educational, intellectual, social, and motivational factors before administering the materials. They should never be administered pell-mell, without a rationale or criteria for selection and matching. Attention must be paid to finding out who can profit by the use of these materials and who cannot. One needs to be continually mindful of the variability among people. What works for one person, couple, or family may not work for another, even with the same pattern of referral. We need, of course, to find out which specific program will work best with which individual characteristics, at what cost, and with what kind of helper.

Programmed writing is not a panacea for all ills. It may not fit with the therapist's style, or, in some cases, some therapists may feel (without evidence) that programmed writing may hinder the process of therapy or distract from the therapeutic relationship. Some problems may be less amenable than others to programmed writing, just as some clients like it better than others. Liking and requesting these assignments may have a great deal to do with positive outcome in therapy. Clearly, in spite of this rationale and our enthusiasm, programmed writing has not been substantiated sufficiently for wholesale application. A great deal of evidence is still needed from sources external to us and to the experience that we have gathered over the last fifteen years before such widespread applications can take place (L'Abate, 1990a).

Burton (1965) enumerated the following potential disadvantages of the use of writing in psychotherapy: (1) it might threaten the dissociation of the therapeutic relationship; (2) it might move the emphasis to ideas rather than feelings, at the cost of less affective involvement by the client; (3) some clients might be unable to write or to use written material; (4) it might provide a distraction and a defense from the honesty of direct confrontation, becoming ultimately another form of defense; (5) therapy might be relegated to writing alone; (6) it might affect the tone and structure of the therapeutic relationship "insidiously" (p. 14); (7) it might become a magical process precluding actional outcomes (that is, it could help some patients avoid direct actions and rest at the level of writing rather than of acting). All these disadvantages need to be evaluated and demonstrated empirically before one can see them for what they really are: possible, even probable, interferences that should be kept in mind by professionals who are willing to take chances with their clients by applying this modality.

Areas in Which Writing Can Help

Writing—whether open, focused, guided, or programmed—can augment both cathartic and cognitive skills. It can facilitate both the expression of feelings and the development of balanced thinking.

Help with Cathartic Skills

Cathartically, writing can increase a client's sense of self-mastery through greater self-disclosure and awareness. For instance, just by keeping appointments and concentrating on a single task, clients begin to feel that they are doing something worthwhile for and by themselves. Writing can improve self-knowledge because clients no longer need to ruminate and obsess but are able to get these recurring thoughts out of the self so that they and their therapists can look at them. Most important, writing can allow approach of painful feelings that cannot yet be expressed verbally. Writing can increase introspection, reflection, and meditation, especially in dealing with impulsive and repetitive behaviors. It can allow the internal monologue to become an internal dialogue: rather than considering just one aspect of an issue, the client may start to consider other aspects of the same issue (Schwartz & Garamoni, 1989).

Painful (hurtful, shameful, traumatic) feelings and memories that we put down on paper can be subjected to the caring and careful scrutiny of a professional. It is indeed easier for some people to write down what they find difficult to disclose in a face-to-face contact or relationship. Writing can bring about the expression of pent-up feelings and forgotten traumas, or, especially in couple and family therapy, it can help hold in check explosive emotionality and uncontrolled feelings. One can express in writing many feelings that are difficult to express verbally. Of course, the reverse may also be true, which emphasizes the need to substantiate these claims empirically.

Help with Cognitive Skills

If thinking is the basis of most behavior, as cognitive theorists and therapists like to stress, faulty thinking is the basis of inappropriate behavior. Many criminals and psychopaths, for instance, show a consistent deficit in the Comprehension subscale of the Wechsler Adult Intelligence Scale, with a parallel decrease in verbal intelligence and a relative increase in manual performance (Picture Arrangement, another nonverbal measure of social comprehension, may also be lowered). Most traditional talk therapies with these people seem to fail because these individuals learn to say what therapists want to hear, and thus they talk without any change in behavior. Some other form of therapy, not based on talk, may be necessary. This is why workbooks that are programmed and self-paced may help acting-out persons of limited educational and intellectual backgrounds to learn bit by bit to think in more constructive and socially acceptable ways. They are asked to give specific answers to specific questions, in writing, and to complete week-long practice exercises in which they apply in their behavior what they have written down on paper.

Programmed materials strengthen clients' cognitive skills and reflectivity (that is, the internal dialogue). Writing is essentially a cognitive activity that requires thinking, perhaps more thinking than is required in the act of talking. If this is indeed true, programmed writing should produce as much change as talking, perhaps at a lower cost.

Completing each lesson and discussing it with others (self, family members, and therapist) involves three feedback loops. For the individual, writing the responses to each question is an interactive process that produces the first loop, from the paper to the respondent, by enlarging an internal monologue to an internal dialogue. Schwartz and Garamoni (1989) argue that some individuals can only monologue; that is, they talk and think internally, but cannot dialogue within themselves. People who can dialogue within themselves are able to look at many sides of an issue, in what we call "contextual thinking," and seem to be better off psychologically than those who can only monologue. The second feedback loop occurs when partners compare, contrast, and discuss their answers at a meeting, producing a dialogue that should also be feedback to each person's monologue. The third feedback loop occurs when persons discuss their answers as well as their discussion with the therapist, receiving additional corrective input that is feedback to their dialogue and their monologue.

Weintraub (1981) compared and contrasted the spoken and the written word, as summarized in Table 2-1. As this table demonstrates, speech is "easier" than writing. By requiring clients to write, therefore, we are fostering thinking and cognitive skills that would not be developed from just talking. Thinking takes place best when we respond to questions according to the old Socratic method, which is what programmed instruction (PI) and computer-assisted instruction (CAI) are all about. In this way, a therapist can assure that more appropriate cognitive skills will be practiced outside of the therapy office, producing new and more positive behaviors than have taken place in the past.

In emphasizing the importance of writing and writing skills, Boyer (1983) concluded:

> Clear writing leads to clear thinking: clear thinking is the basis of clear writing. Perhaps more than any other form of communication, writing holds us responsible for our words and ultimately makes us more thoughtful human beings. . . . Writing is an essential skill for self-expression and the means by which critical thinking also will be taught. (pp. 90, 176)

Table 2-1 A comparison of spoken and written language

Spoken	Written
Learned earlier in life at home	Learned later in life in school
Easier than written language	Harder than spoken language
Takes less effort	Takes more effort
More productive per unit of time	Less productive per unit of time
Learned automatically	Has to be taught
Spontaneous	Deliberate
Dependent on immediate social context	More autonomous of context
More ideas per unit of time	More ideas per number of words
No permanent record	Permanent record
Less syntactically complex	More syntactically complex
Less abstract	More abstract
Less time needed for planning and encoding	More time needed for planning and encoding

Source note: From *Verbal Behavior: Adaptations in Psychopathology,* by W. Weintraub, M.D., pp. 137-151. Copyright © 1981 by Springer Publishing Company, Inc., New York 10012. Used by permission.

Baron and Sternberg (1987) elaborated on this and earlier conclusions:

> As a sustained activity, writing has the potential to develop many of the dispositions associated with the development of thinking skills. Certainly it can foster persistence and precision in both thought and the use of language. Therefore, writing provides opportunities for evaluating many of the dispositions and abilities that accompany good thinking. (p. 232)

Baron and Sternberg (1987), Griffin (1982), Howard and Barton (1986), Meyers (1986), Nystrand (1986), Scinto (1986), and Young (1980), among many others, have suggested, shown, and stressed writing as one of the major tools in developing and fostering thinking, especially critical thinking, in children as well as in adults. Once writing is used as a paratherapeutic or parapreventive tool, all this technology becomes available to helpers (and to clients!). One of the most exciting aspects of this technology is its relationship to cognition and cognitive processes (Gregg & Steinberg, 1980), which makes the whole process of paratherapeutic writing more amenable to research.

Writing and Principles of Behavior Control

To be maximally helpful, writing needs to be coupled with principles of behavior control. Without these principles, writing may become another exercise in futility.

The initial purpose of any intervention is to help individuals, couples, and families achieve change for the better by establishing a certain degree of control over their lives. Assuming that disordered, disturbed, or disturbing behavior is out of either the individual's or the family's control, control becomes an extremely relevant issue to consider in prescribing writing. Writing, of whatever degree of structure, cannot and should not take place at the whim or will of the client. Under these conditions, writing will increase the capricious nature of the behavior. For instance, writing should not take place when the client is depressed or anxious. If that is the case, control will be lost and depression or anxiety will tend to persist.

Hence, it is crucial, if not imperative, that writing be coupled with principles of control. Still, these principles and the notion of control in general seem to have remained outside the notice of the therapeutic and preventive communities. Indeed, Gibbs, a sociologist (1989), has argued that control is the major if not the only unifying notion in sociology. Unfortunately, in his otherwise scholarly treatise, this author fails to tells us how control is achieved in our society.

The first author (L'Abate, 1986b) suggests that writing needs to be paired with three principles of control: (1) planning and preparing; (2) regulation through routine repetition; and (3) keeping a written record. These principles are the same as those used every day in our society by employers to achieve control over their employees. Our employer tells us what time to go to work and what time to leave. Thus, control is first achieved by determining the *duration* of a target behavior. Second, control is achieved by determining the *frequency* of the behavior, according to a routine—in the case of work, five days a week for so many weeks a year. Third, control is achieved through keeping a written record, whether a time card, a performance evaluation, or a production report. This record shows the *intensity* of an employee's behavior—motivation, work performance, commitment to the work, and so on. Thus, the three prerequisites for progress in human behavior are prearranged, regular appointments with a written record.

In keeping with the first principle, control over undesirable emotions, thinking, and behavior can be obtained if we plan in advance to start, rather than trying to stop, the problematic behavior (L'Abate, 1986b; L'Abate & Levis, 1987; Weeks & L'Abate, 1982). *"If you want to stop it, start it!"* Out-of-control behavior (provided it is not lethal or self-destructive) must be planned by making appointments with it at least 24 hours in advance. Society, like therapy, progresses by people coming together at preestablished, agreed-upon hours. Skyscrapers are not built, government does not make laws by haphazard, random coming together of interested parties. We can follow the same principles in assigning the tasks of writing on a prearranged basis. By prearranging, we give clients the chance to delay rather than to respond on impulse, and we give them time to think and to prepare for the task of thinking about the disturbing behavior rather than giving in to it. Up to now the symptomatic or disturbing behavior has been avoided through self-defeating habits, half-baked solutions, and rituals designed to increase avoidance of the pattern. If the start of the undesirable behavior is prescribed, the person, couple, or family must learn to approach the pattern, confront it, and deal with it.

In keeping with the second principle, control is achieved when we can put our energies (thoughts and time) into dealing with the troublesome behavior on a *regular*, routine basis—for instance, once a week at 9:00 P.M. on Thursdays, or twice a week on Tuesdays and Thursdays, or three times a week on Mondays, Wednesdays, and Fridays. Planning the behavior beforehand tends to change the sequence of how the behavior takes place. By establishing regularity and thus predictability, people achieve greater control over their lives. In the past, the target behavior seemed to be outside the client's control or awareness. Now the client's thinking is focused on having to start the behavior at a given time, rather than impulsively, spontaneously, and without control. Most behaviors, emotions, and thoughts can be controlled if we have a plan for dealing with them at regular, prearranged times.

In keeping with the third principle, writing allows us to achieve control over undesirable or troublesome behavior. For instance, instead of reacting immediately to undesirable behavior on a child's part, parents are instructed to log that behavior in a notebook and consider it in the next regular family meeting. Instead of parenting through reactions, parents learn to lead and show that they are in control rather than abdicating control to their children.

Every lesson in programmed materials ends (or should end) with a weekly homework assignment that forces clients to practice and to learn how to control undesirable behavior according to the principles just discussed—planning, regular meetings or appointments, and keeping a written record. No change can take place unless all three principles are fully used. Change takes place through implementing the three steps basic to programmed writing: (1) contracting for appointments at home, in addition to those in the therapist's office; (2) completing and discussing these written assignments with oneself, with a partner, or with family members; and (3) using the corrective feedback of the therapist *after* each lesson has been completed and seen by the therapist. Persons without partners or family members will of course have to bypass the second step and rely directly on their own monologue or internal dialogue and the therapist's feedback.

The purposes of keeping regular appointments and records at home are fivefold: (1) to decrease reactivity and increase the ability to delay and to respond more appropriately; (2) to increase reflectivity by insisting that the predictable, controllable, agreed-upon meeting times and contents are the bases for possible change; (3) to evaluate progress from a record kept by the people involved in the process of change (rather than just by the therapist); (4) to maintain a written record that is less susceptible to the distortions, omissions, and generalizations that inevitably occur when the verbal or nonverbal modalities are the main or only kinds of exchange; and, (5) to enhance generalization from the therapy office to the home.

A Case Example of Programmed Writing at a Distance

The first author has used programmed writing through the mail in many cases with incarcerated individuals who could not be seen in traditional face-to-face verbal psychotherapy. We will describe one such case here.

Ron (not his real name) was a young man in his twenties in jail for a ten-year sentence for burglary. He agreed to participate in this program, accepting the following conditions: (1) full payment of a fee before treatment, with a refund of one-third of the fee on completion of the program, (2) completion of all lessons, and (3) completion of MMPI-2 testing before, directly after, and three months after completion of the program. He agreed in writing to the publication of the results and of a description of the full process of treatment, provided his identity was safeguarded.

While in other cases some degree of personal contact was present, as, for instance, in the initial testing, in this particular case the author did not meet the client, although he did see and work with his extended family. Ron completed 22 lessons from the Social Training program, plus a few extra lessons, and 8 lessons from the Beck Depression program (Levis, 1987) from the posttest (December 15, 1989) to the follow-up (April 12, 1990). The three profiles shown in Figure 2-1 were obtained at the beginning of the program (December 15, 1988), at the end, and at the three-month follow-up.

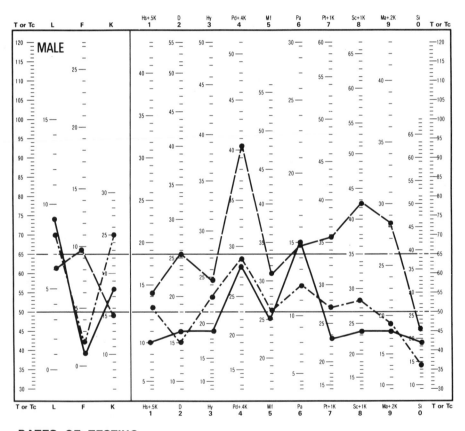

DATES OF TESTING

—— —— —— 12-15-88
————————— 12-15-89
▪—▪—▪—▪—▪ 4-12-90

Figure 2-1. Test results (MMPI-1 for first date and MMPI-2 for second and third date) before, directly after, and three months after participation in a course of programmed writing (Social Training and Beck Depression programs) by a convicted felon.

From the first (MMPI-1) to the second (MMPI-2) testing, a significant decrease in profile elevation and especially impulsivity (scale *Pd*, 4) were noted. While there was improvement in how reliably Ron answered test questions (lower scale *F*), there was also a significant increase in the *Lie* and *K* scales, indicating that this program increased his deceitfulness and his defensiveness. These changes persisted from the second to the third testing. On the basis of these results, one would need to prepare programmed lessons to deal with deceitfulness and defensiveness in individuals who are incarcerated. Nonetheless, this case does demonstrate the feasibility of helping people long distance when they cannot be seen in a face-to-face relationship. This young man may be ready now for such a relationship, especially with his family.

Making Use of Self-Help Books

Conceptually, writing in general and programmed writing in particular are related to mass education. One aspect of popular mass education that has achieved a great deal of success, at least in the United States, is the use of self-help books, supposedly based on "pop" psychology. This trend has achieved such proportions and has such implications for mass education that the American Psychological Association created a task force to evaluate the impact of self-help books. The report by the chair of this task force (Rosen, 1987) raised concerns about the usefulness of these books. Rosen contends that these books do not seem to help, or when they do, the outcome is nearly imperceptible. He has expressed concerns about commercial considerations overshadowing professional standards in the development of self-help manuals; lack of experimental support in their development; and, finally, the potentially damaging effects to readers of self-help treatment books.

Rosen's position concerning the inherent uselessness of self-help books has been disputed on a variety of grounds (Holtje, 1988; Lazarus, 1988). For instance, Mahoney (1988) takes issue with Rosen's negative assertions and argues that "existing literatures on self-administered therapies are rife with methodological and interpretative problems that severely constrain (and, indeed prohibit) the kinds of pat conclusions offered by Rosen (1987)" (p. 598). Mahoney implies that since variability is the norm, before reaching any conclusion, we need to find out and distinguish who is helped by self-administered approaches and why, and who is not helped and why not. He believes that self-help books may "represent a 'developmental bridge' between despair/desperation and the ultimate seeking of mental health services" (p. 598). In other words, we are not yet in a position to dismiss self-help books altogether.

Forest (1988) has presented research data to indicate that self-help books may produce some changes on self-report paper-and-pencil inventories. He suspects that the appeal of self-help books lies in "(a) their low cost; (b) their general availability; (c) their relevance to everyday problems; (d) their positive orientation; and (e) the lack of viable alternatives" (p. 599). Starker (1988a) found that 88.6% of the psychologists ($N = 105$) responding to a survey were prescribing, with various degrees of frequency, self-help books to their clients.

In a second survey, Starker found that in another sample of psychologists (N = 121), 60.3% of those who prescribed self-help books believed them to be "sometimes" or "often" helpful "to supplement their treatment efforts" (p. 599). None of the respondents found them harmful. In a later, more detailed article, Starker (1988b) presented more data on his conclusions, including lists of self-help books most read and most prescribed by responding psychologists (N = 123), rated according to quality and helpfulness.

In our opinion, the major usefulness of self-help books lies in the possibility of reducing them to a workbook format, which forces respondents to practice actively, interactively, and repeatedly with sequential questions. The sequence of questions and answers may stimulate the inner individual dialogue that is, in part, responsible for change. Workbooks, if properly written, require active involvement and repeated practice of desirable behavior. Self-help books usually do not require that practice. Furthermore, by requiring the client to answer and to commit himself or herself to some answer or to certain behavior, a workbook makes whatever the client says or does subject to critical but supportive feedback from the therapist. *Without corrective individualized feedback, any assumedly paratherapeutic or parapreventive approach, even programmed writing, is bound to fail.*

Many therapeutic approaches or treatment-oriented manuals can also be reduced to a workbook format. This has been done in the workbooks created by Stuart and Jacobson (1987) for couples, by Dinkmeyer, McKay, and McKay (1987) for single parents or stepparents, and by Doub and Scott (1987) for families. We can only hope that programmed workbooks will be used increasingly by both primary prevention professionals and by therapists.

Conclusion

Using writing adds tools to the armamentarium of professional helpers. Still, writing in general and programmed writing in particular produce their peculiar sets of problems, for both professional helpers and their clients. Some professional helpers may be so afraid of changing their traditional professional practices that they view the use of writing with distaste and/or with defensively critical reactions without any evidence. To appreciate fully the contribution that writing can make to the helping professions, we need to look at the state of current psychotherapeutic practices, with the ultimate aim of integrating writing into these practices, as we will do in the next chapter.

CHAPTER THREE

Programmed Writing as a Solution to Some Problems in Psychotherapeutic Practice

The theoretical underpinnings of current therapeutic practices are now beginning to crumble under closer critical scrutiny. What about these practices? Can they be any better than the theory underlying them? If there are problems in the practice of psychotherapy, either with individuals, couples, families, or groups, they are due in part to the nature of the spoken medium used to communicate between helpers and clients. By its very nature, talk is usually nonspecific and nonexplicit, especially when the client is upset and troubled. Even if the spoken word is specific and explicit, how will it be remembered? How can it be remembered without distortions, omissions, and generalizations? How can it be remembered in a family or a group, in which each member, even if remembering well, will remember selectively?

Among the many current issues of concern in psychotherapy, at least six are relevant to the practice of programmed writing: (1) the relationship between theory and practice; (2) verifiability; (3) specificity and explicitness; (4) cost and effectiveness; (5) attrition; and (6) the linkage between evaluation and treatment. We will consider each of these issues in this chapter.

Issues of Relationship between Theory and Practice

A psychoanalytically-oriented therapist will spend a great deal of time inquiring about the historical, developmental antecedents of maladaptive behavior, and will never inquire about the reinforcers that tend to increase the probability of that behavior. By the same token, a behaviorist will not inquire into the dreams and associations that may underlie the same maladaptive behavior. Instead of going back into the past, a humanistically-oriented therapist may inquire about the future and expectations related to the fear of the unknown. Hence, a relationship seems to exist between a particular theoretical ideology and the therapeutic approaches followed by representatives of that ideology. This relationship, however, is unclear and subject to distortions.

For instance, we have to rely on therapists' statements of their theoretical biases and therapeutic preferences. However, we do not know how valid these reports are. We presume that a relationship exists between stated theoretical ideology and preferred therapeutic practices, but the extent and type of such a relationship is very difficult to determine (Beutler, 1979; Beutler & Clarkin, 1990; Garfield & Bergin, 1978, 1986; Luborsky, Christopher, McLellan, Woody, Piper, Liberman, Imber, & Pilkonis, 1986). This is because we have to rely on verbal reports of what therapists said or did, and we have no way of verifying these reports unless we have a tape or video record of the therapy session. Furthermore, even if we were to videotape each session, and it takes at least 28 hours of work to decode everything that goes on in a 1-hour session, we have no way of knowing how what the therapist said or did relates to the client's behavior outside of the therapist's office (Luborsky, Christopher, Mintz, & Auerbach, 1988). We do not know, and it is practically impossible to find out, how therapists' theoretical ideology affects their behavior in the therapy room and how this behavior affects clients outside of that room. The major issue of generalization from the therapist's office to the client's home remains a mystery. We really do not know how generalization takes place! If we do not know, how can we make it happen?

By reducing any theoretical position and therapeutic approach to a written workbook format, we can now evaluate the usefulness and efficacy of that position or approach. This evaluation can take place comparatively, when we test two or three different approaches. And different approaches with a modicum of tested—that is, *confirmed*—usefulness can be used in tandem in actual clinical practice. For instance, if two or three workbooks representing two or three different therapeutic approaches are comparable in outcome, then one can be used interchangeably with another, or can be added to increase the options available not only to the therapist but also to the client.

Issues of Verifiability

One criterion that needs to be considered a sine qua non for validating a theory and the efficacy of any therapy is verifiability—namely, to what extent is a theory, or a preventive or therapeutic practice deriving from that theory, reproducible and repeatable, with a minimum of variability from one therapist to another, regardless of what a therapist says or thinks she or he did (L'Abate, 1986b)? Many therapeutic theories, techniques, and practices, especially in the family therapy field, are either not verifiable or are very difficult or expensive to verify. Consequently, many therapeutic interventions remain untested and untestable. How can one verify the spoken word between two or more individuals? As most psychotherapy research shows (Garfield & Bergin, 1978, 1986; Williams & Spitzer, 1984), talk cannot be predicted, controlled, or legislated. The kind of talk that takes place between clients and therapists is too complex and too difficult to control to hope that it will be easily amenable to research. Moreover, the very concept of verifiability is not even considered a criterion for theorizing or practicing in therapy, especially in family therapy (Hansen & L'Abate, 1982; L'Abate, 1986b; Levant, 1984).

Theories, techniques, and therapeutic practices follow a chaotic state of affairs, in which a leader's influence and credibility depend on the charisma of that particular leader (L'Abate & Colondier, 1987; L'Abate & Jurkovic, 1987). Under these chaotic conditions—as long as the criterion of success seems to be the popularity of a particular theorist or therapist, his or her charisma, and the seductive plausibility of his or her theory or technique—it is doubtful that therapeutic practices or their underlying theories can progress. In addition to popularity and plausibility, other criteria for theory and practice are necessary. Verifiability is one of these criteria.

Programmed writing amply fulfills two requirements for the verifiability of both theory and therapy: *explicitness,* through the written rather than the spoken word, and *specificity,* through the use of systematically written materials for specific conditions. Once any method is both specific and explicit, it also becomes verifiable—certainly more easily verifiable than the spoken word.

Issues of Specificity and Explicitness

When one looks at the range of therapeutic practices (Garfield & Bergin, 1978, 1986; Sherman & Fredman, 1986; Williams & Spitzer, 1984), one discovers that most of them consist of ad hoc gimmicks and nonrepeatable procedures, to the point that one cannot even differentiate between a technique and a method. The individual style of the therapist, which is nonreproducible, is confused with the demonstrable and pragmatic methodological contribution of the therapist (L'Abate, Ganahl, & Hansen, 1986). A method is a set or sequence of repeatable steps. A technique is a method loosely applied to the style of the therapist. A method is replicable, but a technique is not, because it is contaminated by the therapist's unique and inimitable style.

In a review of the benefits and limitations of psychotherapy, Karasu (1986) concluded that the field

> is advancing along two ostensibly diametric directions: greater "specificity" in meeting today's needs and tailoring treatments in special populations as well as greater "non-specificity" in the amalgamation of diverse approaches and locating generic factors across different modalities. Indeed, the so-called "specificity–non-specificity dilemma" is one of the pivotal debates of psychotherapy today. (p. 326)

We contend that issues of specificity and explicitness in psychotherapy can be addressed by prescriptive evaluations, programmed homework assignments written to deal with specific referral problems or with specific dysfunctionalities (depression, impulsivity, anxiety, marital conflict, and so on). Nonspecific aspects of psychotherapy are provided by face-to-face contact within the helper-client relationship or, when this interaction is missing, by written feedback correspondence from helper to client.

In commenting on issues of specificity, Karasu (1986) posed the classic question: "What treatment . . . is more effective for this individual with that specific problem and under which set of circumstances?" (p. 328). In posing the same question twenty years earlier, L'Abate (1969, p. 487) added " . . . and at what cost?" Karasu also qualified his question by adding, "However, at the present time, the field of psychotherapy is far from finding the best match of patients with particular methods, types of therapy or styles of therapist" (pp. 328–329). Indeed, Luborsky and his co-workers (1986, 1988) found little support for the "widely held view" that certain therapists are best for certain types of patients and that variations in success rates typically have more to do with the individual therapist than with the type of treatment used. They also found that therapists' success rates differ considerably, as do outcomes achieved by each therapist for particular clients.

It is difficult and expensive to deal with the many complexities of psychotherapy, unless one can start with the major differentiation drawn between specific and nonspecific factors and go from there to identifying and qualifying the contribution of each set of factors in comparison with other sets. The process of psychotherapy is too complex to even try to identify these sets in the therapy office. It may become possible to identify these sets through the use of programmed writing.

Some of these issues have been considered by Giacomo and Weissmark (1987) in terms of the determinism versus indeterminism controversy. Specificity is related to determinism, pragmatism, and demonstrability—all factors that fall within the context of *justification* (L'Abate, 1986a). Nonspecificity is related to nondeterministic factors, such as aesthetics and dialectics—factors that fall within the context of *discovery.* Although both aspects are necessary to a positive outcome in psychotherapy, nonspecific factors have been the mainstay of most therapists. The main goal of programmed writing is to contribute specificity and explicitness to the process of therapy (Garfield, 1984).

A generation ago, in commenting on directions in psychotherapy research, Strupp and Bergin (1973) reached a conclusion that still remains relevant and valid today:

> We have become convinced that further study of the therapeutic process and evaluation of outcomes resulting from traditional therapeutic practice offer little hope for significant scientific advance. While such studies may further expand our understanding of the therapeutic process and lead to refinements of traditional procedures, the potential yield resulting from pursuing other pathways appears comparably greater. . . . New departures appear called for. As we can see it, this means a movement away from the gross, complex and relatively nonspecific traditional therapeutic operations. Stated positively, we must achieve greater specificity and concomitantly, greater power in the sense of making therapeutic operations and strategies count therapeutically. (pp. 792, 793)

Strupp and Bergin concluded further that

> the field as a whole is currently beset with innumerable fads, considerable conceptual unclarity, muddy theories, and grossly unwarranted claims for the effectiveness of simplistic techniques. All of these factors have conspired to impede progress and to retard dispassionate examination of basic scientific issues. . . . With all, a serious return to empirical data is imperative. . . . It can be concluded, then,

that future research in this area must firmly rest on empirical data; it must tend toward increasing explicitness and specificity; and it must seek to isolate psychological principles embedded in, and often obscured by, divergent theoretical formulations. . . . There is no question that greater specificity and a return to empirical data are absolutely essential, but it seems unlikely that the therapeutic process can be effectively broken down into "parts" capable of being studied in isolation . . . and then of being "reassembled." (pp. 795, 797, 800)

In regard to nonspecific factors in therapeutic effectiveness, Strupp (1986) considered this a pseudo-issue beclouding our understanding of the therapeutic process and progress.

The future of psychotherapy should not lie with the isolation of "specific" or "nonspecific" factors; rather we need to become more explicit about what we can do and what we cannot do; what, under ordinary circumstances, we may be able to do in two or three months and what might take several years; and what might be done to refine our understanding of therapeutic principles and their application. (p. 519)*

More recently, Nadelson (1987) commented on the diffusion of the "talking treatments" (p. 494) in terms of enlargement to wider target populations as well as in terms of the proliferation of more than 400 types of therapy, "all claiming efficacy" (p. 494). He concluded that the nonspecific factors of unconditional positive regard, warmth, acceptance, and support, as well as the therapist's use of self, do have "a benign effect" on the therapeutic relationship. He differentiated between treatment and care. Treatment, which consists of a sequential series of replicable steps, is necessary in dealing with symptomatic or dysfunctional behavior. The style of the therapist, what Nadelson calls "care," is all the nonspecific factors that concern dealing with the relationship and the client as a fellow human being and in a nonmethodical fashion. In the same vein, Parloff (1986) maintained that most treatment approaches share the core of nonspecific elements that are responsible for client improvement, such as suggestion, modeling, and placebo effects.

The specificity-nonspecificity controversy could be resolved if one were to accept the importance of both aspects of therapy—specific and nonspecific. While both are important, it is certainly easier to evaluate, control, or change the therapeutic method than the particular style used by the helper. Methods are replicable and verifiable; stylistic techniques that are specific to individuals are extremely difficult to evaluate and to change. Furthermore, one would argue whether the personal style of a therapist should be changed at all. Put another way, it seems more practical to control method than to decrease therapist variability. Programmed writing is a method that can be used by any helper of any theoretical persuasion or style, without doing harm to the helper's ideological or theoretical allegiance. If one does not like a written program, one can create a program to suit one's tastes!

*From "New Directions in Psychotherapy Research," by H. H. Strupp and A. E. Bergin. In H. H. Strupp (Ed.), *Psychotherapy: Clinical, Research, and Theoretical Issues* (pp. 783–805). Copyright © 1973 by Jason Aronson, Inc. Reprinted by permission of the author.

Issues of Costs and Effectiveness

In addition to issues of effectiveness, which have been raised since Eysenck's early criticisms (1952), one needs to consider costs and the relationship of cost to effectiveness in competing, assumedly therapeutic, approaches.

Although mystery seems to shroud this topic, one can surmise that the fee for one hour of therapy may range from $10 or $15 for a student intern to ten times that much for an experienced practitioner. Can these costs be reduced without reducing effectiveness? How can a therapist's effectiveness be improved without reducing the workload? It is difficult to predict the outcome of psychotherapy, except to expect that, after taking into consideration attrition effects (Phillips, Test, & Adams, 1964), of the remainder who terminate, one-third will show definite improvement, one-third will show some improvement, and one-third will either remain the same or deteriorate (Mays & Franks, 1985). Cannot we somehow predict who will fall into which group? Perhaps programmed writing can help us resolve some of these issues.

The question of costs has plagued the therapeutic establishment for some time (L'Abate, 1969). The use of programmed materials can make it quicker and cheaper than ever before to link evaluation with treatment. For instance, the use of programmed materials may decrease the effect of the inevitable variability of therapists, a major factor in trying to match clients with therapy. That process, as a whole, is very expensive and difficult to evaluate.

Programmed materials also can be used to test different theories or models. For instance, one can compare the model of depression developed by L'Abate (1986b) with Beck's well-known model (Beck & Young, 1985). Both have been reduced to a workbook format (Levis, 1987), and with the third program on depression developed from the corresponding Minnesota Multiphasic Personality Inventory-2 (MMPI-2) content scales, we now have at least three different ways of helping people with depressive symptoms. By applying these different programs at random to a depressed population, we can find out which theory is more useful for treatment of depression (L'Abate & Boyce, research in progress; Russ, 1991). One could similarly evaluate competing theories of anxiety or anger.

Dealing with another important issue of cost-effectiveness in psychotherapy, Karasu (1986) quoted Kiesler (1984) as having concluded that "psychotherapy as typically practiced is too labor intensive to be a viable solution to overall national psychiatric problems." Kiesler estimated that "only 2% of those needing help can be indeed helped through psychotherapy" (p. 336). The same conclusion was repeated by Gibbs (1989, p. 413). If this statement is even partially correct, one would be led to conclude that psychotherapy is a drop (and an expensive one at that!) in the bucket of existing mental health and offender rehabilitation practices. Can we do better? Can we reduce part of the process of helping people to mass-producible, cost-effective dimensions? Programmed writing may be one way to achieve the simultaneous goal of offering a mass-producible and reproducible as well as cost-effective addition or alternative to existing therapeutic practices.

Psychotherapeutic practices simply cannot take care of the millions of individuals, couples, and families who need help. As relevant and important as psychotherapy may be for the chosen few, it is not sufficient to deal with the millions estimated to be in need of mental health rehabilitation. There are not enough therapists to go around to deal with all the suffering and dysfunctionality seen today. Psychotherapy is too costly, too complex, and too chancy to be available on a mass-delivery basis. It is tied to a private-practice, crisis-oriented, and necessarily limited model. What we need in addition is a public health model, geared to intervene at all three levels of prevention—primary, secondary, and tertiary—with large masses of people at risk, in need, and in crisis.

To deal with the problems of the American family (Kahn & Kamerman, 1982), for instance, a radically new perspective will be necessary to reconcile preventers and therapists (L'Abate, 1990a). Therapists and preventers do not talk with each other, and use mutually exclusive practices that weaken the whole enterprise of helping individuals, couples, and families (L'Abate, 1990a; L'Abate & Milan, 1985; Levant, 1986). Recognizing the technology of programmed writing as part of a continuum of preventive interventions, as presented in the first chapter, would enable us to intervene with more people at less cost than has been possible heretofore.

Issues of Attrition

One of the primary questions about psychotherapy that has surfaced recently, mostly through the work of Phillips (1985a, 1985b), is, how many individuals drop out of treatment before treatment is terminated? A recent study of attrition for individuals, couples, and families who applied for treatment at a private mental health clinic (Edwards, 1990) showed that the vast majority of clients were no longer in treatment after ten sessions, with individuals lasting slightly longer than couples or families.

Howard, Krouse, and Orlinsky (1986) believe that attrition is due to lack of information: if prospective clients were given more relevant information, attrition rates would decrease. However, they offer no data to support their contention. Phillips (1985a, 1985b), after years of studying this phenomenon, sees it as a naturally occurring result of a mismatch between a patient's needs and the nature of the treatment.

Programmed writing may offer another avenue of intervention to help us deal with problems of attrition. For instance, some people may need to be required to complete specific lessons before being accepted into therapy, as a way to evaluate their motivation for treatment. Some people should not even be seen in a therapist's office until self-defeating aspects of their behavior have been dealt with through correspondence. Programmed writing can also be used to shorten the length of therapy, by requiring that clients match hour per hour their time in therapy with written homework assignments; or to space therapy sessions every two or three weeks by administering written homework assignments in between sessions. After evaluation of the problem, clients could contract, either verbally or in writing, to stay in therapy for a specific number of sessions and to complete a specific number of homework assignments. This approach would remove much uncertainty from the process of psychotherapy.

Problems in Linking Evaluation with Psychotherapy

Among the many issues that beset psychotherapeutic and preventive practices is the inability to prescribe treatment on the basis of an evaluation. As long as psychotherapeutic interventions are based solely on the verbal medium, it will be difficult and expensive, if not impossible, to link initial evaluation of the client with prescribed interventions. This linkage has been the goal of most therapists (Beutler, 1979; Beutler & Clarkin, 1990; Butcher, 1990) for many years. In spite of this desire, no one has yet come out with a positively testable proposal that would solve this problem—a problem that will remain unsolvable as long as words remain the medium of exchange between professional helpers and people in need of help.

Most therapists and preventers do not evaluate clients sufficiently to establish pretreatment baselines and an objective measurement of conditions at referral. This may be because the need to decrease or defuse whatever crisis brought the clients in is more immediate than the need for evaluation, and also because people in crisis find it difficult to give accurate and relevant information. If it is possible, however, to see clients for three sessions of evaluation without treatment, giving the power of evaluation to the client ("It is up to you whether you think that we can be of help to you; we are not the only therapists in town"), this can establish a mutually comfortable context for the possibility of a short-term therapeutic contract. This approach in the long run seems to decrease attrition significantly.

The mental health field should give greater attention to the state of evaluation. Most mental health practitioners use subjective methods of evaluation (the history and the interview). However, evaluation would be more acceptable if it were supported by objective methods (Calam & Elliott, 1987). Unfortunately, too many therapists, especially psychologists, have sold out their knowledge and expertise about evaluation, and do not use it as standard operating procedure in their therapeutic practices. Objective evaluation as a whole has been avoided by most mental health practitioners, most of whom have rationalized evaluation as irrelevant to treatment or useless in evaluating change, since the process of change is multidimensional. This resistance to evaluation makes it impossible to assess whether any form of treatment is effective or which form of treatment is more effective than others.

Moreover, if one applies the same treatment to everybody, there is really no need to differentiate among treatments. The bias toward using verbal psychotherapy, which Kiesler (1966) called one of the myths of psychotherapy, makes it impossible to individualize treatment: the therapist uses the same approach with everybody who comes into the office.

Why should we evaluate? Many reasons have been given over the years by the proponents of evaluation. The primary one is that evaluation is necessary for setting a *baseline* from which to assess changes after treatment. The second reason is to delineate the kind of intervention to be administered and the level of intervention needed. For instance, we should be able to discriminate among individuals, couples, and families who are (1) *at risk* and who would benefit from primary prevention approaches; (2) *in need* of secondary prevention; or (3) *in crisis* and in need of tertiary prevention—that is, therapy and psychotherapy (L'Abate, 1990a). Another reason for evaluation is to obtain comparable data on individuals, couples, and families so that we can establish norms and guidelines that will then enable more specific and explicit treatment.

Evaluation, when it is done at all, has traditionally taken place through time-consuming interviews, producing historical information that is rather difficult and expensive to code and decode. The symptom or the reason for referral may also be used as a basis for arriving at an evaluation of the problem. Symptoms can be classified (albeit unreliably!) according to the quality, intensity, frequency, and duration of the behavior. But even if a diagnostic label can be arrived at, this in itself is not sufficient for a thorough understanding of an individual. Two individuals classified with the same label may be completely different according to other criteria.

Another kind of data gathering that is more useful in unclear or borderline cases and that is relatively more objective and quantifiable than interviews, is psychological tests for individuals, couples, or families (L'Abate & Bagarozzi, in press). Tests serve as a comparative data base from which to judge therapeutic outcome, as measured by comparisons of scores before and after intervention, a comparison that cannot be made with historical and interview information. Tests are, however, time-consuming, expensive, and oftentimes irrelevant in designing a treatment plan. The test market is so chock-full of instruments that one is left to rely on tried-and-true tests to evaluate outcomes of intervention. An initial evaluation is worthless if no reevaluation with the same test or test battery takes place at the end of treatment. Furthermore, both pre- and posttreatment testing is worthless if it is not anchored by long-term follow-up. When it takes meeting all these requirements to properly and professionally manage a case, it's no wonder that the mental health profession cannot live up to these standards.

Perhaps the best source of information on which to base an evaluation *is* intervention. To paraphrase Broffenbrenner (1979): "If we want to know how a system works (or fails to work!), try to change it!" By intervening, one can find relatively quickly how impervious a system (individual, couple, or family) is to attempts to improve it.

As Hayes, Nelson, and Jarrett (1987) have indicated, traditional evaluation has not been used as a basis for specifying which treatment should be applied. These researchers summarized the status of diagnostic testing and evaluation in relationship to treatment as follows: "Assessment is often not integrated into the therapy process. . . . Some clinicians even fear that the assessment process is negatively intrusive on the therapeutic alliance. . . . With specific assessment devices, more specific treatment implications can be explored" (p. 964).

How, then, shall we evaluate? We need to recognize that the information gathered through an interview is necessary, but it is not sufficient. It does not offer an objective baseline from which to evaluate changes in behavior and it varies from one interviewer to another. In addition to the important subjective inferences and conclusions of the interviewer, we need an additional source of information that will help indicate the most appropriate treatment for the client. The subjective inferences and conclusions furnish what is called the *idiographic* (that is, derived from and directed toward the individual) aspects of evaluation. The objective inferences and conclusions from a test or a battery of tests furnish what is called the *nomothetic* (that is, derived from and directed toward norms) aspects of the evaluation. *To help people in trouble we need both forms of evaluation.* We need to reconcile the historically controversial distinction between the two (Howard & Myers, 1990) and create instruments that will assess both the idiographic and the nomothetic aspects of an individual or of a relationship. Programmed writing can be such an instrument.

Further, we need instruments of evaluation that are not only *descriptive* and *predictive*, but also *prescriptive*. That is, we need tests that can prescribe treatment, in addition to fulfilling traditional descriptive and prescriptive functions. Again, programmed writing can fulfill this need. A test becomes prescriptive and therefore linked to treatment *provided* the treatment is clearly defined in writing. Otherwise, the requirement of linkage between evaluation and treatment is bound to remain a wish that cannot be achieved, or that will be very difficult or expensive to achieve as long as treatment is based on the spoken word.

Moreover, we need instruments that assess clients both *directly* and *indirectly*. For instance, to assess conflicts in dyadic relationships *indirectly*, a Problems in Relationships Scale (PIRS) was created to evaluate couples along 20 dimensions of functioning-dysfunctioning. The same 20 dimensions can also be evaluated *directly* through a self-description test using a semantic differential format found in Chapter 6. We need both measures to evaluate the concurrent validity of the instruments. Given two different measures of the same behavior, what is the extent of agreement and congruence between the two?

Programmed writing enables us to link treatment with evaluation in a nomothetic as well as idiographic fashion. For instance, the 20 dimensions of the PIRS just mentioned are isomorphic with 20 lessons covering the very same dimensions measured by the test. The test evaluates which dimensions are conflictful for a particular couple, ranking these dimensions from most to least conflictful. On the basis of this ranking, it is now possible to administer to a couple just those lessons having to do with the dimensions on which they are most conflictful. By the same token, with the MMPI-2, it is now possible to administer a program that is written specifically to deal with each of the 15 content scales (Fraizer, 1991). Consequently, it is now possible to prescribe treatment idiographically outside of one's professional office using nomothetic, programmed, self-administered materials.

The Creation of Prescriptive Diagnostic Instruments

We will now look more closely at the possibility of creating *prescriptive* rather than just *descriptive* assessment instruments. As a recent survey has amply demonstrated (L'Abate & Bagarozzi, in press), most instruments for marriage and family evaluation, including traditional, individually-oriented instruments, are mainly descriptive; that is, they stress the importance of understanding and describing individual, marital, and family patterns. However, none of these instruments leads directly into linking theory with therapy or evaluation with treatment. Both enterprises, up to now, have taken place catch-as-catch-can, without any clear or direct links between theory or evaluation and interventions.

Through the written medium, it is now possible to design instruments that can provide these links. After new ways of intervening with individuals, couples, and families are developed, new evaluative instruments can be designed with that purpose in mind, *provided one uses the written in addition to the spoken medium in therapy* (L'Abate, 1986b, 1987a, 1987b, 1987c, 1990a). When the spoken word is the main or the only medium of dialogue between two or more individuals, it becomes virtually impossible to control what is going on between them, or, if some control is achieved through structuring, myriad variables that we cannot control still intervene. Even when control is established, trying to chart the interaction is costly and time-consuming. However, when the written word is used as an additional, or, under certain conditions, the only medium of exchange, a variety of possibilities emerge. First of all, the influence from a variety of subtle interpersonal variables may be lowered or even eliminated. Second, the whole process can be recorded and reported. Third, once the feasibility and usefulness of this process is established, it becomes possible to use the written word synergistically with the spoken word if that becomes necessary. Fourth, the written word can be reproduced cheaply and in quantity, thus becoming a cost-effective medium when it is used appropriately.

The following examples of *prescriptive* instruments, still experimental and still in the course of validation, illustrate what can be done when writing rather than speaking becomes the preferred medium of paratherapeutic exchange. These prescriptive instruments can be classified in two main categories: theory-free and theory-derived.

Theory-Free Instruments

There are at least three theory-free or theory-independent instruments, two of which are included in Part II of this book. Not all of them, however, can be used for prescriptive purposes. The Social Information Form, for instance, included in Chapter 6, is an objective way of obtaining background, historical, and situational information that may not possess any prescriptive usefulness. However, it does gather quantifiable demographic, personal, and familial background information that eventually may have predictive, even prescriptive, validity.

The Adjustment Inventory
This instrument was developed a few years ago and can be used with individuals, couples, families, or groups. It is easy to administer as a self-report or as a structured interview (L'Abate & McHenry, 1983, p. 378). It is easy to score and to interpret, and has been preliminarily validated by Hall (1987). It

consists of selecting three areas of dissatisfaction—for instance, personality, marriage, and children—and listing three specific unsatisfactory behaviors for each area, plus one extra behavior unrelated to the other nine. These ten behaviors are then ranked in order of importance for change and then given an emotional rating from −5 to +5. By multiplying and then adding the rankings with the ratings, one obtains a total number (usually negative) that indicates the current level of dissatisfaction. This instrument, therefore, is nomothetic in relying on established norms that are now being gathered (L'Abate & McMahan, research in progress). It is also idiographic because it allows one to specify the behaviors that need to be changed in a particular individual, couple, or family. For instance, once we have gathered workbooks reduced from existing self-help books, they can be classified into three different areas: personhood, partnership, and parenting. We can specify these as the three areas of dissatisfaction in the Adjustment Inventory, and from respondents' rankings and ratings, we can then identify and select the workbook or workbooks that seem most appropriate.

The MMPI-2

An old testing standby, the Minnesota Multiphasic Personality Inventory-2 (MMPI-2) is an empirically-derived, theory-free test that can be used in the same fashion as a prescriptive instrument. Thus far, workbooks are available to be assigned on the basis of high scores on Depression (scale 2), Impulsivity (scale 4), and Anxiety (scale 8). In addition, we have developed workbooks based on the 15 new factor scales of the MMPI-2, as contained in Part II of this book. Fraizer (1991) evaluates whether these programs will decrease the high peaks in undergraduate scores with minimal face-to-face contact.

Family Profile Form

This instrument is derived from structured enrichment programs for functional and semifunctional (not for critical or clinical) couples and families in primary prevention (L'Abate, 1985; L'Abate & Weinstein, 1987). These programs, concerning a variety (50, to be exact) of marriage and family topics, consist of three to ten lessons per program, and three to eight exercises per lesson. These exercises rely on the spoken word, even though some of these exercises, lessons, and programs can be converted to the written word and administered as workbooks. We review this instrument here because of its potential use in prescribing various programs, lessons, or exercises in writing rather than orally.

Depending on the population, structured enrichment programs can be used as a primary or a secondary prevention approach. They can be administered by paraprofessionals, trainers, or enrichers, who are instructed to read instructions, verbatim but not mechanically, from the manual. A trainer can select an appropriate program or lessons specific to the stated and observed needs of a given couple or family. For years this selection was made by matching the couple's or family's perceived needs with program titles and the index of lesson topics. Pre-post evaluation with various test batteries, irrelevant to prescription, was routinely administered (L'Abate & Wagner, 1985). However, none of the test batteries could link directly the evaluation and the selection of programs, lessons, or exercises specific to the couple's or family's needs (L'Abate & Young, 1987). Selection, therefore, was cumbersome and strictly subjective, based on the whim and will of the trainer or of the supervisor. How can one select from hundreds of lessons and literally thousands of exercises? Selection was also not sufficiently specific, because it depended a great deal on the clinical experience and knowledge of the supervisor who helped trainers select specific programs or lessons. Not being objective, it was not reproducible and not readily transmittable to others.

The problem became one of finding out whether we could make selection more specific and more objective at the level of exercises rather than only at the level of programs and lessons. We thus started to attempt to classify and code these exercises. As this attempt at classification went on, we came up with objective decision rules that enabled seemingly reliable discrimination and allocation of exercises into nine functional and nonoverlapping categories: (1) brainstorming, (2) description, (3) evaluation, (4) negotiation, (5) play, (6) reflection, (7) role taking, (8) self-expression, and (9) touching (L'Abate & Weinstein, 1987, pp. 498–499). Although the reliability of these discrimination rules has not yet been computed quantitatively, a separate classification of exercises by two judges yielded a 90% to 100% agreement between the two. Because an evident bias is possible here, the reliability of these decision rules still needs to be established quantitatively. Once these categories were used to classify all of the exercises, it became possible to generate items (136, to be exact) that would tap into the nine dimensions. Family members describe their family on each item on a five-point Likert-type scale and indicate, therefore, either by consensus or by disagreement, which of the nine dimensions are more troublesome for them. On the basis of the identification of such dimensions, we can now prescribe which among the 1000+ exercises can be specifically administered to improve the reported area of conflict or of perceived deficit (L'Abate & Weinstein, 1987, pp. 471–476). Research to validate this instrument is now in progress (Kochalka, research in progress).

Theory-Derived Instruments

The Self-Profile Chart

This instrument is partially and loosely based on the work of Wallace (1968) to measure projections of self in the past, present, and future. While the Adjustment Inventory measures change over time from present to future, the Self-Profile Chart measures change over time from the past to the present and into the future. This instrument was developed to measure indirectly the sense of importance one attributes to the self (L'Abate, 1990a; L'Abate & Bryson, in press). The attribution of importance to oneself and other intimates is the cornerstone of a theory of personality development explained in greater detail later. In this chart, individuals are asked to rate themselves along dimensions of personal quality, such as intelligence, health, physical attractiveness, morality, and spiritual status, and to fill in a blank dimension of their choosing. Further ratings deal with success areas as an individual, as a friend, as a spouse, as a parent, as a sibling, as child to one's parents, as in-law to one's in-laws, as a worker, and as self in leisure activities. Ratings from +5 to −5 are to be given for the present, the past, and the future. A total score gives a measure of respondents' view of their importance. Data concerning the validity and reliability of this test have been collected and are being analyzed.

The Problems in Relationships Scale (PIRS)

This scale and associated workbook, mentioned earlier, came into being during the testing of a theory-derived model for couples. The underlying model of personality development (L'Abate, 1990a, 1990b; L'Abate & Bryson, in press) deals with status or self-definition according to the attribution of importance to self and to other intimates (mate, parent, child, friend). From this attribution of importance, four possibilities can be derived: (1) *selfulness,* or attribution of importance to self and to other in an "I win, you win" fashion that leads to equality of importance, reciprocity, and intimacy in marriage; (2) *selflessness,* or attribution of importance to other and denial of importance to self, in a "you win, I lose" fashion; (3) *selfishness,* or attribution of importance to self and denial of importance to other, in an "I win, you lose" fashion; and (4) *no-self,* in which both the self and the other are denied importance, in an "I lose, you lose" fashion. The first possibility leads to functional, even creative, intimate relationships. Here, primary prevention approaches would be most successful. The second and third possibilities lead to many dysfunctionally reactive and manipulative relationships, to the extent that many individuals socialized for selfishness, mainly men, tend to attract and be attracted by persons socialized for selflessness, mostly women. From this population come the highest levels of conflict, divorce, and dysfunctionality. Here, the therapies are necessary. The fourth possibility leads to serious psychiatric dysfunctionalities. Here, medication, hospitalization, and incarceration need to be coupled with other forms of intervention, especially tertiary and secondary ones.

We have thus summarized most marital problems and polarizations in 20 conflictful and polarized dimensions (dominant-submissive, weak-strong) that are the bases for the creation of the PIRS, consisting of 240 items on a five-point Likert scale, and the development of a parallel workbook, whose lessons correspond to the 20 dimensions measured by the test. It is now possible to identify which of the 20 dimensions are the most conflictful for a couple and to rank them from the most to the least conflictful. The couple can then be administered just the lessons that correspond to their most conflictful dimensions. Thus, we have a nomothetic method in the test and in the workbook, while the administration of the specific lessons to each couple is idiographic (L'Abate & Kunkel, research in progress).

Self-Description and Description of Self-in-Relationship Tests

Using the same rationale, we created a simpler instrument to parallel the one just presented, with one form for individuals and another form for couples. The first test is for individuals who are not in a committed or prolonged relationship and who do not have enough knowledge of their partners to rate them, but who can rate themselves. The second test is for individuals in relationships who have sufficient knowledge of their partners to rate both self and other. Both tests follow a semantic differential approach, consisting of simple seven-point ratings for the same 20 dimensions measured more indirectly by the Problems in Relationships Scale (PIRS). Both the Self-Description Test and the Description of Self-in-Relationship Test are more direct and shorter ways to select appropriate lessons for partners from the many lessons contained in Part II.

Conclusion

There is no reason why the approach described here, linking evaluation with programmed writing, cannot be developed with other evaluative instruments. Workbooks, based on the written rather than the spoken word, can be created as paratherapeutic and parapreventive methods to help individuals, couples, and families at risk, in need, or in crisis. One can develop a nomothetic programmed workbook from any nomothetic evaluation instrument and then use the instrument to link deviant scales with idiographic treatment, as it is being done by the first author and his associates with the MMPI-2 and the PIRS.

CHAPTER FOUR

Programmed Writing in the Context of Therapy and Prevention

In this chapter we expand on the implications of combining the practice of programmed writing with existing therapeutic and preventive practices. This combination is based on practical, theoretical, and empirical considerations. We describe here a rationale for the use of writing in the practice of psychotherapy and of primary prevention with individuals, couples, and families, based on a conceptualization of the helping process. We also present guidelines for the preparation and use of programmed materials.

A Skills Rationale for the Use of Writing in Therapy and Prevention

Psychotherapy and primary prevention can be conceptualized as processes requiring two distinct sets of helper skills. These two sets of skills are *relationship* and *structuring* skills. Relationship skills underlie the personal, soft-hearted, aesthetically dialectical *style* of the therapist or preventer as a human being, and structuring skills underlie the professional, sometimes hard-headed, pragmatically demonstrative *methods* used to change or to prevent stubborn or symptomatic behaviors.

Relationship skills are exercised inside the professional's office. Warmth, unconditional positive regard, and empathy are traditionally identified as the primary relationship skills needed by helpers; the skill of positively reframing negative behaviors can also be added (Ascher, 1989; Seltzer, 1986). Relationship skills or style are specific to the therapist's person and personality. They are important to establish rapport and maintain the therapeutic or preventive relationship. By definition, relationship skills are exercised mainly in the face-to-face verbal contact between the professional and the client (Rogers, 1957).

Structuring skills are used in creating interventions inside and outside the therapy office, such as homework assignments, paradoxical injunctions, ordeal work, and prescriptions such as marital and family conferences (L'Abate, Ganahl, & Hansen, 1986). Structuring skills are the basis of method, a series of repeatable and reproducible steps applied to the treatment or prevention of symptomatic or problematic behavior. Structuring skills are less concerned with the personalities of therapists or clients and more concerned with getting results (changing or preventing undesirable behavior) in a planned, programmed, and predictable fashion. Structuring skills are exercised in creating programmed materials that are repeatable and that can be administered by a professional and completed by a client using the medium of writing to communicate.

Both sets of skills, relationship and structuring, are necessary for a positive therapeutic and preventive outcome (L'Abate, 1986b), especially with very disturbing or disturbed psychological conditions. The more disturbed the behavior, the greater the need to rely more on method than on style. While relationship skills, as manifested in verbal contact, are necessary for starting and maintaining a therapeutic relationship, they may be insufficient to produce change, especially in very resistant cases. And while structuring skills, as manifested in assignment of writing, may be insufficient to start and maintain a relationship, they may be more useful in producing change, especially in highly resistant conditions. The spoken and the written modalities can thus be seen to complement each other in their functions. A comparison of these modalities from an interventional viewpoint is presented in Table 4-1.

We can compare relationship and structuring skills along other lines, as well. While relationship skills may be mainly *reactive*, structuring skills are usually *conductive*. The former are based on our immediate reactions to clients in expressing our acceptance of them through verbal and nonverbal behavior, keeping a professional stance, not getting "hooked" to them, and indicating a nonjudgmental attitude toward their behavior and a caring view of their pain.

Table 4-1 A comparison of spoken and written words as modalities of intervention in preventive and therapeutic relationships

Spoken	Written
Necessary for relationships*	Necessary for structuring methods to deal with symptoms
Necessary to start and maintain relationship but insufficient to help produce changes in clients, especially couples and families	Insufficient to start and maintain relationship but necessary to help produce changes in clients, especially couples and families
Adaptive	Standardized
Uncontrollable	Controllable
Unpredictable	Predictable
Unprogrammable	Programmable
Nonprescribable or difficult to prescribe	Prescribable or easier to prescribe than the spoken word
Subject to distortions and/or omissions	Not as subject to distortions and/or omissions as the spoken word

*In some relationships, with clients exhibiting impulsive and/or acting-out character disorders, for instance, the spoken word may be used for manipulative and distracting purposes. Under these conditions, the spoken word may become more of a hindrance than a help in the relationship.

Source: From *Building Family Competence*, by L. L'Abate. Copyright © 1990 by Sage Publications.

The latter indicate that the therapist knows and has thought responsibly about what is to be done. There is a definite plan to alleviate pain, decrease troublesome behavior, and thus increase the level of competence of clients.

Reliance solely on relationship skills may limit the influence of the therapist to the context of the therapy office. On the other hand, use of structuring skills to make written assignments may enable that influence to expand from the context of the office to the context of the home or workplace. To hope that relationship skills will generalize outside of a professional's office is to ask ourselves and our personal styles or techniques to achieve an unrealistic and impossible goal that is not substantiated by the available evidence. Relationship skills may be necessary, but they are not sufficient to produce change (Baucom & Epstein, 1990; Garfield & Bergin, 1978, 1986; Norcross, 1986). In addition to giving of ourselves as persons in the office, we need to give our clients methods that will be used and practiced in the home. Our clients need to know and experience that in addition to warmth, empathy, and positive acceptance, there is a definite, concrete, and clear plan to deal with the referring problem and troublesome behavior. Furthermore, therapeutic plans need to become available to the scrutiny of the psychotherapeutic community to accept, change, or reject. This scrutiny can take place only if these plans and programs are in writing.

Value Positions Underlying the Skills

Philosophically, each set of skills is based on different and, unfortunately for many therapists, mutually exclusive value positions. Relationship skills are based on a value position free of determinism, while structuring skills are based on a value position that stresses determinism. As Giacomo and Weissmark (1987) saw this distinction, therapeutic methods can be classified as either programmable or nonprogrammable: "The problem of indeterminism, which arises from the feature of inconsistencies, cannot be adequately solved using programming methods that assume determinacy, namely, regularities and programs" (p. 440). Relationship skills as nondeterministic in their nature are not programmable, while structuring skills are and should be programmable *in writing* if any significant progress in the fields of psychotherapy and prevention is to be achieved.

Therapeutically, relationship skills have been favored by the humanistic school, while structuring skills have been favored by the behavioristic school (Baucom & Epstein, 1990; Garfield & Bergin, 1978, 1986; McMullin, 1986; Norcross, 1986). An approach based on relationship skills is dear to the hearts of individually-oriented humanistic therapists (Hart & Tomlison, 1970; Maddi, 1985; Mahrer, 1986; May & Yalom, 1984; Meador & Rogers, 1984; Miller, 1989; Raskin, 1985; Rogers, 1957; Tageson, 1982). An approach based on structuring skills is favored by behaviorally-oriented therapists (Meichenbaum, 1985; Rimm & Cunningham, 1985; Wilson, 1984) as well as by marital and family therapists (Foley, 1984; Foster & Gurman, 1985) and preventers (L'Abate & McHenry, 1983).

We need to consider the possibility that these extreme therapeutic stances may produce different outcomes. As Stiles (1982) noted, two hypotheses exist that may explain why we obtain differential therapeutic effects. One hypothesis would maintain that "different psychotherapies promote qualitatively different kinds of psychological health. . . . There may be no common core to the psychotherapies because each is aimed at accomplishing something different" (p. 14). The other hypothesis maintains that "the common process core of the various psychotherapies lies in the clients' revealing their own knowledge or experience through Disclosures and Edifications, rather than in any technical similarity in the behavior of the therapists. . . . On the other hand, there may be many ways to facilitate clients' self-explorations and different clients may be more responsive to different techniques" (p. 14). The differentiation between relationship and structuring skills allows us to reconcile both hypotheses. The first hypothesis, concentrating on differences among people and symptoms, points to the importance of structuring skills, while the second hypothesis points to the importance of relationship skills.

Preventively, relationship issues have been considered secondary or even irrelevant to the administration of a program. Preventers, as a whole, rely more on repeatable methods of intervention than do therapists (L'Abate, 1990a). Still, it is doubtful whether any preventer would deny the importance of relationship skills in the establishment and maintenance of a working relationship with clients. But preventers realize that while relationship skills may be necessary and possibly (but not unquestionably!) sufficient with individuals, this set of skills does not suffice in helping couples and families deal with interpersonal and intimate issues of family living.

In summary, then, relationship skills represent what the therapist or preventer does and says in the office in front of and in contact with clients. Structuring skills represent what the therapist or preventer does to help clients change their troublesome behavior where it matters the most—that is, in clients' kitchens, bedrooms, living rooms, or workplaces. To save time and energy as well as to avoid inevitable distortions, instructions should be put in writing for clients to follow step-by-step, matching one hour of homework for each hour of therapy or of prevention. While relationship skills must rely mainly on the oral and nonverbal modalities, structuring skills need not. Instructions can be given in writing and responded to by clients in writing between therapy sessions. Consequently, the use of writing in psychotherapy allows integration of both relationship skills and structuring skills. Both sets of skills, compared in Table 4-2, are necessary for a successful outcome.

Theory Underlying the Skills

A developmental theory of interpersonal competence that has been detailed in various sources (L'Abate, 1976, 1986b, 1990a, 1990b, in press; L'Abate & Bryson, in press; L'Abate & Harel, in press) postulates that the ability to love and the ability to negotiate define interpersonal competence and are the most fundamental processes for individual, dyadic, and family living. The ability to love is linked to Being, while the ability to negotiate is linked to Doing and Having. Being is characterized by exchange of status and love. Doing is characterized by exchange of services and information. Having is characterized

Table 4-2 A comparison of relationship and structuring skills in therapy and prevention

Relationship Skills	Structuring Skills
Indeterminate	Determinate
Unplanned	Planned
Dialectical: Oriented toward discovery (aesthetics)	Demonstrable: Oriented toward justification (pragmatics)
Nonrepeatable from one therapist to another	Repeatable from one therapist to another
Reactive*	Conductive
Immediate (mainly for office use)	Delayed (for home use and family consumption)
Mainly verbal and nonverbal	Mainly written
Specific to the person and style of the therapist	Specific to the symptomatic behavior to be improved
Idiographic	Nomothetic
Assert clients' inherent worth and importance	Assess and assert the seriousness of referral problem and symptom
Deal with clients as persons and not as objects	Deal specifically with the symptom
Global, holistic, and subjective	Detailed, particularistic, and objective
Emphasize being available emotionally to self and to clients verbally and nonverbally	Assign systematic and planned written homework

*Questionable and open to empirical confirmation or disqualification.

Source: From "The Practice of Programmed Writing (PW) in Therapy and Prevention with Families" by L. L'Abate and K. Platzman, in press, *American Journal of Family Therapy.* New York: Brunner/Mazel.

by exchange of goods and money (Foá & Foá, 1974). Being is expressed personally and interpersonally through *presence,* being emotionally available to self and to significant others. Doing is expressed through *performance,* while Having is expressed through *production.*

Recently, Huston and Rempel (1989) have noted that there are "two almost separate literatures . . . about family and other close relationships. One focuses on general interpersonal attitudes and dispositions such as love, commitment, and trust; the other centers on the analysis of behavioral exchanges, usually concentrating on the detailed examination of behaviors that take place during face-to-face interaction" (p. 177). Huston and Rempel distinguish between these two literatures by referring to them respectively as attitudinal/dispositional and behavioral. In relationship to our developmental theory of interpersonal competence, the attitudinal/dispositional view tends to focus attention on the ability to love, while the behavioral view tends to focus attention on the ability to negotiate.

How does our developmental theory of interpersonal competence relate to the two sets of helping skills? Relationship skills relate to Being—that is, (1) being able to be present and to be available emotionally to oneself and to another verbally and nonverbally without demands for performance, production, perfection, or problem solving; (2) asserting the inherent importance and worth of clients as autonomous, self-determining human beings; through (3) expressions of unconditional positive regard, warmth, and empathy, and positive reframing of negative behaviors. The structuring approach favors Doing and Having, asking clients to perform and produce (services) anytime they are asked to process and complete homework assignments (information). If they want to save money and time (Having), the more they perform and produce in the area of homework assignments the more money they may be able to save in therapy. Homework assignments are administered on a collaborative basis with clients and are subject to negotiation (confrontation, bargaining, and problem solving) between client and helper.

In terms of applying our theory to clients, Being is evaluated in writing through two models, one of self-definition through the attribution of importance to self and to others, and the second through a model of love and intimacy. Both models have either been verified through paper-and-pencil self-report tests (L'Abate & Wagner, 1985, 1988; Stevens & L'Abate, 1989) or are in the process of being verified (L'Abate & Kunkel, research in progress). Doing is measured by *how well* one performs various roles and tasks at home, as a provider, partner, and parent; at work, as an employer or employee; and in leisure-time activities, like hobbies, avocations, games, and sports. Having is measured by *how much* one produces at home, at work, and in leisure-time activities.

Guidelines for the Use of Writing in Therapy and Prevention

After presenting case studies of writing therapy, Phillips and Wiener (1966) gave guidelines on its use. We paraphrase their guidelines freely here, and suggest that writing can be useful in any helping practice, provided that it is additional to individual, marital, or family face-to-face contact (L'Abate, 1986b) or an alternative in working with people who cannot be seen face to face, like people in jails, hospitals, or out of the country.

1. Writing should be done at set times—for example, every other day at 9:00 P.M.—for a constant length of time, such as half an hour or an hour, depending on the topic and its preeminence in the person's life. If a particular issue—for instance, depression—is to be considered (L'Abate, 1986b), clients may need to write about it every other day for at least half an hour at set times, to learn how to control it rather than to be controlled by it. In less extreme cases, once a week may be sufficient.

2. It is usually helpful to suggest a specific topic so that clients focus time and energy on one topic at a time. Once the topic has been suggested, the client should be encouraged to write freely, without paying attention to sentence structure, grammar, or logic.

3. If reading and writing are difficult because of educational level or other factors, the client can do each lesson by listening to tape-recorded questions and speaking answers into a tape recorder or to volunteers who write the responses.

4. If a rationale is to be given, or if clients ask for it, issues of control (L'Abate, 1986b) may be considered ("Do you want the depression to control you, or do you want to learn to control the depression?") in addition to economic issues. Writing in general may help get obsessive thinking out of the head and onto a piece of paper (that is, from the inside to the outside), where it can be evaluated and responded to.

5. Another rationale for writing as a paratherapeutic modality is record keeping. Plans, procedures, and progress in our world are generally recorded. Without written records, we would not be able to evaluate change or progress.

6. Clients' notes can be read during the face-to-face session, or they can be read afterward by the professional and discussed during the next session.

7. For maximum effectiveness, the use of writing and of regular appointments to implement it, should be agreed upon from the very beginning of any therapeutic or preventive contract. Otherwise, clients may think that something new is being sprung on them and may feel betrayed by the professional.

The use of writing in psychotherapy needs to be based on a clear contract from the outset of an intervention. Clients are to spend as much time working on homework assignments as they spend in therapy or in prevention. This contract can be presented paradoxically. Clients do not have to engage in these written homework assignments at stated times and frequencies if they have unlimited finances, want a long period of therapy, and like the professional helper so much that they want to stay in therapy forever. Of course, even with this contract, some clients do show resistance to engaging in and completing assignments. In such cases, part of therapy is to deal with the meaning and context of this resistance to meeting the letter and spirit of the intitial contract.

A major difference between therapy and programmed writing lies in the fact that in therapy, the helper constitutes a "public" in front of whom clients may or may not choose to air their dirty laundry. By contrast, during programmed lessons, there is no "public." When the structure of these materials orchestrates the exposure of very dirty laundry (whether self-incriminating or other-incriminating), no third party is present to serve as referee, moderator, interpreter, counselor, or comforter. Members of a family are solely responsible for experiencing, regulating, and expressing their emotionality, rationality, and activity, during moments when they are highly aroused and understandably defensive and irrational.

The nature of clients' responses to programmed materials imposes certain ethical necessities and professional responsibilities on the helper. Full participation in programmed materials forces individuals, couples, and families to engage in focused self-examination and in critical examination of partner and other family members. It is stressful enough to cope with one's own candid reflections in these areas; it can be even more stressful to be exposed to a mate's or family member's uncensored, sudden, and unprovoked interpretations, reflections, and evaluations of self and others. Self-disclosure may be especially necessary when years of unresolved conflicts have been swept under the proverbial carpet and either mates or family members have collected enough hurts to reach extremely destructive outcomes. Thus, substantial damage can be done by the unsupervised discussion of highly sensitive issues introduced by the workbook, even when the clients are meeting weekly with the therapist. Consequently, it is an ethical necessity and a professional responsibility to ensure that no workbook lesson is assigned until the therapist is fairly certain that it will not exhume issues with which clients are ill-equipped, at that time, to deal.

This ethical consideration brings up another issue. Fortunately, in the last few decades, we have begun to view individuals along a continuum of normalcy rather than seeing some persons as prisoners of psychiatric categories and others as "normal." Although diagnostic characteristics prove useful in suggesting treatments that have worked with others who have exhibited the same characteristics, there may be great value in the premise that every individual has the capacity for adaptive and maladaptive behavior, for rational and irrational behavior, for helpful and hurtful behaviors. Therefore, it may be a disservice to view clients as either in crisis or crisis-free. Certain lessons can be very effective in precipitating crises, even in couples who have been evaluated as not in crisis but perhaps in need. By teaching new skills and fostering deeper self- and other-awareness, this process requires individuals to participate at a level of intrapersonal and interpersonal functioning that may not be in their repertoire. Programmed materials may tell people that they can interact more effectively, but they do not teach them, through practical lessons, how to apply the affective and interpersonal skills necessary to participate in the lesson without defensiveness and oversensitivity. Continuous corrective feedback from the therapist is crucial in this situation.

The omission of the helper's feedback and supervision may have serious consequences. For example, a husband and wife who are not highly competent at accepting each other's differentness might be alarmed at the differences expressed in answers to workbook questions. Family members who are competitive may find programmed lessons an ideal passive-aggressive outlet for putting each other down. This would be especially tempting in the intellectual realm, because of the vocabulary-quiz style of some lessons. This aspect of some lessons may tend to promote performance anxiety (competing with each other) rather than encourage presence (being emotionally available to each other).

Another possible problem the helper should watch out for is related to the objectives for participating. A respondent who is not psychologically invested in the shared benefit of doing the workbook could easily undermine the activity and might be cruel or angry about it. Answers to questions can easily be "salted" to ventilate frustration or resentment. Or they can be "sweetened" to avoid conflict when answers are shared and discussed. Either salting or sweetening retards therapy and relationship building. The supervising therapist must help the couple become aware of this and other dangers, encouraging them in every way possible to learn to communicate honestly but with compassion and tact. Workbooks may roll back the carpet and expose the mound of unresolved conflicts that may have been piling up for years. The therapist should teach people skills that will enable them to deal with the emotional intensity of finally confronting and discussing these conflicts.

It is important for the helper to exercise caution when assigning programmed materials to couples or families in which one partner or family member resists these activities. This outcome is to be expected when one person is less verbal or less emotionally available than the other(s). One family member may do the workbook lesson to obligate or placate others; or may do the workbook under less than voluntary circumstances; or may lose interest in doing the workbook after beginning the project. All these issues need to be considered grist for the therapeutic mill. With acting-out juveniles, who, for instance, may refuse to come for family therapy or may distract and misdirect communication while there, it is possible to see the rest of the family and to make a contract with the juvenile to complete the Social Training workbook but not to attend family therapy sessions.

Should a professional collude with parts of the system (spouse, family members) to urge a reluctant member to participate in the workbook program, it is vital that the following details be made crystal clear:

1. Programmed materials are not therapy. They can be an adjunct to therapy sessions provided they are used properly and professionally.

2. Assignments require approximately one hour a week to complete and discuss the respective answers with a mate or other family members.

3. Completion of each lesson demands a moderate-to-intense expenditure of emotional, mental, and psychological energy. If one cannot commit to this kind of effort, one should not agree to participate in this program.

4. Ground rules for sharing and discussing lessons should be discussed and agreed upon by family members before beginning work. These rules should be written down for review during work on programmed lessons. It may be best if rules are developed by the clients themselves rather than having rules assigned to them by the therapist. This decision should perhaps be made by the therapist.

5. There are no correct or incorrect answers. This provision must be reinforced with families who have problems dealing with each other's differentness or who are too perfectionistic or intellectualized.

6. Participation in the program may at times require more than the one hour allotted for the completion of each lesson; that is, each person answers each lesson independently of all other family members, and then all family members discuss their answers. For some people this process may take less than an hour; for others, it may take longer.

Guidelines for Devising Programmed Materials

Programmed materials can be as varied as the need of the clients and the ingenuity of the professional. Writing assignments can be (1) generated by the professional's own experience and practice for clients with specific presenting problems or complaints; (2) taken from the clinical or research literature and modified for clients' use; and (3) taken from the immense self-help literature and reduced to a programmed, self-administered format, making self-help more active and actually interactive, rather than passively receptive

(L'Abate, 1990a). Currently, these materials can be classified according to their origin: (1) they can be derived from clinical approaches, as are the Social Training and Social Growth workbooks; (2) they can be derived from theory-derived models, as is the Problems in Relationships workbook; and (3) they can be derived from the voluminous self-help literature. The range of programmed materials that can be developed is limitless. The following criteria might be given serious consideration in constructing them.

1. Follow examples of programmed materials already available. At the outset do not worry about length, format, and style. Establish the purpose of the workbook in general, outline the topics you want to cover, assign a lesson for each topic, and follow principles of sequencing between and within lessons.

2. If you consider writing just one lesson, make sure it can stand alone. In writing each lesson, avoid brainwashing and lengthy instructions. If you find yourself explaining too much, break the paragraph into smaller steps, with a minimum of guidance and a maximum of letting the respondent come to find his or her answers, step-by-step, gradually.

3. To write a whole workbook, it may be useful to divide it into sections, each devoted to a different stage of the treatment process. For instance, in preparing a workbook on addiction, you may want to divide lessons into four different sets: (a) *crisis intervention*—at this beginning stage, a lesson or a series of lessons devoted to the topic of crises and how one copes before, during, and after a crisis may be relevant; (b) *treatment proper*—here you may want to detail the steps one must undertake to change one's self and one's relationships; (c) *relapse prevention*—because relapse is a major part of any addictive process, one must plan for it rather than waiting for it to happen; (d) *maintenance or support*—this final part pertains to the long-range outcome; that is, how is one going to take care of oneself and of intimate relationships?

4. Follow a sequence in planning each lesson. Questions within each lesson should follow from the previous ones. For instance, you could start with the most immediate concerns, moving on to short-term and then to long-term concerns (past, present, and future). To increase the respondent's temporal perspective, give some daily, weekly, monthly, yearly, and longer-range goals. Determine what is needed now, what will be needed later on, and what will be needed in the long run. Separate diagnostic from problem-solving questions.

5. Give a title to each of your lessons. Then state the purpose of the lesson; help define terms; describe the costs and rewards of proposed changes or implications of the topic for treatment; and elaborate on ways this topic is relevant to the specific condition or addiction.

6. Make sure that each lesson culminates with a specific assignment of certain relevant behaviors that the client needs to monitor or practice for at least a week. This requirement is important to produce change at the cognitive level. At the beginning of the next lesson, provide space for feedback about the previous lesson. Did the client follow the assignment? If not, why not? How did he or she feel after doing or not doing the assignment? What was the outcome? If the assignment was followed, what happened? If it was not followed, what happened?

7. Make sure that the weekly behavioral assignments are complete, specific, limited in space and time, well-defined, and doable, relatively easy to carry out. If the client talks a good game but does not do the homework assignments, you may need to provide a lesson on duplicity and lying to oneself, loved ones, peers, colleagues, friends, and so on.

8. After you have finished a first draft, show it to another professional colleague or friend for initial critiquing and debugging. Then make a second draft and send it to a few very critical friend-colleagues, asking them for specific reactions and suggestions.

9. Administer your lesson or workbook to a few clients in a selective and appropriate fashion, and on the basis of their feedback revise again. Try the lesson or workbook out yourself or give it to family members and/or friends who are not professionals to get their reactions. Use their reactions to revise again. Pat yourself on the back.

10. Try out the workbook with selected clients and debug it again.

11. Give the workbook to other colleagues to use in their practice; in exchange, ask them to give you their candid feedback.

12. Start thinking about another workbook!

Conclusion

In this chapter we have considered the many theoretical, therapeutic, and practical implications of combining writing and especially programmed writing with the traditional practice of face-to-face therapy and prevention. The process of helping requires two sets of skills—relationship and structuring. In terms of a developmental theory of interpersonal competence, these two sets are related respectively to Being and to Doing and Having.

Once we distinguish between relationship and structuring skills, we are able to locate writing, and especially programmed writing, in the category of structuring skills that require performance and production. While face-to-face contacts between therapists and clients require presence, or emotional availability, writing does not require this modality. With certain individuals, especially driven or acting-out ones, presence may be irrelevant to or even distracting from change. The presence of the therapist may take place (as a reward?) only after acting-out and impulsive behavior has been replaced by more thoughtful and positive behavior that may have been produced by writing, especially programmed writing.

CHAPTER FIVE

Implications of Programmed Writing for the Mental Health Field

The purpose of this chapter is to indicate how programmed writing can help in the delivery of services both in mental health and in offender rehabilitation. We look first at a multilevel approach to service delivery made possible by programmed writing. Then we examine how programmed writing facilitates research, describing some completed and ongoing research projects.

A Multilevel Approach to Delivery of Human Services

Use of programmed writing makes possible a model of service delivery in mental health and offender rehabilitation in which (1) psychodiagnostic evaluation discriminates among three populations classified as at risk, in need, and in crisis; and (2) appropriate levels of intervention are administered by a hierarchy of personnel, differing in training, credentials, and interests, and ranging from professionals (Ph.D. or equivalent) to middle-level professionals (M.A. or equivalent) to paraprofessionals (B.A. or equivalent) (L'Abate, 1990a). Such a model differentiates among levels of intervention, matching the level of intervention to the needs of the population served. Furthermore, it differentiates among levels of expertise necessary to administer different levels of intervention.

If primary prevention consists of psychoeducational skill-training programs (L'Abate & Milan, 1985) for populations *at risk*, while therapy deals mainly with people *in crisis*, then programmed writing could deal with people *in need*—that is, people either at risk or in crisis who have additional requirements. Such people at risk would be administered not only psychoeducational skill-training programs, but also additional writing assignments. By the same token, such people in crisis could benefit by additional writing assignments as well as by additional skill-oriented psychoeducational programs.

Of course, the question arises, with whom, by whom, for whom, and at what price are various levels of intervention most effective? Although some direct and indirect evidence has been published about the applicability of programmed writing (L'Abate, 1990a), and more evidence is being gathered by the first author and his co-workers, this question cannot be answered solely by ourselves. We will need the help of our colleagues to answer it more adequately.

Ideally, the initial evaluation can determine the nature and the level of the self-administered program to be assigned to each individual and whether therapy should be concomitant with programmed writing. For instance, people on waiting lists for psychiatric and psychotherapeutic help might work on specific programmed materials while they wait. Once these clients completed assigned written programs successfully, with a pre- and postevaluation of the specified reason for referral, they could be assigned to more expensive therapies, if still needed, requiring prolonged, face-to-face individual, marital, family, or group contact.

Doctorate-level therapists can serve as front-line personnel in crisis situations, in which evaluation is difficult or impossible. Programs for such emergencies have been written for some couples and families, as shown in Part II, following a methodology for crisis intervention. After the crisis is dealt with, additional written materials can be administered. Face-to-face contact is still necessary in crisis intervention and with people who cannot read or write. However, many of these services with populations that cannot read or write can be performed by persons drawn from the same populations (former alcoholics with alcoholics, former addicts with addicts, former delinquents with delinquents). These preprofessional personnel can be selected from those who can read and write, who have successfully completed the written programs, and who have met the criteria of mastery and satisfaction over time. These persons can become teacher-tutors, provided they are regularly supervised and supported by more experienced personnel.

A Hierarchy of Interventions

We propose a hierarchy of eight possible levels of intervention, proceeding from the most expensive to the least expensive or from the least to the most expensive. Cost is computed in terms of professional time; the higher one goes up the ladder of professionalism, the higher the costs. In primary prevention, for instance, we would start with the least expensive procedures (evaluation) in the hands of pre- or paraprofessionals. They would determine the course of intervention, using face-to-face interviews plus written programs. Clients who needed to learn further skills would be assigned specific programmed homework on the basis of their specific needs. In dealing with crises, one would start with the most expensive level of intervention—that is, face-to-face contact with a professional who, after dealing with the crisis, would assign the client to para- or preprofessionals for further secondary and primary prevention activities. This approach involves essentially a two-stage model: a first stage of therapy to deal with the referring symptom and a second stage of enrichment or primary prevention to help clients learn skills that should help them for the long haul.

The concept of successive levels in human services delivery is not new (L'Abate, 1969; L'Abate & Thaxton, 1981). However, up to now it has been impossible to articulate a more detailed model for lack of a sufficient number of differentiated levels. Implicit in this concept is the practice of proceeding either from a cheaper level of service delivery to a more expensive level in primary prevention, or from a more expensive level to a less costly one in tertiary prevention.

The eight levels of intervention we have identified, from least to most expensive, are as follows:

Level 1: This level encompasses structured enrichment programs for functional and semifunctional couples and families who need to make a good thing better through verbatim instructions delivered by college graduates. Available are 50 different programs covering a wide variety of issues relevant to family living, both structurally and developmentally (L'Abate & Weinstein, 1987; L'Abate & Young, 1987).

Level 2: This level consists of the programmed materials described and found in Part II of this book. They are designed for individuals involved in either tertiary or primary prevention activities with little or no need for professional time except for written feedback. Lessons in these materials can be reviewed by master's-level personnel who have training and experience in this approach.

Level 3: This level encompasses programmed materials to make marital or committed relationships better. It requires covenant contracting, a structured form of marital paratherapy that requires partners to follow a sequence of steps designed to deal with unspoken and spoken aspects of the relationship (L'Abate & McHenry, 1983; Sager, 1976). Because it is less structured than the preceding levels, it requires a manual and more expertise and sensitivity than the preceding levels, and thus should be administered by personnel at the master's level or above.

Level 4: This level encompasses social skills training (L'Abate & Milan, 1985; Levant, 1986), a paratherapeutic movement based on the psychoeducational model—that is, teaching and practicing of personal and interpersonal skills according to a gradual increase in difficulty of problems to be solved.

Level 5: This level encompasses psychotherapy with individuals, couples, families, and groups. Administration requires a minimum of a master's degree plus supervised experience (up to the doctorate) with outpatients.

Level 6: This level encompasses psychotherapy plus medication to keep clients out of hospitals. Administration requires a master's degree plus years of experience and supervision or a doctorate for therapy, or a medical degree for medication.

Level 7: This level consists of temporary, crisis-oriented hospitalization or incarceration. Administration requires an abundance of personnel with varying degrees of skills and experience.

Level 8: This level consists of long-term custodial care or incarceration.

Once successive levels of intervention have been identified, it is possible to deliver a combination of different forms of intervention to meet clients' needs. For instance, family psychotherapy can be combined with different workbooks to meet the different needs of each family member. Even hospitalization or incarceration can be combined with a variety of other forms of intervention according to the specific needs of each client.

A Hierarchy of Personnel

Mental health services can be differentiated and delivered by a hierarchy of professionals, semiprofessionals, paraprofessionals, and subprofessionals. A more experienced professional, preferably with a doctorate degree, can supervise a second tier of less experienced helpers, at the M.A. level. The latter, in addition to seeing clients directly, can supervise subprofessional (A.A. or B.A. degree) personnel, who can administer a plethora of structured enrichment programs or other psychoeducational programs currently available (L'Abate, 1986b; L'Abate & Milan, 1985; Levant, 1986). Use of this diversity of personnel can make services available to much wider segments of the populations in need of quality services at lower costs than have been possible heretofore.

The hierarchical structure we propose is as follows:

Subprofessionals with a high school diploma or the equivalent can perform simple clerical tasks. They can help administer and score objective tests, schedule appointments for other professionals, teach simple skills to persons who are illiterate, and even lead discussion groups with illiterate persons and their families. They can be responsible for data gathering to support efficient and inexpensive treatment. Subprofessionals can be former patients who are being rehabilitated and who can work with populations with the same disorders they have experienced. They can be supervised and supported by paraprofessionals.

Paraprofessionals, who need a college degree or the equivalent, in addition to supporting and supervising the work of providers in the preceding category, can deliver structured enrichment and psychoeducational (preventive) programs; train individuals, couples, and families in social skills (L'Abate & Milan, 1985); deliver self-administered programs; and supervise compliance with the programs and completion of them. This level of personnel, in turn, can be supported and supervised by semiprofessionals.

Semiprofessionals, who have a master's degree or the equivalent, can assess and evaluate referrals through interviews and history taking, provide crisis intervention based on unstructured counseling and psychotherapy, and provide services that the preceding two categories cannot provide. They can be supervised by professionals.

Professionals, who have doctorate degrees or the equivalent, can be responsible for decision making about needed services. For instance, what kind of treatment or approach should be used with a client on the basis of the data gathered by workers in the preceding categories? Professionals can support, supervise, direct, and devise treatment strategies and their implementation.

This hierarchical structure would require a much more responsible and expanded leadership role for full-fledged mental health professionals (Ph.D. or M.D.) than has been envisaged up to now. This professional would be a therapist as well as a preventer, since at least 66% of clients who have terminated therapy are at risk for relapse (Leff & Vaughn, 1985) and can benefit from further psychoeducational training. It is possible to train such leaders. Training at a graduate level could begin with psychoeducational programs and progress gradually to less structured (and more complex) and more difficult family therapy methods (L'Abate, 1985). The multilevel approach we have described is summarized in Table 5-1.

In conclusion, the potential for implementing programmed writing within the context of traditional therapeutic, preventive, and rehabilitative mental health services is immense. But the chances of implementation may be rather slim, since change in the mental health and offender rehabilitation fields is hard to come by. This proposal may be too radical to implement, even on a limited, experimental basis. Too many sacred cows and institutionalized shibboleths are part of the baggage that makes change in the mental health field difficult if not impossible. We want our clients to change, but we want to keep our methods of change as they are—unchanged! But if we do not do it, who will? If not now, when?

Linking Clinical Practice with Research

Programmed writing can bridge the gap between theory and practice. On this topic, Glasgow and Rosen (1978) wrote,

> The possibility of developing empirically validated self-help programs is an exciting one. In addition to the important clinical implications of such programs, there exist implications for the conduct of treatment outcome research. For example, self-administered or minimal contact programs can be used as comparison conditions against which to evaluate the effects of more time-consuming and costly therapist-directed interventions. In addition to providing a cost-effectiveness standard, self-administered or minimal-contact controls may avoid ethical problems associated with delayed or untreated conditions. It also becomes possible to assess treatment and placebo under double-blind self-administered conditions. (p. 17)

Table 5-1 A multilevel approach to mental health service delivery, from least to most costly

Level of Intervention	*Level of Personnel Required to Administer*
1. Structured enrichment	Paraprofessional
2. Programmed materials	Semiprofessional
3. Covenant contracting for couples	Semiprofessional
4. Social skills training	Semiprofessional
5. Psychotherapies (individual, couple, family, and group)	Semiprofessional, professional
6. Medication (outpatient)	Professional
7. Hospitalization or incarceration (temporary, crisis-oriented)	Professional
8. Long-term custodial care or incarceration	Professional

A practitioner using stylistically personal ways of intervening can at the same time act as a researcher of the usefulness of the paratherapeutic process as assessed by written homework assignments. Results from assignments can be collected and coded by the therapist/researcher. Instead of remaining separate enterprises, research and practice can be combined without doing injustice to either. As mentioned before, many therapeutic or preventive techniques and practices are not verifiable because they are specific to the therapist's style and therefore are not reproducible and repeatable. Consequently, they remain untested, and often untestable. Programmed writing, on the other hand, is reproducible and offers tangible proof of improvement as a result of either therapeutic or preventive interventions.

Programmed materials lend themselves easily to a variety of research projects— much more easily than do spoken words. One knows exactly what has gone on in treatment, especially treatment that has been administered long-distance, through the mail. Because in programmed writing a record is kept by the client and eventually given to the therapist, there is less need for the transcription and coding of tapes. Therapeutic writing is much more controllable than talk. And to evaluate the outcome of programmed writing and other treatment and intervention programs, a variety of paper-and-pencil diagnostic instruments are available, some of which were described in Chapter 3.

To illustrate how well programmed writing lends itself to research, we will describe here various research projects at different stages of completion.

A Study of the Negotiation and Intimacy Programs

The purpose of the first study we will describe was to evaluate the usefulness of two interactive programs designed to teach couples how to negotiate and how to be intimate. These programs—the Negotiation and Intimacy programs— were derived from theoretical models that are part of the larger theory of personality development and competence touched on in Chapter 4 (L'Abate, 1986b; L'Abate & Bryson, in press; L'Abate & Colondier, 1987; L'Abate & Harel, in press). This study was completed with the collaboration of Elizabeth Cogswell and John R. Lutz.

Participants
Subjects were volunteer couples who had expressed an interest in participating in an experiment concerning structured communication tasks for couples. They signed consent forms before participation. Sixty-four partners or spouses (32 couples) participated in this study. To be included, couples had to be in a committed relationship (that is, dating each other exclusively for at least six months, engaged, or married). Subjects were secured by one of two means: through personal solicitation by trainers, or through an undergraduate psychology experimental credit requirement in which students in introductory psychology courses earned course credits for participation in research. To safeguard subject confidentiality, personally solicited couples were assigned to another trainer if the couple had had a previous relationship with the soliciting trainer. Couples were randomly assigned to one of three experimental

conditions—control, trainer-assisted, or trainer-conducted—which allowed matching by marital or dating status. Five couples dropped out after starting, four couples dropped out before the completion of the program, and eight couples did not complete the Intimacy program.

Trainers/facilitators were graduate or undergraduate psychology students. Trainers had completed the entire program (either Negotiation or Intimacy) with a spouse, boyfriend or girlfriend, family member, or a close friend in a one-week format to thoroughly familiarize themselves with each of the lessons, the test battery, and the use of the communication principles of feedback and instructions. Behavioral rehearsal was used to help train trainers in their role. The experimenters met with each trainer weekly to deal with questions and to monitor progress and adherence to the experimental design and conditions. All trainers received course credit for their participation. No formal assessment was conducted of the level or the extent of the trainer's existing clinical skill or research experience.

Instruments

A test battery given before and after the program to each partner or couple consisted of four self-report inventories.

1. The Spanier Dyadic Adjustment Scale (DAS) (Spanier, 1976) was used as an index of general dyadic adjustment. Asking subjects to select the level of disagreement across a number of areas relevant to a couple's adjustment (for example, finances, in-laws, friends), the 31-item scale yields four subscale totals (Dyadic Satisfaction, Cohesion, Consensus, and Affective Expression), which are added to yield a total scale score.

2. The Primary Communication Inventory (PCI) (Navran, 1967) is a 25-item measure of married couples' communication practices. It includes both self-report and spouse-report statements and assesses both verbal and nonverbal communication practices.

3. The Marital Issues Questionnaire (MIQ) (Ulrici, 1984) is a developmental-cognitive measure of one's understanding of marital issues and is based on a social prospectivism approach. Consisting of five vignettes that include a problem to be solved or a decision to be made, it requires subjects to rate a series of thoughts or ideas as to their importance in resolving a dilemma. The couple is asked to rank different choices. Ulrici's research (Ulrici, 1984) has shown correlations between age (and possibly marital status) and the ranking of items according to a developmental-cognitive schema of the understanding of relationships. Changes in scores as a result of psychotherapeutic interventions, however, have not been studied.

4. The Sharing of Hurts Scale (SOH) is a 39-item survey measuring the degree of agreement with statements hypothesized to relate to intimacy. It has been found to correlate well with three other established scales of intimacy (Stevens & L'Abate, 1989).

In addition to evaluation by these four inventories, each lesson and the set of lessons as a group were evaluated on feedback evaluation forms. Included on the evaluation form for each lesson were ratings of the lesson's usefulness in facilitating or developing effective communication. Evaluation of each set of lessons included the rank ordering of the lessons in terms of their usefulness and ratings of their effect on the couple's relationship in general, the couple's willingness to recommend the set of lessons to other couples, and their overall usefulness and importance in facilitating or developing effective communication practices. Responses to two open-ended questions on what was learned and how the lessons could be improved were included for each of the individual lessons and for the lessons as a group for the Negotiation program only, after it was found that the evaluation forms did not discriminate among the six Negotiation lessons (Lutz, 1985).

Interventions

Couples in the trainer-assisted group completed each lesson together at home. Once a week, they met with a trainer/facilitator for no more than 15 minutes to turn in their completed worksheets and feedback evaluation forms, to receive feedback on their responses, to ask questions about the target behaviors covered in each lesson, and to receive an introduction to the next lesson. Lessons that had not been completed were reassigned for the following week, along with the next lesson.

Couples in the trainer-conducted group met weekly for at least 45 minutes (longer if needed) and completed each lesson in the presence of the trainer. The trainer introduced each lesson; had the couple read the lesson's introduction, purpose, and instructions; answered questions; modeled communication skill behaviors for each lesson; provided feedback on each partner's responses; and collected the completed worksheets and feedback evaluation forms. The settings for meetings, chosen for convenience, included offices at the Georgia State University Child and Family Clinic as well as the subjects' homes. All couples were trained in individual format—that is, one couple to one trainer.

Procedures

The Negotiation program in this research consisted of six lessons instead of the eight that constitute the complete published program (L'Abate, 1986b). The Intimacy program consisted also of six lessons. The set of six lessons were based on the models of L'Abate (1986b). The six lessons in the Negotiation program, in order of assignment and completion, were (1) "I" Statements; (2) Styles in Intimacy; (3) Options in Responding: Emotional, Rational, and Actional; (4) Options in Responding: Awareness and Contextual; (5) Priorities; and (6) Guidelines for Negotiation. The six lessons in the Intimacy program, in order of assignment and completion, were (1) Caring; (2) Seeing the Good; (3) Forgiveness; lessons 4, 5, and 6 concentrated on Sharing of Hurts.

Each lesson, presented in writing, followed a standard format: Introduction, Purpose or Rationale, Instructions/Directions, Definitions, Examples of Communication Skill Target Behaviors, and Lesson Worksheets, on which responses were recorded. Blanks in which to supply stimulus sentences and situations unique to the couple's relationship were incorporated into each of the lessons so that couples (1) would have to elaborate on each answer, specifying its relevance to their relationship, and (2) would be able to include stimuli that had affective significance for them.

Before the experiment began, each couple completed the test battery. Experimental couples then completed the six lessons, approximately one per week, in the order listed. The evaluation feedback form on the entire set of lessons, along with the second administration of the test battery, were completed one week after the experimental couples completed lesson 6. A third group, the control couples, who received no intervention, completed the test battery twice, once at the beginning and once at the end of eight weeks. Therefore, completion of the entire experiment for all three experimental groups took approximately eight weeks.

Hypotheses

As scores on measures of communication and dyadic adjustment have been shown to correlate positively (Navran, 1967; Yelsma, 1984), the hypotheses in this study were as follows:

Hypothesis 1: Scores for subjects in either of the two programs (Negotiation and Intimacy) and in the two experimental groups (trainer-assisted and trainer-conducted) will reflect changes at posttesting in a positive direction and will be significantly greater than scores for subjects in the control group on measures of communication and cognitive/developmental understanding of marital issues.

Hypothesis 2: Couples participating in the Intimacy program should show greater improvements in scores than should couples participating in the Negotiation program.

Hypothesis 3: Communication and dyadic adjustment scores of couples in the trainer-assisted group will change as much as (that is, will not be significantly different from) those of couples in the trainer-conducted group because of the expressed interest in communication skills by both groups, the identically structured format of the set of lessons for both groups, and the inclusion of trainer contact for both groups.

Results and Discussion

The test scores, separated by gender, pre-post tests, program, and condition (trainer-assisted vs. trainer-conducted) are shown in Table 5-2.

Pre- and postintervention test scores were subjected to correlation analysis and to ANOVA to evaluate the significance of differences in means and standard deviations shown in Table 5-2. The correlation matrix (Table 5-3) indicated that most measures, except the MIQ, were correlated at a significant level of confidence, either in a positive or a negative direction, depending on the dimension. For instance, the DAS and the PCI correlated significantly with the SOH, both pre- and postintervention, indicating an expected inverse relationship between marital adjustment and communication and intimacy; that is, the higher the marital adjustment and the higher the level of communication, the lower the level of sharing hurts. ANOVA yielded the following results for

Table 5-2 Comparison of test scores before and after completion of negotiation and intimacy programs (N = 74)

| | | | Males | | | | Females | | | |
| | | | Pre | | Post | | Pre | | Post | |
Program	Condition	Test	Mean	SD	Mean	SD	Mean	SD	Mean	SD
Negotiation	Trainer-assisted (N = 16)	DAS	99.67	7.79	107.33	10.91	109.44	14.23	114.88	12.40
		MIQ	26.50	4.50	23.17	5.45	28.33	6.54	27.78	4.94
		PCI	87.33	8.43	95.67	6.09	93.00	9.59	95.55	7.79
		SOH	105.33	7.22	99.17	9.58	95.00	10.26	89.67	10.02
	Trainer-conducted (N = 16)	DAS	110.20	12.74	113.00	11.13	109.57	11.77	111.00	11.89
		MIQ	25.10	4.68	27.20	4.80	27.72	4.68	29.86	2.85
		PCI	89.80	7.64	95.40	9.58	96.28	10.45	99.57	7.02
		SOH	97.10	11.61	94.50	12.28	85.28	15.79	88.86	12.17
	Control (N = 10)	DAS	111.60	11.06	108.40	5.08	117.00	5.34	112.40	7.12
		MIQ	25.20	4.87	28.20	3.83	27.00	8.60	26.20	5.88
		PCI	99.20	6.68	95.40	4.16	96.80	8.76	93.40	4.77
		SOH	87.80	10.06	91.60	11.80	88.00	11.00	96.40	6.77
Intimacy	Trainer-assisted (N = 12)	DAS	111.17	7.13	109.83	7.30	117.67	9.89	116.83	9.87
		MIQ	26.17	3.31	29.17	6.14	31.00	2.90	30.17	5.23
		PCI	80.33	16.57	84.00	11.26	87.17	12.27	89.00	13.40
		SOH	84.83	14.17	87.33	11.79	84.50	11.73	81.83	6.43
	Trainer-conducted (N = 14)	DAS	110.43	13.75	110.71	15.26	110.86	14.89	111.71	18.84
		MIQ	26.43	8.16	28.00	4.54	30.14	2.61	32.28	3.68
		PCI	94.86	16.54	87.71	13.94	92.71	13.47	94.00	12.57
		SOH	92.57	19.75	93.43	23.32	87.95	11.16	84.85	16.91
	Control (N = 6)	DAS	105.00	6.08	122.59	12.05	109.67	14.01	120.33	19.29
		MIQ	22.67	1.53	21.67	4.16	29.33	4.93	29.00	1.73
		PCI	104.67	4.04	77.67	19.86	100.33	7.23	102.33	7.64
		SOH	80.33	7.50	83.33	8.14	85.33	12.22	86.67	5.51

Table 5-3 Coefficients of correlation for test scores shown in Table 5-2

Test	PRE-DAS	PRE-MIQ	PRE-PCI	PRE-SOH	POST-DAS	POST-MIQ	POST-PCI	POST-SOH
PRE-DAS		0.14	0.53**	−0.64**	0.75**	0.22	0.36*	−0.32*
PRE-MIQ			0.09	−0.10	0.14	0.54**	0.08	−0.16
PRE-PCI				−0.56**	0.42**	−0.07	0.62**	−0.44**
PRE-SOH					0.51**	−0.22	−0.24	0.69**
POST-DAS						0.26	0.36*	−0.59**
POST-MIQ							0.09	−0.31*
POST-PCI								−0.38**

$*p < .01$
$**p < .001$

Note: We are grateful to the following people, who donated their services and good will above and beyond the call of duty (and of coursework credits) to work on this project: Laura Bond, Jenny Boyce, Tammy Coots, Sallie Mackenfuss, Monique Snellgrove, and Denise Stokes. Many others have helped us in this research and our only regret is that we cannot name them all.

each test. On the DAS there was a significant ($F = 4.33$, $p < .05$) within-cells variance and a very significant condition-by-program interaction ($F = 7.96$, $p < .001$). The MIQ failed to show any significant main effect or interaction; the PCI showed the greatest number of significant main effects and interactions. The two conditions (trainer-assisted vs. trainer-conducted) showed a significant main effect ($F = 10.62$, $p < .001$). The two programs also showed significant main effects ($F = 8.16$, $p < .006$), and two interactions—gender by condition and gender by programs—were also significant ($F = 4.94$, $p < .01$; $F = 8.92$, $p < .004$).

There was also a significant triple interaction in gender by condition by program ($F = 3.26$, $p < .05$). The SOH was slightly affected by conditions ($F = 2.6$, $p < .01$). However, the direction of these pre-post differences is too variable to verify the original hypothesis that the Intimacy program would have greater impact on the SOH scores than the Negotiation program. The PCI showed consistent gains, regardless of condition or program, except for the controls and the males in the trainer-conducted condition. These results are too variable to be anything but suggestive about the potential use of programmed materials to test competing theories or methods of treatment.

Research in Progress

In addition to research already published (L'Abate, 1977, 1990a), at the time of this writing five different research projects have been completed or are about to be completed. Again, we describe these to give an indication of the usefulness of programmed writing as a tool to link practice with research.

Validity and Reliability of Prescriptive Tests
The psychometric properties of the tests described in Chapter 3 are now being evaluated with a large group ($N > 200$) of undergraduates. Their concurrent validity is being compared with two overall MMPI measures of adjustment, mean profile elevation and scatter scores.

Comparative Usefulness of Three Depression Workbooks
A pilot study comparing the use of Social Training, Depression, and Social Growth workbooks with undergraduates in psychology of adjustment classes, where the workbooks were used in various combinations of structured role-playing, lectures, and no contact with the instructor, showed that the Depression workbook seemed to be more helpful than the other two workbooks. The Social Training and Social Growth workbooks are too long to compress into the six or seven weeks of a trimester. Consequently, a comparative study of the paratherapeutic usefulness of three depression-oriented workbooks is now under way with undergraduates scoring high on two scales of depression (L'Abate & Boyce, research in progress). Of the three depression-oriented workbooks, one is based on the cognitive theory of Beck (Beck & Young, 1985), a second is based on an interactive view of depression (L'Abate, 1986b), and a third is based on the MMPI-2.

Application of the Problems in Relationships Scale (PIRS) and
Program with Volunteer Undergraduate Couples
Lessons found in Part II of this book are administered according to the model
explained in Chapter 3. Lessons are selected isomorphically according to scores
received on the PIRS, thus linking "treatment" with evaluation (L'Abate &
Kunkel, research in progress).

Treating High Points on MMPI-2 Content Scales with Workbooks
This project administers lessons according to highest score received on one
of the 15 MMPI-2 content scales. A control group receives no treatment.
Supposedly, the workbooks should reduce the level of the high scores for the
experimental group to a more significant degree than for the control group
(Fraizer, 1991).

Using Workbooks to Deal with Anxiety
In this project, volunteer undergraduates scoring on the upper third of the
anxiety distribution receive one of three programs. The first one is derived
from the MMPI-2 (see Part II), while the other two programs were designed
from two tests of trait versus state anxiety (Russ, 1991).

The Future of Programmed Writing

Of course, we think that the future of programmed writing, as just one of
the many possible applications of writing, is wide open! We believe that the
potential applications of this approach are almost infinite. This optimism,
however, is tempered by an awareness that programmed writing needs to be
solidly founded on empirical bases rather than on conjecture or faith. Without
the firm foundation of empirical results, programmed writing could become
another of the many passing fads in the mental health field.

The future of programmed writing cannot be based just on the assignments
and programs presented here. These programs are limited and limiting.
Instead, we hope that the materials presented here will serve as models (either
to copy or to oppose!) for the creation of many additional and different programs. For example, there are plans for a variety of specific workbooks to go
alongside the traditional treatment of many addictions (L'Abate, Farrar, &
Serritella, in press). Students have written quite a few workbooks from already
existing self-help books.

The future of programmed writing is predicated, then, on (1) the validation
and verification of this approach, using assignments and programs already
existing and presented here, and (2) the creation of new and different written materials, such as new homework assignments for individuals, couples,
and families.

Therapy at a Distance

One of the main implications of programmed writing lies in its immediate applicability as an alternative or additional form of intervention at a distance, without face-to-face contact between clients and therapists. In some instances, this may be the only form of intervention available—for example, with incarcerated persons or missionary and military families abroad. Programmed writing might make help available, through interactive, satellite-delivered telecommunications between a teaching source and potentially inaccessible populations miles away in jails, hospitals, and overseas.

This concept maybe repugnant to scores of therapists who maintain that face-to-face contact is the most important factor in therapeutic change. The introduction of programmed writing would allow us to view this issue along a continuum—that is, from persons who are helped by face-to-face interaction to those who are not. With the latter, especially felons and acting-out individuals, face-to-face contact is expensive and chancy. At best, two-thirds of all individuals, couples, and families who are seen in verbal therapy can be helped additionally through programmed writing. Programmed writing offers the possibility of improving the effectiveness of existing therapies and making help available to populations who could not be helped otherwise. Ultimately, programmed writing, just like any other form of intervention, will need to specify which clients, problems, symptoms, and dysfunctionalities can be helped by this approach and which cannot.

Programmed writing does not and should not detract from established methods of intervention. Instead, it can expand their influence and render them more effective. It can serve as an alternative or an additional paratherapeutic modality, in some instances by itself, but in most instances in combination with other therapeutic modalities, including nontraditional ones, such as structured enrichment (L'Abate & Weinstein, 1987; L'Abate & Young, 1987), covenant contracting (L'Abate & McHenry, 1983), social skills training (L'Abate & Milan, 1985), or medical forms of treatment, including hospitalization.

Extending Programmed Writing to Electronic Media

The development of self-administered, self-paced programs based on the written word is just one step away from extending this technology to use of TV monitors and personal computers. This extension would make programs of this type available to more individuals than can be reached by traditional face-to-face individual or group psychotherapy. However, as we warned in earlier chapters, someone needs to monitor, evaluate, and correct the answers given in writing, catching out-and-out distortions, omissions, and generalizations. Even in this methodology, the human factor cannot be ignored. The professional helper, within this framework, assesses and evaluates progress through pre- and postprogram testing, selects the appropriate lessons or program on the basis of demonstrated improvement, and monitors the process and the progress by correcting erroneous or inappropriate answers in each lesson.

Conclusion

Programmed writing is a reproducible method that complements and supplements the therapist's personal contribution. It offers a method that sensitive, experienced, and knowledgeable professionals and semiprofessionals can use to improve their effectiveness and efficiency. Programmed writing can become a relatively inexpensive, relevant tool in the amelioration of human suffering. It needs to be used responsibly and caringly, and it can be as useful as those who use it want to make it. No one who has methodological and personal reservations about its applicability should use it. It needs to be used selectively and appropriately. It will not cure the ills of humankind. It will, we hope, cure a few of the many.

Its advantages have yet to be fully explored, along with its limitations. More empirical evidence needs to be gathered to support its wider applicability. Because of its cost-cutting and time-saving potential, it deserves more attention from the psychotherapeutic and preventive communities than it has received heretofore.

Programmed Materials for Individuals, Couples, and Families

Introduction: Instructions for the Administration of Programmed Materials

The purpose of Part II is to make available materials for the practice of programmed writing as explained in Part I. These programmed materials consist of evaluation forms, written homework assignments, and workbooks. (When making up question sheets, the helper may want to provide space at the end of each question for the client's answer, or have the client provide answers on a separate sheet of paper.) These materials should not be administered until after the professional helper has read Part I. More specific instructions will be given whenever necessary before different lessons, programs, and workbooks. For a list of all the lessons contained here, see the index.

The professional using these materials should keep in mind that they are all *experimental*. Consequently, these materials should not be administered without previous evaluation, both impressionistic and objective. Certain materials, as explained in the introductory text, cannot be administered without an objective evaluation.

The administration and use of programmed materials contained here should be the outcome of a contractual agreement between a professional helper and clients (individuals, couples, or families) from the very outset of the helping process. Clients are asked to set aside one hour a week to work on these materials individually, as a married couple, or as a family. Clients should agree to match at least one hour of professional help (therapy, counseling, psycho-educational training, interpersonal skills training, and so on) with one hour of programmed writing at home.

With clients resistant to undertaking this contract, the helper may need to discuss and evaluate possible sources of resistance, such as fear of change, fear of the unknown, anxiety about self-disclosure, or fear of hurting self and loved ones. Whether to make therapy or professional help conditional on completing programmed homework assignments is an individual decision that each professional needs to make on the basis of experience and judgment.

Assignment of programmed materials implies that clients are in sufficient control to be able to carry out the completion of these materials. One can find out very readily whether clients are ready to work on these materials by assigning them. In many cases, clients may be too upset to even start working on them. Consequently, one may have to work on lowering the level of stress and disturbance in the client's life before administering these materials. Some, but not all, of the materials contained here may help the professional to lower the level of disturbance in some clients. If these materials do not apply to the disturbance at hand, the principles given in Part I may help the professional write lessons to apply to that disturbance.

It is important that the professional helper be either convinced about the inherent usefulness of these materials or keep an open mind and evaluate results on the basis of subjective and objective evaluation. Clients themselves will be the best source of information about the usefulness of these materials. The helper should be open to the possibility that not all materials will be liked by all clients. There is a great deal of variability in client satisfaction with these materials. The professional helper, on the other hand, will need to look behind apparent client satisfaction to find out whether these materials were indeed useful in the process of help-giving and change.

CHAPTER SIX

Materials for Evaluation

Social Information Form

1. Name (last, first, middle), ID#, date
2. Date of birth
3. Sex
4. Occupation (if under 21, parents' occupations)
5. Home address, phone
6. Business address, phone
7. Ethnic origin (white, black, Asian, American Indian, Hispanic, other)
8. Birthplace
9. Born in a big city (over 250,000), a small city (between 50,000 and 250,000), or a town (below 50,000)?
10. Religious preference (Protestant, Catholic, Jewish, other)
11. Education:
    a. Graduate degree
    b. Some graduate
    c. College graduate
    d. Some college
    e. Vocational-technical school graduate
    f. Some voc-tech school
    g. High school graduate
    h. Finished grade school
    i. Some grade school
12. School record:
    a. excellent
    b. good
    c. fair
    d. barely passing
    e. frequent failure
13. Health in early childhood:
    a. very good
    b. good
    c. fair
    d. poor

14. Physical condition now:
    a. Usually very good
    b. Usually good
    c. Occasionally ill
    d. Frequently ill
    e. Chronically ill
15. Times you moved in the past year
16. On a scale of 1 (not at all important) to 10 (extremely important), how important are sex and sexuality to you?
17. On a scale of 0 (very poor) to 4 (very good), how good are you as a:
    a. Provider
    b. Caretaker
    c. Spouse
    d. Parent
    e. Child to your parents
    f. Sibling to your siblings
18. Job history:
    a. Employed continuously in the same position for the past two years
    b. Employed continuously for the past two years but place of employment changed
    c. Out of work sometimes during the past two years
    d. Unemployed for the past two years
    e. Retired
    f. Other
19. Religious involvement:
    a. Attend church regularly and active in church work
    b. Attend church regularly but inactive in church work
    c. Attend church sometimes
    d. Never attend church
20. Membership in social groups:
    a. Active in one or more social groups (name them)
    b. Attend meetings of one or more social groups but not very active
    c. Not a member of any social group .
21. Friends:
    a. Many close friends (how many?)
    b. Some close friends (how many?)
    c. Only a few close friends
    d. No friends
22. On a scale of 0 (very similar) to 4 (very dissimilar), how similar are your interests to those of the people you know well?
    a. Family
    b. Friends
    c. Co-workers
23. On a scale of 0 (not comfortably at all) to 4 (very comfortably), how comfortably can you talk with the people you know well and who know you?
    a. Spouse
    b. Family

    c. Friends

    d. Co-workers

    e. Others

24. On a scale of 0 (hardly at all) to 4 (very much), how much do people you know well generally approve of you?

    a. Spouse

    b. Family

    c. Friends

    d. Co-workers

    e. Others

25. Ownership of home (or apartment) you are now living in:

    a. Owned by you or your family

    b. Rented by you or your family

    c. Living in a room by yourself

    d. Staying with a friend

26. Automobile available for family use?

    Television set at home?

    Telephone at home?

27. Cigarette smoking:

    a. I do not smoke

    b. I smoke 5–10 cigarettes per day

    c. I smoke one pack per day

    d. I smoke 20–30 cigarettes per day

    e. I smoke two packs or more

28. Drinking:

    a. I drink a lot

    b. I drink often

    c. I drink occasionally

    d. I drink once in a while

    e. I do not drink

29. Drugs:

    a. I use drugs frequently

    b. I use drugs occasionally

    c. I use drugs once in a while

    d. I never use or have used drugs

30. Dieting:

    a. I eat a lot, to the point of being fat

    b. I do not eat regular meals

    c. I eat a lot, but weight is normal

    d. I eat a well-balanced diet

    e. I eat regular meals

31. Sleep:

    a. My sleep is very short

    b. My sleep is very irregular

    c. I never get a good night of sleep

    d. I sleep well with occasional bad nights

    e. I sleep well regularly

32. Other habits (list). For each, does this habit control you?
    a. A lot
    b. Pretty much
    c. Sometimes
    d. Not at all
33. Were you ever disabled by illness or accident?
    a. Not at all, never
    b. For periods of less than one week
    c. For periods less than one month
    d. For as long as six months
    e. Permanently
34. Height, weight
35. How much exercise do you get every day?
    a. I engage in a physically taxing activity every day
    b. I follow a regular schedule of exercise or engage in some sport activity several times a week
    c. I either do mild calisthenics each day or manage to walk a mile or more
    d. I walk about one-half to one mile daily, or equivalent physical activity
    e. I get very little exercise
36. How physically attractive would you say people consider you to be?
    a. Extremely attractive
    b. Moderately attractive
    c. Ordinary or average
    d. Unattractive
    e. Very unattractive
37. Have you ever cohabited? If so, for how long?
38. Have you ever been married? If so, how many times?
39. How satisfied are you in your marriage or cohabiting relationship?
    a. Very
    b. Some
    c. Not at all
40. List your reason(s) for wanting improvement in your life at this time.
41. Present marital status:
    a. Married—never divorced, separated, or widowed
    b. Married—previously divorced, separated, or widowed
    c. Presently divorced, separated, or widowed
    d. Never married
42. Occupation of spouse
43. Partner's health:
    a. Excellent
    b. Good
    c. Fair
    d. Poor
44. Ethnic origin of spouse (white, black, Asian, American Indian, Hispanic, other)

45. Educational level of spouse:
    a. Graduate degree
    b. Some graduate
    c. College graduate
    d. Some college
    e. Vocational-technical school graduate
    f. Some vocational-technical school
    g. High school graduate
    h. Finished grade school
    i. Some grade school
46. If unmarried, are you:
    a. Engaged
    b. Going steady
    c. Living together
    d. Dating frequently
    e. Dating infrequently
    f. Not dating
47. Current living situation:
    a. Living with spouse and children
    b. Living with spouse, no children
    c. Living with children, no spouse
    d. Living alone
    e. Living with other(s) of same sex
    f. Living with other(s) of opposite sex
    g. Living with parent(s)
48. Number of children, sex, age(s)
49. Children's health:
    a. Children healthy
    b. One or more children occasionally sick with minor illnesses
    c. One or more children have severe chronic illnesses—birth injury, retardation, kidney disease, etc.
50. On a scale of 0 (very poor) to 4 (very good), how good is your spouse (mate, companion, partner) as a:
    a. Provider
    b. Caretaker
    c. Spouse
    d. Parent
    e. Parent to his/her parents
    f. Sibling to his/her siblings
51. On a scale of 0 (totally rejecting) to 4 (totally loving), how loving or rejecting do you feel you have been with your children?
52. On a scale of 0 (totally rejecting) to 4 (totally loving), how loving or rejecting do you feel your spouse (partner, mate, companion) has been with your children?
53. Number of times you go out (for pleasure) monthly (individually, as a couple, as a family, other)

54. Father's birthplace
55. Mother's birthplace
56. When you were growing up (ages 6 to 18) were either of your parents in poor health?
    a. All of the time
    b. Frequently
    c. Sometimes
    d. Rarely
    e. Never
57. How many of the following health prolems have you, your father, your mother, your sister, or your brother ever had: arthritis, asthma, bladder troubles, colitis, diabetes, epilepsy, heart condition, high blood pressure, neuralgia, nervous breakdown, sciatica, skin condition, stomach trouble?
58. Is your mother still living? If no, how old were you when she died?
    a. Over 20
    b. Between 16 and 20
    c. Between 10 and 15
    d. Between 6 and 9
    e. Under 6
59. Is your father still living? If no, how old were you when he died?
    a. Over 20
    b. Between 16 and 20
    c. Between 10 and 15
    d. Between 6 and 9
    e. Under 6
60. Were your parents separated/divorced? If yes, how old were you?
    a. Over 20
    b. Between 16 and 20
    c. Between 10 and 15
    d. Between 6 and 9
    e. Under 6
61. When you were growing up, how much did your father work outside of the home?
    a. All of the time
    b. Frequently
    c. Rarely
    d. Never
62. When you were growing up, how much did your mother work outside of the home?
    a. All of the time
    b. Frequently
    c. Seldom
    d. Never
63. When you were growing up, did your parents quarrel:
    a. All of the time
    b. Frequently

    c. Rarely

    d. Never

    Did they agree:

    e. All of the time

    f. Frequently

    g. Rarely

    h. Never

64. When you were growing up, did you ever feel that:
    a. Mother spent too little time with you
    b. Mother wanted to run her children's lives
    c. Mother did not understand you
    d. Mother was always proud of her children
    Comments?

65. When you were growing up, did you ever feel that:
    a. Father spent too little time with you
    b. Father wanted to run his children's lives
    c. Father did not understand you
    d. Father was always proud of his children
    Comments?

66. On a scale of 0 (totally dissatisfied) to 4 (totally satisfied), how satisfied or dissatisfied you do believe your mother is or was with her marriage to your father?

67. On a scale of 0 (totally dissatisfied) to 4 (totally satisfied), how satisfied or dissatisfied do you believe your father is or was with his marriage to your mother?

68. If your parents were separated or divorced, with which parent did you side most during the period of their separation and/or divorce?
    a. Mother
    b. Father
    c. Neither—I was either too young to understand what was happening or too old to be influenced

69. If your parents were separated or divorced, how upset were you by their separation/divorce, on a scale of 0 (extremely upset) to 4 (very relieved)?

70. Overall, on a scale of 0 (competely rejecting) to 4 (completely loving) how loving or rejecting do you feel that your parents have been in their relationship with you?

71. On a scale of 0 (totally authoritarian) to 4 (totally democratic), how permissive or authoritarian do you feel your parents were in raising you?

72. One a scale of 0 to 4 (where 0 is extremely restrictive, 2 is extremely permissive, and 4 is firm and flexible but fair), how would your rate your parents' actions and attitudes pertaining to your dating relationships?

73. Did your parents drink? If so, how much?
    a. A great deal
    b. Sometimes
    c. Never

74. On a scale of 0 (very poor) to 4 (very good), how good was your father as a:
    a. Provider
    b. Caretaker
    c. Husband
    d. Parent
    e. Parent to his parents
    f. Brother to his siblings
75. On a scale of 0 (very poor) to 4 (very good), how good was your mother as a:
    a. Provider
    b. Caretaker
    c. Wife
    d. Parent
    e. Parent to her parents
    f. Sister to her siblings
76. Comment about your parents at will.
77. List your siblings, half-siblings, and/or step-siblings by age and sex beginning with the oldest. Indicate whether they are married, and how many children they have, if any. Include yourself in the list and circle your age and sex.
78. On a scale of 0 (very distant) to 4 (very close), how close or distant were (are) you from your siblings, half-siblings, and/or step-siblings?
79. Did you have a favorite sibling, half-sibling, or step-sibling? If so, on a scale of 0 (very distant) to 4 (very close), how close were you?
80. Did you have a competitive sibling, half-sibling, or step-sibling? If so, on a scale of 0 (very competitive) to 4 (not at all competitive), how competitive were you with each other?
81. On a scale of 0 (not at all important) to 4 (very important), how important are your siblings, half-siblings, and/or step-siblings (if any) to you?
82. Comment about your sibling relationships at will.
83. How frequently do you contact your family of origin, either by letter, by phone, or in person?
    a. Daily
    b. Weekly
    c. Monthly
    d. Yearly
    e. Not at all
84. What was the total annual income of your father and your mother when you were growing up?
    a. Above $100,000
    b. Between $100,000 and $50,000
    c. Between $50,000 and $20,000
    d. Below $20,000
85. What is your income at this time?
    a. Above $100,000
    b. Between $100,000 and $50,000

      c. Between $50,000 and $20,000

      d. Below $20,000

86. Please add any other information or comments that may be important for an understanding of you as a person.

Weights to Score the Social Information Form

Warning: Please note that these weights are still tentative and subject to change. Scorers should use caution and common sense in scoring each item because these weights represent subjective and personal judgment. They can be changed to suit the value system of the scorer.

The direction of these weights is related positively to adjustment and competence. The higher the score, the higher the client's level of adjustment and competence is expected to be. Some items cannot be scored because no value judgment of any kind can be made.

  4. Score 5 points for a professional occupation, 4 for middle-level semi-professional work, 3 for white-collar or clerical work, 2 for blue-collar work, 1 for domestic-janitorial work, and 0 for no occupation.

11. Score 4 points for a, b, and c, 3 for d, e, and f, 2 for g, 1 for h, and 0 for i.

12. 4 for a, 3 for b, 2 for c, 1 for d, and 0 for e.

13. 3 for a, 2 for b, 1 for c, and 0 for d.

14. 4 for a, 3 for b, 2 for c, 1 for d, and 0 for e.

15. 2 for one or two moves, 1 for three or four moves, 0 for five moves or more.

16. 2 for scores between 10 and 7, 1 for scores between 6 and 3; 0 for scores below 3.

17. Use scale score chosen by respondent, for a, b, c, d, e, and f.

18. 3 for a, 2 for b, 1 for c, and 0 for d.

20. 2 for a, 1 for b, and 0 for c.

21. 3 for a, 2 for b, 1 for c, and 0 for d.

23. Use scale score chosen by respondent, for a, b, c, d, and e.

24. Same as 23.

25. 3 for a, 2 for b, 1 for c, and 0 for d.

26. 1 for yes, 0 for no, for each question.

27. 4 for a, 3 for b, 2 for c, 1 for d, and 0 for e.

28. 0 for a, 1 for b, 2 for c, 3 for d, and 5 for e.

29. 0 for a, 1 for b, 2 for c, and 3 for d.

30. 0 for a, 1 for b, 2 for c, 3 for d, and 4 for e.

31. Same as 30.

32. 0 for a, 1 for b, 2 for c, and 3 for d.

33. 4 for a, 3 for b, 2 for c, 1 for d, and 0 for e.

34. 2 for weight appropriate to height, 1 for weight somewhat out of proportion to height, and 0 for weight completely out of proportion to height.

35. 4 for a, 3 for b, 2 for c, 1 for d, and 0 for e.
36. 4 for a, 3 for b, 2 for c, 1 for d, and 0 for e.
38. 3 for married once, 2 for married two to three times, 1 for married four to five times, and 0 for married more than six times.
40. 2 for many good reasons, 1 for one valid reason, 0 for one invalid and irrelevant reason.
41. 3 for a, 2 for b, 1 for c, and 0 for d.
42. Same as 4.
43. 3 for a, 2 for b, 1 for c, and 0 for d.
45. Same as 11.
49. 2 for a, 1 for b, and 0 for c.
50. Use scale score chosen by respondent, for a, b, c, d, e, and f.
51. Use scale score chosen by respondent.
52. Same as 51.
56. 0 for a, 1 for b, 2 for c, 3 for d, and 4 for e.
57. 5 for one problem, 4 for two problems, 3 for three problems, 2 for four problems, 1 for five problems, and 0 for more than six problems.
58. 4 for a, 3 for b, 2 for c, 1 for d, and 0 for e.
59. Same as 58.
60. 4 for a, 3 for b, 2 for c, 1 for d, and 0 for e.
61. 0 for a, 1 for b, 2 for c, and 3 for d.
62. Same as 61.
63. 0 for a, 1 for b, 2 for c, 1 for d; 3 for e, 2 for f, 1 for g, and 0 for h.
64. 0 for a, 1 for b, 2 for c, and 3 for d.
65. Same as 64.
66. Use scale score chosen by respondent.
67. Same as 66.
68. 0 for a or b, 1 for c or d.
69. Use scale score chosen by respondent.
70. Same as 69.
71. Same as 69.
72. Same as 69.
73. 0 for a, 1 for b, and 0 for c.
74. Use scale score chosen by respondent, for a, b, c, d, e, and f.
75. Same as 74.
76. Score from 5 to 10 for positive statements and from 4 to 0 for negative comments.
78. Use scale score chosen by respondent.
79. Same as 78.
80. Same as 78.
81. Same as 78.
82. Same as 76.
83. 0 for a or e, 1 for b or d, and 2 for c.
84. 3 for a, 2 for b, 1 for c, and 0 for d.
85. Same as 84.
86. Same as 76.

Adjustment Inventory

Instructions

1. Set up a page with five columns. In column 1, list three general areas of distress or dissatisfaction in your self, your marriage or intimate relationships, your family, your work, or other important activities in your life.
2. In column 2, for each of the three areas specify further concrete and specific behaviors that are displeasing, unsatisfactory, or painful to you.
3. In column 3, rank these behaviors from 10 to 1 in terms of which behavior needs attention the most. Give a 10 to the behavior that needs attention the most, down to 1 for the behavior with the lowest priority, that needs least attention now.
4. In column 4, rate each behavior on a scale of unpleasantness, distress, or hurtfulness to you from −1 to −5, with −1 being the least unpleasant and hurtful, and −5 being the most unpleasant and hurtful. If any of these behaviors are no longer unpleasant or hurtful to you, rate them from +1 to +5.
5. List one more behavior not already listed, and fill in columns 2–4 for it. In column 5 for each behavior, place the product of multiplying columns 3 and 4.
6. Finally, total the numbers in column 5.

Self-Profile Chart

This is a way to find out how you see, have seen, and will see yourself in the present, past, and future. Completing this chart will help you get a more complete picture of how you see yourself in different areas of your life.

Instructions

1. Set up a page with four columns. In column 1, list the following personal qualities and roles:
   A. Personal Qualities:
   Intelligence
   Physical health
   Attractiveness
   Moral goodness
   Spiritual status
   Other (   )
   B. Roles:
   As an individual
   As a friend
   As a spouse or partner
   As a parent
   As a sibling

As a child to your parents
As an in-law to in-laws
As a worker
At leisure
Other (   )

There is one open area in both categories. If there are particular personal qualities or roles not listed here that you would like to add, write them in the spaces provided.

2. In column 2, headed *NOW,* rate how you feel about yourself in the present. *Rate each area with a number between −5 and +5* to show your present level of satisfaction (positive numbers) or dissatisfaction (negative numbers) with yourself in each area. A rating of +5 means the greatest degree of satisfaction. A rating of −5 means the greatest level of dissatisfaction. A 0 score means you do not feel either way about that area. If a quality or role does not relate to you, like, for example, being a parent, leave it blank.

3. In column 3, headed *Past,* rate your level of satisfaction or dissatisfaction with yourself in each of the same areas in the past. Use +5 to indicate the highest level of satisfaction and −5 to indicate the highest level of dissatisfaction.

4. In column 4, headed *Future,* rate your projected future level of satisfaction or dissatisfaction with yourself in each of the same areas. Please rate all the areas even though you may not think much about that personal quality or role.

5. Total the numbers in columns 2, 3, and 4.

Problems in Relationships Scale

Instructions

On a separate sheet, rate how much each of the following statements applies to you as you see yourself in relation to your partner. There are no right or wrong answers. Answer only how you feel right now. Use these codes:

A—Applies to you a great deal
B—Applies to you somewhat
C—Does not apply to you at all

1. I choose to take care of my partner even when I would like to be taken care of.
2. Finding faults in the past does not help; what matters is that we learn from our mistakes.
3. I am more critical of myself than I am of others.
4. When it comes to family life, I make most of the small decisions, and my partner makes the big decisions.
5. I do not like someone to doubt my trust in them.
6. I am often disappointed in how my partner does things.

7. I feel lost as a boat in the middle of the ocean.
8. When my partner makes a decision, I carry it out without much fuss.
9. In comparison to other people, I really have few shortcomings.
10. Although we have different tastes, my partner and I take an active role in helping each other.
11. I do not feel comfortable talking to others.
12. I like it when my partner and I come out as winners in the same situation.
13. In dealing with my partner, I am used to openly admitting when I am right and when I am wrong.
14. In my relationships with those who are close to me, I don't really care whether I am right or wrong.
15. I like to give and receive attention.
16. When I face and compare my partner with myself, his or her faults get smaller and my faults get bigger.
17. My partner and I value each other very much.
18. I am perfectly happy if my partner makes decisions for me.
19. I am better at doing things than my partner is.
20. Contrary to my partner, I am trustworthy.
21. I am used to accepting decisions made by others.
22. If I think that someone is going to give me trouble, I make trouble for them first.
23. My partner will often say that he or she is trustworthy even though I don't believe him or her.
24. I am resigned to the acceptance of things as they are.
25. I comfort my partner more than my partner comforts me.
26. I am not the one to handle important business in the house.
27. My partner is more important to me than my work.
28. I am more critical of my partner's mistakes than my own.
29. My partner and I think things through before we answer.
30. It seems as though my partner and I have a million ideas and projects to work on together.
31. I have more shortcomings than my partner.
32. I would rather talk to myself than to anyone else.
33. Whenever my partner stops me from doing something, it makes me feel as though he or she is trying to stifle me.
34. It scares me to be right at my partner's expense.
35. I spend most of my energy taking care of my partner and I do not worry about myself.
36. Others are more important than I am.
37. My decisions are better than my partner's.
38. I choose whether or not someone is trustworthy and no one can influence that decision.
39. Sharing our feelings with each other gives us a great deal of pleasure.
40. My partner influences my behavior.
41. I feel I am better equipped than anyone else to handle family responsibilities.
42. I accept my weaknesses and learn from my mistakes.

43. Both my partner and I like to participate actively in whatever we set out to do.
44. I don't have much, if anything, worthwhile to say.
45. I think I am right, but often my partner helps me to see that he or she is right instead.
46. I expect those close to me to pay a lot of attention to me.
47. My partner tells me that I am very critical of others and that I am never critical of myself.
48. I make the most important decisions in our relationship.
49. I am pretty sure that my relationship is based on mutual trust.
50. My partner and I share our fears, hurts, and anxieties with each other.
51. It doesn't matter if I compromise, because my partner gets upset anyway.
52. I am the one who is responsible for the welfare of my family.
53. I am very careful not to make any mistakes.
54. I feel very lonely.
55. I would rather listen to my partner than do much talking myself.
56. In disagreements with others, I am the one who is right about things.
57. I need to think about my interests because I cannot pay attention to the interests of others.
58. I have heard others say that I pay more attention to my needs than to the needs of others.
59. Compared to others, I think of myself as better able to make the right decisions at the right time.
60. Both my partner and I have earned each other's trust and it shows in the way we behave with each other.
61. Both my partner and I share our fears and anxieties with each other without being critical.
62. To keep my partner happy, I accept things even though I don't necessarily agree with them.
63. I don't bother trying to earn my partner's trust, because he or she wouldn't trust me anyway.
64. My partner and I like to do things together but without being perfectionists.
65. I feel as though I have no support.
66. My partner has more exciting things to talk about than I do.
67. I do not like to tell my partner when I am wrong.
68. My partner pays more attention to my needs than I do to his or her needs.
69. I find that when others criticize me or what I do, it is not very useful criticism.
70. Together my partner and I are able to reach good decisions.
71. My partner and I are quite used to expressing our trust in each other.
72. It is not easy for me to get along with others.
73. I have learned that by compromising one gets what one wants.
74. I am in charge of making important decisions, but I leave small responsibilities to my partner.
75. My partner and I are able to laugh at our mistakes.
76. I feel empty and unimportant.
77. I do not like to talk about unpleasant topics with my partner.

78. I am hardly ever wrong.
79. Sometimes I like to spend time with others, but sometimes I also need time for myself.
80. I try to be no more critical of others than I am of myself.
81. I know how to make decisions, but I like to take my partner into consideration.
82. I find it hard to change, even though I know it would be good for me.
83. There is always someone who says that I do not know how to work things out with anybody.
84. There are times when even a little thing from my partner makes me mad and I tend to explode.
85. Our style is to share the responsibility of carrying out decisions with the active support of the partner.
86. I find it hard to stop and think things over.
87. Life has taught me to depend on others for things and support.
88. My interests are usually more exciting than those of my partner.
89. I will admit when I am wrong to my partner.
90. I like to pay attention to my partner, just as my partner likes to pay attention to me.
91. I love myself and my partner in spite of everything that has happened to us.
92. In making important decisions, my partner likes to take me into consideration.
93. Things that do not need change give me the greatest sense of security.
94. I recognize that I have a negative streak in me.
95. Even without being aware of it, I get my partner to do what I want her or him to do.
96. My partner and I carry out together whatever we have agreed on.
97. I am not used to thinking before I act.
98. I limit my independence in order to allow my partner to feel free.
99. There are some topics, like my work, that I do not like to talk over with my partner.
100. I am aware that I am not always right or always wrong.
101. My partner and I like to support each other in a balanced and positive fashion.
102. It does not matter to me whether anyone sacrifices for me.
103. I don't mind leaving the responsibility with my partner.
104. Other people tell me that I am not very flexible.
105. My partner tells me that I use very little imagination when I work with him or her.
106. Whenever someone provokes me, I tend to react very quickly.
107. Our style is to finish together whatever we have agreed on.
108. I do not know how to control my actions.
109. When I compare myself to others, I am very dependent on my partner.
110. I talk to my partner when he or she will listen.
111. Bad luck always stops me from winning.
112. In my life I have neither given nor received much.

113. Doing things or sacrificing oneself for others is just making an excuse for others.
114. I do not like being in a position of responsibility in my relationship with my partner.
115. I am a very flexible person.
116. I do what my partner tells me to do.
117. I do not ask my partner to do anything that I would not willingly do for my partner.
118. I am afraid to fail.
119. I allow myself to take responsibility in many situations very quickly, no matter how much energy I have left.
120. I am a strong believer in being as independent as possible.
121. My partner and I talk together a lot.
122. I usually lose, no matter what.
123. I do not like to owe anything to others, no matter who they are.
124. Whoever says that they have sacrificed themselves for me is just talking.
125. I do not feel responsible for my partner's welfare.
126. I give in to the wishes of my partner.
127. I have been trained to follow what I am told to do without arguments, and for me it is hard to change this training.
128. Both my partner and I respect each other very much.
129. I am afraid of success.
130. I find it hard to say no to my partner and I feel that he or she takes advantage of me.
131. My partner knows that he or she cannot limit my independence.
132. I like to keep my partner informed of what I feel, and I like for my partner to do the same with me.
133. I really don't care whether I win or lose.
134. I have no energy left to either give or receive.
135. I am happy to give of myself for my partner without limits.
136. I recognize that when my partner takes the initiative things go more smoothly.
137. My partner recognizes that I am very flexible when changes have to be made.
138. I do not follow my partner's instructions.
139. Working together means that we both must win with each other.
140. I have no personal goals of any kind.
141. As soon as my partner expresses a wish I am ready to fulfill it.
142. I have chosen my partner because he or she does not mind being dependent on me.
143. My partner and I talk to each other about personal and private things.
144. I don't mind if my partner wins at my expense.
145. I give as much as I can in life, in spite of the fact that I feel like I am losing most of the time.
146. I have always made more sacrifices for my partner than my partner has made for me.
147. I am much more submissive than my partner.

148. My relationship with my partner is very clear because he or she lets me be in charge.
149. Experience tells me that I am better off when I follow my opinions.
150. I do not know how to share my feelings with anyone, even with myself.
151. My partner's career goals are much more important than my goals.
152. I feel like strangling my partner.
153. Both of us know how to walk on our own feet, but we choose to walk together.
154. I am not very responsible.
155. I do not like to win if my partner loses.
156. Usually I tend to let life control me rather than taking control of my life.
157. Everybody says that I sacrifice myself for others without paying attention to myself.
158. Even though I may have my personal ideas about how to run our household, things are organized by my partner.
159. I develop an opinion quickly and it is hard for me to change it.
160. My partner does what I ask him or her to do.
161. My life experiences have taught me that it is better to keep my feelings to myself.
162. My satisfaction lies in helping my partner achieve his or her goals.
163. I get angry and upset very quickly when my partner provokes me.
164. I think that both of us have learned to work together without giving up our individual selves.
165. Everybody tells me that I look very tired.
166. I am afraid to win at someone else's expense.
167. I like and feel obligated to give more than I receive.
168. I expect my partner to pay attention to my needs before anything else.
169. Above all, I expect respect from my partner.
170. In front of others, I do not bend very easily.
171. I like to talk things over openly with my partner.
172. When things do not go well, it's everybody's fault, including mine.
173. To achieve something that is important to me, I need to be pushed by my partner.
174. I tend to act first and talk later.
175. My partner and I both know how to share our sadness, anxieties, and shortcomings with each other.
176. I do not have enough energy to face life.
177. I hate it when my partner wins and I lose.
178. I try to take advantage of what I have now because I know "I can't take it with me" when life is over.
179. I do not like to sacrifice myself for others.
180. When I make a decision I know that my partner will go along with it.
181. Although I may have ideas of my own, I do not mind comparing them with those of my partner, and if necessary, changing them.
182. My partner and I work things out together well.
183. I was raised to help others feel better even if I do not pay attention to myself.

184. Above all I am interested in succeeding personally in whatever I have set out to do.
185. I am able to wait in order to allow my partner the benefit of thinking through a problem before giving me an answer.
186. I fail to see any strengths in myself, only weaknesses.
187. When my partner actively makes a decision, I follow in his or her footsteps.
188. Winning is what matters to me, no matter what.
189. Above all, I like to receive compliments from my partner even when I do not really deserve them.
190. In my partner I have found a person who is willing to sacrifice herself or himself for me.
191. It is a source of pleasure for both of us to share whatever comes in life.
192. Both my partner and I are willing to change our opinions to meet each other somewhere in the middle.
193. My partner is straight and constructive in working with me.
194. I am quick to put myself down.
195. My work interests and activities take precedence over anything else and are not open for discussion.
196. It is important for both of us to talk things over before reaching a conclusion.
197. I really don't feel I do anything well.
198. Even though I would like to take care of some personal interests, I have to give the highest priority to my partner's interests.
199. I like to win at someone else's expense.
200. I receive more than I give.
201. My partner and I help each other in almost everything.
202. Sometimes I follow my partner's lead and sometimes my partner follows my lead.
203. I am able to change the way I do things whenever my partner gives me some good reasons.
204. I do not like to depend on others because I never know when they will change their opinion.
205. I like to put down other people who put me down.
206. My work is my identity.
207. Since I was always told to mind my own business, I do just that.
208. Many times I have heard that I can't do anything right.
209. By always taking care of others, I have completely let go of myself.
210. My partner and I know how to help each other to come out as winners in the struggle of life.
211. As much as possible I try to give as much as I receive.
212. My partner and I have different strengths that add to our relationship.
213. I am happy to share chores and responsibilities with my partner.
214. Making decisions frightens me.
215. I grew up with the idea that no one can trust me and I cannot trust anybody.
216. I can have many jobs but just one partner.
217. My behavior depends on my partner.

218. My partner does things better than I do.
219. I would like for my partner and I to succeed in our relationship.
220. My partner knows how to give me all the compliments I deserve.
221. It seems stupid for people to waste time and energy thinking about the feelings and needs of themselves and of their partners.
222. I do not like myself because of my many shortcomings.
223. For me to make a decision means putting others down.
224. I trust others more than I trust myself.
225. Both of us are committed to helping each other become fulfilled as human beings.
226. I do not work well with other people.
227. I am glad that my partner has fewer faults than I do.
228. I do not understand people who have trouble making decisions.
229. Some people say I am a saint or a martyr to put up with my partner.
230. I do not feel at all important to anybody and especially to my partner.
231. I would like to be completely different from what I am now.
232. I do not know what's good for me or my partner.
233. I take responsibility for what happens in the house.
234. It is important for me to keep on working, no matter what happens in my relationship with my partner.
235. As far as my partner is concerned, I am always wrong.
236. I do not expect any attention from my partner and what attention I do get appears to depend on her or his whims and will.
237. I don't see much good in either myself or my partner.
238. I am more used to depending on others than on myself.
239. I make mistakes like everybody else.
240. In dealing with others, I do not know whether I am right or wrong.

Weights to Score the Problems in Relationships Scale

Warning: Please note that this is an experimental test still in the early phases of construction that needs further psychometric refinement and validation. To ensure greater precision in assigning specific lessons to a couple, also administer the Description of Self-in-Relationship Test to each partner. Assign lessons based on areas of agreement among those tests, this test, and your clinical judgment.

Scoring: Three different sets of weights are possible:

1. Score 2 points for B and 1 point for A or C.
2. Score 3 points for A, 2 for B, and 1 for C.
3. Score 3 points for C, 2 for B, and 1 for A.

The set to use is indicated here after the number of each question. Please note that until we have better criteria to score each item, this scoring is tentative. We are aware of the many questions that can be raised about these weights and we are working on improving them.

1. 1	31. 1	61. 2	91. 2	121. 2	151. 3	181. 2	211. 2
2. 2	32. 1	62. 1	92. 2	122. 3	152. 1	182. 2	212. 2
3. 1	33. 3	63. 3	93. 1	123. 1	153. 2	183. 3	213. 2
4. 3	34. 3	64. 2	94. 1	124. 1	154. 3	184. 1	214. 3
5. 1	35. 3	65. 3	95. 1	125. 1	155. 3	185. 2	215. 3
6. 3	36. 1	66. 1	96. 2	126. 1	156. 3	186. 3	216. 2
7. 1	37. 1	67. 1	97. 3	127. 3	157. 3	187. 1	217. 1
8. 1	38. 3	68. 1	98. 1	128. 2	158. 3	188. 1	218. 1
9. 1	39. 2	69. 3	99. 1	129. 3	159. 3	189. 3	219. 2
10. 2	40. 1	70. 2	100. 2	130. 3	160. 1	190. 1	220. 2
11. 3	41. 1	71. 2	101. 2	131. 3	161. 1	191. 2	221. 3
12. 2	42. 2	72. 3	102. 1	132. 2	162. 2	192. 2	222. 3
13. 2	43. 2	73. 1	103. 1	133. 1	163. 3	193. 2	223. 3
14. 1	44. 3	74. 1	104. 1	134. 3	164. 2	194. 3	224. 3
15. 2	45. 1	75. 2	105. 3	135. 1	165. 3	195. 3	225. 2
16. 1	46. 1	76. 3	106. 3	136. 1	166. 1	196. 2	226. 3
17. 2	47. 3	77. 1	107. 2	137. 1	167. 1	197. 3	227. 3
18. 1	48. 1	78. 1	108. 3	138. 1	168. 3	198. 1	228. 3
19. 1	49. 2	79. 2	109. 3	139. 2	169. 3	199. 1	229. 3
20. 3	50. 2	80. 2	110. 1	140. 3	170. 3	200. 1	230. 3
21. 1	51. 2	81. 2	111. 3	141. 1	171. 2	201. 2	231. 3
22. 3	52. 1	82. 1	112. 3	142. 1	172. 3	202. 2	232. 3
23. 2	53. 1	83. 3	113. 3	143. 2	173. 3	203. 2	233. 1
24. 1	54. 3	84. 3	114. 1	144. 1	174. 3	204. 1	234. 3
25. 1	55. 1	85. 2	115. 1	145. 3	175. 2	205. 3	235. 3
26. 3	56. 1	86. 3	116. 1	146. 3	176. 3	206. 1	236. 3
27. 2	57. 2	87. 1	117. 2	147. 3	177. 1	207. 1	237. 3
28. 3	58. 3	88. 1	118. 3	148. 1	178. 3	208. 3	238. 3
29. 2	59. 1	89. 2	119. 3	149. 1	179. 1	209. 3	239. 1
30. 2	60. 2	90. 2	120. 1	150. 3	180. 1	210. 2	240. 1

How to Evaluate Scores

Conflictful scales: Add the weights for the three items on each scale of the four dimensions of Selfhood. The total of the four scores will give a measure of conflict on each scale *in comparison* to the partner's score. Scores on these scales are meaningless by themselves. They have meaning only in comparison to the scores of a partner. A computer program to score the PIRS is now available from the first author.

So = Selful; Si = Selfish; Se = Selfless; Ns = No self.

1. Winning vs. losing at others' expense

So: 12, 210, 219
Si: 177, 188, 199
Se: 144, 155, 166
Ns: 111, 122, 133

2. Denying vs. unrealistically admitting errors So: 13, 89, 100
                     Si: 56, 67, 78
                     Se: 34, 45, 239
                     Ns: 14, 235, 240

3. Mainly giving vs. mainly receiving love So: 15, 211, 220
                     Si: 178, 189, 200
                     Se: 145, 156, 167
                     Ns: 112, 123, 134

4. Spoiled vs. neglected So: 79, 90, 101
                     Si: 46, 57, 68
                     Se: 1, 35, 229
                     Ns: 221, 230, 236

5. Self-indulgent vs. self-debasing So: 17, 201, 212
                     Si: 168, 179, 190
                     Se: 135, 146, 157
                     Ns: 102, 113, 124

6. Critical of self vs. critical of others So: 2, 80, 91
                     Si: 47, 58, 69
                     Se: 3, 16, 36
                     Ns: 222, 231, 237

7. Dominant vs. submissive So: 191, 202, 213
                     Si: 19, 169, 180
                     Se: 136, 147, 158
                     Ns: 103, 114, 125

8. Determinate vs. "wishy-washy" So: 70, 81, 92
                     Si: 37, 48, 59
                     Se: 4, 18, 21
                     Ns: 214, 223, 232

9. Rigid vs. pushover So: 181, 192, 203
                     Si: 148, 159, 170
                     Se: 115, 126, 137
                     Ns: 82, 93, 104

10. Gullible vs. conning So: 49, 60, 71
                     Si: 5, 20, 38
                     Se: 23, 224, 238
                     Ns: 63, 204, 215

11. Rebellious vs. placating So: 171, 182, 193
                     Si: 138, 149, 160
                     Se: 105, 116, 127
                     Ns: 72, 83, 94

12. Showing vs. hiding feelings So: 61, 39, 50
                     Si: 6, 22, 205
                     Se: 25, 183, 194
                     Ns: 150, 161, 172

13. Manipulative of others vs. manipulative of self So: 117, 128, 139
                     Si: 84, 95, 106
                     Se: 40, 62, 73
                     Ns: 7, 24, 51

14. Driven vs. pushed (or dragged)	So:	27, 216, 225
	Si:	184, 195, 206
	Se:	151, 162, 173
	Ns:	118, 129, 140
15. Authoritarian vs. overly responsible	So:	85, 96, 107
	Si:	41, 52, 74
	Se:	8, 26, 233
	Ns:	207, 217, 226
16. Immediate vs. delaying	So:	29, 185, 196
	Si:	152, 163, 174
	Se:	119, 130, 141
	Ns:	86, 97, 108
17. Perfectionistic vs. sloppy	So:	42, 64, 75
	Si:	9, 28, 53
	Se:	31, 218, 227
	Ns:	186, 197, 208
18. Denying dependency vs. overly dependent	So:	153, 164, 175
	Si:	120, 131, 142
	Se:	87, 98, 109
	Ns:	54, 65, 76
19. Hyperactive vs. passive	So:	10, 30, 43
	Si:	33, 228, 234
	Se:	187, 198, 209
	Ns:	154, 165, 176
20. Overly expressive vs. unexpressive	So:	121, 132, 143
	Si:	88, 99, 110
	Se:	55, 66, 77
	Ns:	11, 32, 44

Selfhood dimensions: Add scores for each of the 4 dimensions of Selfhood on the 20 Conflictful scales. Again, scores on these dimensions are meaningful only in relationship to the scores of the partner.

Selful (So)

Item Numbers: 2, 10, 12, 13, 15, 17, 27, 29, 30, 39, 42, 43, 49, 50, 60, 61, 64, 70, 71, 75, 79, 80, 81, 85, 89, 90, 91, 92, 96, 100, 101, 107, 117, 121, 128, 132, 139, 143, 153, 164, 171, 175, 181, 182, 185, 191, 192, 193, 196, 201, 202, 203, 210, 211, 212, 213, 216, 219, 220, 225.

Selfish (Si)

Item Numbers: 5, 6, 9, 19, 20, 22, 28, 33, 37, 38, 41, 46, 47, 48, 52, 53, 56, 57, 58, 59, 67, 68, 69, 74, 78, 84, 88, 95, 99, 106, 110, 120, 131, 138, 142, 148, 149, 152, 159, 160, 163, 168, 169, 170, 174, 177, 178, 179, 180, 184, 188, 189, 190, 195, 199, 200, 205, 206, 228, 234.

Selfless (Se)

Item Numbers: 1, 3, 4, 8, 16, 18, 21, 23, 25, 26, 31, 34, 35, 36, 40, 45, 55, 62, 66, 73, 77, 87, 98, 105, 109, 115, 116, 119, 126, 127, 130, 135, 136, 137, 141,

144, 145, 146, 147, 151, 155, 156, 157, 158, 162, 166, 167, 173, 183, 187, 194, 198, 209, 218, 224, 227, 229, 233, 238, 239.

No self (Ns)

Item Numbers: 7, 11, 14, 24, 32, 44, 51, 54, 63, 65, 72, 76, 82, 83, 86, 93, 94, 97, 102, 103, 104, 108, 111, 112, 113, 114, 118, 122, 123, 124, 125, 129, 133, 134, 140, 150, 154, 161, 165, 172, 176, 186, 197, 204, 207, 208, 214, 215, 217, 221, 222, 223, 226, 230, 231, 232, 235, 236, 237, 240.

Self-Description Test

Instructions

Each item below names polar opposites on a particular dimension of individual behavior in relationship to others. For each item, rate yourself on a scale of 1 to 7, where 4 represents the middle of the dimension while 1 represents the first extreme and 7 represents the second extreme. Be as open and as frank as you can in rating yourself.

1. Winning at someone else's expense vs. losing at someone else's expense
2. Denying errors vs. admitting errors unrealistically
3. Mainly giving love vs. mainly receiving love
4. Spoiled vs. neglected
5. Self-indulgent vs. self-debasing
6. Critical of self vs. critical of others
7. Dominant vs. submissive
8. Determinate vs. "wishy-washy"
9. Rigid vs. pushover
10. Gullible vs. conning
11. Rebellious vs. placating
12. Showing feelings vs. hiding feelings
13. Manipulative of others vs. manipulative of self
14. Driven vs. pushed (or dragged)
15. Mainly authoritarian vs. mainly overly responsible
16. Immediate vs. delaying
17. Perfectionistic vs. sloppy
18. Denying dependency vs. overly dependent
19. Hyperactive vs. passive
20. Overly expressive of feelings vs. unexpressive of feelings
21. Selfish vs. selfless
22. Selful vs. no self

Description of Self-in-Relationship Test

Instructions

Each item below names polar opposites on a particular dimension of individual behavior in relationship to a partner. For each item, rate yourself and your partner on a scale of 1 to 7, where 4 represents the middle of the dimension while 1 represents the first extreme and 7 represents the second extreme. Be as open and as frank as you can in rating yourself and your partner.

1. Winning at someone else's expense vs. losing at someone else's expense
2. Denying errors vs. admitting errors unrealistically
3. Mainly giving love vs. mainly receiving love
4. Spoiled vs. neglected
5. Self-indulgent vs. self-debasing
6. Critical of self vs. critical of others
7. Dominant vs. submissive
8. Determinate vs. "wishy-washy"
9. Rigid vs. pushover
10. Gullible vs. conning
11. Rebellious vs. placating
12. Showing feelings vs. hiding feelings
13. Manipulative of others vs. manipulative of self
14. Driven vs. pushed (or dragged)
15. Mainly authoritarian vs. mainly overly responsible
16. Immediate vs. delaying
17. Perfectionistic vs. sloppy
18. Denying dependency vs. overly dependent
19. Hyperactive vs. passive
20. Overly expressive of feelings vs. unexpressive of feelings
21. Selfish vs. selfless
22. Selful vs. no self

CHAPTER SEVEN

Materials for Individuals

The programmed materials described in this chapter are directed toward individuals. They can be used in parallel with couples or family therapy or prevention, to deal with an individual's specific self- or other-defeating patterns that may be contributing to the relationship or family disturbance. The prescription of any of these materials must be based on the reason for referral, historical and situational factors, objective test results (preferably but not exclusively the MMPI-2), and the helper's professional judgment.

This chapter consists of a brief lesson for addicted individuals (the Alcoholics Anonymous 12-Step Program); two workbooks, one for acting-out individuals (Social Training) and the other for anxious individuals with generalized, nonspecific symptomatology (Social Growth); and a program for each of the 15 MMPI-2 content scales.

Some of the lessons in one workbook may overlap with lessons in other workbooks. For instance, the Depression program for the MMPI-2 scales is included in two other workbooks available on the same topic (L'Abate, 1986b; Levis, 1987). There are two lessons on anger—one in the Social Training workbook and another for the MMPI-2 scales. This seeming duplication is all to the good. None of these lessons are etched in stone. A sensitive and caring therapist can combine various lessons from different workbooks as deemed necessary by the client's condition. For instance, with depressed individuals, one might administer all the lessons from the three workbooks. There is little overlap, and each has a different focus. The workbook developed by L'Abate has a paradoxical and interpersonal bent. The workbook developed by Levis from Beck's original work is more intrapsychic and focused more on how the individual thinks negatively rather than how she or he behaves in intimate relationships. Both workbooks are oriented toward the process of depression; the MMPI-2 Depression program is more oriented toward the content of depression. Thus, all three approaches may complement and supplement each other. The same goes for combining the two different anger lessons, or any other lessons on the same or related topics.

The Alcoholics Anonymous (AA) 12-Step Program

This lesson, written in collaboration with Michael J. Gill, was paraphrased and developed very loosely from the well-known Alcoholics Anonymous (AA) 12 steps and traditions. It can be used as a structured interview by the therapist or as a self-administered lesson by addicted individuals. The basic requirement to be fulfilled at the end of this lesson, like most lessons in programmed writing, is for the individual to start monitoring how much control the addiction has over his or her overall functioning and welfare. With farther testing, one could then administer either a Depression workbook (if the client admits depression and it shows on the MMPI-2 profile or an equivalent test) or the Social Training workbook (if the testing shows the presence of a character disorder with impulsivity and acting out). Diagnostically, the therapist should be very careful not to confuse character disorder with drivenness. The former is shown by a peak on MMPI-2 scale 4 (*Pd*); the latter shows a peak on scale 9 (*Ma*). A person exhibiting drivenness should not be administered the Social Training workbook but might be administered the Type A lesson for the MMPI-2 (if a peak is also shown on the appropriate content scale).

The Commitment to Change

1. Are you ready to admit to yourself and to others that you are an addict? If your answer is yes, go on with this lesson. If your answer is no, do not go any farther. Apparently, you may need to suffer some more before admitting that (a) you may be powerless to help yourself, and (b) you need help.
2. How powerless do you feel over your addiction?
   a. Completely and hopelessly powerless
   b. Powerless but not hopeless
   c. Somewhat powerless
   d. Not at all powerless
   e. I can lick it all by myself
   f. I do not need anybody's help—help is for weaklings and I am not a weakling

   Write down how you feel about your addiction.
3. Which of these attitudes apply to you?
   a. I know better than anybody else
   b. I can kick my addiction any time I want
   c. I can control my addiction
   d. My addiction controls me
   e. People should leave me alone
   f. I won't be caught

   Write down an attitude not contained in the list above that applies to you.

4. How does your addiction make your life unmanageable? Write down in detail how your addiction has hold of your life.
   a. Relationships with family
   b. Performance on the job
   c. Relationships with friends
   d. Relationships with co-workers
   e. Relationships with others (please explain)
5. Make a list of the times you have gone out of your way to feed your addiction. Go back as far as you can remember. Use an extra page if necessary. Write exactly what you did.
6. How do you spend your free time?
7. Which of these uncontrollable habits do you have?
   a. Going out late at night to get those chocolate cookies or ice cream you've been thinking about
   b. Going out to buy cigarettes
   c. Spending your last dollar for a fix
   d. Daydreaming about the pleasure you will get from your addiction
   e. Thinking only of your addiction and of nothing else
   f. Driving fast to get what you crave
   What other habit(s) do you have?
8. How do these habits relate to your addiction?
9. What other pleasures do you have outside of your addiction?
10. How much has your addiction distorted your thinking and judgment?
    a. A lot
    b. Somewhat
    c. Not at all
    If your answer is c, you must be kidding yourself. Have you ever met an addict who could think straight?
11. If you are thinking straight, how come you are still addicted?
12. Why not have a close friend, family member, or spouse check on your decisions and judgments to see if you are doing the right thing? Please comment.
13. Have you ever known anything in nature that heals itself, without outside help? Does your car, for instance, fix itself? Does your vacuum cleaner? Your toaster? Yet, you expect yourself to fix yourself without outside help? In doing so, you are violating the laws of nature. Please comment.
14. What decisions have you made in the past that have caused you harm and embarrassment? List at least three of them.
15. Make another list of your moral and personal beliefs. Has your addiction caused you to stray from these beliefs? Make a check by those you have not followed because of your addiction, and describe how you have gone against them.

The four assignments that follow should each be completed in one week. Complete Assignment 1 during the first week, Assignment 2 during the second week, and so on. These assignments will not be easy. However, each of them is a small step toward recovery. If you miss any one of them, your recovery will be that much harder.

Assignment 1

This assignment should be accomplished with another person, preferably someone who has already gone through what you are going through at this moment. The person who has gone through this will understand you best. Discuss the answers you gave to the preceding questions and the things you have done because of your addiction. Be as honest as possible, even if it hurts. This is a growing step and takes a great deal of courage.

Do not go on to the next assignment until you have completed this first one.

Assignment 2

Make a list of all the persons you feel you have hurt in the past while feeding your addiction. Be honest and thorough when making your list. Write the name of each person you have hurt, and describe how you have hurt that person.

Now go back to see each person on your list and ask for his or her forgiveness. The only exceptions should be those for whom greater harm would be caused if you saw them. This is very likely the hardest step you will have to take, harder even than quitting your addiction. However, if you cannot forgive yourself first, how can you ask others to forgive you? You really cannot ask anyone's forgiveness unless you have forgiven yourself. The best and only way you will know whether you have forgiven yourself will be your quitting your addiction.

Do not go on to the third assignment until you have completed this second one.

Assignment 3

The most important part of your recovery is daily communication with an understanding person. Talk with or write to this person about any daily compulsions and obsessions you may have regarding your addiction. Make a list of people you can contact, with their addresses and phone numbers, and keep this list with you at all times. Write down what happens with each of the support friends you contact by phone or by mail. How could you make new friends and find more support from them? Write down some very specific steps to reach this goal.

Do not go on to the next assignment unless you have completed this third one.

Assignment 4

Have you made a decision to do what it takes to fight your addiction, no matter what is asked of you? If your answer is no, you will need to hurt yourself and those who love you more. If that is what you want, and you want to avoid the pain and suffering by producing more pain and suffering, no one can stop you. If your answer is yes, then write down in as much detail as possible what plans and fallback plans you are going to follow to fight your addiction. Describe your primary plan, a support plan to ensure that you will follow your primary plan, and a fallback plan you can resort to if your first two plans fail.

If you have completed all four assignments you may be on the road to recovery. Congratulations! You should feel proud of yourself.

What are you going to do now? Are you ready now and strong enough to ask for help? Remember that only healthy people ask for help; unhealthy ones do not.

Social Training Workbook*

Evaluating Participants

The therapist should evaluate participants before they start and after they complete this workbook. For participants who cannot read or write, administer a nonverbal test of intelligence, and possibly a nonverbal test of personality. For subjects who can read and write, administer any available standard tests to measure intelligence and personality, like the Minnesota Multiphasic Personality Inventory (MMPI) or equivalent instrument to measure impulsivity and immediacy in orientation.

Ideally, for each experimental participant who is willing to undergo this program, the therapist should pick another subject to use as a control, who either will not undergo this program, is on a waiting list for this program, or is following another rehabilitation program. This control subject should be matched with the experimental subject in most demographic characteristics (age, sex, socioeconomic level, education, and intelligence). The control subject should be evaluated with the same instruments as the experimental participant at the beginning and at the end of this program. Do not start this program unless the experimental participant has read or has been read and signed the Agreement that precedes the lessons. This Agreement grants informed consent in the presence of a witness. Make one xerox copy of this Agreement. Give the copy to the participant and keep the original in your files.

Description

This workbook consists of 16 basic lessons plus 4 optional lessons that deal with concepts assumed to guide and control a great deal of our behavior. These lessons are as follows:

1. *Goals and Wants.* What does the person want to achieve through this program?
2. *Mistakes.* What past errors is the person willing to admit and take responsibility for?
3. *Control.* How does the person control or fail to control, and what are the consequences of successes or failures in achieving control? At this point, it has been found useful to administer one or more of the optional

lessons on anger, humility, and reactivity, depending on the nature of the controls in the individual.

4. *Law.* Why do we have laws, and what is the most important law that all of us need to follow?
5. *Responsibility.* How does the person take responsibility for his or her own actions?
6. *Self.* How does the person see the importance of the self, and how does the person enhance or debase self and other?
7. *Love.* How does the person give and receive actions that enhance the self? Care, seeing the good, and forgiveness are at least three important components of love.
8. *Care.* How does the person show care of self and others through concrete actions?
9. *Seeing the Good.* This is a cognitive decision; one needs to accept and accentuate positive qualities in one's self in order to see them in others.
10. *Forgiveness.* One needs to accept inherent flaws and give up expectations of perfection in one's self and others.
11. *Respect for Parents.* If one cannot respect one's parents, no matter how flawed, one cannot respect one's self and others, especially authorities.
12. *Situations.* One needs to learn to accept responsibility for what happens in situations that have been in part determined by one's self.
13. *Actions and Decisions.* One needs to discriminate hurtful from helpful actions and be able to behave accordingly.
14. *Emotions and Feelings.* Actions are the outcome of feelings, emotions, and thinking, all of which need to be sharply divided from actions.
15. *Thinking.* This is the connecting link between feelings and emotions and actions; if one cannot use thinking before acting, one is lost.
16. *Putting It All Together.* This lesson is a review and evaluation, to determine whether goals have been achieved and whether other goals are necessary.

In addition to these 16 lessons, 4 optional lessons can be administered as needed.

1. *Goal Setting.* To be used for daily, weekly, monthly, and yearly living.
2. *Anger.* Anger is one of the main feelings experienced by most acting-out individuals. This lesson can be administered at the very beginning if anger is a primary problem in the acting out.
3. *Reactivity.* This lesson examines responding immediately without hurting self or others.
4. *Humility.* This quality is the opposite of arrogance. This is another lesson that can be very usefully administered at the outset.

In each lesson the respondent is asked to answer questions sequentially related to the initial question to define a concept. Most lessons end with concrete examples of how the respondent has applied behavior to real situations. If the person has not completed this part of each lesson, he or she cannot go on to the next lesson.

Administering the Workbook

Participants who can read and write can be given this workbook one lesson at a time, possibly with discussion after each lesson has been completed. Participants can move on to the next lesson when they have completed the homework assignment satisfactorily.

The supplementary lessons on goal setting, anger, reactivity, and humility can be administered on an as-needed basis. For instance, the goal-setting lesson can be administered after completion of the first lesson, if goals and goal setting are still unclear and further specification and elaboration of goals is needed. Otherwise, this lesson can be administered on completion of this program to decrease possibilities of relapse and to continue on an additional program. The lessons on anger, reactivity, and humility can also be administered at the very outset of this program, after completion of the lessons on goals and goal setting. They can be administered at any time during this program if and when anger, reactivity, and arrogance raise their ugly heads.

The choice of an additional program or workbook after completion of this program should be based on how the client did on the Social Training workbook, pre- and post-workbook test results, and goals the client wants to achieve.

*This program is protected by copyright laws and cannot be reproduced without the permission of its author, Luciano L'Abate, Ph.D., who is greatly indebted to Dan MacDougald, J.D., for his help in improving this program and for all of his many years of committed and hard work with Emotional Maturity Instruction, on which the present program is partially based. Whatever errors may be found in this program are due to the author's negligence and not to Mr. MacDougald's.

Instructions to Participant

To be read by participant before signing the Agreement

This program requires you to answer all the questions in each lesson in writing. You will be assigned about one lesson a week. Each lesson focuses on a different concept that seems to influence how we behave. You will need to understand how each concept may affect you. Spend as much time as you can answering each question in as much detail as possible. Feel free to go back to your answers and add to them as you like. It will be up to you to save all of your lessons so that they can be reviewed and you can receive information back about your work. Make sure that each lesson bears your name and/or an identification number like your social security number. Without written work, you will not get any information back, nor will you receive the next lesson. Without written work, therefore, there may not be a chance for improvement. Keep on writing!

Agreement of Informed Consent

I, the undersigned, [please print name], have read the paragraph below and agree to work on this Social Training workbook voluntarily and entirely on my own, free from any kind of pressure, coercion, or force from anyone.

I understand that this workbook deals with the definition and understanding of many key concepts necessary for successful social living. This program means answering a great many questions in writing or on a tape recorder. My writing (or tape recording) may help me change my behavior for the better. My answers will be used to give me back information about what I have written, so that I can improve my behavior. I understand that I can quit this program any time I want, without suffering any consequences or reprisals.

Signed of my own free will on [date]
Signature of Participant
Signature of Witness
(Print name of witness)

Lesson 1: Goals and Wants

1. Why do you want to work on this program?
2. Why is it important for you to change?
3. Why would you want to change?
4. Rank the following goals from the most important to you (1) to the least important to you (8 or 9).

   I want to feel better as a person
   I need to lower the stress I am under
   I wish to improve my behavior
   I want to be more comfortable with myself
   I need to be more comfortable with others
   I would like to understand myself better
   I want to win for a change
   I would like to stop failing all the time
   Other goal (   )

5. Explain why you want to achieve your most important goal.
6. Explain how you are going to achieve your most important goal.
7. Would it be better for you to stay the same? Why not?
8. If you want to stay the same or get worse: *Stop and go no farther!*
9. If you want to change for the better, you will need to follow all the instructions given in the following lessons. If you follow these instructions in detail, there is a chance that you will reach your goal(s). If you do not follow these instructions, you very likely will not change and you will stay the same or get worse.
10. To work on this program, you will need to set aside some quiet place and time. Write down when and where you will work on this program.
11. What do you think will happen to you if you do not work on this program?
12. Whose responsibility is it to work on this program, and why?
13. Please feel free to write down how you feel about your answers to the questions in this lesson or any other comments that would be helpful in understanding why you want to work on this program.

Lesson 2: Mistakes

1. What is a mistake for you?
2. What is the difference between a mistake and an error?
3. What is the difference between an error and a goof?
4. What mistakes have you made this week? List as many mistakes as you can possibly remember. Add past mistakes to this list as they come to you and as you think about them.
5. In looking over your list of past mistakes, can you see any pattern to them? For example, do you keep making the same mistake? What other pattern can you find?
6. Do you like making the same mistake again and again?
7. Have you ever made the mistake of denying you were making a mistake?
8. Why should you want to quit making the same mistake?
9. What will it take for you to quit making the same mistake?
10. How are you going to avoid making the same mistake(s) in the future? Please be as specific and detailed as you can.
11. Write any comments you want to make about the questions in this lesson.
12. During the next week, make at least three mistakes and see what happens to you. Write down what each mistake was and what happened to you after you made each mistake.
13. Also during the next week, see whether you can avoid making at least three mistakes. Write down each mistake you avoided and what happened to you when you avoided it.

Lesson 3: Control

1. What does control mean to you?
2. Who controls you?
3. When have you failed to control yourself? Write down as many times as you can remember when you failed to control yourself.
4. Why should you control yourself?
5. Why should you not control yourself?
6. Why is it better to control yourself than not to control yourself?
7. What happens to you when you fail to control yourself?
8. What happens to you when you control yourself?
9. How do you achieve control of yourself?
10. What will it take for you to be in control of yourself?
11. Which is better for you: being in control of yourself or losing control of yourself? Why?
12. Write down whatever comments you care to make about this lesson.
13. During the next week, notice the times when you lose control. List three of these times and describe what happened.
14. Also during the next week, notice the times when you keep your cool and keep control of yourself. List three of these times and describe what happened.

If you feel you need further help with control, ask your counselor or therapist to give you more lessons dealing with improving your sense of control.

Lesson 4: Law

1. What is the meaning of the word *law?*
2. What laws do you follow for yourself?
3. What is the difference between the authority and the law?
4. Why are there laws? List at least three reasons.
5. Give three examples of when you followed the law. What happened to you afterward?
6. Give three examples of when you broke the law. What happened to you afterward?
7. How do you feel when you break the law?
8. How do you feel when someone rips you off?
9. How do you feel when someone lies to you?
10. How do you feel when someone cheats you?
11. How do you feel when someone steals from you?
12. How do you feel when someone attacks you?
13. How would others feel if you were to rip them off, lie, cheat, steal, or attack them?
14. How would you like to be treated by other people?
15. Why should other people treat you well if you do not treat them just as well?
16. What would happen to you if there were no law to ensure you would be treated the way you want to be treated?
17. What do you want to call this law?
18. Do you want to follow this law? Why?
19. During the next week, see what happens to you when you treat people in a way you would not want to be treated. Write down at least three times when you treated people in ways you would not want them to treat you. What happened to you?
20. Also during the next week, see what happens to you when you treat people the way you want to be treated. Write down three times when you treated people the way you want them to treat you. What happened to you?

Lesson 5: Responsibility

1. What does the word *responsibility* mean to you?
2. Who is responsible for your behavior, and why?
3. Who is responsible for getting you into trouble, and why?
4. Who is responsible for getting you out of trouble (if possible), and why?
5. Why should you be responsible for what you do?
6. What happens to you when you fail to take responsibility for yourself?
7. What happened to you when you took responsibility for yourself in the past? Describe at least four times when you took responsibility for your behavior.

8. What happened to you when you failed to take responsibility for yourself in the past? Describe four different times when you failed to take responsibility for yourself.
9. During the next week, notice when you take responsibility for yourself. List four of these times and describe what happened.
10. Also during the next week, notice when you fail to take responsibility for your behavior. List four of these times and describe what happened.

Lesson 6: Self

1. What does the word *self* mean to you?
2. Do you have a self? Why?
3. What kind of self do you have?
4. What kind of self would you like to have?
5. What happens to you when your self is put down?
6. How do you put your self down?
7. Describe what happened three times when you put your self down.
8. What happens to you when you are pleased with and proud of yourself? Describe three times when you were pleased with and proud of your behavior.
9. Who is responsible to your self? Why?
10. What happens to you when you fail to be responsible to your self?
11. What happens to you when you are responsible to yourself?
12. What does it mean to love one's self as a neighbor?
13. Who is your closest neighbor?
14. What does it mean to act like a selfish person?
15. What happens to you when you act like a selfish person?
16. What does it mean to act like a selfless person?
17. What happens to you when you act selfless?
18. What does it mean to act without a self?
19. What happens to you if you have no self?
20. What does it mean to act like a selful person?
21. What happens to you when you have a self or act selful?
22. Finish the following sentences:
    a. I want . . .
    b. I need . . .
    c. I like . . .
    d. I feel . . .
    e. I am . . .
    f. I . . .
23. What do these sentences have in common?
24. To act *selful* means acting important without taking importance away from others, to act *selfish* means acting important and denying the importance of others, to act *selfless* means denying the importance of self and making others more important than us. *No self* means denying both our importance and the importance of others. During the next week, act out all four ways

of showing or not showing your importance at least once. Write down what happened.

Lesson 7: Love

1. What is the meaning of the word *love* to you?
2. What does it mean to love one's self?
3. What does it mean to love others?
4. Why should we love ourselves?
5. Why should we love others?
6. What happened to you the last time you acted out of love for yourself?
7. What happened to you when you failed to love someone, including yourself?
8. What would happen to you for the rest of your life if you were unable to love yourself?
9. Would you agree that love means acting important without putting others down? You have a choice to either show love and act important without putting others down or to fail to show it, by acting important at someone else's expense. Which of these choices do you make and why?
10. If you had to choose between giving and getting love, which choice would you make, and why?
11. How can you get love if you do not give it?
12. During the next week, notice when you fail to show love for yourself by acting important at the expense of others. List three times and describe what happened.
13. Also during the next week, notice when you show love without putting anyone down. List three times and describe what happened.

Lesson 8: Care

1. What does the word *care* mean to you?
2. Why should you or anybody else care about you? Give at least four reasons.
3. What happens to you if you do not care about yourself?
4. What happens to you if others do not care for you?
5. Why should anyone care for you if you don't?
6. How do you show care for yourself? Write down three ways you take care of yourself.
7. What happens to you if and when others take care of you? Describe three times when you allowed someone else to take care of you.
8. What happens to you when you fail to take care of yourself? Describe three times when you failed to take care of yourself.
9. What happens to you when others fail to take care of you? Describe three times when others failed to show care for you.
10. During the next week, notice times when you show you care for yourself, without taking away care from others. List three times and describe what happened.

11. Also during the next week, notice times when someone shows no care for you. What happened to you and how did you feel? List three times and describe what happened and how you felt.
12. How do you feel about this lesson? Make any comments you want to make.

Lesson 9: Seeing the Good

1. What does seeing the good mean to you?
2. Can you see the good in you? How?
3. Can you see the good in others you know?
4. What happens to you when you fail to see the good in yourself? Describe four times when you failed to see the good in yourself. What were the results of this failure?
5. What happens to you when others fail to see the good in you? Describe four times when this happened. What was the result of this failure for you?
6. What happens to you when you see the bad in yourself? Describe four times when this happened. What were the results for you?
7. What happens to you when you see the bad in others? Describe four times when this happened. What were the results for you?
8. Why is seeing the good better than seeing the bad? Write down four reasons.
9. During the next week, notice times when you see the good in yourself. List four times and describe what happened.
10. Also during the next week, notice times when you see the bad in yourself. List four times and describe what happened.
11. What did you learn from this lesson, if anything? Write down at least four different results that may have helped you.
12. Any other comments you care to make about this or any other lesson you have completed thus far?

Lesson 10: Forgiveness

1. What does it mean to forgive?
2. In case you do not know or are not clear about this concept, it may be useful for you to think of forgiveness as giving up the expectation of perfection in ourselves and in others. This giving up, however, does not mean that we should not try to do as well as we can. How do you feel about this definition? Do you have a better one?
3. When was the last time you forgave yourself?
4. What happened to you when you forgave yourself?
5. When was the last time you forgave another?
6. What happened to you when you forgave another?
7. Are you worthy of being forgiven? Why?
8. How do you know or how can you show that you have really forgiven yourself?
9. If we really forgive ourselves we will not make the same mistake twice. Describe four times when you forgave yourself and you did not make the same mistake again.

10. If you have not forgiven yourself, you will keep repeating the same mistake. Describe four times when you did not forgive yourself and ended up repeating the same mistake.
11. If you do not forgive yourself, why should others forgive you? Describe four times when others did not forgive you.
12. During the next week, notice times when you forgive yourself and others. List four times and describe what happened and how you felt after you forgave.
13. Also during the next week, notice times when you do not forgive yourself or others. List four times and describe what happened and how you felt.
14. What did you learn from this lesson and how are you going to apply it to yourself every day of your life?

Lesson 11: Respect for Parents

1. Who was your major female caretaker as you grew up?
2. What was your major female caretaker like? Tell as much as you can about her.
3. How did she raise you? What did she do to make you mind her?
4. How close were you to her as you grew up?
5. How did your caretaker reward you?
6. How did your caretaker punish you?
7. Recall one particular memory from your relationship with her that is especially pleasant and pleasurable for you to remember.
8. Recall one particular memory from your relationship with her that is especially painful and unpleasant for you to remember.
9. How did you behave with your caretaker? What did you do to make her job as caretaker easier?
10. What did you do to make her job harder?
11. What kind of feelings do you have left over about her?
12. What do you think of her now?
13. Did she love you because you minded her? Or did she love you no matter how you behaved?
14. Who was your major male caretaker as you grew up?
15. What was your male caretaker like? Tell about him in detail.
16. How did he raise you? What did he do to make you mind him?
17. How close were you to him as you grew up?
18. How did he reward you?
19. How did he punish you?
20. Recall a particular memory from your relationship with your male caretaker that is especially pleasant and pleasurable for you to remember.
21. Recall a particular memory from your relationship with your male caretaker that is especially painful or unpleasant for you to remember.
22. How did you behave with your male caretaker? What did you do to make his job easier?
23. What did you do to make his job harder?
24. What kind of feelings do you have left over about him?

25. What do you think now of your male caretaker?
26. Can you forgive and forget what either of your caretakers may have done to you that is still painful and hurtful for you to recall?
27. What are you doing now, either as a human being, partner, or parent, that is better than either of your parents?
28. If you cannot forgive them, how are you going to forgive yourself?
29. If you cannot forgive either of them, how are you going to learn from your experience?
30. If you cannot accept and respect your parents as human beings who did the best they could under their situations at the time, how are you going to respect any kind of authority?
31. What happened to you in the past when you did not respect the importance of authority? Describe four times when you did not respect authority.
32. What is going to happen to you in the future if you do not respect or pay attention to authority?
33. What will authority do to you if and when you do not respect it? Who will lose?
34. During the next week, notice what happens to you when you respect and pay attention to authority. List four different times it happened.
35. Comment on how important or unimportant this lesson was for you. What did it mean to you?

Lesson 12: Situations

1. What is a situation?
2. Who controls situations that hurt you?
3. Who is responsible for situations that happen to you?
4. How much are you responsible for situations that hurt you?
5. How much are you responsible for situations that help you?
6. Who makes a situation helpful or hurtful to you?
7. Whether a situation is helpful or hurtful to you depends on how you behave in that situation. Describe four situations where you behaved helpfully. What happened to you then?
8. Describe four situations where you behaved hurtfully. What happened to you then?
9. For the next week, notice how you behave in situations that are helpful to you. List four situations and describe what happened to you.
10. Also during the next week, notice how you behave in situations that are hurtful to you. List four situations and describe what happened to you.
11. You have the power to choose whether a situation is going to be helpful or hurtful to you. Which of these choices do you want, and why?
12. If you get hurt in a situation, how should you behave afterward? Should you hurt those who hurt you? If you do, what will happen to you?
13. Comment on the meaning of this lesson for you.

Lesson 13: Actions and Decisions

1. What does it mean to act?
2. What does it mean that a person is known by his or her actions?
3. What kinds of actions get you into trouble? Describe four actions that get you into trouble or have gotten you into trouble in the past.
4. What kinds of actions get you good results? Describe four actions that get you good results or got you good results in the past.
5. Who chooses whether your actions will be hurtful or helpful, you or others?
6. If you act hurtfully toward others, why should you expect others to act helpfully toward you?
7. What happens to you when you let others control your actions? Write down four results that hurt you when you let others control your actions.
8. Your actions can be either helpful or hurtful. Which of these choices do you make, and why?
9. Who is responsible for your acting helpfully? What happens to you then? Describe what happened to you four times when you acted helpfully.
10. Why should you act helpfully? Write down four reasons.
11. Who is responsible for your acting hurtfully? What happens to you then?
12. Describe what happened to you four times when you acted hurtfully toward others.
13. Write down four reasons why you act hurtfully.
14. During the next week, notice helpful actions on your part. List four actions and describe what happened to you as a result of those actions.
15. During the next week, notice hurtful actions on your part. List four actions and describe what happened to you as a result of those actions.

Lesson 14: Feelings and Emotions

1. What are feelings and emotions to you?
2. List as many feelings and emotions as you can. If you need help, ask other people. Keep adding to this list.
3. Why are feelings and emotions important? Give four reasons.
4. What happens to you when you do not stay with your feelings and instead go into action right away?
5. What happens to you when you cannot split your feelings and emotions from your actions? Describe four times when you did not split your feelings from your actions. What happened to you?
6. What happens to you when you mix feelings and emotions with actions? Describe four times when you mixed feelings and emotions with actions. What happened to you?
7. What happens to you whenever you go into action because you feel bad, sad, mad, or because something unpleasant or painful happened to you? Describe four times when you felt bad and you jumped into action. What happened to you?

8. Give four reasons why we must split feelings and emotions from actions.
9. What did you learn from this lesson about feelings, emotions, and actions?
10. During the next week, notice times when you hurt yourself by jumping into action and not staying with your (bad) feelings. List four times and describe what happened.
11. During the next week, notice times when you help yourself by staying with your (bad) feelings and avoiding jumping into action. List four times and describe what happened.

Lesson 15: Thinking

1. What is thinking?
2. What does thinking do for you? Describe four ways in which thinking helps you.
3. Describe four times when you did not think before you acted. What happened to you?
4. From what you just wrote, what happens to you when you do not think before you act?
5. What is the difference between poor thinking and good thinking?
6. Would you agree that good thinking helps you, while poor or bad thinking hurts you? Please comment.
7. Describe four times when good thinking was helpful to you and got you out of trouble.
8. Describe four times when poor or bad thinking was hurtful and got you into trouble.
9. During the next week, notice what happens when you think badly or poorly. List four times when you did not think well. What happened to you?
10. Also during the next week, notice what happens when you think well. List four times when you used good thinking to help rather than to hurt yourself. What happened?
11. What did you learn from this lesson about thinking?
12. Why is good thinking better than bad thinking? Write down four reasons.

Lesson 16: Putting It All Together

If you have come this far, you should be congratulated for finishing this program. Congratulations! You deserve a good pat on the back!

1. What have you learned about yourself since you started work on this program?
2. Did you reach your goal, as stated in Lesson 1? If yes, how? If no, why not?
3. Why did you choose to change? Write down four reasons for changing.
4. Write down four behaviors that you changed because of what you learned in working on this program.
5. Which lesson from this program did you like the best, and why?
6. Which lesson did you like second best, and why?

7. Which lesson did you like the least, and why?
8. Which other lesson from this program did you not like, and why?
9. Write down three things you want to do in the future—one this month, one before the end of this year, and one next year.

Thank you for finishing this program. You can be very proud of your achievement!

Supplementary Lesson: Goal Setting

Daily Goals

1. Set your goal for today. What do you plan to do for today that will make this and every future day an important and exciting one for you?
2. How do you plan to reach your goal for today? Please explain in detail, even if the details do not seem important to you.
3. At the end of the day, check on whether you did what you set out to do. Did you reach your stated goal?
4. If you reached your daily goal, write down in detail how and why you think you reached it.
5. If you did not reach your goal, write down how and why you think you did not reach it. What was in your way? How did you fail to reach it?
6. If you did not reach your goal, question whether the goal you set for yourself could not be reached. Did you set yourself up to fail? Please comment.

Weekly, Monthly, or Yearly Goals

1. Now write down your goal(s) for this week, month, or year (circle which one). What do you plan to do this coming week (month, year) that will make this week (month, year) an important and exciting one for you?
2. Write down in detail how you plan to reach each of your goals.
3. At the end of the week (month, year) check back on your answers to questions 1 and 2 and write down whether you think you reached or failed to reach your stated goals.
4. How did you reach your goals? Write down in detail how you did it.
5. How did you fail to reach your goals? Write down how and why you think you failed to reach your goals.
6. If you failed to reach your goals, think of easier goals that you can reach and that lie within your ability to reach. Get another copy of this lesson and start again from the beginning. This time make sure you set goals you can reach!

Supplementary Lesson: Anger

1. What does anger mean to you?
2. What do you do when you get angry?
3. When do you get angry?
4. How often do you get angry?
5. How much anger do you feel when you get angry?
6. How much of your anger is a way to control others?

7. Comment on how you could be using anger to control others.
8. Does your anger control you and your life, or do you control it?
9. What would you like to see happen: learn how to control your anger or have your anger control you? Why?
10. What is the cost of your anger controlling you and your life? Write down three results of your not being able to control your anger and your anger controlling you instead.
11. What will be the reward if you learn to control your anger? Name at least three rewards that you will reap if you learn to control your anger.
12. What will happen to you for the rest of your life if you let your anger control you?
13. Please complete the following sentences:
    a. I get angry when . . .
    b. I also get angry when . . .
    c. I also get angry when . . .
    d. I also get angry when . . .
    e. When I get angry, I . . .
    f. When I get angry, I do . . .
    g. When I get angry, I say . . .
14. What would happen to you if you were to talk about your anger right away through words rather than through actions? During the next week, say "I am angry!" as soon as you feel anger or whenever someone or something makes you angry. List four times when you said "I am angry!" and describe what happened.
15. During the next few weeks, plan ways and means of expressing your anger helpfully rather than hurtfully. Write down three of these ways.

Supplementary Lesson: Reactivity

1. Reactivity means a pattern of answering or reacting to certain situations right away and without thinking, in a explosive, revengeful, angry, and destructive way. How does this pattern apply to you?
2. How reactive are you?
3. What happens when you react?
4. Who controls you when you react?
5. Do you or anyone else learn anything from your reactions?
6. How do you feel after you have reacted?
7. Complete the following sentences:
    a. I react when . . .
    b. I also react when . . .
    c. I also react when . . .
    d. When I react, I . . .
    e. When I react, I also . . .
    f. When I react, I also . . .
8. If you react, why shouldn't everybody else react, too? What would be the result of everybody reacting to everybody else?
9. What happens when others react to your reactions?

10. Complete the following sentences:
    a. When I am in charge of myself, I feel . . .
    b. When I am in charge of myself, I also feel . . .
    c. When I am in charge of myself, I also feel . . .
11. Give four reasons why it is better to be in charge of ourselves than to react.
12. During the next week, watch how and when you react and lose control of yourself. List four times when you reacted, and describe what happened and how you felt.
13. Also during the next week, notice if and when you do not react and are in charge of yourself. List four times when you did not react, and describe what happened and how you felt.
14. Please comment on what you learned from this lesson.

Supplemenaty Lesson: Humility

1. What does the word *humility* mean to you? Please define it the best way you can.
2. What is the opposite of humility? What would you call it and how would you define it?
3. What does the word *arrogance* mean to you? Please define it the best way you can.
4. Sometimes lack of humility, or arrogance, shows itself in an "I know better" attitude. Please describe how this "I know better" attitude may apply to your behavior.
5. Please complete the following sentences:
    a. I know better because . . .
    b. I also know better because . . .
    c. I also know better because . . .
    d. I also know better because . . .
6. Think of four times in the past when you had this attitude of "I know better" and write down what happened to you.
7. Think of four times in the past when you kept an open mind and an attitude of humility. Write down what happened to you.
8. Now write four arrogant statements.
9. How do you feel now?
10. Now write four humble statements.
11. Write down how you feel now.
12. Which of the feelings you described above do you like best, and why?
13. Which of these two feelings are you going to keep, and why?
14. Write down four reasons why you think humility works better than arrogance for you.
15. During the next week, act arrogant at least four times and do not use an attitude of humility. Write down what happened and how you felt.
16. Also during the next week, have an attitude of humility at least four times. Write down what happened and how you felt.
17. Which of the two attitudes, humility or arrogance, is best for you in the long run, and why?

Programs for the MMPI-2 Content Scales

These programs have been created to accompany the second revision of the Minnesota Multiphasic Personality Inventory (MMPI-2), which consists of 15 content scales (Butcher, Graham, Williams, & Ben-Porath, 1989). Although each scale is matched by just one lesson, each lesson requires homework that may take place over a period of weeks; this is the reason for calling these assignments "programs." The Social Training and Social Growth workbooks are based on strictly *linear* perspectives. Many of these lessons, on the other hand, are based on *circular* perspectives, in which seemingly paradoxical prescriptions are administered. Homework in almost all lessons includes a pre-scription of the undesirable behavior, according to the principles of control enunciated in Chapter 2 of this text. It is, of course, important to reevaluate the client upon completion of each lesson (or whenever the therapist and the client consider reevaluation necessary) to see whether or not the lesson helped decrease the influence of the problem area. Each lesson also requires the client to keep written or tape-recorded notes. These notes are one indication of the client's motivation to work on the problem area (Butcher, 1990).

The programs matched with the 15 content scales of the MMPI-2 are as follows:

1. *Anxiety.* Anxiety is perhaps one of the most pervasive and common individual symptoms. Usually it consists of inadequately defined behaviors, such as internal tension, fidgety behavior, or dread of undefined situations.
2. *Fears.* Fears and phobias have very specific sources, the destructive influence of which needs to be recognized and acknowledged.
3. *Obsessiveness.* Obsessive thoughts are one of the many symptoms that leave many therapists buffaloed. Unless one has a clear plan for dealing with them, they are very difficult to control. There are two programs, one on obsessiveness proper and one on compulsiveness.
4. *Depression.* As mentioned earlier, this is one of three programs available on depression. It can be used in tandem with the other two and helps us deal with one of the most common referral problems.
5. *Health Concerns.* Somatizing, especially in introversive and internalizing individuals, may become such an obsession that this lesson may need to be paired with others, such as the lesson on obsessiveness.
6. *Unusual Thinking.* Many hospitalized persons show this characteristic. Treatment may pair antipsychotic medication with this program.
7. *Anger.* This is a common symptom in acting-out or impulsive persons. Additional lessons on anger can be found in the Social Training and Social Growth workbooks. One missing component in this and the other lessons concerns the manipulative role of anger. An additional lesson should be written, or specific questions should be asked about this role.
8. *Cynicism.* Skeptical, untrusting persons may show low motivation for therapy. This cynicism, however, should be considered as a defense and dealt with accordingly.

9. *Antisocial Practices.* This is a straightforward lesson in which, however, the antisocial practices cannot and must not be prescribed. What can be prescribed are the two attitudes underlying many of these practices: "I know better" and "I won't get caught."
10. *Type A Behavior.* Workaholics, driven individuals, and perfectionists can be detected relatively easily by asking, "What do you do when you do nothing?" Many Type A persons cannot "do nothing."
11. *Low Self-Esteem.* This is conceived as one of the many determinants of psychopathology, especially depression. Ultimately, a positive sense of self-importance may be a decision that each of us must make, because the cost of not thinking well of ourselves is too high.
12. *Social Discomfort.* Social phobias or fear of crowds or closeness are much more pronounced than we might think. Ultimately this discomfort may relate to loneliness and fear of closeness.
13. *Family Problems.* It is doubtful whether any deviant personal pattern takes place in a vacuum, devoid of family problems, whether or not the individual recognizes those problems.
14. *Work Interference.* A great many anxieties and pressures are brought home from the workplace, which is being increasingly recognized as a relevant source of stress in our society (LaBier, 1986).
15. *Negative Treatment Indicators.* Many persons cannot or do not want to change, or, to put it another way, they are too vulnerable and fragile to admit that they need professional help. Seeking help is seen as equivalent to admitting to "being crazy." In fact, only healthy persons can admit to that. An additional source of motivation for negatively oriented persons can be found in the Change Program in L'Abate and Weinstein (1987). It could be administered in writing rather than verbally.

For experimental reasons, the instructions for each lesson can be changed to ensure comparability of sessions from one scale to another. Thus far, it has been found useful to limit the number of lessons to five (Fraizer, 1991).

Anxiety

1. What is anxiety for you? Please define it as it applies especially to you and to no one else.
2. Explain in detail which of the following problems with anxiety apply especially to you.
   a. Tension
   b. Physical problems in general
   c. Physical problems in particular, like heart pounding, shortness of breath, loose bowels, sweating, or any other physical problem not listed
   d. Trouble with sleep
   e. Worries about (fill in your particular worries)
   f. Trouble concentrating
   g. Fears of losing my mind, not making it in life, losing my family, losing my job, losing my friends, or any other fear

3. Focus on the problem that upsets you the most, either listed above or one that is particular to you and that is not listed above.
   a. What is the problem that upsets you the most?
   b. How often does this problem upset you?
   c. How does this problem upset you?
   d. How does this problem upset your family?
   e. How does this problem upset your friends?
   f. How does this problem upset your work?
   g. How does this problem upset your leisure time?
4. Now focus on the second most troublesome problem in your life and answer in the same way you have done above.
   a. What is the problem that upsets you the second most?
   b. How often does this problem upset you?
   c. How does this problem upset you?
   d. How does this problem upset your family?
   e. How does this problem upset your friends?
   f. How does this problem upset your work?
   g. How does this problem upset your leisure time?
5. Focus on your third most troublesome problem and answer like you have done above.
   a. What is the problem that upsets you the third most?
   b. How often does this problem upset you?
   c. How does this problem upset you?
   d. How does this problem upset your family?
   e. How does this problem upset your friends?
   f. How does this problem upset your work?
   g. How does this problem upset your leisure time?
6. Focus on your fourth most troublesome problem and answer like you have done above.
   a. What is the problem that upsets you the fourth most?
   b. How often does this problem upset you?
   c. How does this problem upset you?
   d. How does this problem upset your family?
   e. How does this problem upset your friends?
   f. How does this problem upset your work?
   g. How does this problem upset your leisure time?

Do you want to learn to control your anxiety or do you want your anxiety to control you? If you want your anxiety to control you, do nothing and go on as you always have. If you want to learn to control your anxiety and you really mean it, then you might find it helpful to do the following homework.

Homework for Week 1
During the next week, make regular appointments with your most troublesome problem (for instance, on Monday and Friday nights at exactly eight o'clock). Make sure that no one will bother you, so you can concentrate on this problem. Make sure that you have plenty of writing paper. During this time (either

30 or 60 minutes, depending how long you want to work on this problem), concentrate on your problem. Make it as real as you can in your mind. Write about it in as much detail as possible for at least 30 minutes. The idea here is for you to start the problem rather than to try to stop it. *Remember: If you want to stop your problem in your mind, start it in your mind!* Return your written notes according to the directions you have been given.

P.S. If you cannot write, then use a tape recorder and record by talking into it in the same way that you would write.

Homework for Week 2
Which problem did you identify last week as the second most troublesome problem in your life?

Focusing on this problem, follow the same procedure as last week, making appointments with it and writing down whatever comes into your mind when you start thinking about the second most troublesome problem. Return your written notes according to the directions you have been given.

Homework for Week 3
Which problem did you identify two weeks ago as the third most troublesome problem in your life?

Focusing on this problem, follow the same procedure as last week, making appointments with it and writing down whatever comes into your mind when you start thinking about the third most troublesome problem. Return your written notes according to the directions you have been given.

Homework for Week 4
Which problem did you identify three weeks ago as the fourth most troublesome problem in your life?

Focusing on this problem, follow the same procedure as last week, making appointments with it and writing down whatever comes into your mind when you start thinking about the fourth most troublesome problem. Return your written notes according to the directions you have been given.

Fears

1. What are fears to you?
2. Rank the following fears, giving a 1 to the fear that upsets you the most, 2 to the fear that upsets you next most, and so on.

Blood	Dogs	Dark places
High places	Other animals	Being indoors
Money	Leaving home	Being outdoors
Snakes	Fire	Dirt
Mice	Storms	Any other fear (please list)
Spiders	Water	

3. Now focus on the fear that you have ranked as #1.
   a. How did this fear start?
   b. How often does this fear control you?
   c. How strongly does this fear control you?
   d. How does this fear control you and your life?
   e. How does this fear control your family?
   f. How does this fear control your friends?
   g. How does this fear control your work?
   h. Hows does this fear control your leisure time?
4. Now focus on the fear that you have ranked as #2.
   a. How did this fear start?
   b. How often does this fear control you?
   c. How strongly does this fear control you?
   d. How does this fear control you and your life?
   e. How does this fear control your family?
   f. How does this fear control your friends?
   g. How does this fear control your work?
   h. How does this fear control your leisure time?
5. and 6. Ask the same questions for 3rd- and 4th-ranked fears.

Now you have to make up your mind. Do you want to learn to control your fears or do you want your fears to control you? If you want your fears to control you, do nothing and go on as you have always done in the past. If you want to learn how to control your fears, then the following homework may help you.

Homework for Week 1

During this week, make appointments with your fear at regular times for regular periods of time—for instance, on Tuesday and Thursday at 9:00 P.M. for 30 to 60 minutes. During these times, make sure that you can work on your fears without anyone or anything disturbing you. Focus on fear #1 and try to make yourself as fearful as possible. As soon as you start feeling fearful, start writing down whatever you feel or whatever comes into your mind. Allow yourself to become as fearful as you can and immediately write down what comes into your mind. *Remember, if you want to learn to stop your fear you need to start it at preset, regular times!*

Return the notes you have written to your therapist according to agreed-upon arrangements.

Homework for Week 2

Which fear did you rank as #2?

Focusing on this fear, follow the same procedure as last week, making appointments with it and writing down whatever comes into your mind when you start thinking about the fear. Return the notes you have written to your therapist according to agreed-upon arrangements.

Homework for Week 3
Which fear did you rank as #3?

Focusing on this fear, follow the same procedure as last week, making appointments with it and writing down whatever comes into your mind when you start thinking about the fear. Return the notes you have written to your therapist according to agreed-upon arrangements.

Homework for Week 4
Which fear did you rank as #4?

Focusing on this fear, follow the same procedure as last week, making appointments with it and writing down whatever comes into your mind when you start thinking about the fear. Return the notes you have written to your therapist according to agreed-upon arrangements.

Obsessiveness

This condition shows itself in different ways. Please describe how it shows itself in any of these ways in your everyday behavior:

1. Trouble in making decisions
2. Thinking too much about issues and problems
3. Causing others to be impatient with you
4. Trouble with changes
5. Compulsive behaviors—that is, behaviors that repeat themselves often and unnecessarily without your control. In fact, these behaviors control you. Compulsions can include
   a. hand washing
   b. hoarding (collecting useless things)
   c. counting
   d. other compulsions (list your own)

Rank the obsessive behaviors you have identified, giving a 1 to the behavior that concerns you the most. If you rank behaviors 1 through 4 as being of most concern to you, then complete the section entitled "Obsessiveness-O." If you rank behavior 5 as your primary concern, then complete the section entitled "Obsessiveness-C."

Obsessiveness-O
1. Describe in detail what you feel, think, and what happens to you before, during, and after you have done the obsessive behavior you ranked #1.
2. How often does this behavior take place? Daily? Weekly? Monthly?
3. How strongly does this obsession affect:
   a. Your life in general?
   b. Your marriage (if you are married) or your relationships with the opposite sex?
   c. Your parents?

    d. Your children (if you have any)?

    e. Your friends?

    f. Your work?

    g. Your leisure time?

4. If you have more than one obsession, focus now on the behavior you ranked #2. Answer the same questions about it that you answered for obsessive behavior #1.

5. Obsessive behavior may come about from our inability to link feelings, thinking, and actions. What do you think of this possibility? If you think that this possibility may apply to you, please comment on the various relationships within yourself among:

    a. Thinking and acting

    b. Acting and feelings

    c. Thinking and feelings

Homework for Week 1

Part of this homework assignment may not make sense to you. However, try to follow these instructions. What do you have to lose? First of all, you have to make the decision whether you want your obsession(s) to control you or whether you want to learn to control your obsession(s). If you want your obsession(s) to control your life, go no farther. You do not need to complete this assignment. If you want to learn how to control your obsession(s), follow these instructions consistently and to the letter:

1. Set specific times when you can start your obsession(s). At the beginning, these times may have to be closely spaced, according to how often you think about your obsession(s). For instance, if you think about your obsession(s) 10 times a day, set 12 times when you are going to think about your obsession(s), once every hour on the hour for 12 hours a day for a week.

2. Schedule at least two appointments to write about your obsession(s) during the week (for example, on Monday and Thursday at 8:00 P.M. for 30 to 60 minutes). Describe in detail what you feel, think, and what happens to you before, during, and after your obsessive behavior(s).

Turn your writing in to your therapist according to the arrangements that have been made.

Warning! Do not try to rush and accelerate your progress. Follow exactly the instructions given.

Homework for Week 2

1. Last week you thought about your obsession(s) a number of times a day for 7 days. This week see if you can start decreasing how often you think about your obsession(s) every day. For instance, instead of 12 times a day, can you go down to 10 times a day for a week, always at prearranged times? In this case you may want to think about your obsession(s) every hour and a half rather than every hour. It is important that you follow the schedule you set beforehand; that is, if you have scheduled yourself to think about it

every hour, use a clock or timer to remind yourself at the time you scheduled and not at any other time.
2. Schedule at least two appointments to write about your obsession(s) during the week. Describe in detail what you feel, think, and what happens to you before, during, and after your obsessive behavior(s).

Turn your writing in to your therapist according to the agreed-upon arrangements.

Warning! Do not try to rush and accelerate your progress. Follow exactly the instructions given.

Homework for Week 3
1. Once again this week, see if you can decrease how often you think about your obsession(s) every day. For instance, instead of 10 times a day, can you go down to 8 times a day for a week, always at prearranged times? In this case you may want to think about your obsession(s) every two hours rather than every hour and a half. As before, it is important that you follow the schedule you set beforehand.
2. Schedule at least two appointments to write about your obsession(s) during the week. Describe in detail what you feel, think, and what happens to you before, during, and after your obsessive behavior(s).

Turn your writing in to your therapist according to the agreed-upon arrangements.

Warning! Do not try to rush and accelerate your progress. Follow exactly the instructions given.

Homework for Week 4
1. Once again this week, see if you can decrease how often you think about your obsession(s) every day. For instance, instead of 8 times a day, can you go down to 6 times a day for a week, always at prearranged times? As before, it is important that you follow the schedule you set beforehand.
2. Schedule at least two appointments to write about your obsession(s) during the week. Describe in detail what you feel, think, and what happens to you before, during, and after your obsessive behavior(s).

Turn your writing in to your therapist according to the agreed-upon arrangements.

Warning! Do not try to rush and accelerate your progress. Follow exactly the instructions given.

Obsessiveness-C
1. Describe in detail what you feel, think, and what happens to you before, during, and after you have done the compulsive behavior.
2. How often does this behavior take place? Daily? Weekly? Monthly?

3. How strongly does this compulsion affect:
   a. Your life in general?
   b. Your marriage (if you are married) or your relationships with the opposite sex?
   c. Your parents?
   d. Your children (if you have any)?
   e. Your friends?
   f. Your work?
   g. Your leisure time?
4. If you have more than one compulsion, focus now on your second compulsion and answer the same questions about it that you answered for your first compulsion.
5. Compulsive behavior may come about from our inability to link feelings, thinking, and actions. What do you think of this possibility? If you think that this possibility may apply to you, please comment on the various relationships within yourself among:
   a. Thinking and acting
   b. Acting and feelings
   c. Thinking and feelings

Homework for Weeks 1–4
Part of this homework assignment may not make sense to you. However, try to follow these instructions. What do you have to lose? First of all, you have to make the decision whether you want your compulsion(s) to control you or whether you want to learn to control your compulsion(s). If you want your compulsion(s) to control your life, go no farther. You do not need to complete this assignment. If you want to learn how to control your compulsion(s), follow these instructions consistently and to the letter:

1. Set specific times when you can start your compulsion(s). At the beginning, these times may have to be closely spaced, according to how often you follow your compulsion(s). For instance, if you wash your hands 10 times a day, set 12 times when you are going to wash your hands, at least once every hour on the hour for 12 hours a day for a week.
2. Once you have completed this task for a week successfully—that is, starting your compulsion(s) the number of times a day you scheduled for 7 days— see if during the second week you can start decreasing how often you follow your compulsion(s) every day. Instead of 12 times a day, can you go down to 10 times a day for a week, always at prearranged times? In this case you may want to follow your compulsion(s) every hour and a half rather than every hour. It is important that you follow the schedule you set beforehand —that is, if you have scheduled yourself to wash your hands on the hour every hour, use a clock or timer to remind yourself to wash your hands right at the time you preset and not at any other time.
3. If you are successful in performing this assignment for the second week, see if you can decrease how often you follow your compulsion(s) every day during the third week, always at preset times. Keep track of how well you follow your schedule and discuss it with your therapist.

4. If you have completed the previous step, see if you can now decrease how often you follow your compulsion(s) every day during the fourth week, always at preset times. Discuss your progress with your therapist.

Warning! Do not try to rush and accelerate your progress. Follow exactly the instructions given.

Depression

1. Depression means different things to different people. What does depression mean to you? Please define it and describe it as you see it.
2. Following is a list of feelings related to depression. Which of these feelings apply specifically to you? Please explain.
   a. Feeling blue
   b. Uncertainty about the future
   c. Lack of interest in living
   d. Broodiness
   e. Unhappiness
   f. Crying often
   g. Feeling hopeless and empty
   h. Thinking of killing oneself
   i. Wishing to be dead
   j. Feeling sinful and lacking forgiveness
   k. Lacking supports
   Any other feeling(s) not yet listed?
3. Now rank the feelings just listed, giving a 1 to the feeling that is the strongest for you, a 2 to your second strongest feeling, and so on.

Homework for Week 1
1. Focus on the feeling that you rated #1. During all of next week, make appointments with yourself to write everything you can think of about that feeling. Your appointments need to be set beforehand, at least 24 hours in advance, like Monday and Thursday from 8:00 to 9:00 P.M. If during the week or in between appointments other depressive thoughts come, make sure to make a written note of them. Save this note for expansion during your next appointment.
2. For this week's feeling, write about the following:
   a. How did this feeling develop?
   b. What makes it come about?
   c. What makes it go away?
   d. Other related thoughts
3. After you have written about this feeling, return your writing to your therapist according to the directions you have been given.

Homework for Week 2
Which depressive feeling did you rank as #2?
   Focusing on this feeling, follow the same procedure as last week, making appointments with it and writing about it. Return your writing to your therapist according to the directions you have been given.

Homework for Week 3
Which depressive feeling did you rank as #3?

Focusing on this feeling, follow the same procedure as last week, making appointments with it and writing about it. Return your writing to your therapist according to the directions you have been given.

Homework for Week 4
Which depressive feeling did you rank as #4?

Focusing on this feeling, follow the same procedure as last week, making appointments with it and writing about it. Return your writing to your therapist according to the directions you have been given.

Health Concerns

1. How often (once a day, week, month, year?) and how strongly (very much, some, very little?) do the following physical symptoms affect you?

    Gastrointestinal
    constipation
    nausea
    vomiting
    stomach trouble
    other (describe)

    Neurological
    convulsions
    dizziness
    fainting spells
    paralysis
    other (describe)

    Sensory
    hearing
    eyesight
    smell
    balance

    Cardiovascular
    heart
    chest pains
    other (describe)

    Skin
    rashes
    itching
    acne breakouts

    Pains
    headaches
    neckaches
    lower back pain
    other (describe)

Respiratory
coughing
hay fever
asthma
emphysema
other (describe)

2. What have you done about these symptoms?
3. What have you done about feeling healthy and keeping healthy?
4. What have you done about your diet?
5. What have you done about exercising regularly?
6. What have you done about your mental and emotional attitude toward your body?
7. What do you think is the relationship between your physical symptoms and painful past events in your life?
8. What do you think is the relationship between your physical symptoms and stressful events in your present life?
9. When was the last time you received a thorough physical examination from a competent physician?
10. Rank the following areas in reference to how much interference they cause in your life. Rank as #1 the area that causes the most interference, as #2 the next area, and so on.
    a. Gastrointestinal
    b. Neurological
    c. Sensory
    d. Cardiovascular
    e. Skin
    f. Pains
    g. Respiratory

Homework for Week 1

To gain control over your health concerns, you must understand what causes the symptoms and how you can keep them from appearing. To do this, make appointments with yourself during the next week to think and write about your symptoms. These appointments should be scheduled in advance for a time when you can write without being disturbed—for instance, Mondays and Wednesdays from 9:00 to 9:30 P.M. During this time, think and write about how the symptoms in the area you ranked as #1 affected you in at least three situations in the past. For each situation, write about the following:

1. Describe the situation.
2. When did you first notice the symptoms?
3. How did you feel physically before you noticed the symptoms?
4. How did you feel emotionally before you noticed the symptoms?
5. What do you think you could have done differently that may have kept the symptoms from appearing in that situation?
6. What long-range changes and plans can you make that may keep the symptoms from returning?

Return your writing to your therapist according to agreed-upon arrangements.

Homework for Week 2
Which area of symptoms did you rank as #2?

Focusing on this area, follow the same procedure as last week, making appointments and writing about it. Return your writing to your therapist according to agreed-upon arrangements.

Homework for Week 3
Which area of symptoms did you rank as #3?

Focusing on this area, follow the same procedure as last week, making appointments and writing about it. Return your writing to your therapist according to agreed-upon arrangements.

Homework for Week 4
Which area of symptoms did you rank as #4?

Focusing on this area, follow the same procedure as last week, making appointments and writing about it. Return your writing to your therapist according to agreed-upon arrangements.

Unusual Thinking

1. Have you experienced hallucinations or visions of any kind recently? For instance, have you:
   a. Heard something very unusual or strange lately? What? When? How often have you heard it? Can you control what you heard?
   b. Seen something very unusual or strange lately? What? When? How often have you seen it? Can you control what you have seen?
   c. Smelled something that you have never smelled before? What? When? How often have you smelled it? Can you control what you have smelled?
2. Describe any strange or peculiar thoughts that have come into your head lately.
   a. When do you have these thoughts?
   b. How often do these thoughts come into your head?
   c. Can you control these thoughts?
3. Do you find that you cannot trust anybody these days and that you are suspicious or fearful that:
   a. Others may speak ill of you?
   b. Others are plotting against you?
   c. Someone is trying to poison you?
   d. Someone is trying to hurt you or your reputation?
   e. Somebody is trying to cheat you?
   f. Somebody is after you?
   g. Somebody has it in for you?
4. Do you think that you are on a special mission?
   a. If yes, what is this special mission about?
   b. What will you get if and when you finish this special mission?
5. Do you think you have received special powers?
   a. If yes, who granted you these powers?
   b. What do these special powers consist of?

Homework for Week 1
If you want to keep hearing, seeing, or smelling strange things or if you want to keep peculiar thoughts and stay suspicious of others, go on your special mission, or keep your special powers, do nothing more. You do not need to do this homework assignment. However, if you want to get rid of strange and peculiar thoughts, follow these instructions to the letter, even if they seem crazy and make no sense to you.

1. Make two appointments with yourself this week at preset times (for instance, Monday and Thursday at a specific time, like 9:00 P.M., for one hour at the most). Set a clock or timer to make sure that you spend just one hour with yourself.
2. During this hour, try to hear, see, smell, or think whatever you have experienced lately. As you make yourself start these things, write down everything you see, hear, smell, feel, and think in as much detail as you can. If you cannot write, talk into a tape recorder. Return your writing or tapes to the therapist according to the directions you have been given. If these things come into your head at other times, write a brief note on a piece of paper and use it during your next appointment.

Homework for Week 2
Follow the same procedure as last week, making appointments with yourself and writing in detail about whatever peculiar things you have experienced lately. If you cannot write, talk into a tape recorder. Return your writing or tapes to the therapist according to the directions you have been given.

Homework for Week 3
Follow the same procedure as last week, making appointments with yourself and writing in detail about whatever peculiar things you have experienced lately. If you cannot write, talk into a tape recorder. Return your writing or tapes to the therapist according to the directions you have been given.

Homework for Week 4
Follow the same procedure as last week, making appointments with yourself and writing in detail about whatever peculiar things you have experienced lately. If you cannot write, talk into a tape recorder. Return your writing or tapes to the therapist according to the directions you have been given.

Anger

1. Is anger a problem for you? If anger is not a problem for you, then you should not be doing this lesson. Ask your therapist or supervisor why you have been given the wrong lesson since it is clear that this lesson does not apply to you.
2. If you admit to having a problem with anger, welcome to the club! Anger and hostility show themselves in various ways. Write in detail about how,

when, how often, and how strongly you express your anger in the following ways:

  a. Irritability
  b. Grouchiness
  c. Impatience
  d. Hotheadedness
  e. Annoyance
  f. Stubbornness
  g. Swearing
  h. Smashing or breaking things
  i. Loss of control, temper tantrums
  j. Verbal abuse of others
  k. Physical abuse of others
  l. Any other way

3. Now rank the problems with anger just listed, giving a 1 to the way you most show your anger, 2 to the next most frequent way you show your anger, and so on.

Homework for Week 1

If you want to learn to control your anger, you need to practice showing it when you plan it and when you have control of it rather than becoming angry when others make you angry. Therefore, you need to make appointments with yourself at preset times—for instance, Monday, Wednesday, and Friday at 10 A.M., 3 P.M., and 8 P.M. The angrier you are, the more appointments you will need to make to get angry. *Remember: If you want to stop your anger you have to start it!* You will learn to control your anger to the extent that you make it come on when you want it and not when others want it.

At your appointments this week, focus on your most frequent way of getting angry. Think about how you express your anger in this way and immediately write down what comes into your head while you are trying to get angry. Return your writing to your therapist according to the agreed-upon arrangement.

Homework for Week 2

Which way of showing anger did you rank as #2?

Focusing on this way, follow the same procedure as last week, making appointments with your anger and writing about it. Return your writing to your therapist according to the agreed-upon arrangement.

Homework for Week 3

Which way of showing anger did you rank as #3?

Focusing on this way, follow the same procedure as last week, making appointments with your anger and writing about it. Return your writing to your therapist according to the agreed-upon arrangement.

Homework for Week 4

Which way of showing anger did you rank as #4?

Focusing on this way, follow the same procedure as last week, making appointments with your anger and writing about it. Return your writing to your therapist according to the agreed-upon arrangement.

Cynicism

Cynicism is a big word. It means a lot of things. Some of these things may apply to you and some may not. Please find which of these things apply to you and which do not by answering the following questions.

1. Distrust of others
   a. Are you distrustful of others?
   b. If yes, how distrustful are you?
   c. What is it that you distrust?
   d. Whom do you distrust the most?
   e. Whom do you distrust next most?
   f. Whom do you distrust the least?
   g. How does this distrust affect you?
2. Negativity and negative motivation
   a. How negative are you?
   b. What are you negative about?
   c. What does your negativity get you?
   d. How did you learn to think negatively?
   e. Give an example of your negativity and what it got you in the end.
   f. How can you learn to replace your negativity with positivity? If you do not know, ask your therapist or supervisor for help.
3. Most people are honest because they fear being caught.
   a. This statement, if you believe it to be true, would mean that you believe that most people are dishonest. Is that what you believe? What does honesty mean to you?
   b. While we cannot control other people's honesty and there is little we can do about it except to make sure they behave honestly with us, there is a great deal we can do to make sure we strive to be as honest as possible. Why?
4. People cannot be relied upon.
   a. Why not?
   b. What past, painful experiences have led you to believe that statement to be true?
   c. If you cannot rely on other people, can other people rely on you? If so, why should they?
   d. Instead of making a general statement, would it be better to say that some people can be relied upon and some cannot? Please comment.
5. Friendliness cannot be trusted.
   a. If you believe this statement to be true, you must have felt let down a lot. What experiences led you to believe the truth of that statement?

List at least three past, painful experiences that led you to not trust friendliness.

b. Between friendliness and coldness can you find a middle point where you can be yourself without turning people off?

6. Distance from others is the best policy.
   a. Do you believe this statement to be true?
   b. If you believe this statement to be true, why do you?
   c. What would be the outcome for you of keeping distance from others?
   d. Rather than making one flat statement for everybody, could you agree that there are some people that we want to keep distant from us? On the other hand, there are people whom we need and want to be close to. What kind of people do you want to keep distant from? Why? What kind of people would you like to be close to? Why?

7. People are out to take advantage of others.
   a. Do you believe this statement to be true?
   b. If you believe this statement to be true, what experiences in your past have led you to believe it to be true?
   c. What kind of people are more likely to take advantage of you?
   d. What kind of people are more likely not to take advantage of you?
   e. What do you think about this statement? Certain people are more likely to take advantage of us if we let them.

Now you have to make up your mind. Do you want to learn to control your cynicism or do you want your cynicism to control you? If you want your cynicism to control you, do nothing and go on as you have always done in the past. If you want to learn how to control your cynicism, then the following homework assignment may help you.

Homework for Week 1

Rank the following statements according to how well they apply to you. Give a 1 to the one that applies to you the most and that you believe to be more true than the other statements. Give a 2 to the one that you believe to be the next most true, and so on.

Most people are honest because they fear being caught.
People cannot be relied upon.
Friendliness cannot be trusted.
Distance from others is the best policy.
People are out to take advantage of others.

Pick the statement you ranked as #1 and during the next week look for instances where you find this statement to be true. Make appointments to write about these instances—for example, on Monday and Thursday at 9:00 P.M. for 30 to 60 minutes. During this time, make sure you can work without anyone disturbing you. Describe at least three instances when your behavior was controlled by this belief, and write down what the results of that belief were in each situation. Return your writing to your therapist according to agreed-upon arrangements.

Homework for Week 2
Which statement did you rank as #2 last week?

This week, look for at least three instances of this belief operating in your life and write about the results of your beliefs. Like before, make appointments to write about these instances. Return your writing to your therapist according to agreed-upon arrangements.

Homework for Week 3
Which statement did you rank as #3 two weeks ago?

This week, look for at least three instances of this belief operating in your life and write about the results of your beliefs. Like before, make appointments to write about these instances. Return your writing to your therapist according to agreed-upon arrangements.

Homework for Week 4
Which statement did you rank as #4 three weeks ago?

This week, look for at least three instances of this belief operating in your life and write about the results of your beliefs. Like before, make appointments to write about these instances. Return your writing to your therapist according to agreed-upon arrangements.

Antisocial Practices

1. Please list the kinds of discipline or conduct problems you had during your school years.
2. Have you ever been in trouble with the law? How, how much? When? Where?
3. How much shoplifting have you done in the past? When? Where?
4. How much stealing have you done in the past? When? Where?
5. How much lying have you done in the past? When? About what?
6. Have you ever set fires? To what? When? Where?
7. One of the major beliefs that produces antisocial behavior is "I know better."
   a. How does this belief apply to you?
   b. How did you develop it?
   c. What does this belief get you?
   d. How can you change this belief if it gets you into trouble?
8. A second belief that leads to antisocial behavior is "I won't be caught."
   a. How does this belief apply to you?
   b. How did you develop it?
   c. What does this belief get you?
   d. How can you change this belief if it gets you into trouble?

Homework for Week 1
If you want to give up antisocial behavior, you will need to work on the two beliefs just listed. For the first week, think about how the belief "I know better" gets you into trouble. Describe in writing at least three recent instances when you held this belief and what the result was for you. Return what you have written to your therapist according to the agreed-upon arrangement.

Homework for Week 2

Think about how the belief "I won't get caught" gets you into trouble. Describe in writing at least three recent instances when you held this belief and what the result was for you. Return what you have written to your therapist according to the agreed-upon arrangement.

Homework for Week 3

Think about how the belief "I know better" gets you into trouble. Describe in writing at least three recent instances when you held this belief and what the result was for you. Return what you have written to your therapist according to the agreed-upon arrangement.

Homework for Week 4

Think about how the belief "I won't get caught" gets you into trouble. Describe in writing at least three recent instances when you held this belief and what the result was for you. Return what you have written to your therapist according to the agreed-upon arrangement.

Upon completion of these homework assignments, if these two beliefs still apply to you and you want to work on changing them but are unsure of how to do that, ask your therapist to give you lessons from the Social Training workbook.

Type A Behavior

Type A is a label used for individuals who are also described as workaholics. This condition means an intense and burning involvement and investment in work. Work is the major source of satisfaction in the lives of Type A individuals. This is often at the expense of other aspects of their personality and of relationships with other people in their lives.

1. How do you qualify for this label?
2. How is work the most important priority in your life?
3. How did you develop this priority?
4. How does this priority affect:
   a. The rest of your life?
   b. Your marriage (or significant relationship if there is one)?
   c. Your children (if you have any)?
   d. The rest of your family (parents, siblings, in-laws)?
   e. Your friends (if you have any)?
   f. Your leisure time (if you have any)?
5. One characteristic of Type A personalities is drivenness.
   a. How does this characteristic apply to you?
   b. How did you develop this drivenness?
   c. Can you enjoy doing nothing?
   d. How would you feel if you did nothing?
   e. Do you feel that you have to justify your existence? Why?
   f. Can you enjoy your vacations?

g. Do you take work with you when you go on vacations?

h. Do you get headaches on Sundays?

6. Another characteristic of Type A individuals is immediacy. This is the feeling behind the motto "Never leave to tomorrow what can be done today!" *Now* is the important word here.

   a. How does this characteristic apply to you?

   b. How did you develop this characteristic?

   c. What does this characteristic get you? How does it affect your significant other? Your children? The rest of your family? Your friends? Your leisure time?

7. One of the major effects of drivenness and immediacy may be a deficit in awareness of other people's needs, wants, and desires. Sometimes this attitude is expressed in the phrase "Don't interrupt when I am interrupting!"

   a. How does this phrase apply to you?

   b. Are you able to listen to others rather than to only yourself?

   c. Are your feelings, thoughts, and actions more important to you than the feelings, thoughts, and actions of others? Why?

   d. How would you reply to the proverb "No person is an island unto oneself"?

8. Another characteristic of the Type A personality is a restriction in time perspective, as if life were too short and time were also short.

   a. How does this perspective apply to you?

   b. How did you develop this restricted time perspective?

   c. How does this perspective affect you? Your family? Your friends? Your leisure time?

9. Another characteristic of some Type A personalities is the belief that bluntness is the best policy.

   a. How does this characteristic apply to you?

   b. How does it affect your family? Your friends? Your relationships with the people you work with? Your subordinates? Your peers? Your superiors?

10. Many of the previous characteristics bring about a pattern of using and manipulating others for your own gains and profits.

    a. How does this pattern apply to you?

    b. How did you develop it?

    c. Who do you use?

    d. How do you manipulate others?

    e. What does this pattern get you?

11. Of course, one of the major characteristic goals of the Type A personality is to achieve SUCCESS through hard work. Success, however, is defined in terms of externals or tangibles, such as money, objects, or fame and glory.

    a. What does money mean to you?

    b. What do material rewards like objects and things mean to you?

    c. What do fame and glory mean to you?

12. If your sense of self-importance and self-esteem comes from all these externals, how are you going to feel if or when they are no longer available to you?

Homework for Week 1

If you want to change your behavior, you need to think and write about your feelings on certain topics. During the next week, make appointments with yourself at regular times each day to think and write—for instance, from 9:00 to 9:30 each night. Be sure that you can write without being disturbed. Think about each of the following topics and write down everything that comes into your head concerning each topic.

1. Work as your most important priority in your life.
2. Who gets shortchanged by this priority?

Return your writing to your therapist according to the agreed-upon arrangement.

Remember: it is doubtful that you will be able to change if you do not make appointments to think and write each day at preset times!

Homework for Week 2

This week, during your scheduled daily appointments, think and write about these topics:

1. With work as your most important priority, what other priorities in your life get shortchanged?
2. How does your drivenness affect others?

Return your writing to your therapist according to the agreed-upon arrangement.

Homework for Week 3

This week, during your scheduled daily appointments, think and write about these topics:

1. What makes you think you are invulnerable to heart attack, burnout, or breakdown?
2. Why do you need everything now? Why can't you wait until tomorrow?
3. What will happen to you and your family if you keep up the pace you have kept thus far?

Return your writing to your therapist according to the agreed-upon arrangement.

Homework for Week 4

This week, during your scheduled daily appointments, think and write about these topics:

1. Why should people be nice to you if you are not nice to them?
2. If your self-esteem is linked to externals, what will happen to you if these externals disappear?
3. Are money, things, fame, and glory more important than what your spouse, children, and family think of you?

Return your writing to your therapist according to the agreed-upon arrangement.

Low Self-Esteem

There are many ways of not feeling good about oneself. We shall consider eleven harmful and hurtful beliefs about oneself.

1. *I do not like myself.*
   a. How does this belief apply to you?
   b. How did you develop it?
   c. Why do you believe it?
2. *I am not important.*
   a. How does this belief apply to you?
   b. How did you develop it?
   c. Why do you believe it?
3. *I am not good-looking enough.*
   a. How does this belief apply to you?
   b. How did you develop it?
   c. Why do you believe it?
4. *I am not bright enough.*
   a. How does this belief apply to you?
   b. How did you develop it?
   c. Why do you believe it?
5. *I am not rich enough.*
   a. How does this belief apply to you?
   b. How did you develop it?
   c. Why do you believe it?
6. *I am clumsy.*
   a. How does this belief apply to you?
   b. How did you develop it?
   c. Why do you believe it?
7. *I am awkward.*
   a. How does this belief apply to you?
   b. How did you develop it?
   c. Why do you believe it?
8. *I am useless.*
   a. How does this belief apply to you?
   b. How did you develop it?
   c. Why do you believe it?
9. *I am a burden to others.*
   a. How does this belief apply to you?
   b. How did you develop it?
   c. Why do you believe it?
10. *I am afraid of what others think of me.*
    a. How does this belief apply to you?
    b. How did you develop it?
    c. Why do you believe it?
11. *Negativity controls me.*
    a. How does this belief apply to you?
    b. How did you develop it?
    c. Why do you believe it?

12. Consider the following two points about the previous eleven statements.
    a. At one time in your life, you decided to think negatively about yourself or to believe the negative things that others may have said about you. The decision to believe negatively, however, was entirely yours. What do you think about this statement?
    b. None of the eleven statements have anything to do with the external, objective reality, however; you have made them your reality by deciding to believe negatively rather than positively. What do you think about this statement?
13. Rank each of the eleven statements according to how well they apply to you. Rank the belief that applies to you the most as #1, the next belief in order of application to you as #2, and so on.

Homework for Week 1

The power to think negatively or positively about yourself is entirely yours. You have the power to choose. What will you choose? You have to decide whether you want negativity or positivity to control your life. If you want to go on thinking negatively about yourself, do nothing. However, if you want to learn to think positively about yourself you will need to control your negativity. During the next week, allow the belief you ranked as #1 to control your life. Force yourself to be controlled by this belief and notice what happens to you. Note at least three times when your behavior was controlled by this belief, and write about these three times. What was the result of that belief in each situation? Return what you have written to your therapist according to the agreed-upon arrangement.

Homework for Week 2

Which negative belief about yourself did you rank as #2?

This week, allow the belief you ranked as #2 to control your life. Force yourself to be controlled by this belief and notice what happens to you. Note at least three times when your behavior was controlled by this belief, and write about these three times. What was the result of that belief in each situation? Return what you have written to your therapist according to the agreed-upon arrangement.

Homework for Week 3

Which negative belief about yourself did you rank as #3?

This week, allow the belief you ranked as #3 to control your life. Force yourself to be controlled by this belief and notice what happens to you. Note at least three times when your behavior was controlled by this belief, and write about these three times. What was the result of that belief in each situation? Return what you have written to your therapist according to the agreed-upon arrangement.

Homework for Week 4

Which negative belief about yourself did you rank as #4?

This week, allow the belief you ranked as #4 to control your life. Force yourself to be controlled by this belief and notice what happens to you. Note at least three times when your behavior was controlled by this belief, and write about these three times. What was the result of that belief in each situation? Return what you have written to your therapist according to the agreed-upon arrangement.

Social Discomfort

1. Being socially uncomfortable means a variety of things to different people. What does it mean to you to be socially uncomfortable? There are a variety of reasons to explain why people are socially uncomfortable. Which of the following reasons apply to you?
2. *I am shy.*
    a. This is one of the main reasons used to explain social discomfort. How does it apply to you?
    b. How shy are you?
    c. If you answered "a great deal" or "some," then explain how this shyness developed in you.
    d. What does shyness get you?
3. *I am afraid of being discovered.*
    a. How strong is this fear?
    b. What are you afraid that people will discover about you?
    c. What are you afraid will happen if or when they discover what you do not want them to find out?
    d. What is the worst thing that could happen to you after they discover it?
    e. Has it ever happened to you, and if so, how?
4. *I like my company better than the company of others.*
    a. Why is the company of others so uncomfortable to you?
    b. How did this fear of others develop in you?
    c. What is the worst thing that could happen to you if you developed some acquaintances, or worse, some friendships?
5. *I am afraid of getting close to people.*
    a. How afraid are you?
    b. If your answer is "a lot" or "some," how did this fear develop in you?
    c. What is the worst thing that could happen if you learned to get close to people?
6. *If people discover what a* _____ [stupid, clumsy, ugly, or such] *person I am, they won't have anything to do with me.*
    a. How did you develop this idea?
    b. What does this idea get you?
    c. Why is what people think of you so important?
    d. Why can't you think on your own two feet?
7. *Parties are awful.*
    a. Why?
    b. Aren't you entitled to fun and pleasure?
    c. How are you going to meet people and make friends?
8. *I do not like crowds.*
    a. Why?
    b. What does this dislike get you?
    c. What is the worst thing that could happen to you if you were in a crowd?

9. Give your own reason for social discomfort.
   a. How did this idea develop?
   b. What does this idea get you?
10. Rank each of the preceding reasons for social discomfort in order of how much they apply to you. Rank as #1 the major reason for your social discomfort, rank as #2 the next most applicable reason, and so on.

Homework for Week 1

You have two choices. You can do nothing and continue to feel socially uncomfortable, or you can start to understand how your negative thinking causes you to be socially uncomfortable. During the next week, notice how the reason you ranked as #1 affects you in at least three social situations. Write down what these situations were and what the result was in each of them. *Remember, if you want to take control of your social discomfort, make appointments with yourself to think and write about how it affects you!* Return what you have written to your therapist according to the agreed-upon arrangement.

Homework for Week 2

Which reason for your social discomfort did you rank as #2?
   This week, notice how the reason you ranked as #2 affects you in at least three social situations. Write down what these situations were and what the result was in each of them. Return what you have written to your therapist according to the agreed-upon arrangement.

Homework for Week 3

Which reason for your social discomfort did you rank as #3?
   This week, notice how the reason you ranked as #3 affects you in at least three social situations. Write down what these situations were and what the result was in each of them. Return what you have written to your therapist according to the agreed-upon arrangement.

Homework for Week 4

Which reason for your social discomfort did you rank as #4?
   This week, notice how the reason you ranked as #4 affects you in at least three social situations. Write down what these situations were and what the result was in each of them. Return what you have written to your therapist according to the agreed-upon arrangement.

Family Problems

Which of the following problems describe your family best?

1. Arguments and fights
   a. How do these arguments and/or fights happen?
   b. How often do these arguments and/or fights take place?
   c. How strong are these arguments and/or fights?
   d. How long do these arguments and/or fights last?

    e. What are these arguments/fights about?

    f. Are the results of these arguments/fights positive or negative? Please explain.

2. Inability to love
   a. How is this inability to love shown in your family?
   b. How did this inability to love develop in your family?
   c. In some families the inability to love is shown through giving love but not getting or receiving it. How does this statement apply to your family?
   d. In some families the inability to love is shown through getting and receiving love rather than giving it. How does this statement apply to your family?
   e. What are some of the ways that your family fails to show love? These ways might include abuse (physical, verbal, chemical, alcohol), neglect (lack of attention, busyness, incompetence), stress on doing and performing at the expense of being together and available emotionally to each other, stress on things and money at the expense of being together and available emotionally to each other, or stress on togetherness and being available emotionally for each other at the expense of doing or having.

3. Unpleasantness
   a. How is unpleasantness shown in your family?
   b. What does this unpleasantness do to your family?
   c. Does anybody gain anything from this unpleasantness?

4. Anger and hate
   a. How are anger and hate shown in your family?
   b. What are the results of anger and hate in your family?
   c. How did anger and hate develop in your family?

5. Abuse and neglect in childhood
   a. How many of your present family problems are due or related to childhood experiences?
   b. If your answer is "a great deal" or "some," please expand on these past, painful experiences.
   c. Has the pain of these experiences ever been shared in the family?

6. Family of origin
   a. Where do these problems come from?
   b. What kinds of problems have been present in your family of origin?
   c. What have these problems done to your family?

7. Present relationships
   a. What kinds of problems exist in your present family relationships?
   b. What do these problems do to you?
   c. What do these problems do to your partner (companion, mate, spouse)?

8. Problems peculiar to your family and to no one else
   a. What kinds of problems exist in your family that were not listed or considered above?
   b. How did these problems develop?
   c. What do these problems do to you?

9. Rank the problems just presented, in terms of how applicable they are to you and your family. Rank as #1 the problem that affects your family the most, rank as #2 the problem that affects your family the next most, and so on.

Now you have to make up your mind. Do you want to improve your family relationships or do you want your family relationships to remain the same? If you want your family to remain the same, do nothing and go on as you have always done in the past. If you want to learn how to help your family, then the following homework assignments may help you.

Homework for Week 1
During the next week, look for instances of the problem you ranked as #1. Make appointments with yourself to write about these instances—for example, on Monday and Thursday at 9:00 P.M. for 30 to 60 minutes. During this time make sure you can work without anyone disturbing you. Describe at least three instances of your problem and the results in these instances. Return the notes you have written to your therapist according to agreed-upon arrangements.

Homework for Week 2
Which family problem did you rank as #2?
   This week, look for instances of this problem. Record three instances of this problem and their results. Return the notes you have written to your therapist according to agreed-upon arrangements.

Homework for Week 3
Which family problem did you rank as #3?
   This week, look for instances of this problem. Record three instances of this problem and their results. Return the notes you have written to your therapist according to agreed-upon arrangements.

Homework for Week 4
Which family problem did you rank as #4?
   This week, look for instances of this problem. Record three instances of this problem and their results. Return the notes you have written to your therapist according to agreed-upon arrangements.

Work Interference

There are many ways of interfering with work performance. Which of the following ways affect you?

1. Low self-confidence
   a. What does your low self-confidence consist of?
   b. How did you develop it?

    c. What does this low self-confidence say about you as a person?

    d. How does your low self-confidence relate to your work performance?

2. Trying too hard to please others

    a. Why are you making others more important than you?

    b. What does pleasing others get you?

    c. How did you learn to please others at your expense?

    d. How would you react to the statement "To please others means killing oneself?"

3. Trouble concentrating

    a. How troublesome is your inability to concentrate?

    b. How is your trouble in concentrating related to your work performance?

    c. How did this trouble in concentrating develop?

4. Conflicts with authority

    a. What kinds of conflicts with authority do you have?

    b. How did these conflicts with authority develop?

    c. How do these conflicts affect your work performance?

5. Conflicts with co-workers

    a. What kinds of conflicts with co-workers do you have?

    b. How did these conflicts with co-workers develop?

    c. How do these conflicts affect your work performance?

6. Inability to make decisions

    a. How are you unable to make decisions?

    b. What kinds of decisions do you have trouble making?

    c. How does this inability to make decisions affect your work performance?

7. Uptightness and inability to relax

    a. How uptight and unable to relax are you?

    b. How did this uptightness and inability to relax develop?

    c. How much does this uptightness and inability to relax affect your work performance?

8. Lack of family support for career choice

    a. How did this lack of support for your career choice develop?

    b. Does this lack of family support of your career choice apply also to other parts of your life? How?

    c. Why do you lack family support for your career choice?

    d. How does this lack of family support affect your work perfomance?

9. Questions about career

    a. What questions about your career do you have?

    b. How did these questions develop?

    c. Why do you have these questions?

    d. How do these questions affect your work performance?

10. Another way not listed above (please list)

    a. How did this develop?

    b. How does it affect your work performance?

11. Rank the forms of work interference just listed, in the order of how much they apply to you. Rank as #1 the thing that most interferes with your work performance, as #2 the thing that interferes second most, and so on.

Homework for Week 1

Make an appointment with yourself each week—for instance, from 8:00 to 9:00 P.M. each Tuesday—to write down a plan for dealing with or solving the things that interfere with your work. For this week, focus on the issue you ranked as #1 and write down a plan for dealing with or solving that issue. If you do not have any suggestions, ask friends and relatives for theirs. Write down all their suggestions and put them together to find a solution. Write about what would work and what would not work, and why. Try to implement the best suggestions. *Remember to make an appointment with yourself to write about the issues that interfere with your work performance!*

Return what you have written to your therapist according to agreed-upon arrangements.

Homework for Week 2

Which issue interfering with your work did you rank as #2?

Focusing on this issue, follow the same procedure as last week, making an appointment with yourself to write down a plan for dealing with this issue. Return what you have written to your therapist according to agreed-upon arrangements.

Homework for Week 3

Which issue interfering with your work did you rank as #3?

Focusing on this issue, follow the same procedure as last week, making an appointment with yourself to write down a plan for dealing with this issue. Return what you have written to your therapist according to agreed-upon arrangements.

Homework for Week 4

Which issue interfering with your work did you rank as #4?

Focusing on this issue, follow the same procedure as last week, making an appointment with yourself to write down a plan for dealing with this issue. Return what you have written to your therapist according to agreed-upon arrangements.

Negative Treatment Indicators

Following is a list of various negative, self-defeating, and destructive attitudes that make psychological treatment, psychotherapy, and professional help very difficult. Which of these attitudes apply to you?

1. Negative attitudes toward receiving help from others in general
   a. What are these attitudes in you?
   b. How did these negative attitudes develop in you?
   c. Under what conditions would you accept help?
   d. Under what conditions would you *not* accept help?
2. *No one can understand me or my problems.*
   a. Why do you think so?
   b. How did this attitude develop in you?

    c. You can use your hopelessness to destroy you or to improve you. Which is your choice and why do you choose it?

3. *I do not need anybody to help me solve my problems.*
   a. Have you ever heard the expression "No one person is an island unto oneself?" What does it mean to you?
   b. How did you develop this destructive attitude?
   c. What have you done to solve your problems by yourself?
   d. How successful were you?

4. *I know better.*
   a. What does this attitude get you?
   b. How did you develop it?
   c. If you know better than anyone else, no one can ever tell you anything. Is that right? Please comment.
   d. Why is being right more important to you than things like being successful, effective, competent, and close to people you love and who love you?

5. *Doctors are incompetent.*
   a. Of course, every profession has its share of incompetents. Are there incompetent people where you work? How do you spot them?
   b. What does this attitude get you?
   c. Do you get your sense of importance by putting other people down?
   d. This attitude says that you elected yourself judge and jury of others. What happens when others do it to you?

6. *My problems belong to me and to no one else.*
   a. How did this attitude develop in you?
   b. What do you get by holding onto your problems?
   c. Are you the only one who has these problems? Should other people hold onto them as you do? What would happen to them then?

7. *I like my life the way it is.*
   a. No matter what the price is?
   b. No matter how it affects those who love you?
   c. How did you develop such a negative attitude?
   d. Apparently you are thinking only or mainly of yourself. What would happen if everybody thought the way you do?

8. *I cannot change my life.*
   a. Why do you feel so hopeless?
   b. How did you develop such hopelessness?
   c. What does hopelessness do to you? What do you get?

9. *No one can help me.*
   a. Why do you feel that way?
   b. How did you develop such an negative attitude?
   c. What does this attitude do to you? What does it get you?

10. *I like trouble in my life, because as long as there is trouble, I do not have to take responsibility for my behavior. I can blame others!*
    a. How did you develop such a negative attitude?
    b. What does this attitude get you?
    c. What does this attitude do to those who care for you?

11. *My car can be fixed but I cannot be fixed.*
    a. What makes you think you cannot be fixed?
    b. Do you know of anything in nature or in your experience that fixes itself?
    c. If you cannot ask for help and want to stay the same, what will those who love you do?
    d. Please comment on the following: "If I cannot change, why should anybody else?"
12. Another negative attitude not listed above (please list)
    a. What does this attitude get you?
    b. How did this negative attitude develop?
    c. How does it affect those you love?
13. Rank the various negative attitudes in the preceding list, according to how much they apply to you. Rank as #1 the negative attitude that most applies to you, as #2 the attitude that applies to you the next most, and so on.

You have at least two choices. One choice is to do absolutely nothing. Keep on doing exactly what you have been doing all along. Do not change in any way possible! This will ensure that you continue to have a negative attitude. The other choice is to think about your negative attitude. By thinking about and writing about your negative attitude, you will see how it affects you and others you come into contact with.

Homework for Week 1
During the next week, apply the attitude you ranked as #1 to as many situations as you can. Answer in writing the following questions about each situation:

1. What was the situation?
2. What was the result of your negative attitude?
3. Were you improved by this behavior?
4. Was the other person (if there was one) affected by your behavior? How? Was it for the better?
5. Think about this statement and write down your feelings regarding it: "We make our choices, we pay our price!"

Return what you have written to your therapist according to agreed-upon arrangements.

Homework for Week 2
Which negative attitude did you rank as #2?
During the next week, apply this attitude to as many situations as you can. For each situation, answer in writing the first four questions you answered last week. Then think about this statement and write down your feelings regarding it: "Only strong people ask for help because weak people cannot." Return what you have written to your therapist according to agreed-upon arrangements.

Homework for Week 3
Which negative attitude did you rank as #3?

During the next week, apply this attitude to as many situations as you can. For each situation, answer in writing the first four questions you answered in week 1. Then think about this statement and write down your feelings regarding it: "People who do not change simply fear the unknown." Return what you have written to your therapist according to agreed-upon arrangements.

Homework for Week 4
Which negative attitude did you rank as #4?

During the next week, apply this attitude to as many situations as you can. For each situation, answer in writing the first four questions you answered in week 1. Then think about this statement and write down your feelings regarding it: "Change is possible but it takes hard work and effort." Return what you have written to your therapist according to agreed-upon arrangements.

Social Growth Workbook

Warning: In spite of this workbook's having been designed originally to deal with anxiety and fearfulness, results thus far do not justify such a specific application. Consequently, this workbook should be considered as a general, all-purpose way to gather relevant information from clients either prior to therapeutic or pretherapeutic interventions or during the process of such interventions.

Administering the Workbook

Each participant should sign the consent form provided on page 147 after the nature of this program has been explained and the instructions for following the program have been read and understood. Each lesson should be given to participants to complete on their own. Questions concerning this workbook, or any other programmed materials for that matter, should be answered to the participant's satisfaction. A lesson should be given only after the preceding one has been fully completed. Depending on the participant's goals, some lessons may be inappropriate or irrelevant and can be skipped or substituted for other lessons. This decision should be made as far as possible in advance of administering this program, so that the participant will know beforehand the total number of lessons that will be administered.

Description

The Social Growth workbook was written with the goal of creating an additional paratherapeutic experience for persons who cannot afford weekly therapy sessions but who are motivated to learn and to change, with a minimum of professional feedback and help. It consists of 13 lessons concerning a variety of issues that all of us have to face—for instance, family of origin, achievement, sexuality, and relationships with the opposite sex. Even though most of the lessons were derived from the interview schedule developed by Kagan and Moss (1972), many changes have been made for which the original authors are not responsible. Any failure resulting from this workbook is not the responsibility of Drs. Kagan and Moss.

Each lesson in this program is described in terms of (1) its relevance to anxiety; (2) its position in relationship to the preceding and the following lessons; and (3) the potential usefulness of normal, or normative, personality functioning.

1. *Checklist of symptoms* and a psychosomatic inventory listed according to intensity and frequency. Many anxiety reactions (or panic) are coupled with physical symptoms.
2. *Recall of childhood* events in relationship to parental socialization practices and discipline. Many anxiety reactions may be related to painful or traumatic events in the past.
3. *Sex roles* and a description of stereotyped gender roles as related to one's choice of identity. Gender issues are the basis of many anxiety reactions.
4. *Sexual behavior* for single and married subjects, from dating to intercourse. Sex and sexuality are also components of many anxiety reactions.
5. *Relationships with authority* figures, with a special lesson concerning the attitudes of college students toward their instructors.
6. *Vocational choices* since leaving high school; current job and opportunities for the future; with separate sections for housewives and mothers, house-husbands, and fathers.
7. *Recognition and achievement* in relationship to organizations, leadership roles, life goals, leisure activities, and hobbies.
8. *Compulsive tendencies and decision making,* such as being on time for appointments, daily routines, decisions about money and possessions.
9. *Anxieties about social interactions,* with new people, in one's home, with old friends, and with acquaintances.
10. *Hostility-aggression* in relation to feelings experienced and expressed, likes and dislikes.
11. *Self-esteem* in relationship to personal satisfactions, self-ratings, competence.
12. *Dependency-nurturance* in relation to asking for help when needed, using available support people as well as family and friends.
13. *Conclusions,* about what was learned from this program and which lesson was most helpful.

Instructions to Participants

Write your answers to the best of your abilities and feel free to go back to expand and elaborate on each of them as you like, even a few days later. If you have additional thoughts for which there are no relevant questions, but that are related to the topic of each lesson, feel free to write down these thoughts on paper, in as much detail as you can. Bring your answers and your thoughts to your helper for discussion. Thank you.

Agreement of Informed Consent

I, the undersigned, [print name], agree to answer all the questions asked of me in this program to the best of my abilities and of my own free will, without pressure or coercion of any kind from anyone. This workbook has been explained to me fully and to my satisfaction. I have also read the instructions for this program and I understand its functions and purposes. My written answers will be discussed and evaluated by whomever is helping me with my work on this program. I can terminate at any time I wish. No pressure will be brought to bear on me for quitting this program.

Signed of my own free will on [date]
Signature of Participant
Signature of Witness
(Print name of witness)

Lesson 1: Symptoms and Psychosomatic Inventory

1. Which of the following conditions have you had this year? How strong and frequent have they been?

Fears
Nightmares
Insomnia
Sleepwalking
Acid stomach
Vomiting
Constipation
Loose bowels
Nausea
Hives
Rashes
Acne
Pains in heart or chest
Obesity
Headaches
Asthma
Hay fever
Heart pounding
Breathing irregularity
Twitches
Hot-cold spells
Faintness
Nervous habits
Stuttering
Back pain
Muscle pain
Chronic illnesses

2. Any other physical condition not listed above? Please note how strong and frequent this condition is.
3. List illnesses or physical disabilities experienced in your life.

Lesson 2: Recall of Childhood

1. Many parents tend to raise their children somewhat differently from the way they were raised. Can you remember similarities and differences between what you did and what your father (or mother) did concerning the following?
   a. Punishment for disobedience
   b. Stress on being clean, on being honest
   c. Punishment for hitting or destruction
   d. Stress on good grades
   e. Stress on religion and going to church. What is your attitude toward religion?
   f. Sex information
2. As you grow older, you get a better picture of your childhood and your parents. How would you describe each parent with respect to the following?
   a. Strictness
   b. Kind of punishment
   c. Push to achieve in school
3. What would you say were your mother's strengths? Weaknesses?
4. What would you say were your father's strengths? Weaknesses?
5. What is your earliest memory?
6. What is your earliest memory of you with your mother?
7. What is your earliest memory of you with your father?
8. Most children feel that each parent had specific preferences for them or their siblings. Do you recall such preferences?
9. Do you remember any childhood fears?
10. How about traumas and painful episodes in your childhood?

Homework: During the next week, ask your parents, siblings, relatives, and longtime friends to give you more details about unusual, painful, or especially traumatic happenings or events in your childhood that you may have forgotten, with special attention to how you behaved under the circumstances. Report these details in writing.

Lesson 3: Sex Roles

1. Write about your hobbies and interests.
2. What do you think are the advantages of male roles?
3. What do you think are the disadvantages of male roles?
4. What do you think are the advantages of female roles?
5. What do you think are the disadvantages of female roles?
6. Have you ever thought about being of the opposite sex? Why?
7. Do you think childbirth is gratifying? Painful?

8. What are your attitudes toward menarche? Menstruation?
9. What is more important to you, playing a role or being your own person?
10. What kinds of myths or stereotypes about the opposite sex did you grow up with?
11. What kind of marriage did your parents have from the viewpoint of traditional sex or gender stereotypes?

Homework: During the next week, observe and report in great detail on cultural or stereotypical differences that you see and meet every day between males and females in the United States.

Lesson 4: Sexual Behavior

For Single Persons
1. When did you start dating? (Give a brief history of your dating.)
2. Did you go steady or not?
3. How often did you go out in the beginning?
4. How often do you go out now?
5. What did your sexual behavior consist of? Did you neck a lot? Pet? Have intercourse?
6. What are the things you look for in a lover?
7. What are the things you dislike in a lover?
8. What are the strengths and weaknesses of your current lover?
9. How is your past and present sexual behavior related to the way you were raised?

Homework: During the next week, concentrate on finding out and recording what pleases and pleasures you the most and what pleases and pleasures the most your sex partner, if you have one. If you do not have a partner presently, concentrate on writing what you remember that pleased and pleasured you the most in past sexual experiences.

For Persons in Committed Relationships (Including Marriage)
1. When did you start dating? Can you give a history of your dating?
2. Did you go steady or not?
3. How often did you go out in the beginning? Now?
4. Did you neck a lot? Pet? Have intercourse?
5. What are the things you look for in a lover?
6. What are the things about your current partner that attracted you?
7. What are his or her weaknesses?
8. What are his or her strengths?
9. How often do you have intercourse now? During first year of relationship or marriage?
10. Comment on how you feel about your sexual behavior and your sexuality.

Homework: During the next week, concentrate on finding out and recording what pleases and pleasures you the most and what pleases and pleasures the most your sex partner.

Lesson 5: Relationships with Authority

For Working People

1. Write about the positive and negative sides of your current boss. What do you like and dislike about him/her?
2. Do you feel any tenseness when you are talking with authorities (boss, professor, police officers, and such)?
3. Write about the positive and negative sides of your past bosses.
4. How do you react and feel when your boss criticizes you?
5. How do you feel when your boss tells you to do something in a hurry?
6. What do you do in situations where you are ordered around?
7. Do you talk with the boss about problems in your job?
8. Give a detailed description of your last meeting with your boss.

Homework: During the next week, watch and write about various meetings between you and your peers and between you and persons in authority (parents, professors, bosses, landlords, and such). At the end of the week, go back to review these notes and see if you can find any differences between how you behave with peers and with persons in authority. Note any conclusions you may reach about these differences.

For Students

1. What do you like the most about your favorite teachers (instructors, professors)?
2. What do you dislike the most about less favorite teachers?
3. What is the ideal teacher for you?
4. What is the worst kind of teacher for you?
5. Give a detailed description of your most recent meeting with a teacher. How did you feel after that meeting?
6. What is your reaction to papers with a deadline?
7. Do you usually work (study) before the deadline or at the last minute? Why?
8. What is your reaction to exams?
9. What is your reaction when a teacher criticizes you for something you have written?
10. How do you feel about going to a teacher with a question and talking with him/her?
11. How often do you go to teachers with questions?
12. What are your reactions to a bad grade or a negative review?

Homework: During the next week, watch and write about various meetings between you and your teachers as well as any specific meetings between your fellow students and teachers that particularly impressed you, especially those meetings that differed considerably from your own.

Lesson 6: Vocation

For Employees

1. Write down what has happened to you since leaving high school. What forces have influenced your behavior?

2. What are the main things you like about what you're doing now?
3. What are some of the reasons you picked your current vocation?
4. How did your parents (spouse) feel about this choice?
5. How important was the security of the job you chose?
6. For some people, the prestige of a job influences their choice. In choosing this job, did you think about its prestige?
7. Did you know someone who did this kind of work and who might have influenced your choice?
8. What do you think is the ideal job for you?
9. Everybody has some heroes or heroines they look up to. Who are the three people you admire most? Why?

Homework: During the next week, allow yourself to daydream about three possible jobs you would like to have. Describe in detail what each job would involve in terms of (1) duties or the nature of the job description, (2) its pros, and (3) its cons. Then write about your expectations and plans for balancing demands from home (family, partner, children) with demands from work; demands from home with leisure time; demands from work with leisure time; demands from self with demands from others; and demands from self with demands from family.

For Housewives and Mothers
1. What are the most enjoyable aspects of being a wife or a mother?
2. What don't you like about being a wife or a mother?
3. What changes would you make to make your job more enjoyable?
4. Who are the people you admire most?
5. How much are these people a source of inspiration for you?
6. What do you think would be the ideal job for you?
7. How can you balance work at home and work outside the house? What problems does this balance create for you?

Homework: During the next week, think and write about various conflicts that you do or will face between your role as a person and your role as a partner; your role as a person and your role as a parent; your role as a homemaker and your role as a woman; any other role conflict you experience. Feel free to add any comments related to these questions.

For Househusbands and Fathers
1. What are the most enjoyable aspects of being a husband or a father?
2. What don't you like about being a husband or a father?
3. What changes would you make to make your job more enjoyable?
4. Who are the people you admire most?
5. How much are these people a source of inspiration for you?
6. What do you think would be the ideal job for you?
7. How can you balance work at home and work outside the house? What problems does this balance create for you?

Homework: During the next week, think and write about various conflicts that you do or will face between your role as a person and your role as a partner;

your role as a person and your role as a parent; your role as a homemaker and your role as a man; any other role conflict you experience. Feel free to add any comments related to these questions.

Lesson 7: Recognition and Achievement

1. What organizations do you belong to?
2. How do you feel about their ideas?
3. Do you hold any leadership roles?
4. Some people like to be leaders, and some don't. What about you?
5. What are the important goals of your life?
6. What are some of the things you want to do or to obtain in the next year?
7. What are your hobbies and interests? Reading? Sports? Carpentry or a manual skill? Music? Any other hobby or interest?
8. What are some of the things you are very good at?
9. What do you do in your spare time?
10. Is it important for you to feel a sense of accomplishment? How do you feel about not doing more with your life?

Homework: During the next week, allow yourself to daydream about three different hobbies you would like to pursue further. Describe them and note their pros and cons. Write down three steps you can take to develop the hobby you prefer. Then put each of these steps into action.

Lesson 8: Compulsive Tendencies and Decision Making

1. Some people tend to keep a great many things in order. Others are compulsively sloppy. Which kind are you? Do you tend to keep your personal things in order? Which things are kept orderly and which are not (for example, books, clothes, checking account, tools, recipes, hobby equipment)?
2. Are you usually on time for appointments?
3. Describe in detail your first hour of activity after waking up this morning. (Attend to your routine and the organization of activity.)
4. Do you find yourself saving papers, nails, letters, and such?
5. Do you reach a decision quickly or do you mull over your decisions?
6. Give a detailed description of a few of the most recent decisions you have made.
7. How do you handle money?
8. What does money mean to you?
9. How can you improve how you handle your money and your possessions (things)?

Homework: During the next week, write down a budget with your income on one side (or whatever your parents give you to go to school) and expenses on the other side. Divide your expenses into three different categories: (1) fixed, like rent, car payments, mortgage; (2) necessary but variable, like food, clothing, transportation; (3) variable and strictly voluntary, like entertainment, travel. After you have finished this budget, what conclusions can you reach about your lifestyle and about yourself?

Lesson 9: Anxiety about Social Meetings

1. Do you have a lot of friends? Close or distant?
2. Do you look forward to meeting new people?
3. Do you look forward to having people over to your house?
4. Are you active in a lot of clubs or organizations?
5. Do you tend to be a bit tense when meeting new people?
6. Write in detail about the last time you went to a gathering of strangers.
7. Tell what you did last Sunday (all day).
8. Tell what you did for the past seven evenings.
9. What does friendship mean to you?
10. How do you tell the difference between acquaintance and friendship?

Homework: During the next week, make at least one new social contact that may or may not develop into a deeper acquaintance or even friendship. Describe in detail what you did to reach that goal.

Lesson 10: Hostility-Aggression

1. People differ in which situations make them irritated or angry. Which situations tend to anger you? What do you do?
2. What kinds of people do you tend to dislike (for example, talkative, conceited, stupid, homely, authoritarian)?
3. Can you recall the most recent time you were mad or irritated? Why were you mad or irritated? What did you do?
4. Can you tell the difference between anger and hurt? How?
5. How do you show your hurts?
6. How do you show your anger?
7. With whom do you share your hurts?
8. Against whom do you direct your anger?
9. Can you tell the difference between how you feel and how you show your feelings?
10. Comment on the following: "What we feel is one thing. How we show our feelings is another thing."
11. What does the following statement mean to you? "We have a right to our feelings. However, we do not have the right to destroy others with them."
12. How much of your anger is hurt?
13. How can you show both feelings of anger and hurt in ways that are good for you?

Homework: During the next week, plan to show your feelings of anger, frustration, hurt, or whatever, as soon as the feeling comes up. Say: "I am angry!" "I feel frustrated!" or "I hurt!" depending on the situation. Whatever you may feel, make sure that you use the pronoun *I* to tell how you feel. Describe these situations in writing. What happened to you afterward? Comment on the importance of this lesson. How much did you learn about separating your emotions from your actions?

Lesson 11: Self-Esteem

1. What are some of the things about yourself you are most dissatisfied with?
2. What are some of the things you are most satisfied with?
3. What would you like most to improve in your personality?
4. How do you rate different parts of your personality? Be specific and open.
   a. Intelligence
   b. Attractiveness to opposite sex
   c. Responsibility
   d. Athletic ability
   e. Other

Homework: During the next week, watch for and write about at least three situations where you acted dumb. If no situation presents itself, pretend to act dumb for the purpose of this lesson. Also observe and write about at least three situations where you acted smart. Who was responsible for your acting dumb or smart? What is the difference between these two types of behavior?

Lesson 12: Dependency-Nurturance

1. When you are stumped by some decision you have to make, what do you usually do? Can you recall the most recent time when such a situation took place?
2. To whom do you usually go when you want to talk about a problem?
3. How often do you talk over personal things with your parents, friends, peers, authorities, other people?
4. What would you do under these conditions?
   a. Not sure of a certain purchase; not sure whether to buy it for yourself; not sure whether it's worth the money
   b. Don't feel well
   c. Thinking of changing jobs
   d. Thinking about which college to go to
   e. Thinking about what kind of car to buy
5. How are the finances handled in your family? Who writes the checks? Who fills out tax forms?
6. Some people don't like asking for help or advice. Does this apply to you?
7. Do you like to have a lot of friends?
8. If a friend asked you to go out with him/her and you didn't want to go, would you go? Why?
9. Do you feel bad if someone doesn't go out with you after the first or second date?
10. Would you like to be able to make friends more easily?
11. Do you tend to worry if you feel you have accidentally insulted a friend?
12. Do you sometimes feel left out of things?
13. Do you keep in contact with your parents by writing, calling, or visiting?
14. Do you sometimes talk about your problems with your mother or father?
15. When you're away from home, do you tend to miss your family?

16. Would you like your partner to take more responsibility?
17. Would you like to assume more responsibility?

Homework: During the next week, talk with whomever you trust about how you could take on additional, helpful, and more important responsibilities and commitments, relinquishing some trivial or irrelevant responsibilities that are not helpful to you. Write down the result of this process.

Lesson 13: Conclusions

1. What did you get out of this program?
2. What did you wish you had gotten that you did not get out of this program?
3. Which lesson was the most useful to you, and why?
4. Which lesson was the least helpful to you, and why?
5. How could this program be improved?

CHAPTER EIGHT

Materials for Couples

In this chapter we have included programs and workbooks that address a range of relationships, from conflictual and dysfunctional relationships, as in Arguing and Fighting, to functional and semifunctional relationships, as in Building Relationships. None of these programs, however, can be administered without the supervision and feedback of an experienced professional. These programs can be administered in the context of individual, group, marital, and family therapy, where the major influence is exerted by the relationship between two committed partners. They can be administered by prevention-oriented professionals working with functional and semifunctional couples who could benefit by an additional and different approach.

Arguing and Fighting Workbook

One of the major problems with couples who ask for professional help consists of their inability to love and to negotiate. Both deficits are shown through inordinate arguing and frequent fights. More often than not, one partner is confronting while the other is "fight-phobic"; that is, one is willing to approach and confront issues while the other wishes to avoid them. This reactive and manipulative interaction usually escalates into a heated discussion, moves on to an argument, and eventually ends up in a fight, characterized often by verbal or physical abuse. Most arguments and fights arise from reactive-repetitive or abusive-apathetic styles of relating (L'Abate, 1986b, 1990a, 1990b). Consequently, the following program proceeds from a focus on the couple to the individual styles of each partner. This program has been found useful also with adolescents and their families, where frequent and heated arguments and fights are the norm.

No constructive confrontation can take place under crisis conditions. It is practically impossible to teach any skills to people in crisis, or worse, to couples who are in an uproar. Arguments and fights indicate out-of-control conditions that need to be regulated before any meaningful learning can take place. Conflictful couples need to learn how to confront and solve issues by routine appointments in order to learn how to be in control of themselves and of the arguments ("Do you want your fights to control you or do you want to control your fights?"). To establish control, we need to set spatial ("your living room") and temporal ("once a week") limits on when, for how long, and how these appointments are to take place. To achieve control, we need a structure, as discussed in Chapter 2, concerning the pairing of programmed writing with three principles of behavior control (routine appointments with a written record).

At its outset, this program follows the same sequence as the one followed in programs for families, namely description, explanations, and detailed prescription of the symptomatic behavior. However, this program differs from the other ones in that the first three lessons are considered the beginning of the program, for the purposes of obtaining information that will be used for a more specific administration of additional lessons.

Lesson 1: This lesson contains detailed questions about the frequency, duration, intensity, outcome, and content of arguments or fights. Each partner (or the parent and the teenager) needs to do this lesson individually. After answering these questions they can come together to compare and contrast their views, keeping running notes of their discussion to bring to therapy.

Lesson 2: In this lesson, each respondent must answer by ranking multiple positive reframings—that is, "explanations"—of the arguments or fights. If they do not like or agree with these explanations they can come up with one of their own. Again, they have to get together at an appointed time to discuss their individual answers.

Lesson 3: Now the arguing or fighting is prescribed in greater detail, including time of appointment, duration (no more than one hour), and place. The argument has to be tape-recorded to be useful. The couple is told how to fight—dirty! They should follow as much as possible six suicidal ("they kill the self") rules: (a) use statements with the "you" instead of the "I" or "we" pronouns; (b) bring up the past; (c) read the other's mind; (d) make excuses for self and not for the other; (e) make threats or deliver ultimatums; and (f) use emotional blackmail and bribery. The rationale for and more detailed description of these initial lessons can be found in L'Abate and Levis (1987). However, since then, a further refinement has been added.

Lesson 4: After the couple or family brings the tape of their argument, they are given individual tally or scoring sheets. They are to listen to their tape individually, and to record on these sheets how often they hear themselves use each of the six suicidal patterns or any additional seventh pattern that may be peculiar to them. This is essentially a content analysis of their fight, with the discovery of any additional pattern (often attempts to distract for men and use of the "poor little me" ploy for women).

Lesson 5: On the basis of scores on the tally sheets, each partner is then handed the lesson that deals with her or his predominant pattern. For instance, if one partner shows the highest frequency of "you" statements, he or she receives the lesson dealing with "you" statements. If the other partner brings up the past more often, then he or she is given the lesson that deals with bringing up the past. Each lesson covers the developmental origins of the pattern, its pros and cons, and ends with an assignment to monitor the outcome of three situations in which this pattern is used and of three situations in which it is not used.

Lesson 6: After a discussion of the previous lesson, each partner is handed the lesson that covers the suicidal pattern that is second in frequency. We have not found it necessary to go beyond this lesson, except to assign an additional lesson to deal with whatever particular pattern is peculiar to a couple's interaction.

Lesson 1: Description

1. Define what an argument or fight is for you.
2. How does it take place in your home?
3. How often do you have these arguments or fights?
   a. Once a day or more
   b. Two or three times a week
   c. Once a week
   d. Once a month
   e. Once every two or three months
   f. Never or hardly ever
4. How long do these arguments or fights last?
   a. Sometimes the whole day or more
   b. A couple of hours or half a day
   c. About an hour or more
   d. Less than thirty minutes
   e. One minute at the most
5. How heated, strong, or intense are these arguments or fights?
   a. Very strong, to the point of physical violence
   b. Very intense, but without physical violence
   c. Strong and verbally abusive
   d. Not very strong
   e. We get excited but we calm down soon
   f. Usually we keep cool and rational
   g. We never lose our cool, we just avoid each other
   h. We do not argue or fight, we just bicker
   i. Other [explain]
6. How do these arguments or fights get started?
   a. I usually start them.
   b. My partner usually starts them.
   c. Sometimes I start them, sometimes my partner starts them.
   d. I don't know.
   e. Other [explain]
7. How do these arguments or fights end?
   a. We kiss and make up.
   b. We stay mad for hours.
   c. We stay mad for days.
   d. We stay mad for weeks on end.

e. We stay away from each other until we have another argument or fight.

f. Other [explain]

8. What are the major problems that start the argument or fight? Rank as #1 the most troublesome problem, #2 the second most troublesome, and so on down to the least troublesome.

   a. Money

   b. Sex

   c. Working hours and schedule

   d. Children

   e. Parents or in-laws

   f. Friends

   g. Neighbors

   h. Other [explain]

9. Add whatever information you feel is important to understand your arguments or fights better. After you have answered these questions, make an appointment (at least 24 hours in advance) with your partner to look over your answers and to talk about them together.

Lesson 2: Explanations

1. Here is a list of what arguments or fights usually do for families. Read it carefully *on your own* and think about which of these explanations applies specifically to your relationship or family.

   a. Arguments are a good way of being involved, because as long as we spend energy on each other, we do not have to waste this energy either on our selves or outside of the family.

   b. Arguments are one way of showing we care passionately about our family. Usually we do not argue or fight with strangers or people we do not really care about.

   c. Arguments can be a good form of distraction. As long as we argue, we do not need to worry about bills to be paid, how to set limits on each other, and so on.

   d. Arguments can also be a form of protection. We keep each other busy arguing so that the other one will not get depressed or leave the home or do more destructive things.

   e. Arguments are a good way of finding out how far we can go with each other and other members of the family. Every time we have an argument, we test the limits of each other's endurance and patience.

   f. Arguments are a good way of blowing off steam and expressing ourselves and letting others in the family know how we feel about what we argue about.

   g. Arguments can be good a way of providing excitement where there is nothing but boredom and apathy. They are a good way of proving we are alive.

   h. Arguments are one way of showing we are attracted to someone we love. We usually avoid people we do not like. Therefore, arguments are better than withdrawing and avoiding contact by leaving the house.

    i. Arguments are one form of confrontation that indicates the need for change and progress in the family. Without these confrontations, there would not be any improvement.

    j. Arguments are one form of conflict that is necessary in all families to settle accounts and to even scores among the various parties. Without conflict, family members would not know how and where everybody stands on any problem.

2. Now that you have read these explanations, rank how much they apply to you and to your relationship. Rank as #1 the one that seems to apply the most to you, as #2 the one that applies second most, and down the line to the one that applies least to you.

3. If none of these explanations applies to you, disregard them and write down what you think is the most likely explanation for these arguments or fights.

4. What have you done to improve these arguments or fights?

5. What could you do to improve these arguments or fights? Please explain in detail.

6. What could your partner do to improve these arguments or fights?

7. How are your present arguments similar to or different from those your parents had (or failed to have)?

8. Make an appointment (at least 24 hours in advance) with your partner to look over and talk about each other's answers.

Lesson 3: Prescriptions

Here are *guidelines* on how to argue or fight really dirty, for those who want to learn how to control this behavior. Please note, if you want to argue or fight really dirty without learning to control it, to ensure that both of you and the whole family will lose, disregard completely these guidelines. You may also follow part of these guidelines and ignore other parts, or withdraw completely and avoid confrontation and conflict. If you do not want to learn anything, keep on avoiding having any argument or fight. In this way you will ensure that these arguments will go on. If you are interested in having both you and your partner fail at arguments, as well as in other areas of life, you should not only ignore these guidelines but also find something wrong with the author (he also is no darn good!). If you *do* want to learn to control your arguing and fighting, proceed with this lesson.

    1. Be sure to set an appointment for the fight or argument at least 24 hours in advance. It would be most helpful if you could agree (although it may be impossible) to argue on a regular schedule, like at a specific time on Mondays, Wednesdays, and Fridays, or Tuesdays, Thursdays, and Saturdays, or just on weekends, at 8:00 P.M., 9:00 P.M., and so on.

    2. Locate yourselves in a comfortable setting, preferably at the dining room or kitchen table or in the living room. You will need a table to take notes. Make sure that you sit as close to each other as possible.

    3. Just before the argument or fight is to start, set a timer (in the kitchen) or an alarm clock for just one hour. Stop the argument as soon as the alarm

rings. If your argument has not finished, reschedule the time for another argument at least 24 hours in advance, then separate and go as far away from each other in the house as possible. If or when you meet again for a second argument, make sure you set the timer for one hour.

4. Tape record your argument or fight. This taping is absolutely necessary. If you do not have a tape recorder, borrow or rent one. Also keep detailed written notes of what happened either during or after the argument. Comment on what you think or feel went on during the argument.

5. Follow as much as you can the following six suicidal patterns that take place with most couples in trouble. In case you follow a suicidal pattern not contained in these instructions, make detailed notes of this new pattern, describe it in detail, and bring it up the next time you meet with your therapist. In arguing, be sure to follow these six suicidal patterns as closely as possible.

Use "you" statements exclusively, accusing, blaming, and name-calling each other as much as you can. For instance, use "You never . . . " and "You always . . . " statements as much as possible. Do not use either "I" or "we" statements under any conditions.

Keep bringing up the painful past in as much negative detail as possible. Keep remembering dates, places, situations, and occasions where you were hurt deeply. Keep on hurting each other by reliving as much as possible all of your past painful experiences in this relationship that were obviously the fault of your partner. See if each of you can top the other in remembering as many painful details as possible. Do not forget (let alone forgive!) any single possible past hurt!

Read each other's minds. Tell what the other one thinks or feels. Disclose to each other all of the many evil intentions each of you knows the other holds. Bring up all of the possible nasty thoughts or feelings that your partner is guilty of thinking and feeling, let alone doing.

Use emotional blackmail and bribery. For instance, say "If you do not do what I want, I will leave you," or "If you do not give me what I want, I will call the lawyer," or "Either you quit [drinking, gambling, or such] or I will take the children away."

As part of the preceding pattern, *give each other ultimatums.* Threaten each other with the worst possible consequences that will follow from each other's behavior. Make sure to specify dates and circumstances when you will follow up on your ultimatum.

Make as many excuses as you can to justify your own behavior, especially by using your partner's behavior as an excuse: "I did such-and-such because you did such-and-such." Do not allow your partner to make any excuses for his or her behavior. Follow the principle that it is perfectly acceptable to behave miserably as long as your partner behaves miserably as well!

Have a really dirty argument. Bring the tape to your therapist.

Lesson 4: Scoring

After recording the argument or fight prescribed in Lesson 3 with a tape recorder, listen to the tape of the argument or fight by yourself, without your partner. Following is a list of the six suicidal patterns you were told to follow, plus whatever other pattern you have discovered is peculiar to your arguing and/or fighting. Listen to the tape carefully and tally each time *you* (not your partner) indulge in any one of these patterns.

1. "You" statements
2. Bringing up the painful past
3. Mind reading
4. Blackmail and/or bribery
5. Ultimatums or threats
6. Excuses
7. Your peculiar pattern

Share and discuss these results with your partner after she or he has completed the same assignment. Then show them, along with a written summary of your discussion, to your counselor, facilitator, or therapist. He or she will give you lessons specifically geared to deal with the two or three suicidal patterns that have the highest total scores.

Lesson 5: Your Most Frequent Suicidal Pattern

Complete the portion of this lesson that deals with your most frequent suicidal pattern.

Making "You" Statements
1. How often do you think and speak about your partner?
   a. All the time
   b. Quite often
   c. Often enough
   d. Sometimes
2. When do you think about your partner?
   a. Only when I am angry
   b. Only when I am sad
   c. Only when I hurt
   d. Only when I am upset
   e. Only when [please complete]
3. How would you describe your thoughts about your partner?
   a. All negative
   b. More negative than positive
   c. More positive than negative
   d. All positive
4. Why do you think so much and/or negatively about your partner?
   a. It keeps me busy and alive.
   b. It distracts me from becoming sad.
   c. It shows how much I care for my partner.
   d. It takes away from my worries.
   e. As long as I think and worry about my partner, I do not have to worry about myself.
   f. Because [give your own reason]

5. What are your reactions to the possibility that thinking about your partner takes away from you and weakens your identity, killing your self?

6. What do you think about this other possibility: "I do not have to take responsibility for my behavior, because as long as I focus my energy on my partner, it leaves very little energy left for me to take care of myself and possibly change my behavior"?

7. What do you think about the possibility that thinking excessively and/or negatively about your partner puts the whole burden of change on your partner rather than on you?

8. Now think about the usual result of your thinking too much and/or negatively about your partner.
    a. What does it do to you?
    b. What does it do to the relationship?
    c. What does it do to your partner?
    d. What is the result, then, of your thinking excessively and/or negatively about your partner?

9. What would be the result if your partner were to do exactly what you are doing (that is, thinking excessively and/or negatively about you)?

10. Our language has mutually exclusive pronouns. If and when we use *you*, it is impossible for us to use the pronouns *I* or *we*. What do you think about this statement?

11. What are your reactions to the statement that using the pronoun *you*—that is, thinking and talking about your partner excessively and/or negatively—is the cancer of relationships?

12. Think of one or more positive reasons for going on in using the pronoun *you* in thinking and talking about your partner.

13. Go back to the title of this lesson. Why do you think that the term *suicidal* was used? What does it mean to you?

14. *Suicidal* means that it kills the self. What do you think about the idea that using the pronoun *you* instead of the pronouns *I* and *we* kills?

Homework: For the next week, see what happens to you and to your partner when you use the pronoun *you* instead of *I* or *we*. Make sure you use *you* at least three times. Describe in detail what happened and what the outcome was. If you want to have a miserable relationship, or if you want your relationship to end, all you have to do is to go on thinking excessively and/or negatively about your partner by using the pronoun *you*. But if you want to change, during the next week notice three times when you use the pronouns *I* or *we* instead of *you*. Describe in detail what happened before, during, and after you used them. After you have completed this assignment, make an appointment at least 24 hours in advance with your partner to share and discuss your answers and their implications for the future of your relationship. Record and summarize your discussion.

Bringing Up the Painful Past

1. How often do you bring up the painful past when dealing with your partner?
    a. Almost every day
    b. At least once or twice a week

    c. Once every two or three weeks

    d. Once a month or less

    e. Once in a blue moon

    f. Never

2. When do you bring up the painful past?

    a. Only when we are fighting

    b. Only when we make love

    c. Anytime I feel bad, mad, or sad

    d. When [please complete]

3. What does it get you to bring up the hurts from the past?

    a. It makes me feel better about myself.

    b. It makes my partner look bad.

    c. I enjoy it.

    d. It makes my partner mad.

    e. It [give your own reason]

4. What kinds of things (memories, events, episodes, hurts) from the past do you enjoy bringing up?

    a. Always pleasant

    b. Sometimes pleasant

    c. Mostly hurtful

    d. Mostly unpleasant

    e. Always unpleasant

5. What does bringing up the painful past do to you? To your relationship? To your partner?

6. What do you think about this statement: "As long as we keep on bringing up the painful past, we have no time or energy left for a pleasant present or a better future"?

7. What would happen to you if your partner kept on bringing up the painful past in the same way you do? To your relationship? To your partner?

Homework: During the next week, note how often you bring up the painful past, and write down what happened in at least three instances, to you, to your relationship, and to your partner. Make an appointment with your partner at least 24 hours in advance to share, compare, and discuss your answers. Summarize and record your discussion.

Mind Reading

As part of your caring for and commitment to your relationship, you might be spending a great deal of time and energy wondering what your partner feels, thinks, and does. Often you may even be sure that you *know exactly* beforehand and without asking or checking it out what your partner feels, thinks, or does. This kind of behavior is frequent in couples who care a great deal about each other but who cannot separate one's self from the other's self. Does this behavior apply to you? If your answer is no, do not go any farther. If your answer is yes, go on.

1. How often do you wonder about your partner's feelings, thinking, motives, and behavior?
   a. All the time
   b. Very often
   c. Often enough
   d. Rarely
   e. Almost never
2. What do you really *know* about your partner? Describe in detail her or his feelings, attitudes, thinking, motives, behavior, and any other area you can think of.
3. Are there special or particular times when you wonder and know what your partner is feeling or thinking?
   a. When we fight
   b. When we make love
   c. When we are apart
   d. When I feel sad
   e. When I am angry
   f. When [please complete]
4. What does reading your partner's mind do for you?
   a. It makes me happier.
   b. It makes my partner happier.
   c. It keeps me busy.
   d. It makes him or her mad.
   e. It makes me sad.
   f. It makes me feel better about myself.
   g. It [please complete]
5. What does reading your partner's mind do for your relationship?
   a. It improves it considerably.
   b. It keeps it exciting.
   c. It renews it.
   d. It makes it worse.
   e. It's the pits!
6. Describe in greater detail what reading your partner's mind does for you and for your relationship.
7. What would happen to your relationship if your partner read your mind the way you do?
8. Why do *you* think mind reading is a suicidal pattern in any close and prolonged relationship?
9. What would happen to you if you did not read your partner's mind?
10. What would happen to your relationship if you did not read your partner's mind?

Homework: During the next week, note every time you find yourself reading your partner's mind. Record what happened to you and to your relationship in three instances. Note three times when *you did not read* your partner's mind and instead you asked and checked out what he or she was feeling, thinking, or planning to do. Write about what happened. After you have finished this assignment, make an appointment with your partner at least 24 hours in advance to share and discuss your answers. Summarize your discussion in writing and bring your notes to your next therapy session.

Blackmail/Bribery

Most examples of this suicidal pattern are emotional, and they are usually preceded by an *if*, as in: "If you do not do what I want, I will leave you." In other words, emotional blackmail or bribery are abusive forms of control, coercion, and manipulation that we use to have our way.

1. Do you use this pattern in your relationship? If your answer is no, you may as well quit this lesson. If your answer is yes, go on.
2. How often do you use it?
   a. Very often
   b. Often
   c. Sometimes
   d. Seldom
3. How and when do you use blackmail? Describe in detail.
4. How and when do you use bribery?
5. What do you get out of using either blackmail or bribery?
6. How does this pattern affect your relationship?
7. How does this pattern affect your partner?
8. What would happen if your partner were to use this pattern with you?
9. See if you can remember how you learned this pattern. When did you start using it?
10. Are you ready to give it up? If your answer is no, don't go any farther. If your answer is yes, then do the following homework assignment.

Homework: During the next week, use this pattern at least three times. Remember that *if you want to stop it you have to learn to start it*. Write in detail about what specific kind of *blackmail* you used and the situation in which you used it. What was the result? Also during the next week, record three times when you used *bribery*. How did you use it and what was the result? After completing this homework, make an appointment with your partner to share and discuss your answers to this lesson. Summarize your discussion in writing, and bring your notes to your therapist.

Ultimatums

1. What does the word *ultimatum* mean to you?
2. Would you agree that an ultimatum consists of a deadline or of an action that would have negative consequences for your partner?
3. How often do you use ultimatums?
4. When do you use ultimatums?
   a. When my partner makes me mad
   b. When I make my partner mad
   c. When I am under pressure

  d. When I don't know what else to do
  e. When I [please complete]
5. What kinds of ultimatums do you give your partner? Give at least three examples.
6. Why do you give ultimatums?
  a. Because I enjoy it
  b. Because it makes me feel good
  c. Because it gives me a sense of satisfaction
  d. Because in this way I can control my partner
  e. Because it worked for my parents
  f. Because [please complete]
7. What do ultimatums do to you? To your relationship? To your partner?
8. How did you learn to use ultimatums?
9. What would happen to your relationship if your partner were to give you ultimatums?

Homework: During the next week, use as many ultimatums as you can. List at least three of them, and describe (a) what kind of ultimatum you used, (b) with whom, and (c) what kind of result you got. After completing this assignment, share and discuss it with your partner. Write a summary of what you two discussed and bring your notes to your next therapy session.

Excuses

Oftentimes, excuses are used to explain or justify our behavior. For instance, we may use our partner's (rotten!) behavior to justify our own actions: "I did this and that because you did this and that." Usually, we do not accept the same excuses from our partner. The principle behind this pattern is that it is perfectly acceptable to behave miserably as long as our partner behaves miserably as well!

1. How often do you use this pattern?
  a. Very often
  b. Often
  c. Sometimes
  d. Seldom
  e. Never
2. How do you make excuses? Describe in detail.
3. What does this pattern indicate?
  a. I am unable to take responsibility for myself and my behavior.
  b. It means that I behave better than my partner.
  c. It means that my partner is wrong and I am right.
  d. My behavior is excusable, but my partner's behavior is not.
  e. As long as my partner behaves miserably, I have the same right.
  f. It means [please complete]
4. How do you react to the following statement: "Children find excuses for their behavior; adults take responsibility for their actions"?
5. What do you get out of making excuses for your behavior?

6. What would happen to your relationship if both you and your partner made excuses about your behavior?
7. How did you learn to make excuses?

Homework: If you want to learn to stop this pattern, follow these instructions. During the next week, find at least three situations where you can make excuses for your behavior. Describe each situation in detail and report on the results. After you have completed this assignment, make an appointment with your partner at least 24 hours in advance. Share and discuss your answers with your partner. See whether together you can come up with more helpful ways to take responsibility than just finding excuses. Summarize your discussion and show your notes to your therapist.

Your Peculiar Pattern

By listening to the tape of your last fight, you might have been able to find a peculiar suicidal pattern that is specific to how you two argue or fight. Congratulations for your care and sensitivity in finding this extra pattern! Not many partners can! Do you want to replace it or do you want to keep it? If you want to replace it, read on.

1. Define and describe in detail this peculiar pattern. What does it consist of?
2. Discuss the advantages and disadvantages of this peculiar pattern.
3. How often is it used?
   a. Almost always
   b. Very often
   c. Often enough
   d. Occasionally
   e. Once in a while
4. When does it take place?
5. What does it get either one of you?
   a. It shows we love each other.
   b. It keeps us busy.
   c. It allow us to make contact.
   d. It keeps us excited.
   e. It keeps us from being bored.
   f. It [please complete]
6. Do you enjoy it? How?
7. If you enjoy it, keep it up and stop answering these questions. If you do not enjoy it, you may want to replace it with a more positive pattern. If so, complete the following homework assignment.

Homework: During the coming week, make sure that either one of you will use this peculiar pattern at least three times. If necessary, flip a coin to decide which of you should use it first. Write down how this pattern was used and what the result was. After completing this assignment, make an appointment with your partner at least 24 hours in advance to discuss how you could replace this peculiar pattern with a more positive pattern. Record your discussion.

Codependency Program

This program, written in collaboration with Lisa Mahon, aims to help symbiotically enmeshed couples. At least one of the partners (the selfish one, according to the formulation presented in Chapter 6 and in the Problems in Relationships workbook later in this chapter) is addicted to a substance, a specific behavior, or an obsession; the other (the selfless one) is usually addicted to the addict. Neither can live without the addiction. Until recent years the concept of codependency was unknown in the addiction field. Treatment was focused on establishing sobriety or independence from addictions in the individual, but it ignored the needs of the family, especially the spouse. Yet, addictions have come to be recognized as conditions that affect every member of the family. The term *codependency* describes a process in which the nonaddicted partner tries to adapt in order to protect and enable the addict (Whitfield, 1984). Subby and Friel (1984) have expanded this definition by describing codependency as ''a dysfunctional pattern of living and problem solving which is nurtured by a set of rules within the family system'' (p. 32).

Within the addict's family, this dependency is based on the desire for security and comfort, through the avoidance of feelings of fear, insecurity, and loneliness (Capell-Sowder, 1984). One function of codependency is to help a person avoid keeping in touch with himself or herself. In codependency, a person's intense overresponsibility and need for self-affirmation are confused with loving and being loved (Schaef, 1986). The codependent then becomes preoccupied with the control of the addicted partner, upon whom she or he depends to feel needed and important (Wegscheider-Cruse, 1984). The spouse may learn controlling behavior to protect the addict and the self from self-discovery and to maintain social and economic equilibrium. Wegscheider-Cruse (1984) wrote that codependents share two features: first, "they are hiding fears, shame and sadness," and second, "their rigidity precludes changing that" (p. 2). The codependent frequently displays symptoms of addiction in the ways he or she relates to the primary relationship. Wegscheider-Cruse goes on to warn that many codependents deny their own addictive symptoms and imagine that if they left the addictive relationship everything would be fine. What codependents fail to recognize is that they will continue these addictive behaviors and responses until they learn new ways of communicating and interpersonal relating based on a stable sense of self (Capell-Sowder, 1984).

Within a nonaddictive system there can be room for interdependence, mutual growth, trust, openness, and sharing of feelings. The treatment goals for codependency should stress reciprocity and mutuality, with interdependence and a strong sense of self (selfhood). Equality of power must be established. To achieve this goal, the partners must have the ability to negotiate. The individual and the family must learn to express their feelings and needs and to believe that they will be heard. Codependents must learn to be responsible to the self and responsive to others (Bepko, 1989).

The codependent operates in the role of a "good," responsible, independent person; the addicted person operates as the underresponsible, dependent, "bad" person (Bepko, 1989). This inequality, however, is never acknowledged because addicted persons take pride in never being one-down, and codependents deny the need for power and control because they believe that they are taking charge only when they must. Subby (1984) believes that the rules in codependency prevent the open expression of feelings as well as the direct discussion of personal and interpersonal problems. To break these rules results in intense shame. Codependents become progressively out of touch with their feelings or learn to distort them. Codependents fear abandonment and can become obsessed with another person. A family rule is not to talk about problems and not to express feelings openly. Codependents behave as if communications are best when they are indirect, one person often acting as a messenger between two others (triangulation). At whatever cost, the codependent is not to rock the boat and is to keep the peace within the family (Schaef, 1986).

Codependents are known for being supreme controllers, believing that they must be in control at all times. Spouses of addicts are described as over-responsible, with the characteristic of grandiosity and a need to feel all-powerful. Doing is valued over Being. Doing (controlling) gives codependents a false sense of worth, one that is based on the other person (Bepko, 1989). Mendenhall (1989) called the spouse of the addicted alcoholic "the chief enabler." The chief enabler tries to protect the addicted person from the consequences of the chemical use or to control the situation so as to remove any possible reason for the addicted person to use chemicals. The enabler thus becomes a chronic worrier, neglecting the self and withdrawing from activities outside the home. Overall, these behaviors help the codependent cover up a feeling of being inherently bad, and avoid facing feelings of depression and a lack of self-worth. The message is to be strong, good, even perfect, and to deny the self. Recently, Mellody and Miller (1989) have published a workbook to deal with codependency.

Lesson 1: Description

1. Define what codependency is and how it takes place in your home.
2. Would you accept a definition of codependency as an addiction to an addicted partner? The codependent cannot do without the addiction of the partner, who is thought to be more important than the codependent's self.
3. How often does an act or pattern of codependent behavior take place?
   a. Every day, more than once
   b. Every day, at least once
   c. Two to three times a week
   d. At least once a week
   e. Once every couple of weeks
   f. Once a month
   g. Other [explain]
4. How long do these acts last?
   a. Days (continuously)
   b. Hours
   c. At least one hour
   d. Less than an hour

    e. Less than 30 minutes
    f. Between 10 and 30 minutes
    g. Less than 10 minutes
    h. Less than 5 minutes

5. How strong or intense are these acts?
    a. Extremely intense, resulting in physical violence
    b. Extremely intense, with verbal abuse but without physical violence
    c. Extremely intense, without verbal or physical abuse
    d. Intense enough to be upsetting
    e. Uncomfortable and unpleasant
    f. Mildly unpleasant
    g. Usually rational and detached (no feeling)
    h. Always rational and under control
    i. Other [explain]

6. How do these acts get started? Tell in detail.
7. What seems to trigger these acts?
8. Describe in detail a typical act of codependent behavior. How does it get started? How does it develop? How does it end?
9. What have you done in the past to end these acts or patterns? List all the ways you have tried and the resources you have used to resolve these acts.
10. How do these episodes affect you? How do they affect your spouse (partner)? How do they affect your children (if any)?
11. Record any other feelings or thoughts that come to you about your codependent behavior.

Lesson 2: Explanations

1. Here is a list of some of the most common explanations for codependency and what it may do for families. Get together for at least one hour and discuss which of the following explanations applies specifically to your family.
    a. Codependence shows that you really do love each other. As long as you continue this behavior, you can prove your dedication to the family and not waste time on yourself or outside the family.
    b. Codependent behavior ensures that you will stay involved with each other in ways that are familiar to you. It is a good way to keep your life predictable.
    c. Codependent behavior is excellent modeling for your children, showing them how to be good caretakers for others and to be self-sacrificing. Consequently, you need to keep up the good work.
    d. Codependency allows you to feel special, the center of the other person's world. In this way you can feel adequate and worthwhile.
    e. As long as you maintain your codependency, staying busy taking care of your partner, you allow him or her to stay off the hook and not be an independent adult. We would not take so much time with someone we did not care about.

    f. Codependency allows you not to have to deal with your own feelings. In this way it can protect you from having to acknowledge your hurts and disappointments.

    g. Codependency allows you not to take risks or make friends, have fun, or play. Since you are uncomfortable doing these, codependency will keep you from having to be anxious about any of them.

    h. Codependency allows you to feel valued for what you do. In this way you do not have to worry about who you are. If you can do for someone else, it protects you from feeling guilty and selfish.

    i.   Codependency allows you to protect the rules of the family. This is one way you have of proving your family loyalty. It shows you are really trying and involved.

    j. Codependency ensures you of feeling in control. It keeps you from dealing directly with the chaos in the family and it protects your social and economic position.

    k. If the codependent behavior goes on, perhaps this is better than thinking about and confronting all the problems in this family.

    l.   Because things would change drastically if the codependent behavior were to change, one should not act quickly and should think seriously about doing anything at all that might endanger the family's solidarity and balance.

2. Now that you have read and discussed these explanations, rank how much they apply to your family. Rank as #1 the one that seems to apply the most, as #2 the one that applies second most, and down the line to the one that applies least to your family.

3. If none of these explanations apply to you, forget about them, and write down what you think is the most likely explanation for these acts of codependency.

4. How do you think these acts of codependency could be improved? Explain in detail.

Lesson 3: Prescriptions

If you do not want to achieve control over this codependent pattern, do not follow these guidelines. If you *do* want to achieve control, follow these guidelines. Although they may seem strange to you, consider these guidelines a step toward the goal of establishing better relationships within your family. The first step is to achieve control over an undesirable behavior. The second step is to learn more desirable behavior.

    1. Set an appointment for a codependency meeting at least 24 hours in advance. It will be helpful if you can agree to schedule your codependency sessions regularly, at a specific time, like 9:00 P.M. for an hour on Monday, Wednesday, and Friday or Tuesday, Thursday, and Saturday, or just on weekends. Be sure everyone knows when and where the session is to be held.

    2. Choose a comfortable setting for the meeting, preferably at the dining room or kitchen table or in the living room. You will need a table on which to take notes.

3. Set a timer for the length of time you have decided on, preferably for one hour, but not to exceed one hour. Stop all codependent behavior as soon as the alarm sounds. Separate and go to different parts of the house at the end of the meeting. Even if you do not feel finished when the alarm rings, do not continue with your codependent behavior until the next scheduled appointment. You are only to use codependent behavior during this scheduled meeting.

4. Keep detailed records of everything that is said and done during the meeting. Be sure to include who is speaking and how each person speaks. The records can be written or tape recorded. Either way, the records are to be reviewed after the meeting so you can comment on what you think and feel was going on during the session.

5. If or when family members start codependent behavior between the scheduled meetings, remind them that they will need to wait until the next scheduled meeting. If they persist, walk away from them and go to a different part of the house. If they persist, call an emergency family conference to make sure that the whole family will have a part in this behavior.

6. During codependency meetings, *do not change past patterns of behavior.* Instead, follow closely the same pattern of codependent behavior that has been destructive to good communication in the past. You will need to practice these patterns until you are so sick of them that you want to leave them behind. However, you are not ready, as yet, to leave them behind. Therefore, be sure to make only "you" statements, blame others, bring up the past, read their minds, threaten others if they do not change, tell them what they should do. At all costs do not take any responsibility for your own happiness. Never be open and direct about what you are feeling, and deny your needs. When possible, send all messages through a third party. If someone expresses a feeling, tell that person not to have the feeling by denying it, instruct them about it, explain, counsel, or in some way try to control the feeling. Make sure that no conflict flares up and that all confrontations are avoided. If a family member gets emotional, help her or him achieve control. Remember that the watchword of codependency is *control, control, control!* Your happiness depends on the other person.

7. Bring your tape and/or notes to your next therapy appointment.

Sexuality Program

This program was written in collaboration with David A. Russ. A major issue in dealing with sexuality seems to be synchronicity. How can two persons with different temporal perspectives, schedules, and commitments ever get together when daily responsibilities and routines make this coming together very difficult? One can conceive of sexuality not only in terms of physical but also emotional, temporal, and spatial synchronicity. Coming together, then, assumes a different meaning. It implies a reconciliation of perspectives, values, and priorities. Sexuality is dealt with in terms of temporal synchronicity in the first lesson and in more specific terms in the next two lessons.

Lesson 1: Description

Answer the following questions:

1. What time do you feel best about getting up?
   a. 5 to 6:30 A.M.
   b. 6:30 to 7:45 A.M.
   c. 7:45 to 9:45 A.M.
   d. 9:45 to 11 A.M.
   e. 11 A.M. to noon
2. How easy is it for you to get up in the morning?
   a. Not at all easy
   b. Not very easy
   c. Fairly easy
   d. Very easy
3. How tired do you feel the first half hour after getting up?
   a. Very tired
   b. Fairly tired
   c. Fairly refreshed
   d. Very refreshed
4. If you had to take a test or examination tomorrow and you needed to set the time you think you would perform best, which would you choose?
   a. From 8 to 10 A.M.
   b. From 10 A.M. to 1 P.M.
   c. From 1 to 5 P.M.
   d. From 5 to 7 P.M.
   e. From 7 to 9 P.M.
5. If you had to remain awake between 4 and 6 A.M. to carry out a night watch and you had no commitments the next day, which choice would suit you best?
   a. Not to go to bed until the watch was over
   b. To take a nap before and sleep after
   c. To sleep before and take a nap after
   d. To take all the sleep you could before the watch
6. A friend invites you to jog with her. She goes between 7 and 8 A.M. How do you think you would perform?
   a. Well
   b. Reasonably well
   c. Would find it hard to do
   d. Would find it very hard to do
7. If you have to wake up at a specific time every morning, how dependent are you on an alarm clock?
   a. Not at all dependent
   b. Slightly dependent
   c. Fairly dependent
   d. Very dependent

8. At what time in the evening do you feel tired and need sleep?
   a. 8 to 9 P.M.
   b. 9 to 10:15 P.M.
   c. 10:15 P.M. to 12:45 A.M.
   d. 12:45 to 2 A.M.
   e. 2 to 3 A.M.

Scoring:
1. Give yourself 5 points for a, 4 for b, 3 for c, 2 for d, and 1 for e.
2. Give 1 point for a, 2 for b, 3 for c, and 4 for d.
3. Give 1 point for a, 2 for b, 3 for c, and 4 for d.
4. Give 4 points for a, 3 for b, 2 for c, 1 for d, and 0 for e.
5. Give 1 point for a, 2 for b, 3 for c, and 4 for d.
6. Give 4 points for a, 3 for b, 2 for c, and 1 for d.
7. Give 4 points for a, 3 for b, 2 for c, and 1 for d.
8. Give 5 points for a, 4 for b, 3 for c, 2 for d, and 1 for e.

A high score means positive sleep habits, while a low score means negative sleep habits. What is important here is that you both have compatible or working sleep habits so that you can get together sexually in a reasonable frame of mind and with a relaxed body.

9. Compare and contrast your answers and scores with your partner to see whether you are an owl or a lark or neither. What did you conclude about your sleep patterns and those of your partner?
10. How do you experience time in terms of (a) your interest and involvement in the past, the present, or the future, and (b) your experience of time as passing slowly or quickly?
11. How often do differences in sleep patterns and time involvement cause conflicts between you and your partner?
    a. More than once a day
    b. Once a day
    c. Two or three times a week
    d. Once a week
    e. Every couple of weeks
    f. Once a month
    g. Other [explain]
12. How strong are these differences?
    a. Very strong, causing a lot of conflict between us
    b. Very strong, but we manage to handle them
    c. Strong enough
    d. Moderate
    e. Hardly strong at all
    f. Other [explain]

13. What areas of your relationship are most affected by differences with your partner or your family considered in questions 1 and 3? Rank the most affected #1, the second most affected #2, down to the least affected.
    a. Chores around the house
    b. Schedules
    c. Sex
    d. Money use and budgeting
    e. Relationships with others
    f. Children and child rearing
    g. Health
    h. Other [explain]
14. Do the different speeds at which you and your partner work affect your relationship? Please explain.
15. What have you done to resolve some of these differences?
16. Of the troublesome areas listed in question 13, pick the one that you would like to change the most. Explain why.
17. How does the past affect this problem area?
18. How does the present affect this area?
19. How does the future affect this area?

Homework: Get together with your partner and talk and think about various ways of dealing with this problem area. Write down possible solutions.

Lesson 2: Explanations

1. The following is a list of what different experiences of time do for families (in this case spouses or partners) with regard to sex and sexuality. Get together for at least one hour and discuss which of the following explanations applies specifically to your relationship.
    a. Experiencing sex at a slow pace is a way of relishing the event and making me feel cared about.
    b. Experiencing sex at a fast pace is a way of feeling passion that is much stronger.
    c. Bringing up past sexual experiences is a way of affirming our current relationship. People don't compare relationships unless these relationships are very important to them.
    d. Sexual problems are a good opportunity to discuss important issues that otherwise might not get brought up. These kinds of discussions are important to a relationship because they offer a chance to grow.
    e. Different speeds are very useful in different situations. Going at different speeds is a good way of expressing individuality.
    f. Experiencing the present only is a good way of enjoying the moment and the sensual pleasure of the moment. Not worrying about the past or the future is a good way of expressing complete interest in your mate.
    g. Fantasizing about the future is a good way of finding out what you wish for. This is important for setting goals and acting upon them.

    h. Having differences in your experience of time that upset you is proof that you care deeply about one another. People who don't love each other don't care and don't get upset.

    i. Going very slowly as you experience sex and refusing to speed it up is a way of saying how important your mate is because you want this experience to last for a long time.

    j. Not having time for sex could be due to the intense schedules you keep to take care of your family.

2. Now that you have read and discussed whether or not these explanations apply to you, rank them from 1 (most important) to 10 (least important).

3. If none of these apply to you, write down what you think is the most likely explanation for the problem(s) you have.

Homework: How do you think your experience of time in sex can be improved? Explain in detail. Go back to what you wrote at the end of the first lesson and write down in detail your own (not your partner's!) step-by-step plan to deal with these issues. Compare and contrast your plan with the plan written by your partner. See if the two plans can be put together. Each of you should then write down what possible solutions could be worked out by putting both plans together. Do not talk about these plans. Do all of the communication in writing if you want to find a solution. If you do not want a solution, keep on talking and see if you find one.

Lesson 3: Prescriptions

If you do not want to resolve the difficulties concerning your time differences in the area of sexuality, then you should ignore these guidelines. If you *do* want to resolve your difficulties, follow these guidelines. Although they may seem strange, just consider them steps toward your goal of a better sex life. You have been putting so much energy into having a positive sexual experience that you may have lost control of yourselves. Now put your energies into planning and having a bad sexual experience. In this way you may become free to have a better experience.

    1. Set an appointment at least 24 hours in advance to fail in your sexual experience. *It is important that you do everything you can to make this experience not work.* It needs to be planned in the future as well so that you can prepare for it. Set a time when sex would most likely occur naturally. Make sure that you will not be interrupted by the phone or by children. Set a timer for 30 minutes. Then go ahead and begin to use completely different speeds and other time factors, such as bringing up the past and fantasizing about the future, or whatever will most likely cause you to fail.

    2. Follow these instructions without talking about this project. Do this as naturally as you can. However, do pay attention to what is happening so that you can discuss it afterward. Be sure to support each other so that one of you will not give in and fail in this project by having a good sexual experience. It is important that neither of you give up.

3. You may even make this experience more extreme by exaggerating the time elements that cause you to fail.

4. Plan to do this experience at least three times during the next two weeks. You can discontinue this project only if the problem disappears. If this problem comes back when you are not trying to fail, implement the same procedure immediately. Go ahead and make that experience as unsuccessful as possible.

5. Take notes of the conversations that you have about your experience as well as about what happened in the experience. Bring these to your next therapy appointment.

Problems in Relationships Workbook

The purpose of this workbook is to help couples who are opposing each other in intimate relationships or who are polarized on some dimensions. These couples have agreed to disagree with each other, reacting to each other with minimal provocation. One partner may be more involved in achievement, success, money, things, and receiving love (that is, sex), while the other partner may be more involved in nurturing—giving love, emotional closeness, and vulnerability. Regardless of their personal values and involvements, they have agreed to relate to each other through defeats rather than through victories. They do not know how to win with each other, very likely because their past models—that is, their parents—did not know either.

This workbook was designed especially to test a model of selfhood or self-definition (L'Abate & Bryson, in press) based on the attribution of importance to self and to others (spouse, partner, parent, child, friend). To elaborate on the theory summarized in Chapter 4, this sense of importance and its attribution are assumed to be the basis for winning or losing outcomes in intimate relationships, producing four different possibilities: (1) "I win, you win," derived from selfulness, leading to equality ("Both of us need to win; otherwise, both of us lose"), reciprocity, and intimacy; (2) "I win, you lose," derived from selfishness and self-absorption; (3) "You win, I lose," derived from selflessness and debasement; and (4) "You lose, I lose," derived from no-self, or the inability to win under any conditions.

A recent rush of popular books relating to sex or gender differences (Forward & Torres, 1987; Langley & Levy, 1977; Leman, 1987; Norwood, 1985, 1988) has highlighted dangerous polarizations between the genders. Most of the scientifically relevant literature on sex and gender differences has been reviewed (L'Abate & Bryson, in press). The sources cited here have focused, in one way or another, on the relative masochism of women and the relative sadism and narcissism of men in our society. None of them, however, has dealt with the issue that many women (we estimate at least 40%) are still being socialized for selflessness, whereas many men (we estimate at least 40%) are still being socialized for selfishness.

The dimension of selflessness-selfishness has implications for understanding in greater detail and more accurately the eternal battle of the sexes. A great many, if not all, of the major pathologies affecting most women, such as depression and self-defeating behavior, can be traced to socialization for selflessness in women; Type A drivenness, criminalities, and addictions can be traced to socialization for selfishness in men. Last but not least, conflict, distress, and divorce prevail among couples made up of persons who are characterized by extremes on this dimension. Selfless women seek out, or are sought out by, selfish men.

In addition, selfish men are the product of the child-rearing practices of selfless mothers, women who cannot say no to them and maintain firm, consistent boundaries. These men, more often than not, model themselves after their fathers and define themselves in opposition to their mothers. They learn from their fathers that women can be demeaned, ignored, and debased, that they are unimportant and below a man's needs and wants. Most selfless women model themselves after their selfless mothers and in opposition to their fathers, who they see as cruel and uncaring toward their mothers. Unfortunately, many of these women marry men like their fathers! Once a selfless woman marries a selfish man, their relationship cannot be anything but oppositional. This adversarial relationship can be evaluated by the amount of reactivity between the partners, as discussed in greater detail elsewhere (L'Abate & Bryson, in press).

This classification has serious and important implications for personality development in the family and for the origin of many psychopathological conditions. Although selfulness leads to creativity in intimate relationships, selfishness leads to many addictions and criminalities. Selflessness leads to many self-defeating, depressed, and manic-depressive conditions. No-self leads to psychosis and schizophrenia.

Reactive, oppositional couples (L'Abate, 1986b; L'Abate & Bryson, in press) can be identified by (1) history, (2) observed behavior, and (3) reports (from one informer about the other) that characterize the relationship as polarized on a variety of dimensions (some of these dimensions may be very specific to a particular couple). In addition to these three criteria, one can use the scores on the two tests especially devised to identify individuals in dyads who score at extreme positions, on either side of each dimension—the Problems in Relationships Scale (PIRS) and the Semantic Differential about Problems in Relationships. These lists are included in Chapter 6 of this book. Because both tests are derived from the very same dimensions considered in this workbook, it will be possible to find out which dimensions are the most extreme for each couple. There is no reason to administer lessons on dimensions where there does not appear to be any conflict. Couples should be given only the lessons concerning dimensions on which they are conflictful. For instance, a couple who seems conflictual on 5 or 6 of the 20 dimensions should be administered only the 5 or 6 lessons that correspond to those conflictual dimensions. This workbook, therefore, is based on a nomothetic approach that allows an idiographic (that is, specific to each couple's particular needs) treatment of each couple. The workbook becomes a menu from which a therapist can select lessons according to the clients' needs. Treatment, therefore, can be tailor-made specifically and explicitly from the evaluation, linking one with the other in ways that are not possible when speech is the only medium of communication and treatment, as discussed in the introductory text of Chapter 3.

Although other workbooks may be theoretically and therapeutically eclectic and may have been derived from a variety of sources and from experiences in clinical practices, this workbook specifically tests the model of selfhood proposed in Chapter 4. It shows how a workbook can be derived from theoretical models as well as from many other sources (self-help books, clinical experience). In this fashion, treatment based (in part!) on workbooks can compare the relative and comparative effectiveness of competing theoretical models. For instance, this workbook could be compared with a workbook derived from a competing theory. Instead of comparing theories ad infinitum on a rational basis, their effectiveness can be evaluated in the therapist's office, provided that homework assignments are administered according to programmed writing procedures.

In summary, the Problems in Relationships workbook is designed to address the reactivity found in intimate but oppositional relationships. It is derived from a theoretical model of selfhood, or self-definition. The workbook includes lessons addressing a variety of dimensions along which couples may be opposing each other. In retrospect, a lesson missing from this workbook is one dealing with one of the basic polarizations in reactive, repetitive relationships: "Pushing the Limits" in the selfish stance versus "Not Drawing Lines" in the selfless stance (L'Abate & Hewitt, 1989). The workbook is intended to reduce the oppositional behaviors of couples by increasing the attribution of importance to self and to others. The desired outcome should be one of selfulness for both partners.

Description of Lessons

The lessons in this workbook are based on dimensions along which a couple's relationship may be polarized. Each lesson was developed as a catalyst for the couple's movement to the midpoint of a specific dimension and away from the extremes. The titles of each lesson are self-explanatory of each dimension of polarization.

1. *"I win, you lose"* vs. *"You win, I lose"*: Defeats, like victories, can be the glue that holds a relationship together. One can use these suicidal rules, six of which were described in the Arguing and Fighting workbook, to check on how partners are destructive and how destructive partners are in arguing or fighting: (a) using "You always . . . " or "You never . . . "; (b) bringing up the past; (c) ambushing and gunnysacking—guerrilla fighting; (d) attributing negative, evil motivation by mind reading and speaking for the other—"You are bad", "I am good"; (e) delivering threats, ultimatums, blackmailing, and bribing: "If you do this I'll do that"; (f) avoiding confrontation altogether; (g) making excuses for oneself but not for one's mate; (h) distracting verbally and nonverbally.

2. *Denial vs. unrealistic admissions of errors:* "It's all my fault" versus "It's all your fault." As long as the partners use the word *fault,* they are not going

to be able to assume responsibility for themselves, because they lack awareness of personal errors.

3. *Mainly giving vs. mainly receiving love:* Selfish individuals are good at receiving love and not reciprocating. Selfless individuals are good at giving love but not at receiving it.

4. *Spoiled vs. neglected:* Looking back into the past, how was the individual trained to have his or her way, know better, win at others' expense? How was he or she ignored, put down, called names, made fun of?

5. *Self-indulging vs. self-debasing:* "Me first, you second," or the opposite.

6. *Critical of self vs. critical of others:* "I can't do anything right" versus "You can't do anything right." The critical, judgmental side is based on an attitude of "I know better."

7. *Dominant vs. submissive:* "I want it done my way" versus "Whatever you want."

8. *Determinate vs. wishy-washy:* "This is what I want" versus "I am not sure what I want."

9. *Rigid vs. pushover:* "My way or no way at all" versus "We can do it your way this time and my way next time."

10. *Gullible vs. conning:* "I believe whatever you tell me" versus "Do you doubt that I would tell you the truth?"

11. *Placating-obedient vs. rebellious:* "There are certain rules to follow, and I will follow them" versus "I am not going to allow anyone to tell me what to do."

12. *Showing vs. hiding feelings:* This concerns directing feelings outward versus directing them inward.

13. *Manipulating of others vs. manipulating of self:* This concerns manipulating others to meet personal needs and desires versus denying one's own personal needs and desires.

14. *Driven vs. pushed:* The extremes are the pushing of limits versus the inability to set limits.

15. *Mainly authoritarian vs. mainly responsible:* One partner may take the authority to make decisions while the other partner accepts the responsibility to carry out decisions that have been made by the other.

16. *Immediate vs. delaying:* Acting before thinking versus thinking before acting.

17. *Perfectionistic vs. sloppy:* The extremes are being overconcerned with order and details versus being unconcerned with order and details.

18. *Overly dependent vs. denying dependency:* This dimension concerns the issue of being dependent on another versus the struggle to gain independence from another.

19. *Hyperactivity vs. passivity:* These extremes concern how individuals in a relationship deal with each other and with their daily lives in terms of being either too active or too passive.

20. *Overly expressive vs. unexpressive:* Being articulate about one's feelings and thoughts versus not talking and being inarticulate about one's feelings and thoughts.

21. *Developing your own lesson:* This lesson allows partners to include a specific problem area not addressed by the other lessons.

22. *Becoming selful: "I win, you win":* Both need to win, or both lose. If one wins at the expense of the other, that is not victory; it's a defeat and a loss. Learning how to draw lines: (a) literally, answering the question "What will you put up with, and what will I put up with?"; (b) nonverbally rather than verbally (words are cheap!), such as going on strike and not talking at all; (c) through a Bill of Rights (L'Abate & L'Abate, 1988), writing down what one will and will not do, with at least three reasons for doing it and three reasons for not doing it.

Instructions to Therapists

1. Have both partners sign two copies of an informed consent agreement form loosely patterned after the consent forms included at the beginnings of the Social Training and Social Growth workbooks (Chapter 7). Give one copy to the couple and retain the other copy for your records.

2. After administering the Problems in Relationships Scale (PIRS) from Chapter 6 to both partners, score the answers and rank order the dimensions in which the couple is most conflictful, from the most conflictful to the least conflictful.

3. Assign the first lesson ("I Win, You Lose" vs. "You Win, I Lose") to every couple as a matter of routine. Then, assign whatever lessons are related to conflictful polarizations, as evaluated by your clinical judgment, results from the Problems in Relationships Scale (PIRS), and the Semantic Differential, starting with the most conflictual. Stop assigning lessons when it is clear that there are no longer conflictful polarizations in the couple and that whatever complementarity may exist is based on reciprocity. After completion of the most conflictual lessons, assign Lesson 21 (Developing Your Own Lesson), and on completion, Lesson 22 (Becoming Selful: "I Win, You Win").

Instructions to Partners

These lessons are designed to help improve your current relationship by building upon basic ideas and patterns that are important to positive relationships. The degree of improvement is dependent mainly upon your individual commitment to change and to the completion of each lesson assigned to you. Likewise, your partner must be committed to change and to the completion of lessons in this workbook.

Each lesson is to be used as a homework assignment. The completion of each lesson will involve three steps. First, each lesson should be completed individually and your answers recorded in writing. You will need to set aside a place and some time, approximately 15 to 30 minutes, to accomplish this part of the homework. Next, you need to make an appointment to meet with your partner and discuss your answers in each lesson prior to your next therapy appointment. Use this time as an opportunity for you and your partner to give and receive feedback about your relationship. After you have met and shared your responses, summarize and record the conclusions of this meeting in writing. Approximately one hour should be reserved for completion of this step. Finally, you should take your written responses and summary to your next therapy session, to share and discuss with your therapist for additional guidance and feedback.

Make sure to sign the informed consent agreement form given to you by your therapist.

Lesson 1: "I Win, You Lose" vs. "You Win, I Lose"

Defeats are often the glue that hold relationships together. One partner is usually winning at the expense of the other partner, and, of course, this conclusion means that the other can only be defeated. Ideally, intimate and committed relationships are not the place for battles, contests, and losses. These relationships are meant to yield victories for both partners and, as you shall learn, serve as the place for both of you to learn how to win with each other.

1. Tell how it feels to be defeated.
2. Write down how it feels to win at your partner's expense.
3. Give two examples of how you have been defeated by your partner.
4. Give two examples of how you have won over your partner.
5. Between the extremes of "I win, you lose" and "You win, I lose" represented on the following scale, where would you say you are in your relationship? Where would you say your partner is?

	1	2	3	4	5	6	7	8	9	10	
I win, you lose											You win, I lose

6. On the same scale, where would you like yourself and your partner to be?
7. If there is a difference between the real and the ideal ratings for yourself and your partner, what is a possible explanation for this difference?
8. What steps might you take to change your position on the scale?
9. What steps might your partner take to change her or his position on the scale?
10. Set aside one hour this week to meet with your partner and talk about your ratings. How can the two of you work out any differences between your ratings of each other, and between your real versus ideal ratings?
11. Write down what you learned from your talk.

Lesson 2: Denial vs. Unrealistic Admissions of Errors

Denial of obvious or painful realities and refusal to take responsibility for what has happened in one partner ("It's not *my* fault, it's all *your* fault," "It's not *my* problem, it's *yours*") is usually met by an unrealistic admission of errors ("It's all *my* fault"). Either extreme can be very damaging to a relationship.

1. There is a problem when couples use the word *fault* in their relationship— for example, "It's all my fault" versus "It's all your fault." How is the word *fault* used in your relationship?

2. What happens when you blame someone else for your own personal errors? How do you think they might feel?
3. What happens when someone else blames you for their own personal errors? Tell how you feel.
4. What happens when both parties take responsibility (rather than fault!) for their own personal errors? How does each party feel?
5. Why is it important to take responsibility for one's own behavior and not take responsibility for the behavior of another?
6. Between the extremes of denial of errors and unrealistic admission of errors represented on the following scale, where would you say you are in your relationship? Where would you say your partner is?

	1	2	3	4	5	6	7	8	9	10	
Denial of errors											Unrealistic admission of errors

7. On the same scale, where would you like yourself and your partner to be?
8. If there is a difference between the real and the ideal ratings for yourself and your partner, what is a possible explanation for this difference?
9. What steps might you take to change your position on the scale?
10. What steps might your partner take to change her or his position on the scale?
11. Set aside one hour this week to meet with your partner and talk about your ratings. See whether you can work out any differences between your ratings of each other, and between your own real and ideal ratings.
12. Write down what you learned from your talk.

Lesson 3: Mainly Giving vs. Mainly Receiving Love

In some relationships, one partner can mainly give love while the other can mainly receive love. It would be better if both partners were able to give and to receive love in equal amounts (if we could weigh love!).

1. How does the giving and the receiving of love work in your relationship? Be specific.
2. What happens when you mainly give love and do not receive love?
3. What happens when you mainly receive love and do not give love?
4. Why is it important for you to be able to both give and receive love in this relationship?
5. Give two examples of how you give love to your partner.
6. Give two examples of how you receive love from your partner.
7. Between the extremes of mainly giving love and mainly receiving love represented on the following scale, where would you say you are in your relationship? Where would you say your partner is?

	1	2	3	4	5	6	7	8	9	10	
Giving love											Receiving love

8. On the same scale, where would you like yourself and your partner to be?
9. If there is a difference between the real and the ideal ratings for yourself and your partner, what is a possible explanation for this difference?
10. What steps might you take to change your position on the scale?
11. What steps might your partner take to change her or his position on the scale?
12. Set aside one hour this week to meet with your partner and talk about your ratings. See whether the two of you can work out any differences between your ratings of each other, and between your own real versus ideal ratings.
13. Write down what you learned from your talk.

Lesson 4: Spoiled vs. Neglected

Some people have been raised and trained to have their way, to know better, and to win at others' expense. They are raised to be spoiled. On the other hand, some people have past experiences of being ignored, put down, called names, made fun of, and such. They are raised as neglected.

1. How do these two ideas of spoiled and neglected work in your relationship?
2. Give two examples of how you were spoiled in your family.
3. Give two examples of how you were neglected in your family.
4. What happens now when you act spoiled or neglected?
5. What happens when your partner acts spoiled or neglected?
6. Between the extremes of spoiled and neglected represented on the following scale, where would you say you are in your relationship? Where would you say your partner is?

	1	2	3	4	5	6	7	8	9	10	
Spoiled											Neglected

7. On the same scale, where would you like yourself and your partner to be?
8. If there is a difference between the real and the ideal ratings for yourself and your partner, what is a possible explanation for this difference?
9. What steps might you take to change your position on the scale?
10. What steps might your partner take to change her or his position on the scale?
11. Set aside one hour this week to meet with your partner and talk about your ratings. See whether the two of you can work out any differences between your ratings of each other, and between your own real versus ideal ratings.
12. Write down what you learned from your talk.

Lesson 5: Self-Indulging vs. Self-Debasing

Some people indulge themselves with a "me first, you second" approach. Other people debase themselves with a "you first, me second" approach.

1. How do these two approaches work in your relationship?
2. Give two examples of how you are self-indulging.
3. What happens when you are self-indulging?
4. Give two examples of how you are self-debasing.
5. What happens when you are self-debasing?
6. Why do relationships need to have partners who are neither self-indulging nor self-debasing in their behaviors?
7. Between the extremes of self-indulging and self-debasing represented on the following scale, where would you say you are in your relationship? Where would you say your partner is?

	1	2	3	4	5	6	7	8	9	10	
Self-indulging											Self-debasing

8. On the same scale, where would you like yourself and your partner to be?
9. If there is a difference between the real and the ideal ratings for yourself and your partner, what is a possible explanation for this difference?
10. What steps might you take to change your position on the scale? How can you enhance yourself without debasing your partner?
11. What steps might your partner take to change her or his position on the scale? How can your partner enhance herself or himself without debasing you?
12. Set aside one hour this week to meet with your partner and talk about your ratings. See whether the two of you can work out any differences between your ratings of each other, and between your own real versus ideal ratings.
13. Write down what you learned from your talk.

Lesson 6: Critical of Self vs. Critical of Others

Some couples may find themselves playing the role of either "victim" or "persecutor." The "victim" is usually critical of self and allows herself or himself to be blamed by a willing party. The "persecutor" is usually critical of others and finds someone to blame.

1. How do the roles of "victim" and "persecutor" work in your relationship?
2. Give two examples of how you have been a "persecutor" by being critical of your partner.
3. Give two examples of how you have been a "victim" by being critical of yourself.
4. Give two examples of how your partner has been a "persecutor" by being critical of you.

5. Give two examples of how your partner has been a "victim" by being critical of self.
6. What happens when one partner plays either the role of the "persecutor" or the "victim"? Who or what rescues (saves) you?
7. Between the extremes of critical of self and critical of others represented on the following scale, where would you say you are in your relationship? Where would you say your partner is?

	1	2	3	4	5	6	7	8	9	10	
Critical of self											Critical of others

8. On the same scale, where would you like yourself and your partner to be?
9. If there is a difference between the real and the ideal ratings for yourself and your partner, what is a possible explanation for this difference?
10. What steps might you take to change your position on the scale?
11. What steps might your partner take to change her or his position on the scale?
12. Set aside one hour this week to meet with your partner and talk about your ratings. See whether the two of you can work out any differences between your ratings of each other, and between your real versus ideal ratings.
13. Write down what you learned from your talk.

Lesson 7: Dominant vs. Submissive

Members of couples often find themselves in either a dominant or a submissive position in their relationships. To be in either a dominant or a submissive position means to be either one up or one down but never on an equal footing with each other.

1. How do these positions of dominant versus submissive work in your relationship?
2. Give two examples of how you are dominant.
3. Give two examples of how you are submissive.
4. Give two examples of how your partner is dominant.
5. Give two examples of how your partner is submissive.
6. Why is it important for both of you to be equally important?
7. Between the extremes of dominant and submissive represented on the following scale, where would you say you are in your relationship? Where would you say your partner is?

	1	2	3	4	5	6	7	8	9	10	
Dominant											Submissive

8. On the same scale, where would you like yourself and your partner to be?
9. If there is a difference between the real and the ideal ratings for yourself and your partner, what is a possible explanation for this difference?
10. What steps might you take to change your position on the scale?
11. What steps might your partner take to change her or his position on the scale?
12. Set aside one hour this week to meet with your partner and talk about your ratings. See whether the two of you can work out any differences between your ratings of each other, and between your own real versus ideal ratings.
13. Write down what you learned from your talk.

Lesson 8: Determinate vs. Wishy-washy

This lesson looks at how certain people are able or unable to make decisions. Decision making includes taking the responsibility for making incorrect decisions, as well as having the power to make correct ones.

1. Tell how problems with decision making work in your relationship.
2. Tell about times when you are determinate.
3. Tell about times when you are wishy-washy.
4. Tell about times when your partner is determinate.
5. Tell about times when your partner is wishy-washy.
6. Between the extremes of determinate and wishy-washy represented on the following scale, where would you say you are in your relationship? Where would you say your partner is?

	1	2	3	4	5	6	7	8	9	10	
Determinate											Wishy-washy

7. On the same scale, where would you like yourself and your partner to be?
8. If there is a difference between the real and the ideal ratings for yourself and your partner, what is a possible explanation for this difference?
9. What steps might you take to change your position on the scale?
10. What steps might your partner take to change her or his position on the scale?
11. Set aside one hour this week to meet with your partner and talk about your ratings. See whether the two of you can work out any differences between your ratings of each other, and between your own real versus ideal ratings.
12. Write down what you learned from your talk.

Lesson 9: Rigid vs. Pushover

Some people are unable to change their thoughts, ideas, or actions concerning some things, topics, or behaviors. Others adapt to everything and are agreeable to anything.

1. How do these two extremes work in your relationship?
2. Give two examples of how you are rigid.
3. Give two examples of how you are a pushover.
4. Give two examples of how your partner is rigid.
5. Give two examples of how your partner is a pushover.
6. Why is it important that both of you maintain a sense of flexibility?
7. Between the extremes of rigid and pushover represented on the following scale, where would you say you are in your relationship? Where would you say your partner is?

Rigid   1   2   3   4   5   6   7   8   9   10   Pushover

---

8. On the same scale, where would you like yourself and your partner to be?
9. If there is a difference between the real and the ideal ratings for yourself and your partner, what is a possible explanation for this difference?
10. What steps might you take to change your position on the scale?
11. What steps might your partner take to change her or his position on the scale?
12. Set aside one hour this week to meet with your partner and talk about your ratings. See whether the two of you can work out any differences between your ratings of each other, and between your own real versus ideal ratings.
13. Write down what you learned from your talk.

Lesson 10: Gullible vs. Conning

Couples in relationships can be gullible or conning. To be gullible means trusting too naively, too soon, and as a result, not showing one's sense of self-importance. To be conning means betraying the trust of someone by lies and by untrue statements.

1. How do these two extremes work in your relationship?
2. Give two examples of when or how you have been gullible.
3. Give two examples of when or how you have been conning.
4. Give two examples of when or how your partner has been gullible.
5. Give two examples of when or how your partner has been conning.
6. Explain why it is important to be neither gullible nor conning.
7. Between the extremes of gullible and conning represented on the following scale, where would you say you are in your relationship? Where would you say your partner is?

Gullible   1   2   3   4   5   6   7   8   9   10   Conning

---

8. On the same scale, where would you like yourself and your partner to be?
9. If there is a difference between the real and the ideal ratings for yourself and your partner, what is a possible explanation for this difference?
10. What steps might you take to change your position on the scale?
11. What steps might your partner take to change her or his position on the scale?
12. Set aside one hour this week to meet with your partner and talk about your ratings. See whether the two of you can work out any differences between your ratings of each other, and between your own real versus ideal ratings.
13. Write down what you learned from your talk.

Lesson 11: Placating-Obedient vs. Rebellious

Some people choose to be placating and accommodating—that is, they obey and do whatever they are told. Other people choose to be rebellious and do the opposite of what they are told to do. In a relationship, when one partner becomes rebellious or unconventional while the other partner placates or accommodates obediently, the two extremes can create tensions, anxieties, and conflicts.

1. How do these extremes work in your relationship?
2. Give two examples of when or how you placate and accommodate your partner.
3. Give two examples of when or how you rebel against your partner.
4. Give two examples of when or how your partner placates and accommodates you.
5. Give two examples of when or how your partner rebels against you.
6. Between the extremes of placating and rebellious represented on the following scale, where would you say you are in your relationship? Where would you say your partner is?

	1	2	3	4	5	6	7	8	9	10	
Placating											Rebellious

7. On the same scale, where would you like yourself and your partner to be?
8. If there is a difference between the real and the ideal ratings for yourself and your partner, what is a possible explanation for this difference?
9. What steps might you take to change your position on the scale?
10. What steps might your partner take to change her or his position on the scale?
11. Set aside one hour this week to meet with your partner and talk about your ratings. See whether the two of you can work out any differences between your ratings of each other, and between your own real versus ideal ratings.
12. Write down what you learned from your talk.

Lesson 12: Showing vs. Hiding Feelings

Sometimes one partner in a relationship tends to show feelings like anger and excitement. The other partner, on the other hand, may hide feelings like fear, sadness, and anxiety. Anger and excitement are usually expressed and shown outside for everybody to see, while fear, sadness, and anxiety are kept inside one's self, to make sure no one sees them.

1. How are these feelings dealt with in your relationship?
2. Give two examples of how you show your feelings outside.
3. Give two examples of how you keep and hide your feelings inside.
4. Give two examples of how your partner shows feelings outside.
5. Give two examples of how your partner keeps and hides feelings inside.
6. What happens when one of you shows feelings outside and the other keeps feelings inside?
7. Between the extremes of showing and hiding feelings represented on the following scale, where would you say you are in your relationship? Where would you say your partner is?

	1	2	3	4	5	6	7	8	9	10	
Showing feelings											Hiding feelings

---

8. On the same scale, where would you like yourself and your partner to be?
9. If there is a difference between the real and the ideal ratings for yourself and your partner, what is a possible explanation for this difference?
10. What steps might you take to change your position on the scale?
11. What steps might your partner take to change her or his position on the scale?
12. Set aside one hour this week to meet with your partner and talk about your ratings. See whether the two of you can work out any differences between your ratings of each other, and between your own real versus ideal ratings.
13. Write down what you learned from your talk.

Lesson 13: Manipulating of Others vs. Manipulating of Self

Some people may con or manipulate others to meet their own needs and desires, while other people may con themselves by denying their own needs and desires. Conning or manipulation implies the use of some means other than straightforwardness to gain a desired goal.

1. How do these extremes work in your relationship?
2. Give two examples of how or when you have conned your partner to meet your own needs and desires.
3. Give two examples of how or when you have allowed your partner to con you.
4. Give two examples of how or when you have conned yourself.

5. Give two examples of how or when your partner has allowed you to con her or him.
6. What happens in a relationship when one partner cons the other?
7. Between the extremes of manipulating of others and manipulating of self represented on the following scale, where would you say you are in your relationship? Where would you say your partner is?

	1	2	3	4	5	6	7	8	9	10	
Manipulating of others											Manipulating of self

8. On the same scale, where would you like yourself and your partner to be?
9. If there is a difference between the real and the ideal ratings for yourself and your partner, what is a possible explanation for this difference?
10. What steps might you take to change your position on the scale?
11. What steps might your partner take to change her or his position on the scale?
12. Set aside one hour this week to meet with your partner and talk about your ratings. See whether the two of you can work out any differences between your ratings of each other, and between your own real versus ideal ratings.
13. Write down what you learned from your talk.

Lesson 14: Driven vs. Pushed

Some people feel driven and as a result they tend to push limits in their relationships. Others are unable to set limits or to draw straight and narrow lines in their relationships. They must be pushed to do so.

1. How do these extremes work in your relationship?
2. Give two examples of drivenness (pushing limits) in yourself.
3. Give two examples of how you are unable to set limits.
4. Give two examples of how your partner is pushing limits (drivenness) in the relationship.
5. Give two examples of how your partner is unable to set limits (being pushed).
6. What happens to the relationship when either partner is pushing the limits or is unable to set limits?
7. Between the extremes of driven and pushed represented on the following scale, where would you say you are in your relationship? Where would you say your partner is?

	1	2	3	4	5	6	7	8	9	10	
Driven											Pushed

8. On the same scale, where would you like yourself and your partner to be?
9. If there is a difference between the real and the ideal ratings for yourself and your partner, what is a possible explanation for this difference?
10. What steps might you take to change your position on the scale?
11. What steps might your partner take to change her or his position on the scale?
12. Set aside one hour this week to meet with your partner and talk about your ratings. See whether the two of you can work out any differences between your ratings of each other, and between your own real versus ideal ratings.
13. Write down what you learned from your talk.

Lesson 15: Mainly Authoritarian vs. Mainly Responsible

In close or committed relationships, sometimes one partner takes the authority to make decisions, while the other partner accepts the responsibility to carry out decisions that have been made by the other. In some relationships the same partner may take both the authority *and* the responsibility or, in some relationships, one partner may not make any decisions *or* carry out any decisions.

1. How does this problem work in your relationship?
2. Give two examples of decisions you made without your partner's knowledge or permission.
3. Give two examples of responsibilities you carried out where the decision was made by your partner.
4. Give two examples of decisions your partner made without your knowledge or permission.
5. Give two examples of responsibilities your partner carried out where the decision was made by you.
6. Why is it important for both of you to share in decision making and in the responsibility to carry out those decisions?
7. Between the extremes of mainly authoritarian and mainly responsible represented on the following scale, where would you say you are in your relationship? Where would you say your partner is?

	1	2	3	4	5	6	7	8	9	10	
Authoritarian											Responsible

8. On the same scale, where would you like yourself and your partner to be?
9. If there is a difference between the real and the ideal ratings for yourself and your partner, what is a possible explanation for this difference?
10. What steps might you take to change your position on the scale?
11. What steps might your partner take to change her or his position on the scale?
12. Set aside one hour this week to meet with your partner and talk about your ratings. See whether the two of you can work out any differences

between your ratings of each other, and between your own real versus ideal ratings.
13. Write down what you learned from your talk.

Lesson 16: Immediate vs. Delaying

Some people act first and think later (immediate) while others think first and then act later (delaying).

1. How do these extremes work in your relationship?
2. Give two examples of when or how you act immediately.
3. Give two examples of when or how you act by delaying.
4. Give two examples of when or how your partner acts immediately.
5. Give two examples of when or how your partner acts by delaying.
6. What happens in a relationship when one partner acts immediately and the other acts by delaying?
7. Between the extremes of immediate and delaying represented on the following scale, where would you say you are in your relationship? Where would you say your partner is?

	1 2 3 4 5 6 7 8 9 10	
Immediate		Delaying

8. On the same scale, where would you like yourself and your partner to be?
9. If there is a difference between the real and the ideal ratings for yourself and your partner, what is a possible explanation for this difference?
10. What steps might you take to change your position on the scale?
11. What steps might your partner take to change her or his position on the scale?
12. Set aside one hour this week to meet with your partner and talk about your ratings. See whether the two of you can work out any differences between your ratings of each other, and between your own real versus ideal ratings.
13. Write down what you learned from your talk.

Lesson 17: Perfectionistic vs. Sloppy

In some relationships one partner may be a perfectionist—that is, picky and overly concerned with order and details about certain things. The opposite of being perfectionistic is being sloppy.

1. How do these two extremes work in your relationship?
2. Give two examples of when or how you are perfectionistic.
3. Give two examples of when or how you are sloppy.
4. Give two examples of when or how your partner is perfectionistic.
5. Give two examples of when or how your partner is sloppy.

6. What happens to the relationship when one partner is perfectionistic and the other is sloppy?
7. Between the extremes of perfectionistic and sloppy represented on the following scale, where would you say you are in your relationship? Where would you say your partner is?

	1	2	3	4	5	6	7	8	9	10	

Perfectionistic   Sloppy

---

8. On the same scale, where would you like yourself and your partner to be?
9. If there is a difference between the real and the ideal ratings for yourself and your partner, what is a possible explanation for this difference?
10. What steps might you take to change your position on the scale?
11. What steps might your partner take to change her or his position on the scale?
12. Set aside one hour this week to meet with your partner and talk about your ratings. See whether the two of you can work out any differences between your ratings of each other, and between your own real versus ideal ratings.
13. Write down what you learned from your talk.

Lesson 18: Overly Dependent vs. Denying Dependency

Some relationships struggle with the problem of dependence and independence. One partner may be overly dependent upon the other for a variety of reasons, or one partner may be in a constant struggle to gain independence from the other.

1. How does this problem work in your relationship?
2. Give two examples of how or when you are overly dependent on your partner.
3. Give two examples of how or when you deny your dependency on your partner.
4. Give two examples of how or when your partner is overly dependent on you.
5. Give two examples of how or when your partner denies being dependent on you.
6. How can a couple be both dependent and independent of each other at the same time?
7. Between the extremes of overly dependent and denying dependency represented on the following scale, where would you say you are in your relationship? Where would you say your partner is?

	1	2	3	4	5	6	7	8	9	10	

Overly dependent   Denying dependency

8. On the same scale, where would you like yourself and your partner to be?
9. If there is a difference between the real and the ideal ratings for yourself and your partner, what is a possible explanation for this difference?
10. What steps might you take to change your position on the scale?
11. What steps might your partner take to change her or his position on the scale?
12. Set aside one hour this week to meet with your partner and talk about your ratings. See whether the two of you can reconcile any differences between your ratings of each other, and between your own real versus ideal ratings.
13. Write down what you learned from your talk.

Lesson 19: Hyperactivity vs. Passivity

In a relationship individuals may either be very active or very passive in how they deal with each other and in their daily lives.

1. How do these extremes work in your relationship?
2. Give two examples of how or when you are very active in your relationship.
3. Give two examples of how or when you are very passive in your relationship.
4. Give two examples of how or when your partner is very active in your relationship.
5. Give two examples of how or when your partner is very passive in your relationship.
6. Explain why it is important that both of you have a balance between being active and passive in your relationship.
7. Between the extremes of hyperactivity and passivity represented on the following scale, where would you say you are in your relationship? Where would you say your partner is?

	1	2	3	4	5	6	7	8	9	10	
Hyperactivity											Passivity

---

8. On the same scale, where would you like yourself and your partner to be?
9. If there is a difference between the real and the ideal ratings for yourself and your partner, what is a possible explanation for this difference?
10. What steps might you take to change your position on the scale?
11. What steps might your partner take to change her or his position on the scale?
12. Set aside one hour this week to meet with your partner and talk about your ratings. See whether the two of you can work out any differences between your ratings of each other, and between your own real versus ideal ratings.
13. Write down what you learned from your talk.

Lesson 20: Overly Expressive vs. Unexpressive

There are some people who can talk freely about their feelings and thoughts while their partners cannot do it in the same way.

1. How do these two extremes work in your relationship?
2. Give two examples of when and how you can talk freely about your feelings and thoughts.
3. Give two examples of when and how you cannot talk about your feelings and thoughts.
4. Give two examples of when and how your partner can talk freely about his or her feelings and thoughts.
5. Give two examples of when and how your partner cannot talk about his or her feelings and thoughts.
6. What happens in your relationship when one partner is mostly expressive and the other is mostly unexpressive?
7. Between the extremes of overly expressive and unexpressive represented on the following scale, where would you say you are in your relationship? Where would you say your partner is?

	1	2	3	4	5	6	7	8	9	10	
Overly expressive											Unexpressive

8. On the same scale, where would you like yourself and your partner to be?
9. If there is a difference between the real and the ideal ratings for yourself and your partner, what is a possible explanation for this difference?
10. What steps might you take to change your position on the scale?
11. What steps might your partner take to change her or his position on the scale?
12. Set aside one hour this week to meet with your partner and talk about your ratings. See whether the two of you can work out any differences between your ratings of each other, and between your own real versus ideal ratings.
13. Write down what you learned from your talk.

Lesson 21: Developing Your Own Lesson

Of all the problems that you and your partner may face, there may still be one that was not included in the previous lessons. See whether you can agree on a specific problem area that the two of you wish to develop and complete in this lesson.

1. What problem area do you want to address?
2. How does this problem area influence your relationship?
3. Give two examples of how this problem works for you.
4. Give two examples of how this problem works for your partner.

5. Between the extremes of your particular problem as represented by the following scale, where would you say you are in your relationship? Where would you say your partner is?

	1	2	3	4	5	6	7	8	9	10	
One extreme											Opposite extreme

6. On the same scale, where would you like yourself and your partner to be?
7. If there is a difference between the real and the ideal ratings for yourself and your partner, what is a possible explanation for this difference?
8. What steps might you take to change your position on the scale?
9. What steps might your partner take to change her or his position on the scale?
10. Set aside one hour this week to meet with your partner and talk about your ratings. See whether the two of you can work out any differences between your ratings of each other, and between your own real versus ideal ratings.
11. Write down what you learned from your talk.

Lesson 22: Becoming Selful: "I Win, You Win"

Relationships can be based on defeats as well as on victories. The fact that you have been given this lesson shows that you have gone from a defeating to a winning basis for your relationship. By now you must have realized that you both must win. Otherwise, you both lose. If one partner wins at the expense of the other, there is not a victory. Rather, it is a defeat and a loss.

1. How have you been able to win with each other?
2. Give three examples of how both of you have won in your relationship.
3. Which lesson helped you the most to win with each other, and why?
4. Which lesson helped you the least to win with each other, and why?
5. Between the extremes of being selful and being either selfish or selfless as represented on the following scale, where would you say you are in your relationship? Where would you say your partner is?

	1	2	3	4	5	6	7	8	9	10	
Selful											Selfish or selfless

6. On the same scale, where would you like yourself and your partner to be?
7. If there is a difference between the real and the ideal ratings for yourself and your partner, what is a possible explanation for this difference?
8. What steps might you take to change your position on the scale?
9. What steps might your partner take to change her or his position on the scale?

10. Set aside one hour this week to meet with your partner and talk about your ratings. See whether the two of you can work out any differences between your ratings of each other, and between your own real versus ideal ratings.
11. Write down what you learned from your talk.

Building Relationships Workbook

This workbook was developed to assist couples in improving their relationships. It was not designed for couples whose relationships could be considered critical or clinical, but for couples whose relationships could be characterized as being in a state of need or at risk. In other words, the relationship is functional or semifunctional but could be improved. This workbook could, for instance, be used by therapists after the initial critical stage has been surmounted to help the couple learn some basic skills. It was designed to be administered with any dyadic relationship, intimate or otherwise, in which the partners want to learn more from each other and from working together with a therapist's help.

A great deal of the workbook is based upon a model of personal and interpersonal development over the life span, which is to say that development throughout the individual, marital, and family life cycles is a multiplicative function of the ability to love and the ability to negotiate (L'Abate, 1976, 1990a, 1990b; L'Abate & Bryson, in press). These two functions are basic to both the instrumental and the intimate sections of the workbook.

As is true of all workbooks, one must assess the current level of distress in order to identify the problem and to develop a treatment plan. Typically, the MMPI-2 and some of the instruments presented in Chapter 3, combined with other diagnostically subjective criteria, can be used to determine which couples could benefit from the Building Relationships workbook. After making a decision to administer the Building Relationships workbook, the therapist determines which of the lessons are most suitable for a particular couple. In other words, the therapist decides subjectively and objectively which lessons to administer. It is always helpful, however, to discuss the choice of lessons with each couple in terms of their perceived needs.

The application of the workbook must be given serious attention by any therapist who chooses to administer it. The importance of clinically determining which couple should receive the workbook cannot be underestimated. The couple must meet several conditions: (1) they must not be in a state of crisis; (2) they must be committed to hard and time-consuming work for a minimum of approximately 12 weeks (12 lessons); and (3) they need to be educated about the process involved in completing the lessons. In other words, preparation time must be spent with the couple before administering the first lesson, in addition to the time spent completing the third feedback loop. Please note that these lessons represent a menu from which the therapist as well as the couple can choose according to their needs and wants.

There is no reason why, in principle, the same process followed in the case of the Problems in Relationships workbook could not be followed with the Building Relationships workbook. This process consists of writing three or more test items to correspond to each lesson topic or descriptor, using all of the items derived from all the lessons to develop an objective test instrument, and then assigning lessons on the basis of how each couple responds to the test items.

The following lessons are included in this workbook:

Section I. The Personal Context

1. *Goals and wants:* The individual must examine and clarify the desired path for change.
2. *Victories and defeats:* It is important to learn that victories are the glue for all relationships and that defeats dictate no winners.
3. *Development:* In all relationships individuals are both independent of and dependent on each other.
4. *Personal importance:* It is necessary first to have self-importance before one can assign importance to others.
5. *Fears and anxieties:* The full range of emotions must be explored and shared if a relationship is to be meaningful and lasting.
6. *Activity and passivity:* For compatible interactions, the active and the passive levels of individuals in a relationship need to be explored and perhaps readjusted through negotiation.
7. *Masculinity and femininity:* Gender differences are crucial in relationships and must be fully explored on a personal as well as an interpersonal level.
8. *Conformity and rebellion:* The roles that individuals play within the relationship are important for full understanding by both partners.

Section II. The Instrumental Context

9. *Authority and responsibility:* Who makes decisions and who carries them out are critical areas that need clarification in most relationships.
10. *Big and small decisions:* The power to be in control must be addressed and resolved by both partners in a relationship.
11. *Problem solving:* All relationships have problems; the skills with which to address them are necessary for a strong relationship.
12. *Negotiation:* Both partners must have the skills for successful negotiating while realizing that some things (such as love) cannot be negotiated.

Section III: The Intimate Context

13. *Equality:* A necessary ingredient for any successful relationship, equality allows both partners to share in the victories.
14. *Reciprocity:* In a relationship, love must be both given and received to achieve a harmonious balance.
15. *Sharing feelings:* The sharing of hurt feelings is the true test of a strong relationship. The ability to admit vulnerability makes one strong. It takes strong people to admit to weaknesses. Weak people cannot do this.
16. *Sex and sexuality:* Partners in an intimate relationship must address this area and examine how it applies to them.

Section IV: Conclusions

17. *Looking back and putting it all together:* This summary lesson brings all the relevant points together for the couple. The goals and needs listed at the beginning of the workbook are reviewed to determine the effectiveness of the lessons, assess the desired change, and restate future goals and needs.

Instructions to Therapists

Before administering this workbook, you need to have made it very clear to couples from the outset of the therapeutic contract that you expect to work with them through this medium *in addition to face-to-face therapy sessions,* unless they (1) like you a lot, (2) have plenty of money or (3) have excellent insurance, and (4) want to stay in therapy forever!

Consider this workbook as a menu from which you can choose lessons at will. The lessons of this workbook, like most programmed materials contained in this book, are loosely based on skill training principles of programmed instruction, making the clients work with basic concepts and processes that are deemed to be crucial for building relationships, through the written rather than the verbal medium. *This workbook is not designed for use with couples in crisis.* Lessons in this workbook should not be used as a crisis intervention tool but rather to make the therapeutic process of helping couples more effective. Use of this workbook may be viewed as a paratherapeutic method in couples therapy to divert a crisis or as a constructive method with couples following a crisis in their relationship.

This workbook consists of 17 lessons that are grouped into the different contextual frameworks of personal, instrumental, intimate, and conclusive. The ordering or appropriateness of each lesson will vary depending upon the specific clients to whom you are administering the specific lessons. Therefore, as the therapist, you have the flexibility of choosing which lessons to use in certain situations and of sequencing them as you deem appropriate. For example, depending upon your clinical evaluation of the couple, you may choose to eliminate certain lessons from this workbook and include lessons from other workbooks. Also, you may decide to write your own lesson for a specific need.

Please note that there is a great deal of overlap between some of the lessons in this workbook and those in the preceding Problems in Relationships workbook. If a couple seems unable to go forward on a lesson, you may want to introduce a similar lesson from the other workbook. In fact, the Building Relationships workbook could be thought of as a backup for the Problems in Relationships workbook because of the duplication in many lessons.

These lessons are designed to be essentially self-administered. Clients should be given their own lessons as homework assignments for the week between therapy sessions. Instruct them to complete each lesson individually. Next, they are to make an appointment to meet with each other and discuss their responses in that lesson prior to their next appointment to see you. They should take notes of this meeting and bring their completed lessons to the next therapy session. This process allows the couple to receive feedback on their individual responses, on their interactions as a couple, and on their interactions with a third party, namely, you. A determination should be made that each lesson has been completed to a satisfactory level of mastery before administering the next lesson.

Instructions to Clients*

The lessons in this workbook are designed to help you improve your current relationship by building upon basic concepts and processes that are deemed to be crucial in close and committed relationships. The degree of improvement is dependent mainly upon your commitment to change as a goal and to the completion of each lesson. Likewise, your partner must be committed to change as a goal and to the completion of lessons in this workbook.

This workbook consists of specialized lessons that will be given to you by your therapist as homework assignments. Completion of each lesson will involve three steps. First, each lesson should be completed individually and your responses recorded in writing. You will need to set aside a place and some time, approximately 30 minutes, to accomplish this part of the homework. Next, you need to make an appointment to meet with your partner and talk about your responses in each lesson prior to the next therapy appointment. Use this time as an opportunity for you and your partner to give and receive information about your relationship. After you have met and shared your responses, summarize your meeting in writing. Approximately one hour should be reserved for completion of this step. Finally, you should each take your written responses and summary to your next therapy session, to share and discuss with your therapist for additional guidance and information.

Lesson 1: Goals and Wants

1. Why do you want to work on these lessons?
2. Why is it important for you to change your present relationship?
3. Why would you want to improve this relationship?
4. Rank the following goals for change in this relationship in terms of their importance to you. Rank the most important as #1, and so on down to the least important.
   a. Feel better as a person
   b. Feel better about the relationship
   c. Understand myself better
   d. Understand the relationship better
   e. Be more comfortable with myself
   f. Be more comfortable with the relationship
   g. Improve my behavior
   h. Improve the relationship
   i. Win for a change
   j. Stop losing all the time
   k. Other goal [please complete]

*These instructions are optional, to be given at the therapist's discretion.

5. Choose your most important goal and explain why you want to achieve it.
6. Explain how you are going to achieve your most important goal.
7. Choose your second most important goal and explain why you want to achieve it.
8. Explain how you are going to achieve your second most important goal.
9. Write down one change or improvement you have made in your relationship in the past.
10. Explain how you achieved this change or improvement in your relationship. What was the most important thing you learned from that experience?
11. Would it be better for this relationship to stay the same? (The devil I know is better than the devil I don't know!) Explain.

If you want this relationship to stay the same or get worse, *stop and go no further!*

If you want this relationship to change for the better, you will need to follow all the instructions given in the lessons of this workbook. If you follow these instructions in detail there is a chance that you may reach your goal(s). If you do not follow these instructions and those of your therapist, your relationship very likely will not change and will stay the same or get worse.

To work on this program you will need to set aside a quiet place and some quiet time to work on the homework that comes with each lesson. Be sure to set a place and a time aside for yourself. If you do not complete the homework, do not expect any change for the better.

12. Write down the place(s) where you will work on this program.
13. Write down the time(s) when you will work on this program.
14. Write down in detail how you plan to achieve your goal of working on the lessons of this program.
15. Write down again why you want to work on this program.
16. What will happen to your relationship if you do not work on this program?
17. Whose responsibility is it to work on this program, and why?
18. Meet with your partner to share your answers, and keep notes about what you and your partner talked about. Share your answers and your notes with your therapist.

Lesson 2: Victories and Defeats

1. What is negotiation? Start writing down your thinking on this topic, because we will get back to it in the course of this program.
2. What does winning (in your relationship) mean to you?
3. What does losing (in your relationship) mean to you?
4. What is the difference between winning and negotiating?
5. What is the difference between negotiating and losing?
6. When was the last time you won in this relationship? What did you win?
7. When was the last time you lost in this relationship? What did you lose?
8. When was the last time you negotiated in this relationship? What did you negotiate?
9. Do you most often win, lose, or negotiate in this relationship, and why?

10. Do you most often want to win, lose, or negotiate in this relationship, and why?
11. With your partner, agree upon a situation or problem in your relationship that needs to be negotiated. Practice negotiating to find a solution. Record the experience.
12. Would negotiating improve the quality of your relationship? Why?
13. What would it take for you to start negotiating more in this relationship?
14. If you really want to negotiate more in this relationship, you need a plan. List all the ways you could ensure that you negotiate more often.
15. Share your answers with your partner and together see whether you can work out a plan to negotiate issues. Keep track of your talk and share your answers and notes with your therapist.

Lesson 3: Development

1. What does it mean to be dependent?
2. What does it mean to be independent?
3. How do you feel when you are dependent?
4. How do you feel when you are independent?
5. Describe the last time you were dependent on your partner in this relationship. Tell about the situation and how you felt.
6. Describe the last time you were independent and did not rely on your partner in this relationship. Tell about the situation and how you felt.
7. Describe the last time your partner was dependent on you. Tell about the situation and how you felt.
8. Describe the last time your partner was independent and did not rely on you. Tell about the situation and how you felt.
9. List all the people upon whom you are dependent.
10. List all the people who are dependent upon you.
11. What does being a person mean to you?
12. What does being a partner mean to you?
13. What does being a parent mean to you?
14. How do you link being a person, a partner, and possibly a parent with being dependent and independent at the same time?
15. Can you be dependent and independent at the same time without giving up you as a person? If so, how?
16. What are the responsibilities that go with being both dependent and independent as a partner?
17. What are the advantages that go with being both dependent and independent as a partner?
18. How could you be a person in your own right and a partner in this relationship?
19. In a close and committed relationship, being dependent and independent means that both partners are able to be their own person, and yet, at the same time, they are also dependent upon the other. There should be equal give-and-take between being independent as a person and dependent upon your partner. This give-and-take is called interdependence. How

do you like to be: dependent, independent, or interdependent in this relationship? Why?

20. Share your answers with your partner and keep notes of your talk. Share your answers and your notes with your therapist.

Lesson 4: Personal Importance

1. What does having a "self" mean to you?
2. What does having a sense of self-importance mean to you?
3. How important are you to yourself?
4. Why should you be important to yourself?
5. What does "Love thyself" mean to you?
6. Why should we love ourselves?
7. Do you love anyone more than you love yourself? If yes, who is that person and why? If no, why not?
8. What does the statement "We can't love anyone unless we love ourselves first" mean to you? Explain.
9. List the ways you show you are important.
10. List the ways you show you are not important.
11. Do you allow others to make you less important than you are? If no, why not? If yes, who and why?
12. Write down what you plan to do to show your importance without putting anybody else down.
13. Share your answers with your partner and talk about making sure that you both stress the importance of yourselves as persons, as partners, and, if necessary, as parents. Keep notes on your talk and bring your notes and your answers to your therapist.

Lesson 5: Fears and Anxieties

1. What does the word *fear* mean to you?
2. What does the word *anxiety* mean to you?
3. What does the word *worry* mean to you?
4. What is the difference between fear, anxiety, and worry?
5. List fears, anxieties, and worries that you have experienced in your life.
6. What is your greatest fear in this relationship?
7. Have you shared this fear with your partner? If yes, what happened? If no, why not?
8. Do you share other fears, anxieties, and worries with your partner? Explain.
9. How scared are you of being rejected?
10. Do you ever feel rejected in this relationship? If yes, tell about the situation(s) in which you feel rejected.
11. How anxious are you about being left out in this relationship?
12. How worried are you about not fulfilling your job as a partner?
13. What does it mean to feel lonely?
14. Have you ever felt lonely in this relationship? If yes, describe the situation(s) in which you felt lonely.

15. Do you believe that everyone has felt rejected, left out, or lonely at certain times in their lives?
16. What might you do to feel less rejected, left out, or lonely?
17. What could your partner do to make you feel less rejected, left out, or lonely?
18. During the next week, keep track of and write about situations in which you feel rejected, left out, or lonely. Try to find out what causes these feelings, and how you act on these feelings. What do you do to overcome these feelings? Be as specific as possible in your answers.
19. At the end of the week, after you have written about situations that made you feel rejected, left out, or lonely, make a date to show and share your notes with your partner. Write down what happened at this meeting.

Lesson 6: Activity and Passivity

1. What does the word *activity* mean to you?
2. What does the word *passivity* mean to you?
3. What differences do you see between activity and passivity?
4. Do you see yourself more as an active person or as a passive person? Explain.
5. Do you see your partner more as an active person or as a passive person? Explain.
6. Is there ever a problem between you and your partner over when you need to be active or when you need to be passive?
7. How do you usually solve this problem?
8. Is there ever a problem between you and your partner over when she or he needs to be active or when she or he needs to be passive?
9. How do you usually solve this problem?
10. List areas of your relationship in which you are most active.
11. List areas of your relationship in which your partner is most active.
12. List areas of your relationship in which you are mainly passive.
13. List areas of your relationship in which your partner is mainly passive.
14. How can you and your partner work out differences in activity and passivity within the relationship?
15. During the next week, write about areas in your relationship in which you would like to change from being too active to being more passive, and from being too passive to being more active.
16. At the end of the week, meet with your partner and share your notes on what changes both of you want to make in how active or passive you are in your relationship. Write down what happened.

Lesson 7: Masculinity and Femininity

1. What does being a man mean to you?
2. What does being a woman mean to you?
3. What does it mean to cast in a mold (or stereotype)?

4. List five stereotypes about women in our society.
5. Do you agree with these stereotypes? Why or why not?
6. List five stereotypes about men in our society.
7. Do you agree with these stereotypes? Explain why or why not.
8. Did your parents or caretakers teach you about how women are different from men?
9. How are you following the teachings of your parents in this area? Do you believe them?
10. Outside of clear physical differences, can women do almost everything men do?
11. How comfortable are you with being a man or a woman?
12. How comfortable is your partner with being a man or a woman?
13. How comfortable are you with the way your partner shows being a man or a woman?
14. How comfortable is your partner with the way you show being a man or a woman?
15. Meet with your partner, show and share your answers to this lesson, and talk about this topic at will. Write down what you learned from your talk.

Lesson 8: Conformity and Rebellion

1. What does it mean to you to conform?
2. What does it mean to you to rebel?
3. What is the difference between conformity and rebellion?
4. When is it necessary to conform?
5. Give three examples of areas in your life where you conform.
6. When is it necessary to rebel?
7. Give three examples of areas in your life where you have rebelled.
8. Is it easier for you to conform or to rebel? Why?
9. What usually happens to you when you conform? How do you feel?
10. What usually happens to you when you rebel? How do you feel?
11. In what areas do you need to conform more and rebel less?
12. In what areas do you need to conform less and rebel more?
13. What would you call the middle ground between conformity and rebellion?
14. How could you develop this middle ground without having to resort to either conformity or rebellion?
15. How do conformity and rebellion apply to your relationship? Who, between you two partners, conforms to and who rebels against the other?
16. During the next week, write about the times you find yourself conforming to your partner.
17. During the next week, write about the times you find yourself rebelling against your partner.
18. Make a date with your partner and talk about similarities and differences in your conformity to and rebellion against each other. See whether you can find a middle ground to avoid either blind conformity or childish rebellion with each other. Write down what came out of this talk.

Lesson 9: Authority and Responsibility

1. Tell how authority works in your relationship—that is, how decisions are made.
2. Tell how responsibilities are carried out in this relationship.
3. What is the difference between authority and responsibility?
4. How are decisions made in this relationship?
5. What decisions do you make?
6. What decisions does your partner make?
7. What decisions are usually shared by you and your partner?
8. How are responsibilities carried out in this relationship?
9. What responsibilities do you usually carry out?
10. What responsibilities does your partner usually carry out?
11. What responsibilities are usually shared by you and your partner?
12. Are decisions and responsibilities balanced (or equal) in your relationship? If not, how could they be more even?
13. Are decisions and responsibilities ever negotiated in this relationship? If not, how might you negotiate them?
14. With your partner, identify a decision or a responsibility that needs to be worked out in your relationship. Write down what happened.

Lesson 10: Big and Small Decisions

1. Are you a good decision maker? Why or why not?
2. What steps do you usually follow to make decisions?
3. What decisions do you usually make by yourself?
4. What decisions does your partner usually make without you?
5. What decisions are made together in this relationship? Who makes the major decisions in the relationship?
6. Is there ever a problem between you and your partner over what decision is to be made? Explain.
7. How is this problem usually resolved?
8. Is there ever a problem between you and your partner over who is to make the decision?
9. How is this problem usually resolved?
10. In some relationships, the partner with the greatest authority and the least responsibility makes the big decisions, while the partner with the most responsibility and least authority makes the small decisions. How does this statement apply to your relationship?
11. Do you feel that how you make decisions in this relationship should be improved? If yes, how could you improve? If no, why should things stay the same?
12. Are decisions ever talked over in this relationship? If not, how might you work things out together?
13. Choose a decision that needs to be made this week, and with your partner work out a result you both want. See whether you can make decisions together. Write down what happened.

Lesson 11: Problem Solving

1. What is a problem to you?
2. Are you a good problem solver? Explain.
3. Do you believe that some problems are easier to solve than others? Why?
4. Do you believe that some people are better at solving problems than other people? Why?
5. List the steps you go through when faced with a problem to solve.
6. Do you sometimes find yourself avoiding a problem in hopes that it will go away? What usually happens in this situation?
7. Give three examples of problems that you have solved recently.
8. List three problems that you have delayed or postponed solving.
9. How do you and your partner solve problems?
10. Who is usually first to point out that a problem exists? Why?
11. Who is first to suggest a possible solution to the problem? Why?
12. What problem have you two solved or resolved recently?
13. What problem have the two of you been unable to solve or resolve?
14. Does the problem still exist? What suggestion(s) do you have for a possible (re)solution?
15. During the next week, list some problem(s) that the two of you need to solve in your relationship.
16. During the next week, list some problem(s) that the two of you have been unable to solve in your relationship. Why?
17. Meet with your partner and make a master list of problems that you need to solve together. Number the problems in order of importance to both of you. Make sure you show your therapist this list and ask for the next lesson on negotiation.

Lesson 12: Negotiation

1. What does negotiation mean to you?
2. Would you agree that negotiation means working together in a relationship on an "I win, you win" basis rather than on an "I win, you lose" or "You win, I lose" basis?
3. What is the difference between blackmail or bribery and negotiating?
4. How is negotiating different from losing?
5. Why is it important to negotiate in your relationship?
6. Did you ever negotiate anything with your partner? If yes, what? If no, why not?
7. What are some common problems that you need to negotiate with your partner?
8. Who usually faces problems in your relationship? Why?
9. What is the usual result of your facing problems in the relationship?
10. What seems to be the major problem in facing problems and finding solutions with your partner?
11. How could you two find ways to deal with problems so that you both can be proud and pleased with the results?

12. List three problems that you two have negotiated in recent weeks. What happened?
13. Do you believe negotiation is a useful skill to use in your relationship?
14. During the next week, write down problems that need to be negotiated between you two.

Following is a list of the necessary steps involved in the negotiation process. Study them carefully and put them to use in your relationship!

First, make regular dates at least 24 hours ahead to negotiate anything. Meet at least once a week. Do not meet suddenly or by whim or will. Then, each of you must make clear to yourself and to the other how you feel about the problem or issue to be negotiated. How each of you feels about the problem must be understood by both of you. To be sure that each understands the other, let the other repeat what she or he has understood about the problem.

Second, each of you must rank, in order of importance, the problems that you wrote down in response to question 14. Flip a coin to choose which problem, between those you and your partner rank as #1, should be given attention right away. *Please note:* The partner whose area was not chosen first has the right to second and third choices. Think of and talk about possible solutions or possible courses of action, including their rewards and costs for both of you. Eventually, choose the solution with the most rewards and least costs to each of you. Make sure that whatever solution you choose is written down in detail.

Third, start working on the solution you have finally chosen. Watch what happens for at least three months. See how the results compare with what you both expected. Write down your comments. Do not keep your feelings or thoughts in your head! Put them down in writing if you want to win!

Fourth, at the end of three months, see whether the results make you want to keep that solution or whether you should change to a fallback solution.

15. Were the steps followed as just outlined when you were negotiating? If not, why not?
16. Make sure that you work with your therapist as you go through these steps. Write down what happens.

Lesson 13: Equality

1. What does the word *equality* mean to you?
2. Would you agree that equality means that each of us counts as much as anyone else, no more and no less?
3. How does equality work in this relationship?
4. Do you see yourself as equal to your partner? Explain.
5. Does your partner see you as equal? Explain.
6. Give two examples of when you feel unequal to your partner.
7. Give two examples of when you feel your partner is not equal to you.
8. How do you feel when you see yourself as unequal to your partner? Explain.
9. How do you feel when you see your partner as unequal to yourself? Explain.

10. If it happens, how do you allow your partner to believe that you are less important than him or her?
11. If you do not believe in your importance, why should anyone else?
12. How can you show your importance without taking away from the importance of others, especially your partner?
13. How can your partner show his or her importance without taking away from your sense of importance?
14. What does this statement mean to you: "Equality of importance but difference in responsibilities"?
15. How can you and your partner agree on the importance of equality of importance but difference in responsibilities?
16. During the next week, start listing areas where you feel unequal to your partner. Show each other your lists and see whether you can negotiate these inequalities without putting each other down. Make a master list of these inequalities and show it to your therapist.

Lesson 14: Reciprocity

1. What does the word *reciprocity* mean to you?
2. Would you agree that reciprocity means equality of giving and getting—that is, treating others the way we want them to treat us?
3. What does the word *love* mean to you?
4. What does it mean to love one's self?
5. What does it mean to love your partner?
6. How are reciprocity and love linked together?
7. What would happen to you if you kept on giving without receiving love?
8. What would happen to you if you kept on receiving without giving love?
9. What is the difference between conditional and unconditional love?
10. Have you ever received unconditional love? How and when?
11. Can you love yourself in spite of your stupidity and mistakes?
12. Have you been able to give love to others unconditionally? How and when?
13. If we do not love ourselves unconditionally, in spite of our stupidity, warts and all, how can we love others unconditionally and how can they love us unconditionally in return?
14. Loving unconditionally means forgiving ourselves in spite of our stupidity, giving up expectations of doing everything right or perfectly. What do you think?
15. Loving ourselves means also being emotionally in touch with ourselves. What does that statement mean to you?
16. If we cannot be emotionally in touch with ourselves, how can we be in touch with and support people we love and who love us?
17. It is easier to do and to have than to be in touch with ourselves. What does that statement mean to you?
18. Is love something we can negotiate? Why or why not?
19. During the next meeting with your partner, talk about whether love can be negotiated or not. Write down what you learned from your meeting.

Lesson 15: Sharing Feelings

1. What does it mean to share feelings in a relationship?
2. Do you share your feelings with your partner? If yes, how? If no, why not?
3. Do you share your feelings with any others?
4. How easy or hard is it for you to share feelings with your partner?
5. How easy or hard is it for your partner to share feelings with you?
6. Give three examples of feelings you share with your partner.
7. Do you share the full range of your feelings and emotions (happiness, sadness, fear, hurt, disappointment, loneliness, and so on) with your partner? How?
8. Have you and your partner ever been able to cry together? If yes, how and when? If no, why not?
9. What emotions are easier to share with others than with your partner?
10. Are there emotions that you do not share with your partner? If yes, what are they and why do you not share them?
11. What does your partner do when you share your feelings with her or him?
12. How do you behave when your partner shares feelings with you?
13. Do you ever spend any time sharing feelings with each other?
14. Are you able to share hurt feelings (grief, failures, frustrations, foibles, personal errors, fears of being hurt, and so on) with each other? If yes, how? If no, why not?
15. If you cannot share hurts with each other, what can you share?
16. If you cannot share hurts, how can you share joys?
17. How would you answer the following statement: "The difference between a relationship and a physical, economic arrangement lies in how hurts are shared"?
18. Meet with your partner to show and share your answers. Talk about the importance of just sharing feelings (and no facts!) in a relationship. Write down what you learned from this talk.

Lesson 16: Sex and Sexuality

1. What does sex mean to you?
2. What does the word *sexuality* mean to you?
3. What is the difference between sex as a physical act and sexuality as an act of love?
4. How important is sex in your relationship?
5. Are you satisfied with the sexuality of this relationship? Why?
6. List three ways you share yourself sexually with your partner.
7. List three ways your partner shares herself or himself sexually with you.
8. Has your sex life changed as a couple? If so, when and how did it change?
9. Does your sex life need change? If yes, why?
10. How would you change your sexual relationship?
11. During your next appointment with your partner, talk about the strengths you have as a couple in your sexual relationship. What changes would

you like to make to work out any differences you might have in this area? Write down your answers.

Lesson 17: Looking Back and Putting It All Together

If you have come this far, give yourselves a pat on the back. You have done great and you should feel pleased and proud of yourselves!

1. What have you learned since you started working on the various lessons of this program?
2. Did you reach your goal(s) as stated in the first lesson? If yes, how? If no, why not?
3. How do you feel you have changed? List four ways.
4. If you did not learn anything from this program, why do you feel you failed?
5. Which part of this program—completing the lessons, meeting with your partner, or meeting with your counselor—did you find most helpful, and why?
6. Which part of this program did you find least helpful, and why?
7. Which lesson did you like the best, and why?
8. Which lesson did you like the least, and why?
9. Where would you like to go from here?
10. What other parts of yourself would you like to change for the better?
11. Which of these parts is the most important to you? How could you start to change it?
12. Which other relationships would you like to change for the better?
13. Which of these relationships is most important to you? How could you start to change it?
14. Give four reasons why you want to strive for personal growth.
15. List all of the things you plan to do for yourself in the future.
16. List all of the things you plan to do for your partner in the future.
17. Share your answers with your partner during your next meeting. Write down what you learned from this meeting.

Thank you for finishing this program! You can be very proud of your achievement. Good luck in your future growth!

CHAPTER NINE

Materials for Families

The main assumption behind these lessons, and the symptomatic behavior that they deal with, is that no behavior, especially no symptomatic behavior, starts or flourishes in a vacuum. The meaning (etiology and development) of symptomatic behavior is found in the family context. If such behavior starts in that context, then that context should be the focus of therapeutic efforts.

The procedures to be described and to be administered precede most, if not all, the assignments that help families to deal with depression, learn negotiation skills, and learn the sharing of intimacy (L'Abate, 1986b). They are to be used at the beginning of therapy, when the referring symptom fits into one of the problem areas described or when the therapist finds, during the initial interview, that one of these patterns, either not mentioned by the family or mentioned only in passing, seems to be prominent.

Dealing with these recurring, resistant problem patterns is relatively easy. What is more difficult is to find the underlying condition that is producing these patterns in the family. More often than not, in our experience, these patterns show themselves in either reactively repetitive or abusively apathetic styles. These styles are present in the marital or in the parent-child relationship or both. When these patterns are present, neither negotiation nor intimacy is present. If personhood is incomplete or inadequate, the partnership will not work well. Consequently, it becomes even more difficult to be a competent parent or partner. These styles are usually related to marital depression, which many women readily admit to but which, at least stereotypically in our culture, men usually deny and avoid (L'Abate, 1986b).

If progress in therapy is not taking place, sometimes one of the caretakers, more often the father, is responsible for failing to cooperate in the treatment. Sometimes the sabotage is very covert and indirect. Sometimes one finds a pattern of driven behavior (alcoholism, drug usage, workaholism, gambling, running around) that the father is refusing to bring up or give up. Oftentimes, the wife cooperates with the husband in keeping this behavior hidden from the therapist while the scapegoated member with one of the symptoms listed above becomes the "patient." Under these conditions, one may need help in the form of medication, Alcoholics Anonymous, or limiting treatment goals strictly to symptom reduction.

Problem or critical areas and resistant patterns can be brought under control by eliciting written descriptions, making positive reframings, and following the three behavior control guidelines discussed in Chapter 2. After this initial step in therapy has been successfully completed, and after depression and its derivatives have been dealt with, a more difficult step follows—helping families learn to negotiate and to love.

Applications to Problem Areas in Families

Many repetitive, often strongly and rigidly resistant, individual, marital, and family patterns are very difficult to eliminate before further therapy can be initiated. Unless steps are taken from the outset of therapy, any of these patterns may detour, derail, and defeat the process of therapy. Unless the therapist can intervene forcefully from the beginning, the people seeking help and relief may be quick to abandon therapy. To reduce the impact of the problem areas that are the main cause of many referrals, a variety of written homework assignments have been created to deal with the most common reasons for referrals from families.

These problem areas need to be taken care of at the outset of therapy. After evaluation and after the problem areas have been brought under control, one can deal with any underlying depressive or impulsive patterns or go on to use homework assignments to teach negotiation and intimacy skills. These initial sessions also establish rapport, trust, and confidence in the therapist and his or her procedures. Once this initial confidence has been established and the crisis diminished, the family is ready to deal with the historical and situational factors that usually underlie maladaptive family patterns. When these factors are taken care of, the family can enter another stage of therapy, where they may use homework assignments to learn how to negotiate. A final stage is an attempt to achieve greater intimacy in the family, either through written homework assignments (L'Abate, 1986b) or through structured enrichment programs (L'Abate & Weinstein, 1987; L'Abate & Young, 1987).

The issue here is whether one can produce standard operating procedures that can be followed with couples or families who exhibit resistant patterns. The written word ensures that all the details necessary to carry out the assigned steps are available beforehand. The written forms save time and energy for everybody (including the therapist) and avoid misunderstandings, avoidance, or distortions. The many similarities and the repetitiousness of these problem areas from one family to another led to putting instructions in writing that allow for idiosyncrasies in individuals, couples, and families.

The Homework Assignments

All the homework assignments follow a sequence of three lessons. For each problem area, a series of three lessons focuses on (1) a description of the behavior (frequency, duration, and intensity); (2) a list of multiple, positive reframings of these behaviors; and (3) guidelines, sometimes paradoxical, prescribing the behaviors. The rationale for this sequence of lessons is to be found in the literature on paradoxical strategies in psychotherapy (L'Abate,

Baggett, & Anderson, 1984; L'Abate, Ganahl, & Hansen, 1986; L'Abate & Levis, 1987; Weeks & L'Abate, 1982). These strategies, however, need to be coupled with the principles of control discussed in Chapter 2. Although most of the workbooks have been written according to a linear, step-by-step strategy, these programs of three lessons follow a circular rather than a linear strategy.

Lesson 1: The first lesson in a series of three consists of answering detailed questions designed to elicit specific information concerning the frequency, the duration, and the intensity of a particularly resistant pattern. The lesson also elicits information on how this problem area developed, how often it occurs, and how intense it is, as well as the main repetitive issues around which this pattern occurs. Each person who can read and write and who is involved in the pattern (both spouses, both parents, parent-child dyads) answers in writing, without checking with the other person. This individual assignment is done to flush out any possible (quite common) discrepancies in perceptions of the same pattern. After completing this form individually, family members are to meet at home at an appointed time (preferably agreed upon in the presence of the therapist) to discuss their answers with each other and with any family members who have not completed the lesson. After obtaining relevant information about this particular pattern of the behavior, one can proceed to the explanations for and the prescription of the behavior.

Lesson 2: In this lesson, respondents must answer by ranking multiple positive reframings—"explanations"—of the problem area. The rationale for the use of multiple reframings, especially concerning marital depression, can be found in L'Abate (1986b). In brief, it is doubtful (and documentation here is lacking) that a single positive reframing, no matter how specifically and exquisitely tailored to a particular family, is sufficient. It seems more appropriate to give individuals, couples, and families a variety of positive reframings from which they can choose. Clients are asked to spend one home session discussing and ranking these reframings in terms of how they apply specifically to themselves, their relationship, and the family. If clients believe that none of the reframings apply to them, they can come up with an explanation that seems to apply better to their family.

Lesson 3: These positive explanations should lead, ideally, to a prescription of the behavior. If no connection can be made between explanation and prescription, one can still justify the use of the explanations and their guidelines on the basis of pragmatism rather than on the basis of rational explanation. ("It would take 6 months to find out why this pattern came about. It may take a few weeks to bring this pattern under control. Which do you prefer?")

This three-session method of description, explanation, and prescription is followed in all the programs for families.

Instructions to Therapists

Warning: Therapists using these programs should be familiar with the literature on paradoxical or circular methods in family therapy (Weeks and L'Abate,

1982). These programs must not be used by therapists who do not have experience working with dysfunctional families. These programs are not substitutes for caring, experience, and professional knowledge.

In administering these programs, one may find it helpful to minimize the role of these potentially powerful procedures. They may be presented tentatively, as experimental, or by saying, "It's doubtful whether they will do any good" or "I really do not know what else to do" or "I am quite baffled by what is going on, and these procedures may not help." The therapist can give a completely contradictory message by supporting their successful use with other families but doubting "whether they will be of help in your case." Thus, the administration of these procedures may begin with a tentative, nondogmatic stance, colored with misgivings and doubts: "I doubt whether they will work, but let's try them for the next two weeks or so and see what happens." The rationale for such tentativeness and avoidance of dogmatism can be found in Weeks and L'Abate (1982) and L'Abate and Levis (1987). In other cases, the therapist may take a more authoritative stance, depending on the referral problem and the clients. If the lessons work, the therapist may need to show surprise, perhaps even chagrin or indignation: "I really do not understand how they worked for you!" This reaction may be factually correct: "You did it all. I don't want any credit because I don't want any blame!"

The experienced and knowledgeable therapist should be able to predict possible upsets that may result from the administration of these lessons. The lessons cannot and should not be handed out in a cavalier or offhand fashion. Therefore, the prediction of possible upsets should be coupled with an ability to deal with these upsets. Some of these lessons will provoke strong emotional reactions on the family's part. The therapist should be able to predict them and to deal with them constructively.

The sequence of these programs should be noted. The first two programs deal with general characteristics of dysfunctional families, negativity and verbal abuse. All of the other programs deal with very specific and circumscribed symptoms or problem behaviors. Very likely, many dysfunctional families will exhibit one of the two general characteristics and a specific symptom. On the other hand, some families may screen from the therapist's view either one of the two general characteristics and present the symptom as just an isolated instance of the identified patient's negative characteristics. In some rare cases, the symptom, indeed, may be present without those two general characteristics. In those instances, however, the therapist may need to look for apathy, passivity, and lack of intimacy in the marital and/or parent-child relationship. In other words, most symptoms develop within contexts of either apathy or abuse of some kind, including neglect or withdrawal. Thus, at least two different programs may be necessary for each family. One specific program may be needed to deal with the specific reason for referral, the so-called symptom. The other general one may be needed to deal with the context of the symptom, if the therapist can determine what it is. In some cases, the therapist may have to infer this context, because many dysfunctional families may tend to mask it through the very presence of the symptom.

Therapists should not expect success with all of these programs with all families. Structuring skills, at best, represent only half of the possible outcome of therapeutic interventions. At least half of the outcome is determined by the therapist's own style—relationship skills. These programs, like most programmed materials contained in this book, are designed to help therapists use structuring skills in a more methodical, systematic fashion.

Like all programmed materials, these programs should be administered after a definite therapeutic contract has been reached. This contract states the therapist's clear expectation that the family will need to get together at home for as many times and for the same duration as each therapeutic session. To avoid unpleasant surprises to the family as well as to the therapist, it is necessary to make this expectation explicit to the family in two ways. The first way is verbal, informing the family about how the therapist chooses to work through the assignment of specific homework tasks between therapy sessions. The second way is nonverbal, by the therapist's administering homework assignments consisting of evaluation forms at the outset and lessons later on. Sometimes, depending on the circumstances, a therapist may want to assign one of these programs at the beginning, assessing the family from its reactions to the first assignment. It is important for the therapist to establish an objective baseline from the outset of therapy, to determine the effectiveness of the program administered.

Each adult in the family, and in some specific instances a teenager, should receive one copy of each lesson. Family members should be instructed to answer these lessons by themselves before coming together to compare and contrast answers. The appointment time for the family meeting should be agreed upon by the family before leaving the therapist's office. In some situations, it may be necessary to predict that the so-called identified patient or symptom carrier may not cooperate in meeting with the rest of the family. This noncooperation can be reframed positively as "caring too much for the family to see it change."

With chaotic, multiproblem, critically upset, or educationally deprived families who may not be able to read instructions or understand them, it may be best not to administer these programs for use at home. Instead, the therapist may want to use these lessons as structured interviews or blueprints to follow in the office, administering them verbally rather than in writing. In other words, the therapist should use judgment as to how, when, where, and to whom these programs will be administered. Again, these programs are no substitute for clinical judgment and sensitivity.

Therapists should remember that programmed materials are not set in stone. If a question seems awkward or unclear, it can be rewritten. If a program does not seem to quite fit the family's or the therapist's needs, it can be rewritten. If the therapist cannot find the lesson or program that fits personal, theoretical, or practical views, a new program can be written following this format. There is no limit to what the therapist can do using the written medium, provided it is done with care and responsibility.

Negativity Program

This program was written with the collaboration of Tricia Jones. Since negativity is so pervasive in all kinds of dysfunctionality, it behooves the therapist to take a consistently positive attitude. This positive attitude is shown by the positive reframings made in the second lesson of these programs. It was difficult, almost impossible, to find much information on the subject of negativity/pessimism as it pertains to family functioning and dysfunctioning (L'Abate, 1986b). The paucity of references is unfortunate, since negativity is a major characteristic of dysfunctional families. Schwartz and Garamoni's (1989) model of positive and negative "states of mind" may go a long way toward linking family negativity with individual negativity. This program could be given to almost every family seen in therapy and may be a particularly good starting point before going on into more sensitive issues.

The following points further explain the ten positive reframings in the second lesson:

1. This reframing of negativity as a way of showing care was taken from examples based on "paradoxical positivism" (L'Abate, 1986b, p. 67). This is simply reinterpreting something negative as a positive. Dysfunctional families have difficulty being intimate and showing caring in positively appropriate ways. Here we highlight the crucial importance of caring as basic to the family's seeking help.

2. This reframing deals with negativity as showing involvement with each other. Since dysfunctional families are unable to become involved with each other in positive ways, one alternative is to be involved in negative ways. Defeating each other is another way of being close and keeping involved (L'Abate, 1985).

3. Putting others down is one way to bolster one's sagging self-esteem. Watson and Clark (1984) found that high negative affectivity correlated with poor self-esteem and with tendencies to devalue the self and others. Thus, devaluing others may boost one's poor self-esteem.

4. Sad and depressed feelings can be either internalized or externalized if one does not know how to experience and how to express them appropriately. In dysfunctional families there is a great deal of hurt that typically is not expressed or is not expressed appropriately. As a defense against more hurt, negativity may arise from a position of "I hurt you before you hurt me."

5. Negativity may be a denial of depression and generally indicates that "things aren't quite right." There is much unhappiness in dysfunctional families, but it is usually not expressed properly.

6. Parents who display negative affectivity have learned this mode of expressing feelings and pass it on to their children. For many dysfunctional families, expressing one's feelings negatively is all they know how to do, and many do a good job of it.

7. Negativity may "represent a form of avoidance and an attempt to maintain distance" (L'Abate, 1986b). A negative atmosphere is inevitable in families

characterized by maladaptive interpersonal behavior. Negativity is found both in severely disturbed and in midrange, semifunctional families (Lewis, Beavers, Gossett, & Phillips, 1976). Thus, families coming to therapy with negativity are indeed saying there is a need for change and progress in the form of greater intimacy and more productive and positive behaviors.

8. Lewis et al. (1976) found that families characterized by negativity were minimally individuated. They also found an absence of affirmation. In an attempt to individuate and affirm, individuals may blame and put down others or themselves.

9. This reframing is related to #5. Negativity indicates unhappiness and may be a way of saying "I'm hurting" or "I'm unhappy." Watson and Clark (1984) also found negative affectivity to be related to sadness, rejection, guilt feelings, tension, and worry.

10. Negativity is another way of getting attention. This may be particularly visible in families whose members criticize themselves to get attention and support from others. Individuals may also act out to get attention, even though it may be negative.

Lesson 1: Description

1. Define *negativity* and describe how it takes place in your home.
2. How often do negative words or acts occur in your home?
    a. Continuously
    b. Every day, more than once
    c. Every day, just once
    d. Two or three times a week
    e. Once every few weeks
    f. Once every few months
    g. Other [explain]
3. How long do these negative words or acts last?
    a. For days (continuously)
    b. Hours (how many?)
    c. At least 1 hour
    d. Less than 1 hour
    e. Less than 30 minutes
    f. 10 to 20 minutes
    g. Less than 10 minutes
    h. Less than 5 minutes
4. How strong or intense are these words or acts?
    a. Extremely intense, with physical violence
    b. Extremely intense, without physical violence
    c. Intense enough to be upsetting
    d. Heated but not intense
    e. Just unpleasant
    f. Not intense but continual
    g. Just occasional but a nuisance
    h. Other [explain]

5. How do these negative words or acts get started? Describe in detail.
6. How do they develop?
7. How do they end?
8. How does this negativity affect you? How does it affect your partner or any other adult in the family? How does it affect the children?
9. What have you done in the past to end this negativity? List all the techniques, methods, and resources you have used thus far.
10. Write anything else about negativity that would make it clearer how it takes place in your home.

Lesson 2: Explanations

1. Here is a list of what negativity usually does for families. Get together for at least one hour and talk about which of the following explanations applies specifically to your family.
   a. Negative words or deeds are one way of showing care in the hope that improvements will then be made.
   b. Negative words and deeds are one way of being involved with each other.
   c. Negativity is one way of boosting one's sense of importance, even if this importance is at someone else's expense.
   d. Negativity is a protection against hurts and vulnerability, since one can't be disappointed if the stress is on negatives.
   e. Negativity is one way of showing one's unhappiness about something in the family.
   f. Negativity is one way of expressing one's feelings. Although there may be better ways, this is the best that this family can do for now.
   g. Negativity is one way of saying that things aren't right and it shows the need for change and progress in the family.
   h. Negativity is one way of showing differentness in the family.
   i. Negativity is one way of saying, "I am hurting and I need help."
   j. Negativity is one way of getting attention from others.
2. Now that you have read and talked about whether and how these explanations fit you and your family, rank how well they fit your family. Rank as #1 the one that best fits your family, as #2 the explanation that fits your family second best, and so on down to the explanation that least fits your family.
3. If none of the explanations fits or applies to your family, write down what you think is the most likely explanation.
4. How do you think this negativity could be decreased? Explain in detail.

Lesson 3: Prescriptions

If you do not want to achieve control over negativity, do not follow these guidelines. If you *do* want to achieve control, follow these guidelines exactly. Although they may seem strange, think of them as a step toward making your family relationships more positive. The first step is to achieve control over behavior you do not like. The second step is to learn more positive behavior. Do you want to control negativity or do you want negativity to control you?

1. Set an appointment for a negative meeting at least 24 hours in advance. It will be most helpful if you can agree to have these meetings on a regular schedule, such as at 8:00 P.M. once a week, or on weekends.

2. Gather in a comfortable setting, preferably at the dining room or kitchen table or in the living room. Make sure that everyone sits as close to each other as possible. You will need a table or surface on which to take notes.

3. Just before the negative behavior is to start, set a timer or an alarm clock for 30 to 60 minutes, however long the family wants to meet. Stop as soon as the alarm rings. If you all want to go on, set another appointment at least 24 hours in advance, then split and go as far away from each other as your house or family members will allow. Follow steps 1 and 2 if and when you meet again.

4. Keep detailed records or notes of what happened either during or after the meeting. Tape record it if you can.

5. During this meeting, make sure that each member of the family pretends to be or practices being as negative as possible. For instance, blame, accuse, put down, cut down other family members' accomplishments, intelligence, abilities, appearance, speech, work, and so on. Find whatever faults you can in them. Exaggerate failures, faults, mistakes, and inadequacies in everybody. Find weaknesses in everybody and poke fun at them. Be specific. Use words like "You never . . . " and "You always . . . ," being as critical as you can possibly be.

6. Bring your notes or, better, a tape recording of this meeting to your therapist.

Verbal Abuse Program

Verbal abuse is one of the most frequent indications of dysfunctional behavior in families. Up to the present, verbal abuse has been called by euphemisms like "expressed emotions" (Leff & Vaughn, 1985) and "communication deviance" (Doane, 1985), and evaluated indirectly through the use of inappropriate tests, like the Rorschach or the Thematic Apperception Test (TAT). As important as these indirect ways may be, they are inappropriate when dealing with families who use verbal abuse. The problem needs to be dealt with directly, because euphemisms or indirect ways of measuring this behavior may be therapeutically time-consuming. Would it not be better—that is, more effective—to evaluate this behavior directly by calling it what it is and measuring it directly (Cusinato & L'Abate, research in progress)? Verbal abuse may be a positive correlate of physical abuse, but may be inversely related to sexual abuse. An expanded version of the questions asked in Lesson 1 is available from the first author.

Lesson 1: Description

1. Define verbal abuse and describe how it takes place in your home.
2. How often do acts of verbal abuse take place?
   a. Every day, more than once
   b. Every day, at least once
   c. Two or three times a week
   d. At least once a week
   e. Once every couple of weeks
   f. Once a month
   g. Other [explain]
3. How long do these acts of verbal abuse last?
   a. Days (continuously)
   b. Hours (how many?)
   c. At least 1 hour
   d. Less than 1 hour
   e. Less than 30 minutes
   f. 10 to 30 minutes
   g. Less than 10 minutes
   h. Less than 5 minutes
4. How strong are these acts?
   a. Extremely strong, with physical violence
   b. Extremely strong, without violence
   c. Strong enough to be upsetting
   d. Heatedly unpleasant
   e. Just unpleasant
   f. Not strong, but continual bickering
   g. Just occasional bickering
5. How do these acts get started? What seems to trigger (start) these acts?
6. How do these acts develop? Describe one in detail.
7. How do they end?
8. How do these acts affect you? How do they affect your partner or other adults in the family? How do they affect your children (if any)?
9. What have you done in the past to end these acts? List all the techniques and sources you have used.

Lesson 2: Explanations

1. Here is a list of what acts of verbal abuse do for families. Get together for at least one hour and talk about which of the following explanations applies specifically to your family.
   a. Being verbally abusive is a way of letting off steam when we have allowed our feelings to build up too much. It is one way of keeping from getting emotionally overloaded.
   b. Being verbally abusive toward each other is a way to avoid looking at our own problems, which can be scary and hard to deal with.

   c. Being verbally abusive is one way of keeping our home life emotionally charged. It creates tension and excitement and is a good way to keep things from getting dull and routine.

   d. Being verbally abusive keeps us from getting too close to one another. Many people have fears about becoming too dependent on their family and losing their identity in the process.

   e. Being verbally abusive is a welcome warning sign that there are parts of our relationship that we are not satisfied with. It lets us know we have some work to do as a family.

   f. Being verbally abusive is one way of staying emotionally connected with each other. It is a roundabout way to let each other know we care. After all, we do not get upset with people we don't care about.

   g. Being verbally abusive toward one another is a way of avoiding other duties we have around the house and in the community. After all, if we are regularly getting into fights with each other, it is hard to have any energy left for routine chores of daily life.

   h. Being verbally abusive toward each other is a sure way to keep things the same at home. Many people avoid changing because they find the unknown scary and settle for the security of what they know best, being abusive to each other.

   i. Being verbally abusive toward each other is one way of testing our love and commitment to one another. We both show that we are willing to earn a "purple heart" as proof of our commitment and love.

   j. Being verbally abusive is one way of demonstrating how well we know one another. After all, people have to be really close to allow this kind of behavior.

2. Now that you have read and talked about how these explanations may apply to you, rank how well they fit your family. Rank as #1 the explanation that seems to fit the best, and so on down the line to the explanation that least fits your family.

3. If none of these explanations apply to you, write down what you think is the most likely explanation for acts of verbal abuse.

4. How do you think these acts could be decreased? Explain in detail.

Lesson 3: Prescriptions

If you do not want to achieve control over this pattern of behavior, do not follow these guidelines. If you *do* want to achieve control, follow these guidelines exactly. Although they might seem crazy or strange to you, think of them only as a step toward establishing more positive relationships among you all. If you choose to avoid them, you will guarantee that things will stay the same.

   1. Set an appointment at least 24 hours ahead for you to be verbally abusive on schedule rather than anytime you like. It would be helpful if you could agree to be verbally abusive on a regular schedule, such as at a specific time three days a week, or once a week, or just on weekends.

   2. Get together in a comfortable setting, possibly at the dining room or kitchen table or in the living room. Make sure you all sit as close to one another

as possible. You will need a table and writing materials so that you can write and take notes.

3. Right before you start to be verbally abusive, set a timer or an alarm clock for one hour. Stop being abusive as soon as the alarm rings. If your acts of verbal abuse are not finished, reschedule the time for another meeting at least 24 hours in advance, then split from each other and go as far away from one another as your house will allow. If and when you meet again for a second meeting, make sure you follow steps 1 and 2.

4. Make detailed written records of what happened during and after the meeting, or, even better, tape record this meeting.

5. Although each of you certainly must have some favorite abusive ways of your own, please include some of the following as additional weapons in your arsenal of abuse:

Use sarcasm, exaggeration, and cynicism whenever possible.

Make faces, mimic, and criticize one another at every opportunity.

Always knock one another down for things that each of you could not possibly change; this method ensures that you all will never run out of good targets.

Make up names for one another. Use your imagination; this is a really good way to get at each other.

Keep the heat on. Do not give up. Act as if everybody else is at fault except you.

By all means, raise your voice; this is a great means of drowning out the others.

Whenever possible, make a joke at others' expense; this is a great way to get everybody's goat. Speaking of goats, making animal noises or using animal names is a sure way to upset others.

Show no mercy and take no prisoners.

Have a good abusive meeting!

6. After your meeting check your notes and the tape to see how well you (not the others!) have followed these instructions. Bring these materials to your next appointment with your therapist.

Temper Tantrums Program

Temper tantrums are most likely to occur and to come to the attention of the professional when the child is still young, usually before school age. Consequently, it is doubtful whether the child will understand what is being discussed with the parents. It is important to evaluate whether this is a mono-symptomatic behavior, isolated in an otherwise fairly well-adjusted child and family, or whether this is one of many other symptoms that indicate a much greater degree of dysfunctionality in the child and in the family.

Before using this procedure, the professional must obtain all relevant information about this pattern and attempt to eliminate it by using so-called familiar, straightforward, "linear" techniques. If these techniques fail, then this program may be implemented. From the outset, the child should be congratulated for his or her behavior because of its many positive results.

Lesson 1: Description

1. Define what a temper tantrum is and how it takes place in your home.
2. How often do these temper tantrums take place?
   a. Every day, more than once
   b. Every day, just once
   c. Two or three times a week
   d. Once or twice a week
   e. Once every few weeks
   f. Once every few months
3. How long do these episodes last?
   a. Days
   b. Hours (how many?)
   c. At least 1 hour
   d. Less than 1 hour
   e. Less than 30 minutes
   f. Between 10 and 30 minutes
   g. Less than 10 minutes
   h. Less than 1 minute
4. How intense (strong) are these tantrums?
   a. Extremely intense and violent
   b. Extremely intense, but not violent
   c. Intense enough to be upsetting
   d. Heated and strong
   e. Heated but not too strong
   f. Just unpleasant
   g. Not too strong but bothersome
   h. Just a nuisance
5. How do these tantrums get started? Tell in detail.
6. Describe in detail a typical tantrum.
7. How does it end?
8. How do these tantrums affect you? How do these tantrums affect your partner or other adult caretakers? How do these tantrums affect the rest of your family?
9. Describe whatever methods, techniques, sources, and resources you have used thus far to deal with these temper tantrums.

Lesson 2: Explanations

1. Below are listed some of the most common explanations for temper tantrums in children. Read them carefully and talk about them among yourselves.
   a. Temper tantrums are one form of expression for children. It is one way of letting out steam and a way of expressing oneself.
   b. Temper tantrums show a need for consistent control by both parents or at least by a single parent.

    c. There are, of course, more mature ways of expressing one's feelings. However, at this point this is the best the child can do.

    d. Temper tantrums sometimes are a way of mimicking the parent(s) or main caretaker. Hence, they show that the child is very loyal to the parent who shows the same or similar explosive behavior.

    e. Temper tantrums are one way of showing that the child is unhappy about something in the family. What could that be?

    f. Temper tantrums sometimes are an indication that parental discipline is not working well and that the child wants the parents to start working together in taking care of their children.

    g. Sometimes temper tantrums take place when one parent is more involved with the child than the other parent. Therefore, temper tantrums are a cry for help, because the child wants both parents to pay attention to him or her.

    h. Temper tantrums sometimes take place when the child receives attention only when she or he acts up. Maybe the child needs our attention when she or he is not acting up!

    i. Temper tantrums take place when the child is tired and all of her or his physical and/or emotional resources have been exhausted. She or he may feel helpless and unable to cope. Therefore, these temper tantrums may express this helplessness.

    j. Temper tantrums may suggest that the child needs consistent discipline from both parents.

2. Now that you have read and talked about whether and how these explanations apply to your child, rank how well they apply. Rank as #1 the one that seems to apply the best, and so on down the line to the one that applies the least.

3. If none of these explanations apply to your child, write down what you think is the most likely explanation for these temper tantrums.

4. How do you think these tantrums could be improved? Explain in detail.

Lesson 3: Prescriptions

    1. Inform the child often during the week preceding a specific, agreed-upon time, when she or he will be able to have a temper tantrum, telling him or her exactly when the temper tantrum is to take place and for how long. For instance: "Next Saturday at 10 A.M. when daddy is at home, you will be able to have *your* temper tantrum. Don't forget!"

    2. Make sure that the place where the temper tantrum is to take place is safe and free from dangerous objects. Use a large ball, punching bag, inflated balloons, inner tube, or empty paper boxes for him or her to hit or kick at will.

    3. Set the timer, saying and showing on the dial how long she or he will be able to express feelings. Urge him or her on to hit and/or kick as intensely and as long as she or he likes. Make sure that no harm will come to the child.

    4. If the child refuses or quits short of the allotted time (usually 15 minutes are sufficient), encourage him or her to go on. If necessary, tell the child that the doctor will be very disappointed that the instructions were not followed.

Inform him or her of how much time is still left for completion of the temper tantrum ("You still have 10 minutes to complete your temper tantrum").

5. The more involved parent should be taking notes throughout this process, supporting the less involved parent as much as possible, who should be the one giving instructions to the child.

6. If the child refuses and quits hitting and/or kicking, express disappointment and reassure him or her that the procedure will take place again next week. (With temper tantrums, usually once a week is enough. However, if necessary, these instructions can be followed two or three times a week.)

7. Make sure that this procedure is followed for at least three consecutive times, even if the child refuses to follow it.

8. If the child has a temper tantrum or starts to have one outside of the scheduled time, remind him or her that he or she will have a chance to do so at the time already set.

9. Stop this procedure only after the child refuses to have a temper tantrum at the set times for at least three weeks and fails to have temper tantrums outside of the set times for at least a month.

10. Throughout this process, help the child express his or her feelings of frustration and helplessness by modeling for him or her how to express hurt and anger in a more appropriate manner ("I get awfully mad sometimes"; "I holler so loud when I feel helpless and I don't know what to do").

11. If a temper tantrum seems to be taking place, sit the child in front of you, also sitting, and ask him or her if something is bothering him or her and if he or she cares to talk about it. Encourage the child to talk about whatever is bothering him or her.

12. Bring your notes to therapy.

Shyness Program

This program was written in collaboration with Sue Matthews. This program is especially useful with families in which there are shy children. Unfortunately, shyness in children, especially girls, is so taken for granted that it may be completely ignored by many families. It may come to the attention of family therapists in conjunction with more severe symptoms in the family. Shyness may thus be considered by many an incidental, secondary pattern rather than a condition in need of treatment.

Lesson 1: Description

1. Define shyness and describe how it is shown in your home.
2. How often do acts of shyness take place?
   a. Every day, more than once
   b. Every day, just once
   c. Two or three times a week
   d. Once or twice a week

  e. Once every few weeks
  f. Once every few months
3. How long do these acts of shyness last?
  a. Days
  b. Hours (how many?)
  c. At least 1 hour
  d. Less than 1 hour
  e. Less than 30 minutes
  f. Between 10 and 30 minutes
  g. Less than 10 minutes
  h. Less than 5 minutes
4. How strong are these acts of shyness?
  a. Extremely strong, to the point of total withdrawal from social contact
  b. Extremely strong, with no physical withdrawal but with total verbal withdrawal
  c. Strong enough to cause blushing and stammering
  d. Strong enough to inhibit wanted social contacts, though not physically apparent, like blushing
  e. Unpleasant but not enough to inhibit social contacts
  f. Just occasional shyness, at the beginning of a social contact
5. How do these acts of shyness get started? Describe in detail.
6. Describe in detail a typical act of shyness. How does it develop? How does it end?
7. How does this shyness affect you? How does it affect your partner or another adult in the home? How does it affect your children?
8. What have you done in the past to end this shyness? List all the techniques and resources you have used.

Lesson 2: Explanations

1. The following is a list of some of the most common explanations for shyness in children. Read them together as a family and talk about them among yourselves.
  a. Shyness is one way of seeking privacy without saying so directly.
  b. Shyness is a way of asking others to pursue contact with us and thus assure us that we are wanted.
  c. Shyness is a worry about not knowing who we are. This pattern may be a way of modeling after one's parents.
  d. Shyness is one way children stay close to their parents. It shows a need for closeness. It shows wanting to be with the family rather than to make new friends.
  e. Shyness is an indirect way of saying no to certain social contacts or certain activities without saying so directly.
  f. Shyness results from not being comfortable in social situations. Maybe the child is reacting to the family going out of its way to be comfortable in the same situations.

    g. Shyness is a response to a parent who may not realize the child's need for privacy. If a child feels that Mom or Dad is being too pushy or interfering, what better way to say no without getting into trouble than by being shy?

    h. Shyness is a way to show anger without letting anybody know. We refuse to perform in certain situations that will upset our parents.

    i. Shyness is a way to help others in the family feel very good about their own social skills.

    j. Shyness is a way of asking others to take care of us.

    k. Shyness is fear of being rejected in social situations.

    l. Shyness means feeling inadequate and unable to compete with others in social situations.

2. Now that you have read and talked about whether and how these explanations apply to your child, rank how well they apply. Rank as #1 the explanation that seems to apply the best, and so on down the line to the one that applies the least.

3. If none of these explanations apply to your child, write down what you think is the most likely explanation for shyness in your child.

4. How do you think shyness might be decreased in your child? Explain in detail.

Lesson 3: Prescriptions

    1. Make sure that the child knows beforehand when and how these guidelines are going to be followed.

    2. Set a time when shyness is most likely to take place (for example, when you have company over). Once you have set the time, call the child and remind him or her that he or she has to start feeling shy for the rest of that evening or day, for whatever length of time you have talked about with your therapist.

    3. Select a room where the child will not be disturbed so that she or he can retreat there while the company is visiting (or whenever you have selected a shy time). Allow the child to take into the room some things that she or he enjoys playing with or using.

    4. Make sure the child stays in the room with the door shut, in total privacy, until the visitors leave. Do not allow anyone to disturb the child.

    5. Keep notes on who tries to disturb or rescue the child from the retreat and describe how this is done. Be alert for "sneaky" ways of disturbing.

    6. Keep notes on whether or not the child wishes to come out of the room.

    7. If the child begins to feel shy at any time other than the one agreed upon, make arrangements for the child to have access to the retreat room if the need for privacy and control is expressed directly. For example, when feelings of shyness come out, encourage the child to try saying statements such as: "I would prefer to have some privacy and entertain myself alone right now."

    8. Do not tell anyone outside the family about this arrangement. Do not tell anyone outside the family about the problems this child is experiencing with shyness. Keep notes about who breaks these guidelines and bring them to the attention of your therapist.

9. The more controlled and quieter parent should be the active enforcer of these guidelines. The more talkative parent should keep writing notes.

10. If the child wishes and it seems needed, look into social skills classes. Talk about attending these classes with your child and therapist.

Stealing Program

This program was written with the collaboration of Ernestine Williams. Stealing is a troublesome pattern that needs to be nipped in the bud, before it reaches more destructive proportions. It is important to find out through this program, as is true for all symptomatic behavior, what the stealing means within the context of the family functioning and dysfunctioning. One will need to go beyond the facade of denial that often clouds a clearer perception of how the family functions or fails to function. The "culprit" may be brought up as the scapegoat and any other family problems glossed over or denied. Consequently, the therapist may "cure" the symptom but not the underlying family structure that brought it about. The safest assumption a therapist can make in dealing with symptomatic behavior is that intimacy is absent within the marital relationship and between parents and their children. To find out, check how the family deals with hurts and grief and what the family does when one of its members cries.

A large number of studies have suggested that early family experiences are related to adolescent and adult behavior, that aggressive behavior in children is stable from childhood to adolescence and that patterns of child rearing are related to aggressive child behaviors (Olweus, 1979; Patterson, 1982). Patterson (1982) showed significant differences in the interactional patterns characterizing stealers and those characterizing social aggressors. These studies indirectly support the notion that there is considerable continuity between the antisocial behaviors that occur in the family when the child is relatively young and the antisocial behaviors of the child in the community at a later age. Stealers, such as aggressive boys, tend to show higher rates of coercive behavior than do nonproblem boys (Patterson, 1982). However, parents of stealers seem to reciprocate less the coercive behavior of their children and are characterized by a more nonopposing and distancing behavior than are parents of either aggressive or nondelinquent boys (Reid & Hendricks, 1973). Stealing in children is usually approached from a behavioral stance. Patterson's approach, which has been very successful, is empirically based. His approach helps to demonstrate not only the usefulness of behavioral methods of intervention but also the usefulness of an empirically grounded approach, one that can provide the basis for feedback and change in the family system. Programmed materials can supplement the behavioral approach, since homework assignments involve the family as a whole. Looking at the presenting problem more positively can lessen the scapegoating of a child, while one can assess and identify the roles family members play in the development and maintenance of aggression and stealing.

Lesson 1: Description

1. Tell what stealing is and how it takes place in your home.
2. How often does something get stolen?
   a. Every day, more than once
   b. Every day, at least once
   c. Two or three times a week
   d. At least once a week
   e. Once every couple of weeks
   f. Once a month
   g. Other [explain]
3. How important or costly is the stolen item?
   a. Not too important items (for instance, combs, pens)
   b. Important items (such as keys)
   c. Small amounts of money (change)
   d. Large sums of money
   e. Other [explain]
4. What happens when someone notices something is missing? Describe in detail.
5. What seems to trigger (start) these stealing acts?
6. Describe a typical act of something being stolen. Include how it starts and how it develops.
7. What happens after the stealing has been found out?
8. How do these stealing incidents affect you? How do these stealing incidents affect your partner or other adults in the family? How do these stealing incidents affect children in the family (if any)?
9. What have you done in the past to end the stealing? List all of the methods and resources you have used.

Lesson 2: Explanations

1. Here is a list of what stealing can do for families. Get together for at least one hour and talk about which of the following explanations applies specifically to your family.
   a. Stealing is an easy way of getting something that you want from your family without asking parents to buy the same thing over again.
   b. When something is stolen, the whole family joins together to try and figure things out.
   c. Stealing is a good way of letting someone know that you admire their tastes. It's a compliment to them that you think they really have something worth the trouble of stealing.
   d. Stealing is an indication that the parents are not disciplining well, and that the child wants the parents to become more observant and work together.
   e. Sometimes a child will steal because that's the only time that she or he gets attention. Perhaps she or he needs attention when not acting out.
   f. Stealing is a good safe way of keeping your parents busy so that they won't have to bother with their own problems.

    g. Stealing from your family is safer than stealing from someone outside because they don't care about you and might hurt you.

    h. Stealing is a good way to get back at somebody in your family without yelling or hitting them.

    i. As long as one steals, other siblings are off the hook, because parents will pay more attention to the one who steals.

    j. Stealing keeps one dependent on someone else. This way the one who steals does not have to grow up and take responsibility for the things that are needed.

2. After you have looked these explanations over, rank how well they apply to this family. Rank as #1 the explanation that seems to fit this family the best, as #2 the explanation that fits this family second best, all the way down to #10 for the explanation that fits this family the least.

3. If none of the explanations seems to fit this family, come up with your own explanation of why stealing takes place in this family.

4. How do you think stealing could be decreased in this family? Explain in detail.

Lesson 3: Prescriptions

1. Inform the child as many times as possible, at least once a day, during the week preceding a specified date, when she or he will be able to steal something. For instance: "Next Saturday morning, when everyone is home, you can steal one item from someone in the family. Don't forget, because we are not going to remind you on Saturday morning!"

2. If the child steals something outside of the scheduled time, remind him or her that he or she will have a chance to do so at the time that has already been agreed upon.

3. At the agreed-upon time, set your timer and give the child a specific amount of time to steal the item: "You have 15 minutes to steal what you want."

4. The following day, the child must surrender what was taken, and state the reason why she or he stole that particular item.

5. The more involved parent should keep notes and bring them to therapy, while the less involved parent should be the one to encourage the child to steal something.

6. Whoever has had the item stolen from them should express their feelings about the item that was stolen when the child surrenders it, and state what type of inconvenience they suffered as a result of being without something that belonged to them.

Sibling Rivalry Program

Just like many other resistant patterns in families, sibling rivalry suggests a possible failure of leadership on the part of both parents. It is important that the guidelines be followed by both parents together or, if necessary, adopted by the parent who is less involved. After this pattern is brought under control, one needs to pay attention to underlying, unspoken patterns that the family is either unable or unwilling to bring up, usually a pattern of marital depression, which needs to be considered as a second step in therapy. Furthermore, one aspect of these three lessons that was stressed in previous conceptualizations of control, relies on changing the context of the symptom. Instead of the parent(s) reacting to the child, these lessons make the child react to the parent, thus changing the context of the symptom, and hopefully changing the various contingencies and consequences that have reinforced the behavior in the past (L'Abate, 1986b).

Lesson 1: Description

1. Tell what sibling rivalry consists of and how it takes place in your home.
2. How often does this sibling rivalry take place?
   a. Every day, more than once
   b. Every day, at least once
   c. Two or three times a week
   d. At least once a week
   e. Once every couple of weeks
   f. Once a month
   g. Other [explain]
3. How long does this behavior last?
   a. Days (continuously)
   b. Hours (how many?)
   c. At least 1 hour
   d. Less than 1 hour
   e. Less than 30 minutes
   f. Between 10 and 30 minutes
   g. Less than 10 minutes
   h. Less than 5 minutes
4. How strong or intense is this sibling rivalry?
   a. Extremely strong, with physical violence
   b. Extremely strong, without physical violence
   c. Strong enough to be upsetting
   d. Heatedly unpleasant
   e. Just unpleasant
   f. Not strong, but continuous bickering
   g. Occasional bickering
5. How does this sibling rivalry get started? Describe in detail. How does it develop? How does it end?
6. How does this sibling rivalry affect you? How does it affect your partner or other adults in your home? How does it affect your other children (if any)?
7. What have you done in the past to end this sibling rivalry? List all the techniques and resources you have used.

Lesson 2: Explanations

1. Here is a list of what sibling rivalry does for families. Get together for at least one hour and talk about which of the following explanations applies specifically to your family.
   a. Fighting with each other shows that you care a lot about each other. We usually do not fight with people we do not care about.
   b. As long as you fight, mother and father will not need to bother with their own problems, either as persons or as partners. Therefore, it may be necessary for you to go on fighting with each other.
   c. Fighting with each other assures that you will keep either or both of your parents busy and involved with you.
   d. Fighting with each other shows that you are really each other's best friend, because you spend a great deal of energy and time with each other.
   e. Fighting with each other keeps each of you from taking responsibility for your behavior, because you can always point to your sibling and blame him or her for how you behave.
   f. Fighting with each other protects each of you from taking time and energy to find other friends outside of your family.
   g. Fighting with each other allows each of you to stay dependent on each other. In this way you do not have to grow up.
   h. As long as you fight with each other, you do not have to watch TV or worse, do your homework!
   i. As long as you fight, you allow your other siblings (if there are any) to stay off the hook and do whatever they want, because your parents are too busy paying attention to you both!
   j. Fighting with each other is very good practice for learning how to compete and fight outside the home. Consequently, you may need to practice some more fighting.
2. Now that you have read and talked about whether and how these explanations apply to you, rank them from the one that seems to apply the most (rank #1) to the next most (rank #2), down the line to the one that applies least (rank #10).
3. If none of these explanations apply to you, write down what you think is the most likely explanation for sibling rivalry.
4. How do you think this sibling rivalry could be decreased? Explain in detail.

Lesson 3: Prescriptions

If you do not want to achieve control over this pattern of behavior, do not follow these guidelines. If you *do* want to achieve control, follow these guidelines exactly. Although they might seem crazy or strange to you, think of them as only one step toward establishing better relationships between you and between your children. The first step is to achieve control over undesirable behavior. The second step is to learn more desirable behavior. *This is the first step!*

1. Make sure that the children know beforehand (at least 24 hours in advance) when and how these instructions are going to be followed. Check with them to make sure that they know how and when.

2. Set a time when fighting between them is most likely to take place—for instance, right after school at 3:30 P.M. or after supper at 7:30 P.M. Once you have set the time, call them in to remind them that they have to start arguing or fighting for at least 15 minutes, if not 30 minutes, according to whatever guidelines have been discussed in therapy.

3. Set a timer for 15 or 30 minutes, whichever time you have decided upon, and urge the children to start their argument.

4. Let them argue without intervening (provided, of course, that they are not using any kind of physical means). If the argument escalates to physical extremes, discontinue it by sending them to their rooms or to different rooms to cool off for five minutes. After the five minutes (by the timer) have passed, call them back to go on with their argument.

5. Keep running notes, either on paper or on a tape recorder, on what is going on, what they are saying to each other, how they say it, what they say to you, and so on.

6. If, by any chance, they refuse to argue or fight, tell them that you will follow the same procedure on agreed-upon days (like Mondays, Wednesdays, and Fridays, or Tuesdays, Thursdays, and Saturdays) and at the same time.

7. If they start arguing or fighting at any time other than those agreed upon, remind them that they will need to do it when you say they will. If they go on arguing or fighting, send them to their rooms or to separate parts of the house for five to ten minutes by the timer. If they go on arguing or fighting outside of the set times, call an emergency family meeting to make sure that the whole family will have something to say about this behavior.

8. If they refuse to argue at the specified time, make sure that you schedule other times. Keep on following these instructions even if they refuse to argue or fight for at least four consecutive times. Do not stop this procedure unless you go four sessions without arguing or fighting. At the time of stopping after the fourth session, remind them that if another argument or fight takes place between them, they will start this procedure again and you will follow it without exceptions. Do not use this procedure just once and then quit. It will be worse than if you had never started! Do not forget to bring your notes or tape of the argument or fight to your therapist.

Domestic Violence and Child Abuse Program

This program was written in collaboration with Fran Greenfield. Child abuse and domestic violence are much more pervasive in our culture than we would like to admit (Fantuzzo & Twentyman, 1986; Justice & Justice, 1976; Martin, 1976; Martin, 1983; Ralmar, 1977). Although it is certainly questionable whether we can deal with this pattern in three easy lessons, an initial, positive plan may help us develop further strategies of intervention as the family becomes involved in completing these materials.

Lesson 1: Description

1. What kind of violence takes place in your household? Describe the following.
   a. Who is the person most likely to become violent?
   b. Who is the person most likely to receive the violence?
   c. What objects have been used against the person receiving the violence (a belt, a paddle, and so on)?
2. Which of the following injuries have resulted from the violence? How often and what part of the body was injured? Tell in detail.
   a. Burns (First degree? Second degree? Third degree?)
   b. Cuts (Some bleeding? Heavy bleeding? Number of stitches required?)
   c. Broken bones (How bad?)
   d. Welts
   e. Black eye
   f. Other [explain]
3. How often does this violence take place?
   a. Once a day or more
   b. Two or three times a week
   c. Once a week
   d. Once a month
   e. Once every two to three months
   f. Once every four to six months
   g. Hardly ever
4. How long does the violence last?
   a. Sometimes a whole day or more
   b. Half a day or several hours
   c. About 1 hour or more
   d. Less than 30 minutes
   e. Less than 15 minutes
   f. Five minutes at most
   g. Less than 5 minutes
5. How heated or strong does the violence become?
   a. So strong that I get scared that someone will be killed
   b. So strong that serious injury often takes place before the violence ends
   c. So strong that it is out of control but usually stops before serious injury results
   d. Strong enough to cause moderate physical injury
   e. Strong and very heated but causing only minor injury
   f. Heated but not strong
   g. Not very strong; one of us loses control but stops very quickly before someone gets hurt
   h. Other [explain]

6. Who usually starts and/or takes part in the violence?
   a. I usually start and finish the violence by myself.
   b. My partner starts and completes the violence.
   c. Both of us have started and taken part in the violence.
   d. One partner [who?] does the violence, and the other does nothing.
   e. One partner [who?] does the violence, and the other always tries to break it up.
   f. One partner [who?] always does the violence when the other partner is not home and cannot interfere.
   g. Other [explain]
7. How does the violence get started?
   a. After a hard day when I just can't cope any longer
   b. When I feel tired and worn out
   c. When the baby cries too much
   d. When I get to feeling too lonely, sad, bad, or mad
   e. When the two of us fight
   f. When we fight about money or sex
   g. When the child gets in the way
   h. When I start hearing voices
   i. Other [explain]

Lesson 2: Explanations

1. Here is a list of the most common explanations for violence in the home. Get together as a family for at least one hour to read and talk about whether and how these explanations apply to your family.
   a. *Violence is a way to get respect for authority.* Spare the rod and spoil the child. The child or the partner must learn that his or her behavior is wrong and that I am the judge of what is right or wrong in my house. If we do not make the rules stick, how will the child or my partner know what is right and wrong? The funny thing is that no matter how much we beat someone, they do not seem to learn.
   b. *Violence is a way to keep everybody in line.* We try to be good parents and partners, to give each other and the baby everything needed to grow up and be happy and strong. But all the baby and my partner do is cry. Tears show that we fail in our job. Therefore, the way to stop someone from crying is to hurt them some more. We do not want our child to grow up a sissy or for my partner to cry every time she gets hit.
   c. *We do not mean to hurt anybody.* It just starts happening. All of a sudden we lose control and we cannot take it anymore. Too much is going on in our lives now. Too many changes and too many pressures are all around us. This is the only way we know to deal with stress. We did not mean to take it out on the child—it's just that when the final straw breaks, the child is always the closest thing around.
   d. *Violence is the only way I have ever known.* My parents always beat me, and my father always beat my mother. I swore on my life that I would

never do those things to my children when I grew up. I guess I just don't know any other way.

e. *Violence is my only way of showing how unfair life is.* I never meant to hurt the child, but I get to be like a pressure-cooker inside. I get so angry and tired, having to take care of everybody else all day long. It just kind of eats away at me, and then I start wondering when, when will it be my turn? When will someone take care of me?

f. *Violence happens when I'm feeling cut off from the world.* I can't stand all the responsibility of having to take care of this child day in, day out, all by myself, with no real help from anybody. I just get so sick of not having anyone to talk to. Besides, I never wanted to have this child in the first place. If it weren't for this child, we would never have had to get married, and then I could have done something with my life.

g. *Violence is the best way to show how much we care for each other.* First the husband starts beating up the wife, and then the mother starts beating the child. Sometimes the mother has to hurt the child a little to make sure that the father won't hurt the child worse. Perhaps the child cried too much and we don't know how to stop the crying. Hitting is the only kind of touching we know. Maybe, if we knew how to touch each other better, we could give up the violence, but still show that we care for each other in better ways.

h. *Violence happens because we forget that our child does not know any better.* We want the child to know better than we do. We want the child to be like a little grown-up, and not get into all that dirt and mess. We forget that the child cannot be any better than we are. That child seems to get into trouble on purpose, just to show us who the boss is. We've got to show him or her who the real boss is.

i. *Violence is what happens when one of us has been drinking.* It's just that we get to feeling so bad we can't stand it any longer. However, it is the child who gets the worst deal. Drinking makes us forget our troubles for the time being, but then we know that the troubles won't go away just because we beat the child.

j. *In a roundabout way, violence keeps this family together.* This is the way I show the family I'm the boss. I am the one in charge here, and don't let anybody forget it! This is our own business and nobody else's. As long as we keep the beatings to ourselves, they will be the glue that binds us. What would happen to us if we did not have anything else to keep us together?

2. After you have read these explanations and talked about them in the family, rank them according to how well they fit your family. Rank as #1 the one that applies most to you, rank as #2 the one that applies second most, down to #10 for the one that applies least.

3. If you do not like any of those explanations and you do not think that any of them applies to you, write down what you think is the most likely explanation for the violence in your family.

4. What would it take for the violence to stop in your family?

Lesson 3: Prescriptions

If you want to go on abusing each other to show how much you love each other, every person in the family must have a chance to be both the abuser and the abused. If you want to decrease the abuse that takes place in your family, follow the guidelines below. However, if you want to go on with the abuse, do not pay attention to them. Not paying attention to these guidelines will ensure that the violence and abuse will go on. In fact, they most likely will get worse. On the other hand, if you are interested in taking control of that violence, follow these directions for truly abusive behavior.

1. Make an appointment, at least 24 hours in advance, for a specific time and place for the immediate family to get together for an abuse conference.

2. Choose a place that is comfortable, and in which no one will get hurt. This lesson can succeed only if it is carried out completely through words and not through acts. Absolutely no physical violence or abuse must take place. If one feels like the abuse is coming on, leave the room and do not come back until everybody is sure that no harm will be done.

3. Right before your abuse conference is scheduled to begin, set a timer to allow one family member to be abused for ten minutes and to be the abuser for ten minutes. Each person must have a turn playing each part. Follow as many of these guidelines as you can:

To be truly abusive, remember to *take absolutely no responsibility* for your own feelings or for the feelings of the other person. The point is to make the other person believe she or he is the scum of the earth; that she or he is personally responsible for every injustice, hurt feeling, or evil that has ever been done to you, anywhere, anytime. Do not feel any good feelings for the other person. The other person exists for you to let off steam, nothing more, nothing less.

Blame the other person for everything that has gone wrong for you that day, this week, the last year, or for all the past years.

Scream at the other person for his or her total failure to meet your needs and make you happy. Be particularly angry at the person's stupidity for not knowing what would make you happy without your having to tell him or her.

Make fun of the other person for not being perfect. Point out how stupid, ugly, clumsy, dirty, sleazy, lazy, rotten, fat, and disgusting she or he is.

Curse the other person with all the rage you feel for your helplessness, which is the fault of the other person. It's all his or her fault that you do not know any better.

Accuse the other person in detail of ruining your life. Give as many reasons as you can find, and in some cases, make them up, to put the blame on him or her. In this way, you can avoid looking at how you are defeating yourself.

Tell what kind of pain you would like to inflict on the person.

4. The abused person must respond with total submissiveness, agreeing that she or he is guilty as charged. After each abuse has been thrown at you by the abuser, respond with one of the lines from below. Be sure to feel the part deeply. Remember, you were put on this earth for the purpose of being a doormat. Do not feel any moral indignation. Do not feel any anger. Remember, your feelings do not count here. Do not try to convince yourself you are

a worthy human being; that will get in the way of your playing the part of the abused. Answer to the abuse with any of the following statements:

You are right, everything is my fault.

I have no right to want to be loved.

I am bad and evil and I deserve any punishment I get.

I have no right to want to be safe.

I am everything you say I am.

I do not count, I am not important.

Without you I am nothing.

5. After each of you has had a chance to be both the abused and the abuser, ask yourselves the following questions.

How does it feel to be the abuser?

How does it feel to be the abused?

Did anything either the abused or abuser said really make any sense?

Isn't it true that everyone has a right to be safe?

Doesn't everybody want to be loved?

Is it fair for one person to blame another for everything, the way the abuser blames the abused?

Isn't it sad to think that this is the only way you know how to show your love?

Isn't it time to learn another way?

6. After playing these parts, take another 15 minutes to talk things over. Do not go beyond this time limit. When the meeting is over, split immediately. Do not talk about the meeting for at least 24 hours. After the meeting has taken place and you have all had time to think about it, it is best to wait and bring your reactions to the next family therapy session.

7. Be sure to tape record the meeting, so that you can bring the tape to the therapist or counselor.

Lying Program

This program was written in collaboration with Maureen O'Toole. The literature on lying and deception is vast (Bok, 1982; Eck, 1970; Ludwig, 1965; Mitchell & Thompson, 1986; Wolk & Henley, 1970). However, few of these references relate to its etiology within the family context, as if individuals learned to lie in a vacuum! Consequently, it seemed necessary to develop a specific program, although we recognize the overlap among many of the patterns considered here—for instance, the overlap among stealing, negativity, abuse, and violence.

Lesson 1: Description

1. Define lying and describe how lying takes place in your family.
2. How often does this lying happen?
   a. At least once a day
   b. Two or three times a week

    c. Once a week

    d. Once a month

    e. Once every two or three months

    f. Hardly ever

3. How long does it usually take for the lying to be discovered?

    a. Suspect it at the time it's being told

    b. Usually suspect it the same day

    c. Within two or three days

    d. Within a week

    e. Within a few weeks

    f. Within a month

    g. More than a month

4. How is the lying usually discovered?

    a. The person who lied tells about it.

    b. The person who was lied to checks up on the story.

    c. Someone else in the family tells about the lie.

    d. A friend or neighbor tells about the lie.

    e. Something that indicates lying is accidentally discovered.

5. What is your family's usual reaction to the discovery that someone has lied?

    a. Don't mention the lie and pretend it didn't happen

    b. Act angry but don't talk about the lie

    c. Act hurt but don't talk about the lie

    d. Ask the person why she or he lied and try to be understanding

    e. Confront the person who lied in an angry way

    f. Confront the person who lied with your hurt

    g. Confront the person who lied and punish him or her

6. What are the lies that are told in your family usually about?

    a. Sex

    b. Money

    c. Where someone is going or has gone

    d. What someone is doing

    e. Relationships with other people

    f. Things that happened in the past

    g. Things that the person might be punished for

    h. Things that might hurt other people's feelings

7. Write about what happens when a lie has been told in your family. Be sure to include the following:

    a. What the lie was about

    b. Who told it

    c. Why you think it was told

    d. Who discovered it

    e. How it was discovered

    f. What happened after it was discovered

8. Please write down anything else that you think is important to an understanding of lying in your family.

Lesson 2: Explanations

1. Here is a list of what lies usually do for families. Meet together for at least one hour and talk about which of the following explanations applies specifically to your family. If your children are present, translate these explanations into words they can understand.
   a. Lying is an important way to protect others from things that might hurt them if they knew.
   b. Lying keeps peace and harmony in the family by preventing needless arguments.
   c. Lying is a way to preserve a person's privacy and keep private those things that are none of anyone else's business.
   d. Lying is a way to help someone who feels powerless feel more powerful because he or she knows something that others in the family don't know.
   e. Lying is a way to show someone that his or her opinion matters. We only lie to people whose opinion of us is important to us.
   f. Lying is a way to keep communication going. At least when a person is lying, they are communicating something, rather than just keeping quiet.
   g. Lying is done by someone who is very creative and imaginative and needs to have an outlet for his or her creativity.
   h. Sometimes people just forget or get confused a lot about the truth. They don't mean to lie, but do it accidentally because of forgetfulness or confusion.
   i. Lying is done by people who are very sensitive and just can't handle other people getting mad at them. They must lie to protect themselves from the pain that would be caused by others' anger.
   j. Lying keeps people from realizing things about their relationships that are painful or bad. It works to keep relationships going when telling the truth might break up the family.
2. Now that you have read and talked about whether or not these explanations apply to you and how they do, please rank them. Rank as #1 the explanation that applies the most, as #2 the explanation that applies second most, down to #10 for the explanation that applies the least to your family.
3. If none of these explanations apply to you, write down what you think is the most likely explanation for lying in your family.
4. How do you think the lying in your family could be decreased? Explain in as much detail as possible.

Lesson 3: Prescriptions

These are guidelines on how to make the most of lying and how to get lying to produce helpful effects on your family. If you are not fully prepared to work together to establish the benefits and rewards of lying in your family, continue as you are and do not try this program. This program might turn lying into a family activity, with enjoyment and closeness for all members. If you are not ready for this, please continue to use lying as you have in the past, although you will not completely enjoy it or derive the full benefits from it.

1. Set up a family lying time. This must be a time when all members are present. It must last at least one hour and it must be set up at least 48 hours in advance.

2. Meet together at the appointed time in a comfortable area of the house. Sit so that each person can see each other person. Assign one member to take notes or tape record the session.

3. Set a timer for 30 minutes.

4. Taking turns, each member first announces who may benefit from his or her lie, and then tells that person a lie. The recipient of the lie may not comment on it except to ask for clarification of the lie. No other family members may comment at all.

5. Continue taking turns until the 30 minutes are over. At the end of the 30-minute period, ask if anyone else has another lie that she or he would like to tell in this session, and then allow him or her to tell it.

6. Reset the timer for another 30 minutes.

7. Taking turns, each person names a person by whom she or he would like to be told a lie, and the topic on which she or he would like to be told a lie. The person named responds by telling a lie to the requestor, on the topic named. Do not allow any comments on the lie, other than necessary clarification by the person who requested the lie.

8. Continue taking turns until the 30 minutes are over. Then, ask if anyone else would like to request a lie in this session, and then allow the request to be made and the lie to be told.

9. Allow each family member one vote, and then, together, choose the best lie told in the session.

10. Do not talk about the lies told during this session at any other time during the week.

11. Bring the tape or notes from this session to your next therapy appointment.

Binge Eating Program

This program was written in collaboration with Monique Gray. Our culture's emphases on appearance for appearance's sake and on looking fit and trim have produced vulnerable persons. To them, especially adolescents, their looks are more important than their substance (Chernin, 1981; Roth, 1986). These persons develop and grow in apparently similar home environments—where individuation seems to be a major problem (Kaplan, 1978). The three lessons in this program may help a therapist learn more about how a particular family develops this pattern and consequently to develop more appropriate strategies of intervention.

Lesson 1: Description

1. Define binge eating and describe how it occurs in your home.
2. How often do acts of binge eating occur?
   a. Every day, more than once
   b. Every day, at least once
   c. Two or three times a week
   d. At least once a week
   e. Once every couple of weeks
   f. Once a month
   g. Other [explain]
3. How long do these acts last?
   a. Days (continuously)
   b. Hours (how many?)
   c. At least 1 hour
   d. Less than 1 hour
   e. Less than 30 minutes
4. Are these acts planned? If planned, how far in advance?
   a. At least one week in advance
   b. Less than a week
   c. Hours (how many?)
   d. Less than 30 minutes
   e. Between 10 and 30 minutes
   f. Between 5 and 10 minutes
   g. Less than 5 minutes
5. How strong or intense are these acts?
   a. Extremely strong, involving purging
   b. Extremely strong, involving self-starving for extended periods after each episode
   c. Moderately strong, involving eating until pain is experienced
   d. Eating until full
6. What types of food are consumed during each act?
   a. Meats, vegetables, and starches
   b. Vegetables
   c. Fruits
   d. Fast food (for instance, hamburgers, french fries, pizza)
   e. Desserts
7. How much food is consumed during one act of binge eating?
8. Does the amount of food differ from one act to another?
9. How do these episodes get started? Describe in detail.
10. Tell in detail about a typical act of binge eating.

11. How does this pattern of eating affect you? How does it affect adults in the family? How does it affect children (if any)?
12. What have you done in the past to end these acts? List all the techniques and sources you have used.

Lesson 2: Explanations

1. The following is a list of some of the most common explanations for binge eating. Read and talk about them among yourselves.
   a. Binge eating is a way of showing that you are unhappy about something in the family. What could that something be?
   b. Binge eating is a way of comforting and taking care of yourself.
   c. Binge eating is a way of fighting off feelings of depression.
   d. Binge eating is a way of letting your family know you need their help.
   e. Following binge eating with periods of self-starvation or purging allows you to feel powerful and in control of your body.
   f. Following binge eating with periods of self-starvation or purging shows your family how much you care about them by keeping a weight and an appearance that you feel is acceptable to your family.
   g. Binge eating allows you to protect your family from dealing with feelings of hurt and anger.
   h. Following binge eating with periods of self-starvation or purging is a response to the sociocultural pressure to seek and keep a slender figure.
   i. Binge eating is one way of dealing with inside tensions.
   j. Binge eating fills up feelings of emptiness.
   k. Binge eating is one way of keeping the whole family together.
   l. Binge eating is one way of taking away your family's worries.
2. Now that you have read and talked about whether and how these explanations apply to you and your family, rank them from #1 for the explanation that seems to apply to you the most, to #2 for the next most applicable explanation, down the line to #12 for the explanation that applies least to you.
3. If none of these explanations apply to you and your family, write down what you think is the most likely explanation for binge eating.
4. How do you think this binge eating could be decreased? Explain in detail.

Lesson 3: Prescriptions

If you do not want to achieve control over this pattern of behavior, do not follow these instructions. If you *do* want to achieve control, follow these guidelines exactly. Although they may seem crazy and strange to you, think of them as a step toward establishing better control of your life and better relationships between you and your family. The first step is to control behavior we do not like. The second step is to develop behavior we can be proud of and pleased with.

1. At least 48 hours in advance, schedule a binge eating session. A regular schedule of such family meetings at least once a week—for instance, every Saturday evening at 7 P.M.—should be agreed upon by the whole family.

2. Ask the binge eater to make a list of desired foods. Other family members will be responsible for getting the desired foods.

3. At the beginning of the meeting, set a timer for 15 minutes, informing the binge eater how long the binge will last. Urge the binge eater to eat as much as possible during this period of time, while the rest of the family is watching. If the binge eater wants to purge after this period of time, that should be encouraged.

4. If the binge eater refuses to eat or quits short of the allotted time, encourage him or her to go on. Inform the family member of how much time is left for completion of the bingeing act ("You still have 10 minutes to eat some more").

5. The family member who is most involved emotionally with the binge eater should be taking notes, while the least involved should be the one to set the timer, inform the binge eater of time limits, and encourage him or her to purge if he or she wants to.

6. If by chance the family member refuses to eat, tell him or her that the same procedure will be followed on the same day and at the same time next week.

7. If the family member starts binge eating at any time other than the one agreed upon, tell that family member that she or he will need to do it at a time agreed upon by the whole family. If the binge eating persists outside of the time limits, call a family meeting and repeat the procedure indicated in steps 2 and 3.

8. Stop this procedure only after the family member refuses to binge during the set times as well as outside of those set times for at least four weeks.

9. Throughout this procedure, help the family member talk about whatever feelings of frustration and helplessness may be present, as well as hurts and anger, in an appropriate manner ("I feel . . . "). Share whatever feelings may be expressed without becoming defensive, even if you feel attacked.

10. If bingeing seems to take place again, ask the family member to tell you what he or she is feeling and what is bothering him or her. Encourage this member to express whatever feelings may be present without reacting with judgments, negative comments, or criticisms. Each of us is entitled to our feelings.

11. Make sure that throughout the whole procedure, full notes of whatever happened and was said are taken. Bring these notes to the next therapy appointment.

PART III

Programmed Writing in Action

CHAPTER TEN

The Case of JEF

This chapter presents a case study of the use of programmed writing with a convicted felon. To the knowledge of these authors, this is the first documented case of "treatment at a distance," through correspondence. JEF was the first of a long series of incarcerated clients treated by the first author with the Social Training workbook (contained in Part II). In this particular case, face-to-face contact between the examiner (the first author) and JEF took place only during the initial psychological testing. This client was never seen again and was not charged for this service. He was originally sentenced to ten years in jail, but was subsequently let go from jail after serving one year and six months. He was put on probation and on a later follow-up found to be in group therapy with a colleague of the first author's.* The advantage of programmed writing here, of course, lies in the fact that a complete record of what was said to the client and what the client said and did is available.

The MMPI-1 was administered during the original psychological testing, as part of a whole battery of tests described here. Posttest took place at the end of the program. Follow-up took place three months after completion of the program. The original profile, as well as the other two profiles shown in Figure 10-1, do indicate the presence of a character disorder. JEF is essentially quick to act and react impulsively, with little or no thinking. Over the three tests, the target behavior, as indicated by the *Pd* scale, decreased from the 82nd percentile to the 77th and then to the 70th percentile, a little more than one standard deviation from the mean. Of course, this is by no means the profile of a healthy or functioning individual, or one who has been "cured." In fact, as in the first case presented in Chapter 2, there are still some deceit and defensiveness present in the follow-up test, as shown by increases in the *L* and *K* scales. Since the administration of this program to this young man in 1987, various lessons dealing with goal setting, anger, reactivity, and humility have

*Note: It has been four years since treatment ended, and JEF was recently apprehended for suspicion of bank robbery. I failed to deal with him on "Reactivity," "Humility," and the underlying depression as done in the later case presented in Chapter 2, showing that we (therapists) need to pay more attention to test results than to what criminally-oriented individuals claim or say. His *Pd* Scale (Figure 10-1) was still high enough to show that he needed further treatment (that is, more programmed writing).

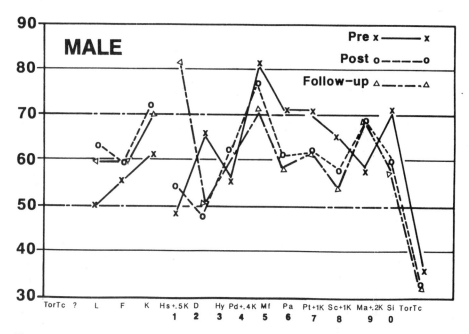

Figure 10-1. Test results for JEF (MMPI-1) before, directly after, and three months after completion of the Social Training workbook.

been added to this program (as reflected in Part II). Further refinements in the MMPI-2 also allow the use of additional workbooks to deal with deviations in the clinical and content scales (Part II).

This chapter reprints all the written materials associated with the evaluation of JEF and administration of the Social Training workbook through the mail. Written permission to reproduce these materials has been granted by JEF.

Psychological Evaluation

JEF   Evaluated: February 3, 1987
White, Male, Single   Location: County Detention
Age: 19 Years   Facility, Georgia

Reason for Evaluation: JEF was referred by Attorney R in relation to JEF's incarceration for burglary, theft, and various other law-breaking acts.

Interview: JEF explained how he got himself in trouble with the law through the use of cocaine, which gave him a false sense of security and clouded his judgment and comprehension of his self-destructive behavior. He felt a variety of pressures building within him since he was dating his first girlfriend in high school.

Before finishing high school, he was raised by his mother as a single parent, because his natural father left them when he was quite small. His mother has been married three times, and apparently was not taking good care of him and his siblings because, in at least one instance, the children were taken away from her by protective or welfare agencies. As he grew up and saw his mother struggle with meager financial resources, he wanted to get out on his own, to avoid being a financial burden to his mother.

His first girlfriend in high school wanted to get married, while he was set on a football career in college. She quit taking birth control pills and consequently became pregnant by him with the idea that then he would have to marry her. Her father had her abort instead. After the abortion JEF got into an argument with the girlfriend's father and could not handle this man's criticisms of him. He lost his job and started experimenting with drugs. Eventually, after he broke up with this girlfriend, he got a job as a car salesman and started doing relatively well. He started going with a second girlfriend, Joy, who is a dental assistant and who is still coming to see him in jail. "She is the only good thing in my life . . . "

Through the continued use of drugs, however, he became less and less interested in the job. His performance on the job started to go down. He started to gamble to pay debts and expenses for his drug habit. He maintained a facade of working and having money even after he was laid off from his job, while he was still thinking of going to college. His misfortunes culminated in his trying to burglarize a home and his being caught after a chase with the police, where he crashed a car he had "borrowed" from his former employer. His mother had to pay the lawyer for him out of an insurance settlement she received as a result of an accident.

He is aware now that one of his worst, hopefully past, attitudes, that was in part responsible for his downfall, was to expect to do very well on any job right away, giving up as soon as he became aware that he could not do the job well. He is aware now that it is better to finish the job started rather than give up because he cannot do it well. He realizes now that he needs to finish what he starts and to give up this perfectionist attitude.

Tests Administered: Figure Drawings, Benton Visual Retention, Michigan Picture Test, Wechsler Adult Intelligence Scale-Revised (WAIS-R), Minnesota Multiphasic Personality Inventory (MMPI), Rorschach Inkblots.

Test Results and Interpretation: JEF is an individual of above-average intelligence who shows a distinct and unusually wide discrepancy between his average verbal skills (WAIS-R Verbal IQ = 101) and his, at times, superior visual-motor assets (WAIS-R Performance = 125). These assets, however, can also become his worst liabilities, because it is in this area that he tends to act out impulsively, especially under pressure.

Even though JEF's verbal skills may come out at an average level, he does show a very high ability and facility to deal with numbers in a routine fashion, while his ability to abstract, as well as his contact with reality, indicate a rather unusual potential for very imaginative, original, and creative thinking. If and when this potential were to be combined with an educationally based channeling of his superior visual-motor abilities, the outcome could be a very skilled craftsman or high-level technician. His average verbal skills should disabuse him, however, of thinking along the lines of further college aspirations. With further help and proper training he could do very well in a technical school.

The major shortcoming, however, that landed him where he is now, is poor impulse control and acting with very little thinking. Interpersonally he thinks in rather unconventional and nonconformist fashion that makes it difficult for him to relate to other conforming individuals. His external macho orientation of direct physical confrontation to assert his insecure and incomplete masculine identity is rather superficial and short-lived. Under stress he would behave like a scared little child, acting out impulsively and inappropriately. Consequently, this uncoventionality in thinking and his poor impulse control would lead him to think like and associate with other rebellious and nonconforming individuals like himself. In other words, there are aspects of his thinking that are still immature and unsocialized. These potentially destructive aspects thus far have overwhelmed his potentially creative aspects, which have not as yet been allowed to come through and express themselves.

Conclusions and Recommendations: On the basis of the foregoing, JEF should receive as much encouragement as possible to use his as yet untapped natural talents in the visual-motor area and in creative thinking. With further assessment or analysis of his mechanical aptitudes, he should be supported in finding a field of technical specialization where he could do well and that he would like to pursue further. Of course, he should be helped in his perfectionistic attitude to complete a job he begins even if he cannot excel at it.

His educational training would need to be coupled with social training, to allow him to alter those aspects of his unconventional thinking and his impulsivity that have gotten him into trouble in the past. He has already embarked on a self-administered program of social training with the present examiner. Completion of this program should help him correct those liabilities in his thinking and actions that have landed him where he is now. The potential here for further training and growth is present and largely untapped, but JEF shows sufficient awareness of his shortcomings and past mistakes to recommend that some concerted efforts at rehabilitation be made, because not to do so would result in a great waste of talent, not only for JEF, but also for the community at large.

Lesson 1: Goals and Wants

Name *JEF*   ID

1. Why do you want to work on this program? *Because I have a sincere desire to find out really what makes me do some of the things I've done.*
2. Why is it important for you to change? *Because if I were to go any further than I have already, I don't think there would be any turning back. I want to make myself, my family, and Joy, proud.*
3. Why would you want to change? *I want to change so I can get rid of these evil ways and show what I know is inside of me. I believe I have a gift to share. Just plain tired of going nowhere and living on the edge!!!*
4. Which of these is the most important goal for change for you? Rank from the most important (#1) to the least important (#8 or #9).

	Rank Number
a. to feel better as a person	2
b. to lower the stress you are under	4
c. to improve your behavior	3
d. to be more comfortable with yourself	6
e. to be more comfortable with others	7
f. to understand yourself better	1
g. I want to win for a change	8
h. I am tired of failing all the time	9
i. Other *goal*	5

5. Pick your first goal and explain why you want to achieve it.   *My first goal would be to understand myself. I need to know what makes me tick because I can't pinpoint the reason for doing really reckless things.*

6. Explain how you are going to achieve your first goal.   *I'm just going to be honest with myself and others and hope and pray that I can find the best way to go about it.*

7. Pick your second goal and explain why you want to achieve it.   *My second goal is to feel better as a person. By this, I want to feel good about who I am, what I stand for, and the work I do.*

8. Explain how you are going to achieve your second goal.   *I hope to rehabilitate and start thinking about a particular profession to train in and also just train my code of behavior so that I am useful and contribute to society.*

9. Pick your third goal and explain why you want to achieve it.   *My third goal is to improve my behavior so that people can see the real me. I can't stand feeling regret for half the things I did and the way I went about them.*

10. Explain how you are going to achieve your third goal.   *I am hoping to express my true self and throw away the reckless things. To set myself guidelines and stand by them. Don't give in!*

11. Would it not be better for you to stay the same? Why not?   *Most definitely not. I could not live with myself much longer and I believe I would lose the people I love so much!*

12. If you want to stay the same or get worse: STOP AND GO NO FURTHER!

13. If you want to change for the better you will need to follow all the instructions given in the lessons of this workbook. If you follow these instructions in detail there is a chance that you may reach your goal(s). If you do not follow these instructions you very likely will not change and you will stay the same or get worse.

14. To work on this program you will need to set aside some quiet place and quiet time to work on the homework that comes with each lesson. Be sure to set this place and this time aside for you. If you do not do the homework do not expect any change for the better.

15. Write down the place(s) where you will work on this program.   *At the time I'm not sure. I guess in my jail cell.*

16. Write down the time(s) when you will work on this program.   *At lock down time or any free time.*

17. To work on this program you will need a pencil or pen to write. Write down here how you plan to achieve your goal of working on the lessons

of this program. Write in detail what you will do to work on this program. *I will set aside the time I need to get all projects done so long as they benefit me. I don't think anyone would be more dedicated to giving their all. I will also be 100% honest with myself.*

18. Write down again why you want to work on this program. *I want to find out my problems that I don't even understand at times. I want this as much as anything I've ever craved.*
19. What will happen to you if you do not work on this program? *I'm truly scared to think about how I might end up.*
20. Whose responsibility is it to work on this program and why? *It is mine and mine alone because I got myself in this and I have to get myself out.*

Lesson 2: Mistakes

Name *JEF*   ID

1. What is a mistake for you? *Something I did wrong, either intentionally or unintentionally.*
2. What is the difference between a mistake and an error? *They are somewhat similar. A mistake would be more serious and not made on purpose.*
3. What is the difference between an error and a goof? *A goof relates to an error like an error relates to a mistake.*
4. What mistakes have you made in this week? List as many mistakes as you can possibly remember. Add to this list past mistakes as they come to you and as you think about them. *As I think back over the week, I can't remember any mistakes I've made but I can remember many mistakes I've made in the past and I can detect a pattern in them.*
5. In looking over your list of past mistakes, can you see any pattern to them? For example, do you keep making the same mistake? What other pattern can you find? *Most of my mistakes were the result of irrational decisions, actions, disrespect, and uncaring ways. My past history.*
6. Do you like making the same mistake again and again? *No!*
7. Have you ever made the mistake of denying you were making a mistake? *No. I am not sure I understand the question.*
8. Why should you want to quit making the same mistake? *Simply because mistakes can be destructive, they can hurt people and that is a mistake.*
9. What will it take for you to quit making the same mistake? *I am training myself to do right: rational thinking, respect, discipline, experience, and knowledge. These are just a few aspects of a positive attitude.*
10. If you really want to quit making the same mistake all over again, write down all of the past mistakes that you have denied in the past.
    a. *Lying—a horrible mistake, always! This action will cause so many negative results. Honesty should be kept and spoken at all times.*
    b. *Being a "con-artist." This relates with lying. I thought I could get anything I wanted by playing the right role at the right time by misleading. I was badly mistaken!*
    c. *Thinking of only myself most of the time. I thought I was doing what I liked most, I was very blind. This mistake hurt so many people—including myself.*

    d. *Abusing drugs and alcohol. This was one of my biggest mistakes. I was ruining my mind and body and as a result look where it put me.*

11. What thread or pattern do you see running all through your past mistakes? Do you see any pattern? Can you explain it? *There is a very definite pattern. All my mistakes result from irrationality, not thinking of the outcome, and they're all negative. They all result from a lack of self-discipline and experience.*

12. How are you going to avoid making the same mistake(s) in the future? Please be specific and detailed. *Actions with discipline, actions from rational thinking, actions with love and caring. I am now in a predicament where I will have to prove who I am, how I think and what I believe if I am to regain the trust, love, and care from others.*

Lesson 3: Control

Name *JEF*   ID

1. What does control mean to you? *"Maintaining." Having the say-so in situations.*
2. Who controls you? *I have the final, ultimate control over myself.*
3. When have you failed to control yourself? Write down as many times as you can remember when you failed to control yourself. *I have failed to control myself many times when ignorance and greed influenced me. Getting drunk, doing drugs, being influenced by others to do something I knew was wrong.*
4. Why should you control yourself? *I must control myself so that the results of my actions will be acceptable and my actions will be positive and rational.*
5. Why should you not control yourself? *The only time I should not control myself is when I am doing something positive, i.e., helping someone, showing enthusiasm, showing love, care and interest.*
6. Why is it better to control yourself rather than not to control yourself? *When I use control my actions will be positive and I will know the difference between right and wrong.*
7. What happens to you when you fail to control yourself? *I do things that I may later regret. I may hurt someone, including myself. The results are negative.*
8. What happens to you when you control yourself? *I am usually happy with whatever the situation or outcome may be.*
9. How do you achieve control of yourself? *Self-discipline, rational thinking, practice, action.*
10. What will it take for you to be in control of yourself? *Rational thinking, self-discipline, and repetition of controlled actions.*
11. During the next week write down at least four times when you failed to maintain control of yourself. What happened to you then?
    a. *I failed to control my patience by writing another letter to the warden about something I wanted. I worried about what he thought.*
    b. *I failed to control my temper toward an officer who was being very disrespectful. I almost received a disciplinary report.*
    c. *I am constantly failing to control my anxiety. This causes me to think negatively. I will battle this until I win.*

d. *I failed to control and budget my time, therefore, I didn't study for a test as much as I should have—lower grade.*

12. During the next week write down at least four times when you did achieve control of yourself. What happened to you then?
    a. *I controlled my temper and attitude several times this past week. This prevented what could've been trouble for me.*
    b. *I controlled some of my anxiety which helped me not to worry about things I could do nothing to change.*
    c. *I controlled my actions. I have a job which gives me access to things that other inmates want to buy and refused to sell to them.*
    d. *I controlled my attitude by keeping my mind in a positive state. It helps me to cope and feel good with life and people.*

13. Which is better for you—being in control of yourself or losing control of yourself, and why? *Definitely being in control. This way I can go for what I know to be best and right. By controlling myself, I can control and see what the future has for me. Without control I would drift aimlessly and probably head directly for trouble.*

Lesson 4a: Law

Name *JEF*   ID

1. What is the meaning of the word *law*? *Rules set down by a government for people of its land to follow and abide by in order to have a controlled society.*
2. What laws do you follow for yourself? *It is obvious that I broke some laws but I believe I would try my hardest to abide by all laws now no matter how difficult they may seem.*
3. What is the difference between the authority and the law? *The authority is what enforces the law.*
4. Why are there laws? List as many reasons as you can find. *1) to keep a controlled society, 2) to protect people, 3) protect people's rights, 4) to keep America going, 5) to protect one's property.*
5. Give one example of when you followed the law last. What happened to you afterward? *I stopped at a red light is the last I can remember. I felt good that I was abiding as opposed to being reckless and not stopping.*
6. Give an example of when you broke the law last time you remember. What happened to you afterward? *The last time I broke the law I ran from the police and drove recklessly until I crashed. I now am serving time for that.*
7. What happens to you when you break the laws? *I almost always seem to get caught sooner or later. I really feel weird and kinda bad about breaking them, too.*
8. How do you feel when someone rips you off? *I feel very angry at first and think of catching them but I always wonder why they would also.*
9. How do you feel when someone lies to you? *I feel like they are betraying my trust. I try and figure why they would lie.*
10. How do you feel when someone cheats you? *I feel like they tried to pull one over me or took me for a fool. I get angry most of the time.*

11. How do you feel when someone steals from you? *I usually instantly get mad and begin investigating. Kind of upset that something was taken that I worked for.*

12. How do you feel when someone attacks you? *I automatically have a dislike and become defensive and usually attack back. I try to figure why they would attack. Ask them maybe.*

13. Write down all the times you have been lied to, cheated, ripped off, and abused. *I was first lied to about my mother and father's divorce. Been lied to, cheated and ripped off in many money making deals that were dishonest, so I deserved to be done all these things to. I've had personal things stolen by petty burglars and have had my car stolen also. I've been lied to by numerous friends to protect themselves I would think. I've been lied to by an ex-girlfriend. My trust has been abused by some so-called friends. I was abused as a child by one of my stepfathers. The list could go on but all pertain to the items already listed.*

Lesson 4b: Law

Name *JEF*   ID

1. How would others feel if you were to rip them off, lie, cheat, steal, or attack them? *I would think they would feel the same way I would. They could be angry, vengeful, annoyed, and probably would feel betrayed.*

2. How would you like to be treated by other people? *I would just like to be treated fair. I, myself, would want people to treat me like the way they feel about me so I will know how they feel.*

3. Why should other people treat you well if you do not treat them just as well? *At first maybe they should continue to treat me well even if I didn't, but I don't think they should continue if I'm too blind to see the good treatment.*

4. What would happen to you if there was not law that would treat you the way you want to be treated? *I guess I would have to try extra hard to earn the way I wish to be treated. It would be hard to stay in control and not retaliate but it would be a must.*

5. What do you want to call this law? *The Human Fairness of Treatment Law.*

6. Do you want to follow this law? Why? *Definitely. If everyone would abide by the law everyone would be able to live comfortably and get the fair treatment they desired.*

7. What would happen to you if there was no law like this one? *I think I would have to tolerate a great deal and surround myself with the ones who wanted the fair treatment like I did.*

8. Keep a record of how many times you followed the law of treating others the same way you want to be treated.

   a. For the next week, write down every time you failed to follow the law that you treat others the way you want them to treat you. Write down what happened to you when you failed. Give at least three examples:

      (i) *I made fun of an inmate because of a mistake he made. I felt bad because I could see it hurt his feelings and that it was really just a mistake he made.*

(ii) *I won in a card game and kind of rubbed it in because an inmate did the same when he was winning. I regretted doing this because I didn't like it when he did.*

(iii) *I didn't pay much attention to a guy when he was telling me something that he worried alot about. I felt really bad inside because he needed someone and I didn't respond. I did have him repeat it later and helped him out.*

b. Also during the next week write down every time you treated others the way you want to be treated. What happened to you? Give at least three examples:

(i) *An inmate asked me for a loan on some candy until he got to the store and I obliged. I felt good that I helped him out and even better when he kept his word.*

(ii) *I made sure a weaker inmate got his tray that was taken by others in the past and I felt really good about this and I would want the same treatment if others abused me.*

(iii) *An inmate came to me with a personal problem and asked my opinion and I gave him my honest advice. I felt good because I would want the same honesty if I asked for it.*

NOTE: NO FURTHER LESSON SHOULD TAKE PLACE UNLESS AND UNTIL THIS HOMEWORK HAS BEEN SATISFACTORILY COMPLETED.

February 20, 1987

Dear Dr. L:

These lessons seem to really help me open up in ways I never did before. I am anxious to start working on a degree. I'm not sure what particular field I want to go into, as yet, and any recommendations will be welcomed. I did want to ask that when you write your final report to be used in court for me, that you might recommend a facility that would be best suited for me to do this. I thank you, sir, for all your help.

Your sincere student-patient,
JEF

P.S. I am not asking for a particular facility and you may not even know one. I'm just asking for any one that would have that type of environment. I'm sure you understand.

February 25, 1987

Dear JEF:

I appreciate the effort and thinking that you are putting into the Social Training program. I hope you realize that what you put on paper is one thing and what you do with yourself and others is another. I would like to think that *both,* what you write on paper and what you do, are consistent and that you are not trying to con anybody, because by now you should have understood that when you con others you are conning yourself!

I have written your evaluation and passed it on to Mr. R. I have written it with the hope that the judge will send you to an institution that is most appropriate for you in terms of training and specialization. Ultimately, the outcome will be determined by you and how you behave there. I can only recommend and, of course, I will support you all I can within my limits. A great deal of my recommendations will be based on: (a) how you behave there and what reports I get from the officers at CCDC, (b) your successful completion of the Social Training program, (c) what test changes, if any, you will show after you have finished Social Training, and (d) whether you can apply what you learned from working on Social Training by perhaps teaching other inmates who cannot read or write. Of course, the last requirement is very optional and completely up to you. I would not use that last requirement (whether you teach others or not) to make any final recommendation. OK?

In reaction to your answers in the last two lessons of the Social Training program on LAW, I would like for you to answer some additional questions before you go on to the next lesson.

Keep up the good works and keep on writing!

Sincerely yours,
Dr. L

Questions Related to Answers to Lesson 4 on the Law

You stress the idea of "fair" and "fairness" in your answers. I do not think that the idea of "fair" or "fairness" is a workable one. Answer these questions and see what you get.

1. Who is going to judge what is "fair" and what is "not fair"? You? The other guy? His or her idea of what is fair may be quite different from your idea. Then what? *A very tough question. I guess the only explanation would be to do what you genuinely feel was right in a situation. Let the other party respond to your actions to let you know if he agrees.*
2. "Fair" and "fairness" are not working or workable criteria because they mean that someone else will have to be the judge of *what is fair.* If you appoint yourself as the judge of what is "fair" for yourself and others, what are the consequences for you? *If you appoint yourself as judge you are taking responsibility of others' actions. You would be frowned upon if not agreed with and you'll probably not always be agreed with.*
3. How about treating others the way you want or would like to be treated? Would not this principle eliminate *who* is going to decide *what* is fair or not? *It would eliminate it if everyone could abide by this principle. Unfortunately, some don't.*
4. What would you call this principle? *The triple "P" principle. "People Fair to People Principle."*

5. How would this principle work for you? What would happen to you if you were to follow this principle for yourself? *Find more peace in myself and my ways. I am practicing this principle daily with excellent results as far as feeling good about my behavior.*

March 13, 1987

Dear JEF:

If your behavior inside and outside your cell matches what you are writing on paper you should be doing great! I hope you do. I still do not think you have thought through the whole idea of treating other people the way you want to be treated. Yet this is the most fundamental law that has ever existed and that will ever exist! It is called THE GOLDEN RULE. I am willing to bet a dollar to a dime that you get in trouble every time you break this law! Of course, the other guy will not follow this law! He or she would not be in jail today if they had not broken this law! It is so much more important, therefore, that since the other guy is not going to follow this law, we should abide by it. What do you think would happen if no one followed this law? Just because the other guy breaks this law, that does not give us the freedom to break it also! Do you understand? Can you write an answer to these questions to reassure me that you have understood how important, crucial, and fundamental this law is *for your own welfare?* I would appreciate it if you did. I am enclosing the next lesson as well, and I am looking forward to hearing from you.

Sincerely yours,
Dr. L

JEF

March 18, 1987

Golden Rule Questions & Answers

1. What do you think would happen if no one followed this rule? *Well, it would definitely be a complete disaster as far as society goes. If no one treated others the way they wished to be treated there would be nothing but cheating, falsehoods, stealing, killing and etc., in the world. It is just essential in our life.*
2. Just because the other guy breaks this law, does this give us freedom to break it too? *It would be ignorant to do such a thing. That would be like jumping off a cliff just because your friend did. You must always do what is right for you and what feels right in your heart. I've learned that through this hell I'm going through now.*

Lesson 5: Responsibility

Name *JEF* ID

1. What does the word *responsibility* mean to you? *When you are in control of a situation or thing it is your responsibility. Responsibility is being held liable for something.*

2. Who is responsible for your behavior and why? *I'm the only one directly responsible for my behavior because I am given a choice like everyone else. Sometimes people do not choose what is best.*

3. Who is responsible for getting you in trouble and why? *I am once again the guilty party. I had some influence but I was reckless with my judgment and behavior.*

4. Who is responsible for getting you out of trouble (if possible) and why? *I don't think I can actually get out of this trouble. I can put it behind me and work to be better and pray that this shows in my appearance to others.*

5. Why should you be responsible for what you do? *You must be responsible for all your actions because you can't blame them on someone else. In my case it will take discipline, which I lack at times.*

6. What happens to you when you fail to take responsibility for yourself? *I fail myself and sometimes others. I'm almost always reckless and might do something I'm sorry for later.*

7. What happened to you when you took responsibility for yourself? Write down at least four examples.
   a. *I took responsibility for this trouble I got myself into. I believe it will turn out for the better by admitting my guilt. I feel better about myself for taking responsibility of my actions.*
   b. *I took responsibility to help out and be accountable for a Little League baseball team. I was trusted with the children and did quite well. They were my pupils and we won the championship.*
   c. *I took responsibility when I took out a $10,000 loan on my first new car. I paid it until I traded in after about two years.*
   d. *I was failing a particular subject my last two quarters of high school so I doubled up my last quarter and not only passed them but got an "A" and a "B+."*

8. What happened to you when you failed to take responsibility for yourself? Write down four different examples of what happened to you.
   a. *I didn't take responsibility when I let myself depend on the chemical cocaine. It changed my life drastically and gave me a motive to do some crimes.*
   b. *I think I failed when I let my girlfriend have an abortion. I knew what I was doing so I should have not let it go through. I regret it now very much.*
   c. *I failed in responsibility when I had a good job at Coca-Cola Bottling Co. and I let personal problems take over my time and let the job go.*
   d. *I failed in responsibility when I got behind the wheel intoxicated severely and hit head-on with another auto. I had to pay fines and 90 days hard labor in a camp.*

9. For the next week, keep track in writing of at least four instances when you were responsible for yourself, and four times when you failed to take responsibility for yourself.
   FOR YOURSELF:
   a. *I was voted Houseman of our cell-block and have done my duties to the best of my ability.*
   b. *I had an argument over store goods with another inmate and just walked away to avoid a fight and another charge against me.*

   c. *After the inmates were locked-down I cleaned up in their spot on the schedule because I think it is the Houseman's responsibility.*

   d.

AGAINST YOURSELF:

   a. *I got into a poker game and started to lose my store goods. Fortunately I won them back but was irresponsible for getting into the game.*

   b. *I lied about an inmate sneaking an extra tray when it is the Houseman's duty to be sure this doesn't happen. It won't happen again though!*

   c. *I skipped a day of my military exercises I do to stay in shape. I consider these important and will do my best to be responsible enough to continue them.*

   d. *I forgot to pray one day to my Lord for keeping me safe and sane through this. This is irresponsible to me for I need his forgiveness and strength and sell myself short by not praying.*

Lesson 6: Self

Name *JEF*   ID

1. What does the word *self* mean to you? *I believe it means for me and what I am. To look out for one's self is to look out for your own welfare or what is good for you.*
2. Do you have a self? Why? *Yes. Everyone has a self. A self is you and what you are, what you believe in and stand for.*
3. What kind of self do you have? *My self is one of pride and compassion. I try to understand others and help them now, but I also won't let anyone take my pride which is part of myself.*
4. What kind of self would you like to have? *I would like to be maybe a little less hot-tempered but other than that I want to be just like I am, not anyone else.*
5. What happens to you when your self is put down? *I immediately try to focus on what caused the put-down. Sometimes I become a little disturbed too.*
6. How do you put down your own self? *By making hasty remarks or decisions that aren't always in my best interest.*
7. Give an example of the last time you put your own self down. *I once went along with the group in here when they poked fun at a guard. This made me no better than them and I let myself down also.*
8. What happens to you when you are pleased with your self? *I feel like I've accomplished a task almost. I feel good inside and pleased with the positive results.*
9. Give an example of the last time you were pleased with your self. *When I helped a guy out getting picked on by a group of inmates.*
10. Who is responsible for your own self? Why? *I am, because I control what I do now and what happens to me. I decide what my actions are.*
11. What happens when you fail to be responsible to your self? *The results are negative and usually hurt me or others. I let myself down.*
12. What happens to you when you are able to be responsible for your self? *I feel in control of what happens to me and it makes me feel like a winner.*

13. What does it mean to love one's self as a neighbor? *It means not to do anything to anyone that you wouldn't do to yourself. Treat your neighbor like you would yourself.*

14. Who is your closest neighbor? *My closest neighbor would be my fiance, Joy. She means the world to me.*

15. During the next week and before you go on to the next lesson write about the differences among these four words.
    a. selfishness *To help only yourself, kind of greedy.*
    b. selflessness *To be uncaring of your own person.*
    c. selfhood *The mere fact of having a self, and the qualities that are with it.*
    d. nonself *To do something against yourself, like being detrimental to your own being. Not really sure though.*

16. What happens to you when you are selfish? *I don't believe I have that problem. I always try to practice unselfishness but I have been selfish before and it makes me feel greedy and rotten inside. Uncaring for others.*

17. What happens to you when you are selfless? *You become almost self-destructive. If you don't have a self you hurt others also.*

18. What happens to you if you have no self? *It's about the same as being selfless I would guess. You become detrimental to you and society.*

19. What happens to you when you have a self? *You have some pride and self-esteem if you care about the self you have. You become responsible.*

20. Complete the following sentences:
    a. I want *to lead a good and prosperous life.*
    b. I need *to practice control and good behavior to be happy.*
    c. I like *playing many physical sports all through the year.*
    d. I feel *better every day that I'm alive now except for this incarceration.*
    e. I am *hoping and praying for freedom so I can be the real me outside.*
    f. I *love my girl, Joy, and long to start a life with her and prove myself worthy.*

21. What do these sentences have in common? *They all have to do with my life and showing what is really inside me which I failed to do before I came here.*

22. What does it take to show that you have a self? *You must be aware of your actions and that you care about what happens to you.*

23. How can you speak for yourself without putting other people down? *You just say what is right and true. Let people know you respect their opinion but speak for your own self as well. Treat others the way you wish to be treated and it should go smooth when speaking.*

March 26, 1987

Dear Dr. L:

In response to the reports you requested from the guards here, you would personally have to ask Chief G if the guards can give any behavior report on me. I asked one of the nicer guards and that is what he said would have to be done. I am the houseman in C-pod, Section 3, and that title carries duties that the guards ask me to perform for them, such as making rosters, getting laundry lists and laundry, counting trays so everyone is fed, and helping inmates with requests, problems, etc. I have been incarcerated four months now and really don't have a good idea on what field I would like to pursue when released. I am interested in working with people and have always been a hard worker. I am also interested in making more than just average income. I am aware it won't all come at once and I have patience and am eager to train and show my worth as well as my potential. Do you know of anyone who could help me achieve my goal or maybe just some suggestions. Thank you for any and all cooperation you may supply, sir.

Sincerely your student,
JEF

March 31, 1987

Dear JEF:

Thank you for your letter of 3-26-87. I consider it *great news* to hear that you are houseman and that you are entrusted with responsibilities and duties that require reliable and sound judgment. Congratulations! This is exactly the kind of external validating I need to judge whether you are making any progress or not. Ultimately, you will be the final judge of whether you have changed for the better and progressed according to your own internal standards.

I appreciate your concern about not being able to choose any particular course of study that would fit your skills and interests. It should not be too difficult to evaluate your aptitudes in various areas of endeavor. If you are interested in such an evaluation, let me know and I will send you the specific tests that evaluate aptitudes and interests. I do know that in terms of your visual-motor performance being quite a bit higher (20 points) than your verbal skills, you would make a terrific high-level technician, where your visual-motor excellence would be rewarded. No problem in, at least, evaluating your aptitudes. Let me know.

Keep up the good works! I am enclosing the next lesson and look forward to hearing from you soon.

Sincerely yours,
Dr. L

Lesson 7: Love

Name *JEF*   ID

1. What is the meaning of the word *love*? *To show compassion or devotion to another. To care a great deal about another's welfare.*
2. What does it mean to love one's self? *It means to care what is best for yourself and what may happen to you. Like having self-pride.*
3. What does it mean to love others? *It means you are expressing your compassion or devotion to the one you have this emotion for.*
4. Why should you love yourself? *If you didn't love yourself you wouldn't care about yourself and it would make it even harder to love others; which is essential in life.*

5. Why should you love others? *You should love others so you can be loved also. It is important to spread love to keep a peaceful society. The bible commands us to love thy neighbor.*

6. What happened to you the last time you acted out of love for yourself? *I had positive results. It is important to do this because one must look out for what is good for himself first.*

7. What happened to you when you failed to love someone, including yourself? *Immediate negative results. When you fail like this, you let down yourself and usually hurt someone else's feelings in one way or another.*

8. What would happen to you for the rest of your life if you are unable to love yourself? *I think you would gradually sink into a deep depression and lose the will to live or just do valuable things to society.*

9. You have a choice to either show love or to fail to show it. Which of these choices do you like and why? *Definitely to show love. I like to see a smile or a person shine when he or she sees that I am showing love toward them.*

10. If you have to choose between giving and getting love, which choice would you like and why? *I really enjoy being loved but I would honestly have to say, giving, because I just immensely enjoy making others happy by giving and showing love. It's just part of me.*

11. How can you receive love if you do not give it? *You may temporarily receive it but that will wear off. You can't get something for nothing and that goes for love most of all.*

12. Is it better to give than to get love? Why? *Yes, I think so. I think this because I believe if one gives love he will get the love he deserves in return. If you are giving love, people recognize this and many want to return the favor. It goes back to, you must give in order to receive.*

13. During the next week, keep track of how often you failed to show love. What happened to you? What happened to others? Give at least four examples.
    a. *I let myself get upset and got into an argument with an inmate when I could have just explained calmly. I felt bad that I cut him down and he was angry at me for awhile.*
    b. *I got a little upset when my sister didn't call my lawyer for me for the second time. I felt badly and she did also but just explained it was a mistake and misunderstood me.*
    c. *There was a group picking on a weaker inmate and I let it go on when I usually don't. I felt I betrayed him and he felt alone, I could tell.*
    d. *My cellmate asked me to write his girl again because he doesn't write English well and I said I was busy with my letter and he got someone else to do it. I felt selfish and he was angry. We resolved it by agreeing to do it after I finished mine.*

14. Also during the next week write down the times you were successful in showing love to others. What happened to you? Give at least three examples.
    a. *When my girlfriend baby-sitted for my sister on the Northside, I called to make sure she was okay and to be sure she made it home safe. I felt good about showing I love her.*

b. *I gave my income tax check to my fiancee to buy herself some new clothes for summer. I felt good that I showed her I cared and was grateful for the times she left money for me.*

c. *I gave an indigent inmate, who is a good fella, some snacks and cigarettes. I felt good about helping and showing I loved and cared for him even if he didn't have anything from people on the outside.*

April 7, 1987

Dear Dr. L:

I sincerely appreciate your letter of March 31, 1987. I am quite interested in the tests that would evaluate my aptitudes and interests. A high-level technician sounds interesting but I'm not too sure what that would involve. I don't know how I would land a job as one even after I received the training unless a school had some sort of job placement program. I want so much to be a success and when I'm free I will work my hardest to achieve that goal. I will also need to know the fee for any of these tests. I am completely broke except for my income tax return and my girlfriend uses that to send me money for the store in here and personal clothing I might need. That is one reason I am hoping I can be placed in a conversion center to work and earn money before I am released. From what I understand this happens in the final stages of incarceration if they even allow me. It would sure help having a little something to at least get some transportation when I'm released. I believe it will help me adjust to the outside (society) better also. I'll be on my own when released so I really can't run up any medical bill while I'm here. Do you understand? I hope so. Thank you for your help, sir.

Your Social Training patient,
JEF

April 7, 1987

Dr. L:

I am supposed to be moved to Henry County Jail either today or in the next couple days. I don't know what my cell number will be yet but the address is: 505 Hwy. 20 McDonough, Ga. 30253.

Thanks again,
JEF

P.S. Check with Mr. R (Attorney) if there is any problem. He will know exactly what you have a question about.

Lesson 8: Care

Name *JEF*   ID

1. What does the word *care* or *caring* mean to you? *To be concerned or show concern for someone or something. It is one of the most precious words to live by in life.*

2. Why should you or anybody else care about you? Give at least four reasons why:
   a. *I should care about myself because I need to be concerned about what happens to myself in order to succeed in life.*
   b. *I should care about myself because if I didn't I would be making it even harder to care for others.*
   c. *I think my girl should care about me because she knows I care a great deal for her and without caring we can't have love.*
   d. *I believe others should care about me because I always try to care for others when the situation calls for me to do so.*

3. What happens to you if you do not care about yourself? *If you don't care about yourself you are self-destructive and it is also hard to care for anyone which is very detrimental.*

4. What happens to you if others do not care for you? *I would feel unwanted and down. I would wonder what can earn myself some caring and try to gain it by actions.*

5. How do you show care for yourself? Write down at least four examples of how you show you care for yourself.
   a. *I for one just bathe and keep up my personal hygiene.*
   b. *I don't get involved in anything that could be damaging to me or my character now.*
   c. *I try to voice my opinion and let it be known where I stand on issues so a decision for a group doesn't hurt me.*
   d. *I don't let my temper go out of control because that usually leads to detrimental results.*

6. How do you show care for others? Write at least four examples of how you take care of others.
   a. *I always call and see how my family and girlfriend are doing so they can still know I care about their welfare.*
   b. *I always try to give a little something from the store to indigent inmates who have less than me.*
   c. *I try to help other inmates with problems of getting in touch with their people by phone with help from my girlfriend.*
   d. *I write my cellmate's letters for him because he cannot write English well.*

7. What happens to you if you care for yourself? Write down at least four results.
   a. *I feel like I am accomplishing a task when a situation calls for me to care for myself and I do so.*
   b. *I feel like I gain some self-esteem and pride.*
   c. *I get positive results that benefit me in the long run.*

    d. *Others realize that caring for myself is good and it is recognized in my reputation.*

8. What happens to you if others care for you? Write down at least four results.
   a. *I feel wanted and good inside.*
   b. *I immediately begin to think of how I can show care for them in return.*
   c. *I feel like I must be valuable to someone if they show some caring for me.*
   d. *It makes me see good in my fellow man when he reaches out to care for me.*

9. What happens to you when you fail to care for yourself? Give at least four results.
   a. *You lose that pride and good feeling inside of yourself.*
   b. *You leave yourself open to be run over by others.*
   c. *You give a signal to others that you don't care about much if you don't care for yourself.*
   d. *You can easily have not caring for yourself lead to something negative and detrimental to you personally.*

10. What happens to you when others fail to care for you? Give at least four results.
    a. *You feel like that person has something against you or something.*
    b. *In some instances you do without something.*
    c. *It can and has made me bitter when someone fails to care for me.*
    d. *You feel unloved and kind of isolated. You begin to wonder why they wouldn't care and try to overcome the problem.*

11. In the next week write about four times when you showed care for yourself (without taking the care away from others).
    a. *I kept up my personal hygiene all through the week to prevent any vermin from infecting me.*
    b. *I went to court and behaved at my best in order to be respected and show I cared about what happens.*
    c. *I had a chance to break the rules and benefit temporarily but I chose not to and did what I knew was right.*
    d. *I completed this lesson as I do every week to try and help myself be better in many ways. It is a whole lot easier to care for yourself when you know what is inside yourself.*

May 1, 1987

Dear JEF:

I have delayed an answer to your last letter and completed lesson on Care because of your impending move to Henry County. Your attorney told me you had been transferred to Alto. Repeated phone calls to obtain your latest address were not answered. Consequently, I have decided to answer your last letter and send you the next lesson, Seeing the Good, in care of your attorney, who should forward it to your latest address. I hope you receive it. Let me know ASAP that you have indeed received it!

While I was in Henry County Courthouse, I ran into the nurse from CCDF who told me how much you had changed for the better. Reports like this make the whole enterprise worthwhile! Keep up the good works, wherever you are.

As far as placement tests that I could give you, we will need to wait for the following reasons: (a) I do not want to interfere with whatever the prison system is doing to place you; (b) I have no idea what your future will be, therefore, it will be very difficult to plan and place someone if I do not know *where to place them and for how long;* (c) it is important that you finish this program before confusing it with other programs. Remember what I told you when I first saw you. If and when you finish this program, *especially,* if you do not have anything else to do, you could become an *instructor* for *Social Training* for inmates who cannot read or write. Naturally, I would help you as you go.

I hope all these moves have not been hard on you. Let me know how you are doing and keep on working on Social Training. I hope it will pay off for you!

Sincerely yours,
Dr. L

Lesson 9: Seeing the Good

Name *JEF*   ID

1. What does seeing the good mean to you?   *It means looking into a situation or inside a person and searching for the positive aspects even though negative ones might be more recognizable.*
2. Can you see the good in you? How?   *Yes, definitely. I know what is inside me and goodness is in my heart. Everybody has a few bad points but I recognize my good ones from how I behave now.*
3. Can you see the good in all others you know?   *Yes, I think so. If I get enough time to talk with them, I can find goodness in them. Some just cover it up, but it's still there.*
4. What happens to you when you fail to see the good in yourself? Write down four results of this failure.
   a. *I may become manipulated in doing something illegal or wrong.*
   b. *I could hurt others' feelings by reacting without goodness at something they do.*
   c. *I would feel like I let myself down after I failed to see good because I knew it was there.*
   d. *I could lose control of my rehabilitation if I continued to fail to see good in myself.*
5. What happens to you when others fail to see the good in you? Write down at least four results of this failure.
   a. *You feel judged without all the facts weighed and kind of cheated.*
   b. *I stop and think that I may not be showing there is good in me and try harder to show just that.*
   c. *When others fail to see the good in you it may frustrate you enough to make the good more evident.*
   d. *I would confront them and show how I stand and that there is good in me also, just as I believe there is good in him.*

6. What happens to you when you see the bad in yourself? List at least four results that work against you.
    a. *It can make me feel down that I even carry bad with me.*
    b. *I can see the bad in myself from these crimes I committed and the results are prison and sorrow for me and loved ones.*
    c. *I can become shut out by some people if I see bad in myself because they can see it too.*
    d. *It doesn't help you inside because it is negative and doesn't create any good feelings for me.*
7. What happens to you when you see the bad in others? List at least four results that work against you.
    a. *Very tough question!! I see how others might think this as "cool" and it tends to draw others but you have to turn away.*
    b. *When someone steals from me here I become mad at first which is not really good for me.*
    c. *I become filled with vengeful feeling when something bad is seen in others but instead should try harder to see good.*
    d. *You see bad in others constantly here in Alto and I try to show them it's not necessary but it can sometimes result in a serious fight or a gang of them against you then.*
8. Why is seeing the good better than seeing the bad? Give at least four reasons.
    a. *It just simply makes one feel better about life in general when looking for good and positive things instead of bad.*
    b. *It kind of rubs off usually on others if you practice this enough.*
    c. *It gives you a sense of love in your heart and caring enough to look for positive and good things in a person.*
    d. *It helps you everytime you practice it so that problem situations become easier to handle when the good is searched for.*
9. In the next few days write down at least four instances when you saw the good in yourself and how you felt.
    a. *I helped out a weaker boy who is always picked on and tried to show the agitators how unnecessary and foolish it was.*
    b. *I became very mad when a guy tried to show how bad he was to me but I instead just worked my way out with goodness instead of fighting.*
    c. *I help guys out here when I can with stamps, shampoo, or whatever I can spare and it makes me feel good and them also.*
    d. *I tried to comfort a guy who was crying because he missed home and left a pregnant wife. It made him and me feel better.*
10. Write down at least four times when you saw the bad in yourself and how you felt after you did.
    a. *I went along and laughed at a boy that is less fortunate than me and felt terrible about jumping on that "bandwagon."*
    b. *I lied about my past once and immediately felt bad about it.*
    c. *I lost my temper at a guy who was a poor sport and cut him down when I could have handled it differently.*
    d. *I talked once in lunch line and felt bad because I try to set sort of an example. I went without eating so I don't talk even when questioned.*

11. What did you learn from this lesson? List at least four results that helped
you.
    a. *It helped me to remember to focus on the good which I try to do now.*
    b. *It reminded me alot of situations that relate directly to this lesson and will
       aid me in handling them.*
    c. *I learned about how other people look at you and how important it is to make
       the good in yourself identifiable.*
    d. *It helped me realize how you can get caught up in wrong things if you don't
       practice seeing the good.*

May 16, 1987

Dear Dr. L,

As you know, I am now imprisoned in Alto and it is nothing like I've experienced in my lifetime. They put on a big front (officials here) of how this place
is improving and it may be in some ways but it has a long, long way to go. About
3/4 of the guards seem to bring their problems at home or somewhere else here.
Some of them like to engage in unjust and sometimes cruel punishment.

The biggest problem are the inmates themselves though. It's kind of like a
war for power here and there is stabbing, raping, and stealing quite often in
here. It's definitely not what I had in mind for rehabilitation. It makes it especially
hard to concentrate on these lessons and even more since I'm still in the
diagnostic unit. I guess the Lord has a reason for sending me here. It's truly
a struggle. I would like to ask you a favor. I would like for you to check with
my attorney and be sure that your report on me has been sent to the Pardons
and Parole Board. I'm having people send letters to testify to my character and
I think yours will be one that will carry alot of weight. I would sincerely appreciate
it if you could do that for me, sir.

I will try my damndest to continue with the lessons because I really enjoy
working with them and how they deal with my self. I'm sorry it has taken so
long to get back into contact but it has been hell adjusting to this place. I hope
you understand.

Your faithful trainee,
JEF

May 25, 1987

Dear JEF:

I appreciate your letter of May 16th very much. I understand how you are finding
yourself in an extremely tough situation that is going to be a real trial for you.
If you can make it there without losing control of yourself, keeping in mind
everything that you have learned so far, hopefully, you will be able to make it
on the outside. In the meantime, keep up the good work, working step by small
step on Social Training, as you are doing now.

I have called your attorney to make sure that my report on you has been or will be forwarded to the Pardons and Parole Board. *If* and when you finish this Social Training program, and if you show an improvement on the test I gave you (which I will give you again at the end of the program), *I promise you that I will go personally to this board* and make available to them the results (if they are positive, of course!). In other words, I will go to bat for you and do all I can to see that you get a fair shake. OK?

I am enclosing the next lesson on Forgiveness. I am looking forward to hearing from you soon. Hang in there! I know it is very hard for you, as well as all the others. Do not let others drag you down to their level! Keep your counsel and stick to the principles you, hopefully, have learned.

Sincerely yours,
Dr. L

Lesson 10: Forgiveness

Name *JEF*   ID

1. What does it mean to forgive? *It is to overlook a wrongdoing by someone. To pardon them.*
2. When is the last time you forgave yourself? *That's tough because I usually ask for forgiveness from God and I forgive myself then. I forgave myself after prayer yesterday for telling a lie.*
3. When is the last time you forgave another? *I forgave a guy in here for trying to steal from me last week.*
4. What happened to you when you forgave yourself? *I feel a sense of cleanness and humbleness inside me. It clears my mind and helps me to better understand what I did wrong.*
5. What happened to you when you forgave another? *I felt sincerely good about it instead of feeling hatred by holding a grudge.*
6. Are you worthy of being forgiven? Why? *Yes, I think so. I believe this because everyone is capable of making mistakes and I would want to be forgiven because I always try to forgive others.*
7. How do you know or how can you show that you have really forgiven? *I express it first by words and maybe a handshake here. You know you have when you don't have that chip on your shoulder and you can still socialize without a mental block preventing you from doing so.*
8. Can you learn from your past mistakes? If you have really forgiven yourself you will not be able to make the same mistake twice. Why? Give four examples of how forgiveness helped you in avoiding making the same mistake twice.
   a. *I made the mistake of getting into drugs and I forgave myself and since then I've had the opportunity here and have walked away.*
   b. *I made the mistake of stealing and since I've been locked up I haven't stolen one thing although I've been asked to help steal.*
   c. *I used to try and show power by starting fights when things didn't go my way but I've controlled myself.*

d. *I used to also get into groups or gangs that caused trouble and although I've been invited numerous times here I've declined.*

9. If you have not forgiven yourself, you will make the same mistake again and again. Write down at least four examples of how you make the same mistake again and again. What happened to you?
   a. *I make the mistake of letting the mass punishment here piss me off. It fills me with hatred for the guard that does it for awhile.*
   b. *I have a problem with saying "God damn" at times still almost subconsciously. I feel bad about saying it.*
   c. *I make the mistake of daydreaming when I should be listening at times. It annoys me but I'm improving on it.*
   d. *I make the mistake of laughing at some tricks guys play on weaker ones. I feel bad but recognize it and improving on it also.*

10. If you do not forgive yourself why should others forgive you? Give four examples of how this happened to you.
    a. *I was playing cards and was using a cheating trick I learned to win candy. I kept on until recently and didn't forgive myself or deserve forgiveness from anyone until I broke down and quit doing it and forgave myself.*
    b. *I never forgave myself for continuing to use cocaine, therefore, I didn't deserve forgiveness from others.*
    c. *I didn't forgive myself for stealing when I once stole and received stolen goods so I sure didn't deserve anyone else's forgiveness.*

11. During the next week keep track of and write down how many times you forgave yourself and others and what you felt after you forgave.
    a. *I forgave a guy for snooping into my personal business and he let me know it was a misunderstanding. I felt good inside that we could still settle it the right way and I practiced control in the situation.*
    b. *I forgave myself for laughing and going along with a trick they played on a guy. I felt better about myself and have refrained from "going along" since then.*
    c. *I forgave a guy for trying to steal my store goods while I was sleeping. I just let him know how I stand on that kind of thing and I won't hold a grudge and forgave him.*
    d. *I forgave myself for telling an untruth about my case in a conversation and have since then told the true story about it. I feel much better each time I do so.*

June 1, 1987

Dear Dr. L:

I am just about to finish your lesson on Forgiveness. It was interesting and, as always, helped me understand another part of myself. I am supposed to go out of this Diagnostic unit this week and into population as a working inmate. I was recommended to the G.I.I. Fire Department by my counselor but am not eligible right now because of my 10 year sentence. You have to be on minimum security and because of the amount of years I have, I am on close security. They say my security level can change in 6 months but my attorney said he thinks the most I'll do is 6 more months. I've already done 6 months. He said the only way I could have it changed was if I knew someone in Atlanta that rules on those things or possibly have someone speak on my behalf to the warden here. It is by far the best and most trustworthy detail here. I will ask my attorney for help and if you think you could be an influence, I would greatly appreciate any help. My diagnostic test scores and behavior have been tops. I'm ready for another lesson and look forward to hearing from you, sir.

Sincerely giving my best,
JEF

June 8, 1987

Dear JEF:

Thank you for your letter of June 1, reassuring me that you had received the lesson on Forgiveness. I am sending you the next lesson which is based on Forgiveness: Respect for Parents.

I was not aware that you were in for 10 years. That is a long time! I am sure you can make it much shorter with good behavior. As I told you in our previous correspondence, let us finish this program, take one of the tests I gave you the first time I saw you, and depending on the results of this test, I will tell you what I can realistically do for you. There is no question that you worked hard on Social Training. If the test comes out OK, I will be glad to either phone or write whomever you tell me to write or phone. If necessary, I will come to Alto personally to talk with whomever will listen to me! OK? I will not move a finger, however, until we have finished this program and you have taken that test again. I hope you are clear about what I am prepared to do for you.

I appreciate your continuing hard work. Remember, taking care of yourself is a full-time job. Do not let others do it for you! I am looking forward to receiving the enclosed lesson along with news on how you are doing there.

Sincerely yours,
Dr. L

June 17, 1987

Dr. L:

How are you today, sir? I'm still surviving here and thought I would write a note to just let you know that things are pretty much the same. I've been working every day but haven't had the chance to register for college because my high school transcript hasn't been sent here yet. My counselor said that I scored in the first and second level of college on most of the categories on the achievement tests they give you here in diagnostics so I was pleased with that. I'm still waiting to hear from the parole board concerning my tentative parole month so I'll at least have something to shoot for. My attorney said he was quite sure I wouldn't do any more than 12 months and I am working on seven now. By the way, I heard he had a mild heart attack or something of the sort and had to be hospitalized for awhile. Do you know how he is doing? If you get a chance to speak with him *please* give him my best and let him know I'm praying for his health to improve. I would appreciate that greatly! I just finished the lesson and am enclosing it. I'll be glad when I get the chance to put what I've learned about myself to work in the free world! Until then I'll just continue to use it in my rehabilitation. It's truly helped in alot of situations I've faced here. Thanks again and I hope you're having a great summer!!

Sincerely yours,
JEF

Lesson 11: Respect for Parents

Name *JEF*   ID

1. What was your mother or your major female caretaker like? Describe her in detail.   *Quite emotional but very understanding. Seemed to be a very proud Mom. Quite outgoing and above average intelligence. Caring and protective.*
2. How did she raise you? What kinds of methods did she use to discipline and/or control you?   *She was alone without a partner raising me and always did her best for me. She paddled and also took away privileges which worked well until I grew older.*
3. How close were you to her as you grew up? Check one:
   a. extremely close
   b. very close X
   c. close
   d. not close
   e. not at all close
   f. very distant
4. How did your mother (or caretaker) punish you?   *Once again she would scold, paddle, and take away privileges. She would always let me know with her attitude that I had not pleased her also.*
5. How did your mother (or caretaker) reward you?   *She might give me a special privilege and would always praise me for good works.*
6. Recall one particular example of your relationship with your mother that is especially painful and hurtful for you to remember.   *When I went to visit her in intensive care after an accident and all she was worried about was how my sister and I were doing.*
7. Recall one particular example of your relationship with your mother that was especially pleasant and pleasurable for you to remember.   *We all worked together and bought our first home of our own.*
8. How did you react to your mother? What did you do in reaction to her methods to raise you?   *I always thought about her ways in raising me and see now how sensible they were. I was a bit rebellious at times though because I felt cheated for not having a dad.*
9. What kind of feelings do you have left over about your mother or female caretaker?   *I love her with all my heart and plan to make her proud now that my head is clear again. I need her love and support just as I did when I was young.*

10. What do you think of your mother now? *She is one-of-a-kind in my book. She deserves all my love and I can never really repay her for supporting me through all this.*

11. What was your father or your major male caretaker like? Describe him in detail. *I saw my father very few times when growing up. He's a good, hard-working man from what I know. I don't know him well, though.*

12. How did he raise you? What kind of methods did he use to discipline and/or control you? *Never participated in raising me.*

13. How close were you to him as you grew up? Check one:
    a. extremely close
    b. very close
    c. close
    d. not close
    e. not at all close   X
    f. very distant

14. How did your father or male caretaker punish you? *N/A*

15. How did you father (or substitute) reward you? *N/A for the most part. He might say congratulations if I told him I did well in sports or something.*

16. Recall one particular example of your relationship with your father that is especially painful and hurtful for you to remember. *When I was telling him about how I did in football one time on the phone and all he was saying in response was how my stepbrother was doing in sports too.*

17. Recall one particular example of your relationship with your father that is especially pleasant and pleasurable to remember. *When we spent a whole day together when he came down for my sister's wedding.*

18. How did you react to your father? What did you do in reaction to his methods to raise you? *N/A—Once again, he didn't have anything to do with raising me.*

19. What kind of feelings do you have left over about your father or male caretaker? *They are mixed really. I love him because he is my father but I don't quite understand how he just kinda forgot my sister and I.*

20. What do you think of your father now? *He's a basically good man whom I love but there is still that empty space in our relationship.*

21. Can you forgive and forget what either of your parents may have done that is still painful and hurtful for you to recall? *I always try and practice forgiveness when it's deserved. I don't believe I can forget.*

22. What are you doing now that is better than either of your parents? *I am learning what makes me tick and how to control all modes of my behavior. I'm also living for the Lord a cleaner, better life for myself and my soul.*

23. If you cannot forgive them, how are you going to learn from your experience? *I do forgive them and I have learned and continue to learn what happened in my earlier years with my mom.*

24. If you cannot forgive them, how are you going to forgive yourself? *I don't believe you can truly start to forgive others until you can forgive yourself first.*

25. If you cannot accept and respect your parents as human beings who did the best they could under their situation at the time, how are you going to respect any kind of authority? *Once again, I never lost respect for my parents and I believe that respecting them starts you off to respecting other authority which I also respect when it is what I believe in.*

26. What happened to you in the past when you did not respect the importance of authority? List at least four specific examples.
    a. *I did not respect authority when I broke the law that has me incarcerated now. That in turn gave me what I deserved—prison time.*
    b. *I did not always listen to the wishes of my mother who was the main authority in my life. It usually got me detrimental results also.*
    c. *I was on a roll when the law didn't mean much to me for awhile and I let that disrespect tear down what I had built up for myself.*
    d. *Not respecting any authority in the past and being rebellious hurt me inside when I stopped and really thought about it. It led to a state of depression because I wasn't happy with myself.*
27. What is going to happen to you in the future if you do not respect or pay attention to authority? *The consequences could be as devastating as this incarceration. Once again it would tear down what rehabilitation I've worked hard to achieve.*
28. If you do not respect authority what will authority do to you? Who will lose? *They always make you pay and usually to the fullest extent for not playing by the rules. The loser is me for sure.*
29. During the next week list at least four examples of what happened to you when you did respect authority.
    a. *I was treated fairly by our cell guard when I showed him respect as both my elder and my authority.*
    b. *I was given an "E" slip for excellent behavior by my work supervisor when I showed him respect at all times.*
    c. *I was granted visitation privileges for two hours for respecting authority this week and showing I could live without getting into trouble in one of the toughest dorms.*
    d. *I was given half of a day off for complying to all of my detail authority's wishes and commands to the best of my ability the whole week.*
30. Comment on how important or unimportant this lesson was for you. What has this lesson meant to you? *It was both important and meant alot to me. The questions opened my eyes to some things that are overlooked and not thought about alot of times. As always, I also learned more about myself which is very important to my rehabilitation.*

June 30, 1987

Dear JEF:

Thank you for your letter of June 17, with news about you and your concern about your attorney. I did check with his wife and he may need surgery. I am sorry. He certainly appreciated your thoughts and prayers. I hope that his illness will not deter or detour your progress. I am hopeful that as soon as you finish this program, I can intervene more actively in your behalf.

You did very well on Forgiveness and Respect for Parents and Authority. You are absolutely right. We cannot forgive others unless and until we have forgiven ourselves and our behavior should show that we have learned from the mistakes we have forgiven. I am enclosing the next lesson and look forward to hearing from you soon. Keep up your spirits and do not give up on yourself. If you can enroll in any kind of course offered there, so much the better. Take as much as you can use that is offered.

Keep in touch. You know that I care about you as an important human being. However, you are the only one that can make your importance known to others positively. I am sure you see every day how one can flaunt one's importance negatively!

Cordially, as ever,
Dr. L

July 3, 1987

Dear Dr. L:

How are you today, sir? I haven't received any lessons lately so I guess you don't know that I've been transferred to another prison. I don't really know why I was placed here. I got some news last week that the parole board said I will be going home sometime before Christmas. I am presently trying my best to influence them with all the character references I can come up with. I am shooting for the earliest month possible before Christmas. The detectives from Henry County that worked my case have already gone up there to the board and I've asked a few others to write or call or perhaps even go in person. I would truly appreciate any help you could be also.

I've truly grown to realize what I can achieve and the lessons that I've completed have helped me tremendously in dealing with my behavior. It's hard to put it all in words but I do know in my heart I can now cope with the outside world and am eager to show what a success I can be.

This prison is even poorer as far as living conditions go than Alto and there is definitely a lot of racial tension in the air. I'm so tired of coping with all of it but I just try to apply all that I've learned in order to just live halfway peacefully. You can believe that prison is harder than most people think it is. I know I've seen that much already.

Well, I've got to clean up but I'm looking forward to starting on the next lesson. Again, I would appreciate any and all help and influence you could be on my behalf, Dr. L, and I hope this letter finds you in the best of health.

Sincerely yours,
JEF

July 16, 1987

Dear Dr. L:

I just finished your lesson on Situations and it is enclosed. It has helped to remind me to always focus on the helpful aspects in a given situation. I'm looking forward to the next one.

I've gotten a job as supply orderly here and it is one of the better and more trustworthy jobs in the institution. I also made the state softball team and we are traveling to Jackson this Saturday to play in the state tournament for institutions.

Well, about all I can say is I sure do miss home as usual but I'm determined to make it through all this with a lesson learned. I hope you are enjoying the summer and, by the way, if you talk to my attorney be sure to send him my best wishes for recovery, please. I need to close but hope to hear from you soon, sir.

Cordially yours,
JEF

Lesson 12: Situations

Name *JEF*   ID

1. What is a situation? *It would be the combination of different conditions at a certain time or given moment.*
2. Who controls situations that hurt you? *I would say that I have the majority of the control because I would be the one to place myself in the situation.*
3. Who is responsible for situations that happened to you? *I am responsible for putting myself into situations. It's a matter of proper timing and choice.*
4. How much are you responsible for situations that hurt you? *There is almost always influence by other parties but I hold the key on how to handle the situation.*
5. How much are you responsible for situations that help you? *Once again, there may be some influence from others involved but it is up to me on the decision as to what to do and how to react.*
6. Who determines whether a situation is helpful or hurtful to you? *I am because I must first kind of analyze how to go about toward the problem and then I would try to determine what would most help me and go for that.*
7. Whether a situation is helpful or hurtful to you depends on how you behave in those situations. Write down four situations where you behaved helpfully. What happened to you then?
    a. *I had a chance along with a few other guys to get a job at Coca-Cola Bottling and I prepared myself and got it.*
    b. *I was asked by a coach to try out for the county track team and trained myself well and accomplished some goals of my own.*
    c. *I was in a situation to make good money in a car sales deal at my work and sold a business account by studying.*
    d. *I once declined to drink at a party after a lot of pressure and drove home and made it clear through a license check.*
8. Write down four situations where you behaved hurtfully. What happened to you then?
    a. *I got into an argument with another inmate and didn't walk away. It caused tense feelings between us for awhile.*
    b. *I was presented with some trying times last year and broke laws instead of using a constructive way out.*
    c. *I had some cocaine offered to me last year and instead of turning away I broke down and did it.*

    d. *My Mom needed my help and I was too self-centered to realize it and now she is having problems I could have helped with.*

9. For the next week write down when you were responsible for four situations that were helpful to you.

    a. *I was in a situation where I had a chance to get a very good work detail and I reacted positively to land the job.*

    b. *I got a chance to try out for the state softball team and worked hard and used discipline to make the team.*

    c. *I had a guy ask me for more clothes at my supply job and I explained I couldn't and the officer was happy the way I handled it.*

    d. *I cleaned up one night when the officer asked someone else and I got rewarded with a phone call home.*

10. For the next week write down when you were responsible for four situations that were hurtful to you.

    a. *I didn't stay to myself when a guy was starting trouble and it resulted in an argument.*

    b. *I didn't follow a rule by forgetting to take off my hat inside the cell and had it taken for a day.*

    c. *I had a chance to earn a slip for a phone call but didn't clean up because I went to bed.*

    d. *I went for a gambling trick and let myself get into a situation where I lost some store goods yesterday.*

11. You have the power to choose whether a situation is going to be helpful or hurtful to you. Which of these choices do you want and why? *I definitely would choose the helpful side. I want to always make the best of a situation by applying the correct behavior I've learned. I want to seek the positive paths in a situation. It makes life better for me and easier to cope as I go along and I may even profit in alot of ways.*

12. If you get hurt in a situation, how should you behave afterward? Should you hurt those who hurt you? If you do, what would happen to you? *I would try to seek out how I went wrong and find a way to improve the next time. I try and learn a lesson from it. I wouldn't retaliate and try to hurt back because it gets you on a downhill negative path when other situations come later on. You can get negative attitudes that stick with you and become detrimental to your self.*

July 23, 1987

Dear JEF:

I want to congratulate you for getting a new job, for getting on the softball team, and for slowly finishing up this program!

    I conveyed to your attorney your best wishes and he thanks you. As soon as we finish the program and have the results, I will let him know, as well as your superintendent (or warden).

    Keep up the good works and let me hear from you soon. I am enclosing the next lesson.

Sincerely yours,
Dr. L

July 31, 1987

Dear Dr. L:

I just finished my lesson and thought I would drop a line to let you know I'm still doing great considering my situation. I've been working every day and have been also studying sociology from texts I've checked out at the library. I'm trying to get my work detail changed to recreation aide so I can start lifting weights again.

I'm glad to hear my attorney has recovered and is back in the swing of things. My prayers were answered. The warden of this institution is a man named G. L. since you asked.

Yes, there is a guy I talk with quite a bit here who is very interested in the Social Training program. He is a very intelligent and all-round good fella. He is serving a 5 to 10 year sentence for vehicular homicide. He's not your typical hardened convict and comes from a loving family. I explained to him what the program consists of and it has benefited me. He knows that there is a fee and he said that he's sure his folks would finance it when he got the details from you. I also explained to him that it is very important to be honest for that is the only way you can evaluate him and that he will benefit only with deep thought and honesty. If you would like me to pass information on to him that would be fine or you could write him yourself. His name is K. A., EF-000 is his state number and his address is the same as mine. He is 19 years old, if that matters or is needed by you. He is sincerely interested from what I can tell and I really would like to see him get this help. He has tremendous potential as a person to be something, just as I believe I do, and if the program helps him better understand his inner self and behavior like it has me, that would be just great. Let me know what you think in your next letter.

I hope things are going good for you, sir, out in that big, free world and I hope to be a part of it myself soon. It's over 100 degrees in these dormitories at times so that makes living conditions miserable but I try to stay busy reading and writing to keep my mind off it. I will make it though! I'll be looking forward to hearing from you soon. The parole board is currently investigating my case so I'd like to have your report on me in there to perhaps influence them to parole me. Times are tough at home and I am needed. I hope and pray it's not too much longer but you can bet I'll continue to work hard and will *never* give up!

Your sincere student,
JEF

Lesson 13: Actions and Decisions

Name *JEF*   ID

1. What does it mean to act?   *To act would mean to produce an effect on a situation. To conduct one's behavior is to act, I believe. It can also mean to pretend.*
2. What does it mean that a person is known by his or her actions?   *It means that a person is judged by his or her behavior in any given circumstance—they gain a reputation from it.*

3. What kind of actions get you into trouble? List four actions that got you into trouble in the past.
   a. *Carelessness on my part when a temptation came to get into stolen goods.*
   b. *I acted foolishly when I began to indulge in drugs because I was sort of depressed.*
   c. *I acted without proper thought when I quit my job and went to making money illegally.*
   d. *I was reckless when I started to just put off responsibilities in order to have fun with so-called friends.*
4. What kind of actions get you some good? List four actions that got you some good in the past.
   a. *I put hard work into my job at Coca-Cola every day and was promoted after a summer.*
   b. *I, at one time, declined to get into drugs and it kept me feeling good and out of trouble.*
   c. *I studied the Toyota product feverishly and prepared myself for sales success.*
   d. *I saved and got a car financed in my own name, which made me feel responsible and mature.*
5. Who chooses whether your actions will be hurtful or helpful, you or others? *I choose because I have the opportunity to see the pros and cons in a situation and then make my choice.*
6. What happens to you when you let others control your actions? Give three results of how you let others control your actions.
   a. *I let others influence me to do drugs again when they showed me "false" happiness.*
   b. *I let others lure me into getting into illegal deals because it looked so easy and gave me time to be lazy.*
   c. *I began to drink and drive again because I would party with others and they thought if you were careful it was all right.*
   d. *When I let others control my actions I become irresponsible and lose my self-identity and pride.*
7. Why should you be helpful? List four reasons for being helpful.
   a. *Being helpful always seems to benefit me because it gives me a feeling of goodness and caring inside.*
   b. *It benefits others and gives you that respect people like to achieve.*
   c. *It lets others know that you are caring and loving toward them.*
   d. *It shows that you're unselfish and responsible enough to lend a real helping hand when they are in need.*
8. What happens to you when you behave hurtfully? List four results from your behaving hurtfully.
   a. *It contradicts anything you might work for that may show you can behave helpfully.*
   b. *I hurt others that may care about me when I behave hurtfully.*
   c. *It gives you a feeling of emptiness from being uncaring.*
   d. *I am incarcerated for behaving hurtfully so that should show how negative it is to do so.*
9. If you behave hurtfully toward others, why should you expect others to behave helpfully toward you? *You can't expect that because it's human nature for people to want to be treated like they are treated.*

10. Who is responsible for your behaving helpfully? What happens to you then? *I am responsible and it always gives me a feeling of accomplishment and boosts my pride.*

11. Who is responsible for your behaving hurtfully? What happens to you then? *I am responsible once again and it always ends up being detrimental to my inner self.*

12. During the next week write down at least four times when you did something helpful. Report what happened to you then.
    a. *I helped a guy with a personal problem just by listening and giving my best advice. It made me feel good about myself.*
    b. *I helped a guy with an overload in his work detail and he was grateful and I was satisfied with myself.*
    c. *I helped a guy out of debt and it made me feel good to keep him from being hurt but I also got a chance to advise him on the danger he can get in.*
    d. *I gave a guy some soap and toothpaste that was stolen and it gave me that "good Samaritan" feeling.*

13. During the next week write down also four times when you did something hurtful. What happened to you then?
    a. *I behaved out of control and lost my temper which made me look as bad as the guy who provoked me.*
    b. *I judged a guy unfairly, which I try never to do, and it got us started on the wrong foot toward each other.*
    c. *I acted without thought when my sister told me some bad news and it hurt her feelings.*
    d. *I didn't listen completely to a guy's story when he was snooping in my belongings and it almost ended in a fight.*

14. If you had the choice to do something hurtful or something helpful, which is your choice and why? Give at least four reasons for your choice.
    a. *I try to be helpful because of the wholesome good feeling I get inside each time.*
    b. *I choose to be helpful because the bible states to do so and that's what I believe in.*
    c. *I choose to be helpful because I enjoy the smiles and happiness others may get.*
    d. *I choose to be helpful because of the way it benefits me inside and the way it tends to come back to help me whenever I may be in need of help from others.*

August 8, 1987

Dear JEF:

Thank you for finishing Lesson 13. You are gradually becoming aware of how you have behaved in hurtful ways toward yourself, let alone others. We are approaching the end of the program and I am enclosing Lesson 14. Two more to go after this one!

I certainly appreciate your suggesting this other young man, K. A., to me. If he is interested, have him write to me directly at the same address. This program costs $240. However, $80, one-third of the cost, is refunded if and when he completes the program. He would have to complete the MMPI (personality test) before, after, and 3 months after the end of the program. If he wants to do it and is willing to pay for it, he can contact me. If there is a problem with the cost of the program, let him discuss it with me.

I am looking forward to your successful completion and hopeful rehabilitation. As I told you, once I get the results of the second test after completion, and if the results warrant it, I will advise your warden, attorney, and the Pardons and Parole Board about it. You certainly worked very hard and should be very pleased and proud of yourself.

I am enclosing the next lesson and looking forward to its completion.

To you, my very best,
Dr. L

August 14, 1987

Dear Dr. L:

I just finished my lesson on Feelings and Emotions and I'll tell ya, it really had me thinking. It gave me such a bright perspective on my behavior when it comes down to acting on my true feelings and emotions. It may sound funny but a lot of these lessons, especially the ones concerning how I react to situations, seem to apply directly to me. I don't think there are really right and wrong answers to most of the questions. I just put down what I truly feel. They are helping me in a great many ways and I thank you for your help.

Well, I'm still making it all right here. I can't wait to go home and if they don't go off the grid sheet guidelines, it shouldn't be too much longer. I hope you are doing well and will be looking forward to the next lesson.

Cordially, your student,
JEF

Lesson 14: Feelings and Emotions

Name *JEF*   ID

1. What are feelings and emotions to you? *Feelings and emotions relate directly to each other. They are your personal opinion. Some are stronger than others.*
2. List as many feelings and emotions as you can. Ask other people if you need help. Keep adding to this list as many names of feelings and emotions as you can get.

a. *love*	h. *doubt*	o. *calm*	v. *flattery*
b. *hatred*	i. *proud*	p. *callous*	w. *bitter*
c. *upset*	j. *contempt*	q. *fulfillment*	x. *friendly*
d. *giving*	k. *peaceful*	r. *evil*	y. *reckless*
e. *fear*	l. *confused*	s. *brash*	z. *compassion*
f. *cry*	m. *envious*	t. *regret*	
g. *trust*	n. *secure*	u. *satisfaction*	

3. Why are feelings and emotions important? Give four reasons for their importance.
   a. *They are a tool that lets one express himself totally.*
   b. *Without feelings and emotions the world would be meaningless because there would be no cause to strive for anything if you didn't have emotions to feel good about it.*
   c. *They give us a code to live by in that we try and respect others and yearn for the same in return.*
   d. *They give us personal identity. Everyone's feelings and emotions are different and we are subsequently judged by them.*
4. What happens to you when you do not stay with your feelings and instead you go into action right away? *The effect is usually detrimental because I'm not acting by what is truly in me.*
5. What happens when you cannot split your feelings and emotions from your actions? Give at least four examples of when that happened to you.
   a. *I've gotten into fights before by acting reckless and putting my feelings and emotions in the pits.*
   b. *I've felt depressed and thus acted foolishly by breaking the law and causing this imprisonment.*
   c. *I felt sort of abused and started acting harsh and abusive toward my mother.*
   d. *I had a feeling of wanting to be accepted by so-called friends and acted without good sense a lot of times.*
6. What happens to you when you confuse feelings and emotions with actions? Give three examples of what happened to you.
   a. *I became resentful toward my father by confusing the two and it didn't help the situation for either of us.*
   b. *I acted irrational when I began to get back into drugs and demoralizing myself. I let the feeling of depression rule my behavior.*
   c. *I let the two get mixed up by doing wrong in my work habits and thus quit and lived recklessly until I was locked up.*
   d.
7. What has happened to you, then, when you went into action as soon as you felt something? Was it helpful or was it hurtful? *I would have to say more hurtful then helpful because I went strictly on impulse and didn't take time to evaluate what's best for me.*
8. Why, then, should you (and everybody else) split feelings and emotions from actions? Give four reasons why you should.
   a. *I should because going with just what you feel first is not always best. I should see what makes me feel that way then act in a way that will show control.*
   b. *If I go with my first emotion in a situation I can easily hurt someone else's feelings.*
   c. *I should because even though I have a strong feeling about something I should still evaluate the best way to behave first, under any circumstances.*
   d. *We are judged by our actions and if I act on feeling or emotion without thinking it out, I would be foolish a lot of times.*

9. What have you concluded from the questions in this lesson about feelings and emotions and actions? *The questions had me in deep thought to be honest and opened my eyes as to how easy it is to be wrong by emotions alone and future guidance.*

10. During the next week, write down four times when you were hurt by jumping into action without staying with your feelings.
    a. *I truly feel that my fiancee loves and cares for me but when she didn't do a very important favor I became upset with her, but came to find out she was quite ill that day.*
    b. *I got mad at a guy I work with here when he was a poor sport instead of just explaining first what he was doing then to perturb me and the others.*
    c. *I got upset and let a guy know it when he kept pestering me about trading store items with him when I should have kept control.*
    d. *I went along with others not caring about another guy because he did something they didn't like instead of pointing out his problem to him. I eventually did because my feeling was to help him.*

11. During the next week write down four times when you were helped by staying with your feelings and avoided jumping into action.
    a. *I was offered marihuana by some guys here but declined because I knew it was wrong.*
    b. *I didn't start a fight with a guy in here when he said something I really disliked. I kept control and avoided the trouble.*
    c. *A guy tried to coax me into tricking an officer so we could do something right then but knew that was also wrong and declined to help him.*
    d. *I had a chance to make some extra store goods by giving a guy extra supplies but I didn't because I felt it was wrong.*

August 26, 1987

Dear Dr. L:

I just finished the lesson on Thinking and it has made me realize how important it is to use proper thought before acting. It may sound like a rerun but the lessons you are sending are applying to my life directly. They make me look back and see how different things would've been if I had practiced a lot of the things. Thanks!

I recently talked with my counselor here and he said I'm doing very well and he also read out the criteria I had to meet for a time cut and when he was through I met all of the requirements. I had excellent behavior and work habits here in prison and he said that he is going to put in for a 90 day time cut from my tentative parole month. Now I am just waiting on a grid sheet that will tell me my TPM. It's supposed to be here in September so whatever month it says, the time cut will take effect and knock off three months! I could be going home soon if things work out. Ninety days is the maximum you can get cut so I'm happy with that.

I hope you're doing fine and things are going well for you. Thanks again and I look forward to hearing from you.

Sincerely striving for success,
JEF

Lesson 15: Thinking

Name *JEF*   ID

1. What is thinking?   *It is when you form a thought or opinion in your mind. Sort of forming a mental picture.*
2. What does thinking do for you? List four things that thinking does for you that cannot be done by any other parts of you.
   a. *It helps you evaluate what to do and how to act on a given situation.*
   b. *It lets you plan first what you might want to do.*
   c. *It allows you to imagine things in many different ways before acting.*
   d. *It is a personal thing that allows you to have secrecy on how you believe without exhibiting it in any way if you don't choose to.*
3. What happens to you when you do not think? Give four results that come from your failure to think.
   a. *It will make you act on a situation when you haven't evaluated what is best for you and that could be detrimental.*
   b. *You can show ignorance when you don't think and that puts you down.*
   c. *You are apt to make many mistakes when you act without proper thought.*
   d. *Again, you could hurt others from not thinking and acting on a situation.*
4. What happens to you if you do not think before you act? Give four results that came from your failure to think before acting.
   a. *Again, you could hurt others from not thinking and acting on a situation.*
   b. *You show irresponsibility possibly when you act and don't think about what you're doing first.*
   c. *When you act before thinking you are apt to be showing a lack of knowledge when it could be the opposite if you thought first.*
   d. *You can show reckless behavior from acting spontaneously. It's damaging to your appearance in a situation. Simply makes you look bad.*
5. What is the difference between poor thinking and good thinking?   *Poor thinking shows irresponsibility, lack of control and knowledge. Good thinking shows the desire to do the best and plan your actions.*
6. Would you accept that good thinking leads to helpful behavior while poor thinking leads to hurtful behavior? Give four times when you used poor thinking that led you into trouble.
   a. *I used poor thinking when I let myself act foolishly and take drugs instead of taking the time to think about what would be best for me.*
   b. *I used poor thinking when I let myself get into fights in the past instead of thinking of a way to solve the misunderstanding.*
   c. *I went along with others and chose to drink and drive because of poor thinking. All I had to do was think about how stupid it was.*

d. *I thought poorly when I began to break the law instead of thinking of a proper way to solve my needs.*

7. Give three times when good thinking got you out of trouble.
   a. *I was offered drugs again here in prison and declined because I thought about how it would damage me.*
   b. *I was supposed to spray paint a rival school with others but I thought about the trouble I could get in and if it was done to me how much I would dislike it.*
   c. *I was offered the chance to do a big robbery with others but I thought about the negative things it would lead to.*

8. During the next week, list four times when you thought poorly. What happened to you?
   a. *I thought poorly when I let a guy have an extra sheet and he got caught and I was leaving myself open for trouble from my stupidity.*
   b. *I argued with a guy about what cleaning should be done and it almost led to a fight because I didn't think of the right things to say to get my point across.*
   c. *I thought poorly when I pushed a guy out of my face for accusing me of something I didn't do over and over and it made me feel bad after he found out the truth. I acted foolishly.*
   d.

9. During the next week, list four times when you used good thinking. What happened to you?
   a. *I refused to let a guy have extra supplies because I knew it was wrong.*
   b. *I helped a guy out of a jam by thinking hard and proper about what would be the best for him to do.*
   c. *I had a meeting with my counselor and used good thinking by planning out what I had to say and thus when everything came together I was put in for a 90-day time cut.*
   d. *My lady wrote me about a problem she had and I used good thought evaluating and using what I learned to handle it. Without good thinking the results could have hurt us emotionally.*

August 28, 1987

Dear JEF:

Thank you for completing the lesson on Thinking. You completed it very well! I am enclosing an additional lesson on Anger because I believe this area needs to be considered to make the Social Training program more effective. Tell me what you think about it. To show my appreciation for working so well on the program, I am also enclosing the LAST lesson of the entire program! CONGRATULATIONS! As soon as I receive these two lessons back, I will send you the MMPI to see whether there has been an improvement or not.

I would appreciate it if you could send me, or have it sent, information *in writing* about your progress in the penal system. They will need your written permission to send me this information. It will be crucial to have it in addition to the MMPI results. I hope you can do it.

Of course, I am delighted by the possibility that you may be released as soon as a few weeks or months. We will need to work on your reentry into society to make sure that it is smooth and working for you instead of against you. What issues will you face? economically? emotionally? employment? I would appreciate your preparing a *realistic* detailed plan for how you are going to succeed rather than fail. Work on this plan after you take the MMPI and submit it when you are finished with it.

Cordially yours,
Dr. L

September 6, 1987

Dear Dr. L:

I just finished the lesson on "Putting It All Together" and must say it summed up all that I've been working for. I can't thank you enough! I have put in a request to see my counselor but it usually takes awhile. The best thing to do, if you have time, would be to call here and ask for him and tell him about the report you need. He has been helpful to me and I'm sure he would be the same to you. His name is Mr. Z and he is here Mon.-Fri. Please let me know what you decide or what happens.

Also, I have another guy who is interested in the Social Training program but his is an entirely different situation from K.A.'s. He is a black guy, named D. B., serving 2 concurrent life sentences for armed robbery. He is a friend of mine and it is really hard to imagine him as a "dangerous" man on the street. I've talked to him about it and he is very interested. He knows he needs the help just as I did. He will write you this week. I hope you don't mind me referring these guys to you, let me know if so. I would like to see him better himself since he has the desire.

I'm still waiting to hear when I may be leaving, and working every day except Saturday and Sunday. I hope you are doing well and I hope to hear from you soon, sir. Take care!

Sincere as ever,
JEF

Lesson 16: Putting It All Together

Name *JEF*   ID

If you have come this far, you should be congratulated for finishing this program. Congratulations! You deserve a good pat on the back!

1. What have you learned since you worked on this program? *A lot more than these 2 lines can hold. I learned ways of handling situations and cleared up confusions in my everyday life.*

2. Did you reach your goal, as stated in Lesson 1?
   a. If yes, how? *Yes, because I understand now how I "operate" inside and how I can handle difficulties that come about in my life.*
   b. If no, how? *N/A*
3. Why did you choose to change? Give at least four reasons for changing.
   a. *I was definitely depressed with myself and wanted the change in order to live with some satisfaction about myself.*
   b. *I was doing reckless things that hurt me and others and I wanted to change and put all that in the past.*
   c. *I was eager to show what I'm truly made of and capable of and that could only be achieved by making a change.*
   d. *I'm craving happiness and success and with a change I believe that it is going to happen.*
4. If you did not learn anything from this program, what reasons do you have for failing it? Read the reasons below and rank them from 1 to 11 from the most important reason (Rank 1) to the least important reason.

   I FAILED BECAUSE　　**(NOT APPLICABLE)**　　*RANK NUMBER*
   a. I am unable to use this program.
   b. I did not do the homework right.
   c. This program was too hard for me.
   d. I did not use the homework.
   e. I do not care about myself.
   f. I like to make excuses for myself.
   g. I am afraid to grow up.
   h. I like to fail and lose.
   i. If I win I may need to become independent.
   j. I like to stay dependent on others.
   k. (Write your own reason)

5. Which lesson from this program did you like the best and why? *Feelings and Emotions was my favorite lesson because it seemed to deal with me directly, answered questions about dealing about myself.*
6. Which lesson from this program did you like second best and why? *Control was also a favorite lesson because I needed a lot of work on that and it gave me guidelines to go by.*
7. Which lesson from this program did you like the least and why? *Every lesson was beneficial to me. Some were more difficult than others. I liked and looked forward to all of them.*
8. Which other lesson from this program did you not like and why? *(See No. 7)*
9. List all of the things that you want to do and can do that will do something good for you in the future.
   a. *I can make a plan for my future in an occupation now because I have the right state of mind and have a better idea of what I'll be best at.*
   b. *I want to be a success in life and can do that because now I've become aware of what controls me and that's me and my desire to go for what I want.*

    c. *I want to love and share my life with my lady and can do that now that I have control of myself and my behavior. I would have been unable to love and support her because I couldn't do it for myself.*

    d. *I want and always have wanted to help others and that is possible now that I know what it takes to change.*

THANK YOU FOR FINISHING THIS PROGRAM. YOU CAN BE VERY PROUD OF YOUR ACHIEVEMENT!

Supplementary Lesson: Anger

Name *JEF*   ID

1. What does anger mean to you? *It is an emotion of disgust concerning anything that may happen to me. It is a loss of control by one if he lets it overtake good thinking.*

2. What do you do when you get angry? *I let out the frustration I have for what I'm angry at. I used to lose control and that can be hurtful. Now I try my best to solve the problem without an outburst.*

3. When do you get angry? *When something seems to be done by someone to hurt me or someone else directly.*

4. How often do you get angry? *I do get angry at times but when I do I try to control it and look for a better solution.*

5. Please rate your anger:
    a. Little X
    b. Some
    c. A lot
    d. A great deal

6. Does your anger control you and your life or do you control it? *I control it because if you let it control you, you behave hurtfully and recklessly.*

7. What would you like to see happen: learn how to control your anger or have your anger control you? Why? *Definitely learn how to control my behavior which I practice every time a situation arises because it shows one has control is not a reckless "hot-head." When anger controls you, detrimental results always seem to come about.*

8. What will be the costs of your anger controlling you and your life? Name at least three costs of your anger controlling you.
    a. *You fail to live with love in your heart for others and yourself.*
    b. *Others tend to see how anger is controlling you and stay clear of you because you could hurt them.*
    c. *You do reckless things that will always hurt you and others. It gives you a bad reputation and leads to trouble.*

9. What will be the rewards of your learning to control your anger? Name at least three rewards that would take place if you learn to control your anger.
    a. *You gain respect by showing how you control the situation without blowing up. Shows maturity.*

b. *You keep yourself out of trouble a lot of times when you control anger. Avoid fights.*

c. *You feel good inside and it continues to build up your control when you practice every time the situation calls for it.*

10. If you let your anger control you, what will happen to you for the rest of your life? *You will continue to live reckless and it will start to take less to make you angry, therefore, trouble and detrimental things will happen over and over.*

11. Please complete the following sentences:

a. I get angry when *I am lied to.*

b. I get angry when *someone hurts me or my family.*

c. I get angry when *I play anything with a poor sport.*

d. I get angry when *I lose self-control.*

e. When I get angry I *always stop and look for a proper solution.*

f. When I get angry I do *let them know it.*

g. When I get angry I say *why I am angry and question why it was done.*

12. During the next week keep in touch with your anger and keep track of situations that get you angry. Write down at least four instances of how you handled your anger and what happened to you afterward.

a. *I got angry at a guy for trying to steal from me but I controlled it and let him know why I was angry afterward, although it was obvious.*

b. *I lost control once when a guy grabbed a drink from me and almost fought with him. We stay away from each other still.*

c. *I got angry at an officer when he confused me with another and made me do a detail but I did it and then explained to the officer the truth and he apologized.*

d. *A fella I work with in supply wasn't helping out with the work so I was angry but just tried to explain what he was doing wrong to him and what his attitude was accomplishing and it ended up helping out.*

13. What would happen to you if you were to express your anger *immediately and through words rather than through deeds?* During the next week try to say: "I AM ANGRY!" as soon as and whenever someone or something makes you angry. It is important that you record and report at least four instances of your saying "I AM ANGRY!" during the next week.

a. *A guy kept trying to turn the channel from what we were watching on TV just to be spiteful. I remembered to say "I am angry" and walked away while he was acting up.*

b. *Two guys were picking on a weak guy and I almost jumped in but I said "I am angry" and then I went over and talked good sense to the guys.*

c. *A guy tried to take advantage of my detail supervisor and instead of blowing up at the guy I said "I am angry" to myself then went to him afterward and got back what he lied for.*

d. *A guy kept prying into my personal business and I was angered by it and told myself "I am angry" and then thought of a way to explain to him why I was angry.*

14. Plan ways and means of expressing your anger helpfully (for you and others) rather than hurtfully (to you and others). In the future, when I get angry I will:

a. *Stop and evaluate what it will take to overcome the problem that angered me.*

  b. *Not blow-up, instead I will try to explain why I'm angry and see if we both can help each other.*
  c. *Use the ways of control that I've learned and see if we can reach an understanding in a mature way with whoever angered me.*

September 11, 1987

Dear JEF:

It is with a great deal of pleasure and anticipation that I am enclosing the MMPI for you to take and return as soon as possible. I am keeping my fingers crossed! Remember that I will need to readminister the same test three months from now to see whether any changes that may have taken place, as a result of the program, are holding up!

I cannot contact your counselor unless he has written permission from you to communicate with me *in writing,* since my records must be *in writing.* If he could send me information about your behavior during the last three months, I would appreciate it.

I appreciate very much your continuous recruitment of possible new blood! I will work with anyone you recommend, provided they are motivated and can, in one way or another, pay for my time. I will make individual contracts and try to work with them according to their specific circumstances to the best of my abilities. OK?

I hope you are making specific, detailed, and realistic plans for your release. I would like to see them in writing if you can do it. Let me hear from you as soon as you can. I will then let you know the results as soon as I score the test! If the results are good, I will let other people know about them. I still need your written permission to publish these results if they are positive, with a complete guarantee of your anonymity.

I cannot tell you how much I appreciated working with you and I look forward to working with you as soon as my services are necessary.

Sincerely and gratefully yours,
Dr. L

September 20, 1987

Dear Dr. L:

How are you today? I just finished the test and man, could I ever see a difference in the way I looked at some of the questions. I hope it shows in the evaluation! Let me know as soon as possible.

I hope this letter does what you need to acquire the information on me. That is the way my counselor said to write it to you. All you need to do is call him here I would guess. Also, when the results are in I'm hoping that you can make the parole board aware of my progress, if there is any. I don't see how there couldn't be for I sure feel 100% better and am anxious to start applying what I've learned out there in the "free" world.

I will send my goals and specific plans for when I'm released as soon as I hear from you about the results of the test. I'm just starting another helpful course here by the name of Science of Success by the Napoleon Hill Foundation. It is sort of like your Social Training course and 10 of us are in it from the entire institution. It can't hurt and I'm eager for knowledge.

Once again, I'm hoping you can help me out with a good report to the parole board and I also want to let you know how much I really appreciate your time and help. You are a man I truly look up to and I promise to show what a change I've made as I continue to strive for success. Thank you so much!

Sincerely,
JEF

October 4, 1987

Dear JEF:

I wish I were able to write positively about your test results. Unfortunately, I am afraid that I communicated my anxiety about them to you and you tried very hard, so hard in fact, that your profile does not seem significantly any better than the profile taken before the program. I think you tried to make a good impression and to appear superhuman and supergood! You did not need to answer that way. I am sorry!

However, there are still two alternatives of finding out whether the program has done any good: (a) get information from Mr. Z and see what he says, and (b) take the MMPI in three months to see whether changes have taken place.

These negative results indicate that we should keep on our toes. You will need to be very, very clear and realistic about what you are going to do when you are released. I hope you will be able to outline *in writing* your plans for the immediate and long-range future. I will need to know where you will be in three months so that I can give you the MMPI again.

Have you given any thought to the possibility of teaching Social Training to those inmates that cannot read or write? If you can get a group interested and willing to pursue further training on a consistent basis (one hour a week for 16 weeks), I will be glad to send you a copy of the program to see whether it can be used for group training. You would read the questions, they would answer, and you would assign to them what they have to do from week to week. I am aware that it would require careful selection of people seriously motivated to improve their past self-destructive ways of behavior. What do you think?

Keep up the good work!

Sincerely yours,
Dr. L

GEORGIA DEPARTMENT OF CORRECTIONS

October 21, 1987

RE: JEF

Dear Dr. L:

In response to your inquiry of October 4, 1987, I am pleased to inform you that inmate JEF has managed to present himself as a model inmate since his arrival here at Youthful Offender Correctional Institution. Not only has he managed to stay clean of disciplinary actions, but in all aspects of his life here, he has demonstrated a willingness to do more than is required. He has earned incentive awards (awards made for performing in an above-average fashion in a 30-day period) on his job and in the dormitory. He is a very enthusiastic member of the self-help group, Science of Success, and is currently enrolled in college classes this quarter. He participates in the institutional softball team which placed second in the playoffs.

Inmate JEF has and continues to demonstrate a control of impulsivity and a desire to achieve success.

I hope this information is helpful to inmate JEF in his collaboration with you.

Sincerely,
L.Z.
Counselor (OR)

November 5, 1987

Dear JEF:

This letter is to let you know that I have received the most glowing response from your counselor, Mr. Z. He indicates that you have been an exemplary, model inmate. I am extremely happy about this report and I hope that your behavior will carry outside of the prison setting.

Please do keep in touch because I will need to give you the MMPI again to see whether I can document more objectively if changes have taken place after completion of the program.

Please let me know if there is anything else I can do to help you.

Cordially,
Dr. L

November 5, 1987

Dear Dr. L:

I'm sorry for delaying so long in responding to your letter but I've been thinking about it and have also been quite busy trying to gain my freedom. My counselor put me in for a 90-day time cut and with my tentative parole month of February, 1988, this would be the month if it is approved. I'm keeping the faith.

I was extremely puzzled by you saying my test results were negative. As I read the questions I could see the difference from the last time I took the test. You said I appeared to try and be supergood but that wasn't my intention. I'm not here to con anyone. I have instilled a positive mental attitude within myself with the help of Social Training and a course named Science of Success that I'm taking here. Example: Do you like women who smoke? I honestly don't like smoking by anyone but I answered the question, "Yes," because I do not dislike anyone for *smoking* or any other reason really. I may not like their actions but I still like them as a person. I used the same frame of mind on all the questions and I definitely see how they differed greatly from the first test I took. Anyhow, my counselor said he has replied to you and just has to get it approved by his supervisor. I'm sure he gave me an excellent recommendation for I have given great effort in rehabilitating myself. I hope what I've been trying to say makes sense. I feel in total control of myself and have gained self-discipline I needed badly.

I cannot yet give you an outline on my long-term goals when I'm free but this is my plan when I do gain freedom. I will live with my common-law wife and her parents at first, and will begin working at a construction company or an electrical company I've had offers from. I will immediately enroll in college, at Clayton State probably, to further my education and prepare myself for my occupation of choice. I also plan to get my own apartment and if things work out as planned I will marry in 1988. My father and grandparents are going to give me financial help if needed but I don't count on it. I can and will make a success of myself regardless, and am learning constantly on how to go about it and to recognize opportunity. Life is a learning process and I'm eager to make my own great contribution, not to just merely exist. I hope you are doing well, sir, and hope to hear from you again soon. I appreciate any help you can be to me and thank you for all you've done so far.

Your sincere student,
JEF

November 13, 1987

Dear JEF:

Your last letter of November 5, 1987, must have crossed with my latest one to you concerning Mr. Z's glowing report about you.

I am glad to hear that you are planning to "keep the faith." I am sure you answered on the MMPI as well as you possibly could. Unfortunately, I have to go by what I see on this test, *as well as* the report from Mr. Z. This is why we need to take it another time, to insure that perhaps the previous results were invalid. This test serves as a baseline to evaluate any possible changes, like the thermometer and fever! I do not want you to spend your time worrying about it, because that would be a waste of energy that you could use in more constructive directions! OK? I will send the test back to you as soon as the three-month period has passed. However, I want you to answer it as well as you can, but not controlled by it. Do you understand?

I am very pleased with how you are doing and all your plans to build your life once you leave jail. Keep in touch and keep the faith!

Sincerely yours,
Dr. L

December 13, 1987

Dear JEF:

I hope everything is all right with you and that you are getting set for the day you will be released. I am writing to ask you three separate and distinct favors. First, I would appreciate it if you could retake the MMPI for a third time. I am aware that this process is hard on you. However, just answer as well as you can and do not let it get to you. It is absolutely crucial that I have this third administration to show how well you have done.

Secondly, in working with you and other young people in trouble, I have failed thus far to deal with the important issue of teaching *goal setting.* Consequently, I have written a whole lesson for this purpose. You can make as many copies of this lesson as you please, so that you can use it on a daily, weekly, monthly, and yearly basis. I would like to see your answers so that this lesson can become an integral part of the Social Training program. I could use any extra feedback you can give me on this lesson, to improve it.

Thirdly, I would like to receive, on a separate piece of paper, your written permission to publish your record of work and examinations with the *absolute guarantee of anonymity.* No one ever will know or could find out because I will change pertinent facts in the case, so that no one could trace this case to you. Please keep this letter in your file as my personal guarantee of complete confidentiality. I hope you can trust me on this matter. Just write that you allow publication under conditions of confidentiality and anonymity.

I look forward to receiving the MMPI back, your completed lesson on goal setting, and your permission to publish your case under the conditions I have personally guaranteed. Please, let me know if there is anything else I can do to help you. I wish you a relatively Happy Xmas and hope that the New Year will be a good one for you and your family.

Sincerely yours,
Dr. L

January 16, 1988

Dear Dr. L:

I first would like to apologize for being so late in returning this work to you. I've had such a hectic time at work and with trying to get word on my parole date that I've gotten behind in my studies and Social Training. I also had to cram to finish my Science of Success course. Anyhow, I've been sent back up here to Clayton County jail for a year-old misdemeanor charge. I went to court yesterday and Mr. R had it dead-docked so I should now be paroled any day. I'm anxious to start on my goals and definite major purpose. The lessons on Goals you sent covered it very well. It should definitely be a plus factor for the course. You might ask what one intends to give in return for the realization of their goals. Also, caution students to keep their plans to themselves, for the most part, to avoid negative influence from others because of envy, jealousy, or other negative thoughts. This would be especially important with younger people, I would think.

Concerning your request for my permission to publish my case. I have no problem at all with it but there are a few things I would like to talk about concerning it first. I should be free within a week so I will contact you immediately afterward. I thank you, once again, for your help. With hard work and a positive mental attitude, I will achieve great feats for myself and perhaps benefit others along the way. Thanks again, sir!

JEF

Social Training: Lesson on Goal Setting

To be administered after completion of the program to decrease possibilities of relapse. Setting goals is a very important activity. Without goals our lives would have no meaning.

Name *JEF*   ID

Daily Goals
1. Set your goal for today. What do you plan to do for today that will make this and every future day an important and exciting one for you?   *Today I plan to concentrate on bettering my speech instead of using so many slang words.*
2. How do you plan to reach your goal for today? Please explain in detail, even if the details do not seem important to you.   *I will pay attention to how I express myself in situations and use self-discipline to catch myself.*
3. Did you reach your stated goal? At the end of the day check on whether you did what you set out to do. Write down whether you did or did not. *Yes, I definitely did.*
4. If you reached your daily goal, write down in detail *how* and *why* you think you reached it.   *I put my mind to accomplishing the goal I set and didn't give up. I made it my desire to do it and used a positive attitude.*
5. If you did not reach your goal, write down how and why you think you did not reach it. What was in your way? How did *you* fail to reach it?   *N/A!!*

Name *JEF*   ID

Weekly, Monthly, or Yearly Goals
1. Now write down your goal(s) for this week (month, year). What do you plan to do this coming week (month, year) that will make this week (month, year) an important and exciting one for you?
   Goal 1. *To control all of the times I'm tempted to lie, even if just a "white" lie.*
   Goal 2. *To be more attentive when others are speaking to me even if I, at first, don't have a genuine interest.*
   Goal 3. *To budget my time to be most profitable to myself.*

2. Write down in detail how you plan to reach each of these three goals.
   Goal 1. *When the situation comes about that I am tempted to lie to spice-up a story, etc., I will stop then and be truthful with use of control.*
   Goal 2. *I will keep an attitude of enthusiasm or cheerfulness in order to focus on the speaker and maybe learn something in the meantime.*
   Goal 3. *I will devise a sort of plan on how I will separate my time in order to get things done that need done.*
3. At the end of the week check back on your answers to questions 1 and 2 and write down whether you think you reached or failed to reach your stated goals.
   Goal 1. *I definitely reached this goal!*
   Goal 2. *I've done* much *better but still not as well as I would like.*
   Goal 3. *Reached this goal and results were excellent!*
4. How did you reach your goals? Write down in detail how you did it.
   Goal 1. *I first convinced myself to be just that, myself. When I felt the temptation to fib, I would dash it.*
   Goal 2. *I used a different attitude toward the speaker in that I tried to focus in on his thoughts.*
   Goal 3. *I stuck to the format I set up on how I would use my time to get studies done and things I would put off otherwise.*
5. How did you fail to reach your goals? Write down how and why you think you failed to reach your goals.
   Goal 1.
   Goal 2. *At times I would be tired, etc. and wouldn't be in a listening mood and sort of shut the other off.*
   Goal 3.

For monthly or yearly goal setting, use the same sheets you have just used for weekly goal setting. Follow the same format for monthly or yearly goal setting you have used for weekly goal setting. Good luck!

January 17, 1988

Dear JEF:

I hope this letter will cross with your answer to my previous letter of a few weeks ago. Then I sent you a copy of the MMPI and goal-setting lessons to avoid the possibility of relapse and recidivism. Without a third administration of the MMPI, I would not be able to show any long-term change, that is, after three months from termination of the Social Training program. Goal setting is another crucial task without which there is always the possibility of relapse.

I hope to receive these materials back. I would like to receive them completed by you. However, if, for whatever reasons of your own that I cannot and will not fathom, you choose not to complete them, please send them back to me. I cannot give these materials away to anyone.

Please keep in touch and let me know how things are going with you.

Sincerely yours,
Dr. L

January 31, 1988

Dear JEF:

Thank you for completing the materials I sent to you. Your MMPI profile shows definite changes, even though it looks like you might have developed some physical symptoms without a clear physical basis. Your impulsivity still needs watching, while your thinking about reality could stand a small dosage of conventionalism.

All in all, you need to watch yourself carefully and make sure you set realistic goals you can meet successfully. You do not seem to cope well with failure and rejection. Hence, you need to make sure you write down in a very detailed fashion how you will react positively when you meet either one (because we all meet failure and rejection often in our lives).

As you know, I will be very interested in how you are getting along. Please drop a note from time to time to reassure me that you are doing all right. Let me know if there is anything else I can do to help.

Sincerely,
Dr. L

REFERENCES

Allport, G. W. (1942). *The use of personal documents in psychological science.* New York: Social Science Research Council.

Ascher, L. M. (Ed.). (1989). *Therapeutic paradox.* New York: Guilford.

Atkinson, R. C., & Wilson, H. A. (Eds.). (1969). *Computer-assisted instructions: A book of readings.* New York: Academic Press.

Baker, E. K. (1988). Use of journal writing for psychologists. In P. A. Keller and S. R. Heyman (Eds.), *Innovations in clinical practice: A source book,* Vol. 7 (pp. 269–282). Sarasota, FL: Professional Resource Exchange.

Baron, J. B., & Sternberg, R. J. (Eds.). (1987). *Teaching thinking skills: Theory and practice.* New York: W. H. Freeman.

Baucom, D. H., & Epstein, N. (1990). *Cognitive-behavioral marital therapy.* New York: Brunner/Mazel.

Beck, A. T., & Young, J. E. (1985). Depression. In D. H. Barlow (Ed.), *Clinical handbook of psychological disorders* (pp. 206–244). New York: Guilford.

Bepko, C. (1989). Disorders of power: Women and addiction in the family. In M. McGoldrick, C. Anderson, & F. Walsh (Eds.), *Women in families: A framework for family therapy* (pp. 406–426). New York: W. W. Norton.

Beutler, L. E. (1979). Toward specific psychological therapies for specific conditions. *Journal of Consulting and Clinical Psychology, 47,* 882–887.

Beutler, L. E., & Clarkin, J. F. (1990). *Systematic treatment selection: Toward targeted therapeutic interventions.* New York: Brunner/Mazel.

Birren, J. E., & Hedlund, B. (1987) Contributions of autobiography to developmental psychology. In N. Weisenberg (Ed.), *Contemporary topics in developmental psychology* (pp. 394–415). New York: Wiley.

Bok, S. (1982). *Secrets: On the ethics of concealment and lying.* New York: Pantheon.

Boyer, E. L. (1983). *High school: A report on secondary education in America.* New York: Harper & Row.

Broffenbrenner, U. (1979). *The ecology of human development: Experiments by matter and design.* Cambridge, MA: Harvard University Press.

Burton, A. (1965). The use of written productions in psychotherapy. In L. Pearson (Ed.), *The use of written communications in psychotherapy* (pp. 10–16). Springfield, IL: Charles C Thomas.

Butcher, J. N. (1990). *MMPI-2 in psychological treatment.* New York: Oxford.

Butcher, J. N., Graham, J. R., Williams, C. L., & Ben-Porath, Y. (1989). *Innovations in MMPI-2 interpretation: Development and use of the MMPI-2 content scales.* Minneapolis, MN: University of Minnesota Press.

Calam, R. M., & Elliott, P. A. (1987). Why are we "too busy"? Problems of practitioner research in family therapy. *Journal of Family Therapy, 9,* 329–337.

Capell-Sowder, K. (1984). On being addicted to the addict: Co-dependency relationships. In *Co-dependency: An emerging issue* (pp. 19–24). Pompano Beach, FL: Health Communications.

Chaneles, S. (Ed.). (1983). Current trends in correctional education theory and practice. *Journal of Offender Counseling, Services, and Rehabilitation, 7.*

Chernin, K. (1981). *The obsession: Reflections on the tyranny of slenderness.* New York: Harper & Row.

Clements, D. H. (1986). Effects of LOGO and CAI environments on cognition and creativity. *Journal of Educational Psychology, 78,* 309–318.

Clements, D. H., & Gullo, D. F. (1984). Effects of computer programming on young children's cognition. *Journal of Educational Psychology, 76,* 1051–1058.

Cusinato, M., & L'Abate, L. (research in progress). The validity and reliability of three measures of verbal abuse.

de Vries, B., Birren, J. E., & Deutchman, D. E. (1990). Adult development through guided autobiography: The family context. *Family Relations, 39,* 3–7.

Diem, R. A., & Knoll, J. F. (1981). Technology and humanism: New approaches in correctional education. *Journal of Correctional Education, 33,* 4–6.

Dinkmeyer, D., McKay, G. D., & McKay, J. L. (1987). *New beginnings: Skills for single parents and step-family parents.* Champaign, IL: Research Press.

Doane, J. A. (1985). Parental communication deviance and offspring. In L. L'Abate (Ed.), *Handbook of family psychology and therapy* (pp. 937–960). Homewood, IL: Dorsey Press.

Docherty, J. P. (1984). Implications of the technological model of psychotherapy. In J. B. W. Williams & R. L. Spitzer (Eds.), *Psychotherapy research: Where are we and where should we go?* (pp. 139–149). New York: Guilford.

Doub, G. T., & Scott, V. M. (1987). *Family wellness workbook: Survival skills for healthy families.* P.O. Box 3303, San Jose, CA, 95156.

Eck, M. (1970). *Lies and truth.* London: Macmillan.

Edwards, J. H. (1990). *Attrition in family and marital therapy: A decay curve approach.* Unpublished doctoral dissertation, Georgia State University, Atlanta.

Ellis, A. (1955). New approaches to psychotherapy techniques. *Journal of Clinical Psychology, 11,* 208–260.

Ellis, A. (1965). Some uses of the printed, written, and recorded word in psychotherapy. In L. Pearson (Ed.), *The use of written communication in psychotherapy* (pp. 21–29). Springfield, IL: Charles C Thomas.

Eysenck, H. J. (1952). The effects of psychotherapy: An evaluation. *Journal of Consulting Psychology, 16,* 319–324.

Fantuzzo, J. W., & Twentyman, C. T. (1986). Child abuse and psychotherapy research: Merging social concerns and empirical investigation. *Professional Psychology: Research and Practice, 17,* 375–380.

Farber, D. J. (1953). Written communication in psychotherapy. *Psychiatry, 16,* 365–374.

Foá, U., & Foá, E. (1974). *Societal structures of the mind.* Springfield, IL: Charles C Thomas.

Foley, V. D. (1984). Family therapy. In R. J. Corsini (Ed.), *Current psychotherapies* (pp. 447–490). Itaska, IL: F. E. Peacock.

Forest, J. J. (1988). Self-help books. *American Psychologist, 43,* 599.

Forward, S., & Torres, J. (1987). *Men who hate women and the women who love them.* Toronto: Bantam.

Foster, S., & Gurman, A. S. (1985). Family therapies. In S. J. Lynn & J. P. Garske (Eds.), *Contemporary psychotherapies: Models and methods* (pp. 377–418). Columbus, OH: Charles E. Merrill.

Fraizer, L. (1991). The usefulness of prescriptive programs to deal with MMPI-2 peak scores in undergraduates. Paper read at the annual GPA convention, Atlanta, Georgia.

Garfield, S. L. (1984). Psychotherapy: Efficacy, generality, and specificity. In J. B. W. Williams & R. L. Spitzer (Eds.), *Psychotherapy research: Where are we and where should we go?* (pp. 295–305). New York: Guilford.

Garfield, S. L., & Bergin, A. E. (Eds.). (1978). *Handbook of psychotherapy and behavior change: An empirical analysis.* New York: Wiley.

Garfield, S. L., & Bergin, A. E. (Eds.). (1986). *Handbook of psychotherapy and behavior change: An empirical analysis* (3rd edition). New York: Wiley.

Gelcer, E., & Schwartzbein, D. (1989). A Piagetian view of family therapy: Selvini-Palazzoli and the invariant approach. *Family Process, 28,* 439–456.

Giacomo, D., & Weissmark, M. (1987). Toward a generative theory of the therapeutic field. *Family Process, 26,* 437–459.

Gibbs, J. P. (1989). *Control: Sociology's central notion.* Urbana, IL: University of Illinois Press.

Glasgow, R. E., & Rosen, G. M. (1978). Behavioral bibliotherapy: A review of self-help behavior therapy manuals. *Psychological Bulletin, 85,* 1–23.

Gregg, L. W., & Steinberg, E. R. (1980). *Cognitive processes in writing.* Hillsdale, NJ: Erlbaum.

Griffin, C. W. (1982). *Teaching writing in all disciplines.* San Francisco: Jossey-Bass.

Gurman, A. S., & Kniskern, D. P. (Eds.). (1981). *Handbook of family therapy.* New York: Brunner/Mazel.

Hackley, J. C., & Hagan, J. L. (1975). Work and teaching machines as delinquency prevention tools: A four-year follow-up. *Social Science Review, 49,* 92–106.

Haley, J. (1984). *Ordeal therapy.* San Francisco: Jossey-Bass.

Hall, W. C. (1987). *The efficacy of the marital contracting approach to the treatment of remarried couples.* Unpublished master's thesis, Georgia State University, Atlanta.

Hansen, J. C., & L'Abate, L. (1982). *Approaches to family therapy.* New York: Macmillan.

Hart, J. T., & Tomlison, T. M. (Eds.). (1970). *New directions in client-centered therapy.* Boston, MA: Houghton Mifflin.

Hartley, J. (Ed.). (1972). *Strategies for programmed instruction: An educational technology.* London: Butterworths.

Hausser, D. (1976). *Application of computer-assisted instruction to interpersonal skill training.* Orlando, FL: Naval Training Equipment Center.

Hayes, S. C., Nelson, R. O., & Jarrett, R. B. (1987). The treatment utility of assessment: A functional approach in evaluating assessment quality. *American Psychologist, 42,* 963–974.

Holtje, H. F. (1988). Comment on Rosen. *American Psychologist, 43,* 600.

Howard, G. S., & Myers, P. R. (1990). Predicting human behavior: Comparing idiographic, nomothetic, and agentic methodologies. *Journal of Counseling Psychology, 37,* 227–233.

Howard, K. L., Krouse, M. S., & Orlinsky, D. E. (1986). The attrition dilemma: Towards a new strategy for psychotherapy research. *Journal of Consulting and Clinical Psychology, 54,* 106–110.

Howard, V. A., & Barton, J. H. (1986). *Thinking on paper.* New York: William Morrow.

Huston, T. L., & Rempel, J. K. (1989). Interpersonal attitudes, dispositions, and behavior in family and other close relationships. *Journal of Family Psychology, 3,* 177–198.

Johnson, T. B., Levis, M., & L'Abate, L. (1986). Treatment of depression in a couple with systematic homework assignments. *Journal of Psychotherapy and the Family, 2,* 117–128.

Justice, B., & Justice, R. (1976). *The abusing family.* New York: Human Science Press.

Kagan, J., & Moss, H. (1972). *From birth to maturity.* New York: Wiley.

Kahn, A. H., & Kamerman, S. B. (1982). *Helping America's families.* Philadelphia, PA: Temple University Press.

Kaplan, L. (1978). *Oneness and separateness: From infant to individual.* New York: Simon & Schuster.

Karasu, T. B. (1986). The psychotherapies: Benefits and limitations. *American Journal of Psychotherapy, 40,* 324–342.

Kazdin, A. E., Kratochwill, T. R., & VandenBos, G. R. (1986). Beyond clinical trials: Generalizing from research to practice. *Professional Psychology: Research and Practice, 17,* 391–398.

Kelley, P., & Williams, B. (1988). The use of assigned writings as an adjunct to therapy with individuals, couples, and families. *Journal of Independent Social Work, 29,* 298–299.

Kersh, B. J. (1964). *Directed discovery vs. programmed instruction: A test of a theoretical position involving educational technology.* Monmouth, OR: Oregon State System of Higher Education.

Kiesler, D. J. (1966). Some myths of psychotherapy research and the search for a paradigm. *Psychological Bulletin, 65,* 110–136.

Kiesler, D. J. (1984). The 1982 interpersonal circle: An analysis of DSM-III personality disorders. In T. Millon & G. L. Klerman (Eds.), *Contemporary directions in psychopathology: Towards the DSM-IV* (pp. 571–597). New York: Guilford.

Kinger, J., & Worcester, D. A. (1965). *The effectiveness of auto-instruction.* Tucson, AZ: University of Arizona.

Kochalka, J. (research in progress). *Validation of a scale to specify enrichment interventions* (tentative title).

L'Abate, L. (1968a). The laboratory method as an alternative to existing mental health models. *American Journal of Orthopsychiatry, 38,* 296–297.

L'Abate, L. (1968b). Screening children with cerebral dysfunctions through the laboratory method. In C. H. Haywood (Ed.), *The diagnosis of brain damage in school-age children* (pp. 128–158). Washington, DC: National Education Association.

L'Abate, L. (1969). The continuum of rehabilitation and laboratory evaluation: Behavior modification and psychotherapy. In C. M. Franks (Ed.), *Behavior therapy: Appraisal and status* (pp. 476–494). New York: McGraw-Hill.

L'Abate, L. (1973). The laboratory method in clinical child psychology: Three applications. *Journal of Clinical Child Psychology, 2,* 8–10.

L'Abate, L. (1976). *Understanding and helping the individual in the family.* New York: Grune & Stratton.

L'Abate, L. (1977). *Enrichment: Structured interventions with couples, families, and groups.* Washington, DC: University Press of America.

L'Abate, L. (1979). Aggression and construction in children's monitored play therapy. *Journal of Counseling and Psychotherapy, 2,* 137–158.

L'Abate, L. (1985). A training program for family psychology: Evaluation, prevention and family therapy. *American Journal of Family Therapy, 13,* 7–15.

L'Abate, L. (1986a). Prevention of marital and family problems. In B. A. Edelstein & L. Michaelson (Eds.), *Handbook of prevention* (pp. 177–193). New York: Plenum.

L'Abate, L. (1986b). *Systematic family therapy.* New York: Brunner/Mazel.

L'Abate, L. (1987a). The practice of programmed family therapy: A radical proposal. In L. L'Abate, *Family psychology: Theory, therapy, enrichment, and training* (pp. 109–121). Washington, DC: University Press of America.

L'Abate, L. (1987b). The practice of therapeutic writing. In L. L'Abate, *Family psychology II: Theory, therapy, enrichment, and training* (pp. 138–151). Latham, MD: University Press of America.

L'Abate, L. (1987c). Therapeutic writing through homework assignments. In L. L'Abate, *Family psychology: Theory, therapy, enrichment, and training* (pp. 123–136). Washington, DC: University Press of America.

L'Abate, L. (1990a). *Building family competence: Primary and secondary prevention strategies with families.* Newbury Park, CA: Sage.

L'Abate, L. (1990b). A theory of competencies x settings interactions. In D. G. Unger & M. B. Sussman (Eds.), Families in community settings. *Marriage and Family Review, 15,* 253–269.

L'Abate, L. (in press). A family model of coping. In B. N. Carpenter (Ed.), *Personal coping: Theory, research, and applications.* New York: Pergamon.

L'Abate, L. (in preparation). *The laboratory method in clinical psychology.*

L'Abate, L., & Bagarozzi, D. A. (in press). *Sourcebook for marriage and family evaluation.* New York: Brunner/Mazel.

L'Abate, L., Baggett, M. S., & Anderson, J. S. (1984). Linear and circular interventions with families of children with school-related problems. In B. S. Okun (Ed.), *Family therapy with school-related problems* (pp. 13–27). Rockville, MD: Aspen Systems.

L'Abate, L., & Boyce, J. (research in progress). The comparative usefulness of three depression workbooks.

L'Abate, L., & Brown, E. C. (1969). An appraisal of teaching machines and programmed instruction. In C. M. Franks (Ed.), *Behavior therapy: Appraisal and status* (pp. 396–414). New York: McGraw-Hill.

L'Abate, L., & Bryson, C. (in press). *A theory of personality development.* New York: Brunner/Mazel.

L'Abate, L., & Colondier, G. (1987). The emperor has no clothes! Long live the emperor! A critique of family systems thinking and a reductionistic proposal. *American Journal of Family Therapy, 15,* 19–33.

L'Abate, L., Farrar, J., & Serritella, D. (Eds.). (in press). *Handbook of differential treatments for addictions.* Needham Heights, MA: Allyn & Bacon.

L'Abate, L., Ganahl, G., & Hansen, J. C. (1986). *Methods of family therapy.* Englewood Cliffs, NJ: Prentice-Hall.

L'Abate, L., & Harel, T. (in press). Deriving a theory of developmental competence from resource exchange theory: Implications for preventive interventions. In U. G. Foá (Ed.), *Recent contributions and applications of resource exchange theory.*

L'Abate, L., & Hewitt, D. (1989). Power and presence: When complementarity becomes polarity. In J. F. Crosby (Ed.), *When one wants out and the other doesn't: Doing therapy with polarized couples* (pp. 136–152). New York: Brunner/Mazel.

L'Abate, L., & Jurkovic, G. (1987). Family systems theory as a cult: Boom or bankruptcy? In L. L'Abate (Ed.), *Family psychology II: Theory, therapy, enrichment, and training* (pp. 10–28). Latham, MD: University Press of America.

L'Abate, L., & Kunkel, D. (research in progress). Resolving the idiographic-nomothetic controversy: Concurrent validity and reliability of a problems in relationships scale.

L'Abate, L., & L'Abate, B. (1988). Women clients with resistant husbands: Some suggestions for therapeutic interventions. *Family Therapy Today, 3,* 1–4.

L'Abate, L., & Levis, M. (1987). Paradoxical therapeutic strategies: Current practice and research. In P. A. Keller & S. R. Heyman (Eds.), *Innovations in clinical practice, VI: A source book* (pp. 79–91). Sarasota, FL: Professional Resource Exchange.

L'Abate, L., & McHenry, S. (1983). *Handbook of marital interventions.* New York: Grune & Stratton.

L'Abate, L., & McMahan, O. (research in progress). Resolving the idiographic-nomothetic controversy: Concurrent validity and reliability of two theory-free rating scales.

L'Abate, L. & Milan, M. (Eds.). (1985). *Handbook of social skills training and research.* New York: Wiley.

L'Abate, L., & Platzman, K. (in press). The practice of programmed writing (PW) in therapy and prevention with families. *American Journal of Family Therapy.*

L'Abate, L., & Thaxton, L. M. (1981). The differentiation of resources in mental health delivery systems: Implications for training. *Professional Psychology, 12,* 761–768.

L'Abate, L., & Wagner, V. (1985). Theory-derived, family-oriented test batteries. In L. L'Abate (Ed.), *Handbook of family psychology and therapy* (pp. 1006–1032). Homewood, IL: Dorsey Press.

L'Abate, L., & Wagner, V. (1988). Testing a theory of developmental competence in the family. *American Journal of Family Therapy, 16,* 23–35.

L'Abate, L., & Weinstein, S. (1987). *Structured enrichment programs for couples and families.* New York: Brunner/Mazel.

L'Abate, L., & Young, L. (1987). *Casebook of structured enrichment programs for couples and families.* New York: Brunner/Mazel.

LaBier, D. (1986). *Modern madness: The emotional fallout of success.* Reading, MA: Addison-Wesley.

Lambert, M. J., Shapiro, D. A., & Bergin, A. E. (1986). The effectiveness of psychotherapy. In S. L. Garfield & A. E. Bergin (Eds.), *Handbook of psychotherapy and behavior change* (pp. 157–211). New York: Wiley.

Landsman, T. (1951). The therapeutic use of written materials. *American Psychologist, 6,* 347.

Lange, A., & van der Hart, O. (1983). *Directive family therapy.* New York: Brunner/Mazel.

Langley, R., & Levy, R. C. (1977). *Wife beating: The silent crisis.* New York: Dutton.

Lazarus, A. A. (1988). Right aim, wrong target. *American Psychologist, 43,* 600.

Leff, J., & Vaughn, C. (Eds.). (1985). *Expressed emotion in families.* New York: Guilford.

Leman, K. (1987). *The pleasers: Women who can't say no and the men who control them.* Old Tappan, NJ: Fleming H. Revell.

Levant, R. F. (1984). *Family therapy: A comprehensive overview.* Englewood Cliffs, NJ: Prentice-Hall.

Levant, R. F. (Ed.). (1986). *Psychoeducational approaches to family therapy and counseling.* New York: Springer.

Levis, M. (1987). *Treatment of depression through written homework assignments.* Unpublished doctoral dissertation, Georgia State University, Atlanta.

Lewis, J. M., Beavers, W. R., Gossett, J. T., & Phillips, V. A. (1976). *No single thread: Psychological health in family systems.* New York: Brunner/Mazel.

Luborsky, L., Christopher, P., McLellan, A. T., Woody, G., Piper, W., Liberman, B., Imber, S., & Pilkonis, P. (1986). Do therapists vary much in their success? Findings from four outcome studies. *American Journal of Orthopsychiatry, 56,* 501–512.

Luborsky, L., Christopher, C., Mintz, J., & Auerbach, A. (1988). *Who will benefit from psychotherapy? Predicting therapeutic outcomes.* New York: Basic Books.

Ludwig, A. M. (1965). *The importance of lying.* Springfield, IL: Charles C Thomas.

Lutz, J. R. (1985). *Empirical validation of a set of structured communication tasks with couples: Homework assignment/practice versus traditional workshop format.* Unpublished master's thesis, Georgia State University, Atlanta.

Mace, D. R. (Ed.). (1983). *Prevention in family services: Approaches to family wellness.* Beverly Hills, CA: Sage.

Maddi, S. (1985). Existential psychotherapy. In S. J. Lynn & J. P. Garske (Eds.), *Contemporary psychotherapies: Models and methods* (pp. 191–219). Columbus, OH: Charles E. Merrill.

Mahoney, M. J. (1988). Beyond the self-help polemics. *American Psychologist, 43,* 598–599.

Mahrer, A. R. (1986). *Therapeutic experiencing: The process of change.* New York: Norton.

Martin, H. P. (Ed.). (1976). *The abused child: A multidisciplinary approach to developmental issues and treatment.* Cambridge, MA: Ballinger.

Martin, J. (1983). *Gender-related behaviors of children in abusive situations.* Sarasota, FL: CARE Publishers.

Matarazzo, R. G., & Patterson, D. R. (1986). Methods of teaching therapeutic skill. In S. L. Garfield & A. E. Bergin (Eds.), *Handbook of psychotherapy and behavior change* (pp. 821–843). New York: Wiley.

May, R., & Yalom, I. (1984). Existential psychotherapy. In R. J. Corsini (Ed.), *Current psychotherapies* (pp. 354–391). Itaska, IL: F. E. Peacock.

Mays, D. T., & Franks, C. M. (Eds.). (1985). *Negative outcome in psychotherapy and what to do about it.* New York: Springer.

McKee, J. M., & Seay, D. M. (1968). *How to with PI: A systematic approach to the use of programmed instruction.* Vol. 3 of the Draper Project Final Report. Elmore, AL: Draper Correctional Center.

McMullin, R. E. (1986). *Handbook of cognitive therapy techniques.* New York: Norton.

Meador, B. D., & Rogers, C. R. (1984). Person-centered therapy. In R. J. Corsini (Ed.), *Current psychotherapies* (pp. 142–195). Itaska, IL: F. E. Peacock.

Meichenbaum, D. (1985). Cognitive-behavioral therapies. In S. J. Lynn & J. P. Garske (Eds.), *Contemporary psychotherapies* (pp. 261–286). Columbus, OH: Charles E. Merrill.

Mellody, P., & Miller, A. (1989). *Breaking free: A recovery workbook for facing codependency.* San Francisco: Harper & Row.

Mendenhall, W. (1989). Co-dependency definitions and dynamics. *Alcoholism Treatment Quarterly, 6,* 3–17.

Merley, S., & Laying, T. (1976). In-patient psychiatry and programmed instruction: Application and research in constructional theory. *Improving Human Performance Quarterly, 5,* 35–46.

Messinger, E. (1952). Auto-elaboration: An adjuvant technique in the practice of psychotherapy. *Disorders of the Nervous System, 13,* 339–344.

Meyers, C. (1986). *Teaching students to think critically: A guide for faculty of all disciplines.* San Francisco: Jossey-Bass.

Miller, I. J. (1989). The therapeutic empathic communication (TEC) process. *American Journal of Psychotherapy, 48,* 531–545.

Mitchell, R., & Thompson, N. (1986). *Deception: Perspectives on human and non-human deceit.* New York: State University of New York Press.

Monte, C. F. (1980). *Beneath the mask: An introduction to theories of personality.* New York: Holt, Rinehart & Winston.

Muehlenhard, C. L., & McFail, R. M. (1983). Automated assertion training: A feasibility study. *Journal of Social and Clinical Psychology, 1,* 246–258.

Nadelson, T. (1987). The inhuman computer: The too-human psychotherapist. *American Journal of Psychotherapy, 41,* 489–498.

Navran, L. (1967). Communication and adjustment in marriage. *Family Process, 6,* 173–184.

Norcross, J. C. (Ed.). (1986). *Handbook of eclectic psychotherapy.* New York: Brunner/Mazel.

Norwood, R. (1985). *Letters from women who love too much.* New York: Pocket Books.

Norwood, R. (1988). *Women who love too much.* New York: St. Martin's Press.

Nystrand, M. (1986). *The structure of written communication: Studies in reciprocity between writers and readers.* Orlando, FL: Academic Press.

O'Day, E. F. (1971). *Programmed instruction: Techniques and trends.* New York: Appleton-Century-Crofts.

Olweus, D. (1979). Stability of aggressive reaction patterns in males. A review. *Psychological Bulletin, 86,* 852–875.

Parham, J. D. (1974). *Training effect on helping relationship response tendencies of workshop para-professionals.* Unpublished doctoral dissertation, University of Wisconsin, Madison.

Parloff, M. B. (1986). Frank's "common elements" in psychotherapy: Nonspecific factors and placebos. *American Journal of Orthopsychiatry, 56,* 521–530.

Patterson, G. R. (1982). *Coercive family processes.* Eugene, OR: Castalia.

Pearson, L. (Ed.). (1965). *The use of written communication in psychotherapy.* Springfield, IL: Charles C Thomas.

Pennebaker, J. W. (1989a). Confession, inhibition, and disease. *Advanced Experimental Social Psychology, 22,* 211–244.

Pennebaker, J. W. (1989b). Stream of consciousness and stress: Levels of thinking. In J. S. Uleman & J. A. Bargh (Eds.), *Unintended thought* (pp. 322–350). New York: Guilford Press.

Pennebaker, J. W., & Beall, S. K. (1986). Confronting a traumatic event: Toward an understanding of inhibition and disease. *Journal of Abnormal Psychology, 95,* 274–281.

Pennebaker, J. W., Colder, M., & Sharp, L. K. (1990). Accelerating the coping process. *Journal of Personality and Social Psychology, 58,* 528–537.

Pennebaker, J. W., Hughes, C. F., & O'Heron, R. C. (1987). The psychophysiology of confession: Linking inhibitory and psychosomatic processes. *Journal of Personality and Social Psychology, 52,* 781–793.

Pennebaker, J. W., Kiecolt-Glaser, J. K., & Glaser, R. (1988). Disclosure of traumas and immune function: Health implications for psychotherapy. *Journal of Consulting and Clinical Psychology, 56,* 239–245.

Phillips, E. L. (1985a). *Psychotherapy revised: New frontiers in research and practice.* Hillsdale, NJ: Erlbaum.

Phillips, E. L. (1985b). *A guide for therapists and patients in short-term psychotherapy.* Springfield, IL: Charles C Thomas.

Phillips, E. L., Test, L. R., & Adams, N. M. (1964). Multiple approaches to short-term psychotherapy. *American Psychologist, 19,* 475.

Phillips, E. L., & Wiener, D. N. (1966). *Short-term psychotherapy and structured behavior change.* New York: McGraw-Hill.

Primakoff, L., Epstein, N., & Covi, L. (1986). Homework compliance: An uncontrolled variable in cognitive therapy outcome research. *Behavior Therapy, 17,* 433–446.

Progoff, I. (1975). *At a journal workshop.* New York: Dialogue House Library.

Progoff, I. (1980). *The practice of process mediation: The intensive way to spiritual experience.* New York: Dialogue House Library.

Raimy, V. (1965). The use of written communication in psychotherapy: A critique. In L. Pearson (Ed.), *The use of written communication in psychotherapy* (pp. 47–65). Springfield, IL: Charles C Thomas.

Ralmar, R. (Ed.). (1977). *Child abuse: Perspectives on diagnostic treatment and prevention.* Dubuque, IA: Rendal/Hunt.

Raskin, N. J. (1985). Client-centered therapy. In S. J. Lynn & J. P. Garske (Eds.), *Contemporary psychotherapies: Models and methods* (pp. 155–190). Columbus, OH: Charles E. Merrill.

Reid, J. B., & Hendricks, A. (1973). A preliminary analysis of direct home intervention for treatment of pre-delinquent boys who steal. In L. A. Hameslynck, L. C. Handy, & E. J. Marsh (Eds.), *Behavior therapy: Methodology, concepts, and practice* (pp. 209–220). Champaign, IL: Research Press.

Reiner, T. (1978). *The new diary.* Los Angeles: Tarcher.

Ricci, R. C. (1958). The status of the autobiography. *Peabody Journal of Education, 36,* 33–36.

Richmond, W. K. (1965). *Teachers and machines: An introduction to the theory and practice of programmed instruction.* London: Collins.

Rimm, D. C., & Cunningham, H. M. (1985). Behavior therapies. In S. J. Lynn & J. P. Garske (Eds.), *Contemporary psychotherapies: Models and methods* (pp. 221–259). Columbus, OH: Charles E. Merrill.

Rogers, C. R. (1957). The necessary and sufficient conditions of therapeutic personality change. *Journal of Consulting Psychology, 21,* 95–103.

Roid, G. H. (1974). Issues in judging the cost-effectiveness of self-instructional programs: A case study in programmed dental instruction. *Improving Human Performance Quarterly, 3,* 49–55.

Rosen, G. M. (1987). Self-help treatment books and the commercialization of psychotherapy. *American Psychologist, 42,* 46–51.

Roth, G. (1986). *Breaking free from compulsive eating.* New York: Signet.

Russ, D. A. (1991). The use of written homework assignments as a treatment for anxiety. Department of Counseling and Psychological Services, Georgia State University, Atlanta, GA. Ph.D. dissertation.

Sager, C. J. (1976). *Marriage contracts and couple therapy.* New York: Brunner/Mazel.

Scandura, J. M. (1984). Cognitive instructional psychology: System requirements and research methodology. *Journal of Computer-Based Instruction, 11,* 32–41.

Schaef, A. W. (1986). *Codependence: Misunderstood—mistreated.* San Francisco: Harper & Row.

Schwartz, R. M., & Garamoni, G. L. (1981). Cognitive balance and psychopathology: Evaluation of an information processing model of positive and negative states of mind. *Clinical Psychology Review, 9,* 271–294.

Scinto, L. F. M. (1986). *Written language and psychological development.* Orlando, FL: Academic Press.

Seltzer, L. F. (1986). *Paradoxical strategies in psychotherapy: A comprehensive overview and guidebook.* New York: Wiley.

Selvini-Palazzoli, M., Cirillo, S., Selvini, M., & Sorrentino, A. M. (1989). *Family games: General models of psychotic processes in the family.* New York: Norton.

Shaffer, E. E., Jr. (1954). The autobiography in secondary school counseling. *Personnel and Guidance Journal, 32,* 395–398.

Shaw, L. W. (1978). *A study of empathy training effectiveness: Comparing computer assisted instruction, structured learning training, and encounter training exercises.* Unpublished doctoral dissertation, Syracuse University, Syracuse, NY.

Shelton, J. L., & Levy, R. L. (1981). *Behavioral assignments and treatment compliance: A handbook of clinical strategies.* Champaign, IL: Research Press.

Sherman, R., & Fredman, N. (1986). *Handbook of structured techniques in marriage and family therapy.* New York: Brunner/Mazel.

Siegel, M. A. (1978). Computer-based education in prison schools. *Journal of Educational Technology Systems, 7,* 239–256.

Solly, R., & Lloyd, R. (1989). *Journeynotes: Writing for recovery and spiritual growth.* San Francisco: Harper & Row.

Spanier, G. (1976). Measuring dyadic adjustment: New scales for assessing the quality of marriage and new co-dyads. *Journal of Marriage and the Family, 38,* 15–28.

Starker, S. (1988a). Self-help "treatment" books: The rest of the story. *American Psychologist, 43,* 599–600.

Starker, S. (1988b). Psychologists and self-help books: Attitudes and prescriptive practices of clinicians. *American Journal of Psychotherapy, 42,* 448–455.

Stevens, E. F., & L'Abate, L. (1989). Validity and reliability of a theory-derived measure of intimacy. *American Journal of Family Therapy, 17,* 359–368.

Stiles, W. B. (1982). Psychotherapeutic process: Is there a common core? In L. E. Abt & I. R. Stuart (Eds.), *The newer therapies: A sourcebook* (pp. 4–17). New York: Van Nostrand Reinhold.

Strupp, H. H. (1986). The nonspecific hypothesis of therapeutic effectiveness: A current assessment. *American Journal of Orthopsychiatry, 56,* 513–520.

Strupp, H. H., & Bergin, A. E. (1973). New directions in psychotherapy research. In H. H. Strupp (Ed.), *Psychotherapy: Clinical, research, and theoretical issues* (pp. 783–805). New York: Jason Aronson.

Stuart, R. B., & Jacobson, B. (1987). *Couple therapy workbook.* Champaign, IL: Research Press.

Subby, R. (1984). Inside the chemically dependent marriage: Denial and manipulation. In *Co-dependency: An emerging issue* (pp. 25–30). Pompano Beach, FL: Health Communications.

Subby, R., & Friel, J. (1984). Co-dependency: A paradoxical dependency. In *Co-dependency: An emerging issue* (pp. 31–44). Pompano Beach, FL: Health Communications.

Tageson, C. W. (1982). *Humanistic psychology: A synthesis.* Homewood, IL: Dorsey Press.

Test, L. R. (1964). *A comparative study of four approaches to short-term psychotherapy.* Unpublished master's thesis, George Washington University, Washington, DC.

Ulrici, D. K. (1984). *An objective assessment of developmental stages of marital understanding.* Unpublished doctoral dissertation, Georgia State University, Atlanta.

Wallace, A. E. C. (1968). Identity processes in personality and culture. In R. Jessor & S. Feshbach (Eds.), *Cognition, personality, and clinical psychology.* San Francisco: Jossey-Bass.

Watson, D., & Clark, L. A. (1984). Negative affectivity: The disposition to experience aversive emotional states. *Psychological Bulletin, 96,* 465–490.

Weeks, G. R., & L'Abate, L. (1982). *Paradoxical psychotherapy: Theory and practice with individuals, couples, and families.* New York: Brunner/Mazel.

Wegscheider-Cruse, S. (1984). Co-dependency: The therapeutic void. In *Co-dependency: An emerging issue* (pp. 1–4). Pompano Beach, FL: Health Communications.

Weintraub, M. D. (1981). *Verbal behavior: Adaptations in psychopathology.* New York: Springer.

West, P. T. (1979). *Three models of training alcoholics in interpersonal communication skills: A comparative study.* Unpublished doctoral dissertation, University of Western Ontario, Ontario, Canada.

Whitfield, C. (1984). Co-dependency: An emerging problem among professionals. In *Co-dependency: An emerging issue* (pp. 45–54). Pompano Beach, FL: Health Communications.

Widroe, H., & Davidson, J. (1961). The use of directed writing in psychotherapy. *Bulletin of the Menninger Clinic, 25,* 110–119.

Williams, J. B. W., & Spitzer, R. L. (1984). *Psychotherapy research: Where are we and where should we go?* New York: Guilford.

Wilson, G. T. (1984). Behavior therapy. In R. J. Corsini (Ed.), *Current psychotherapies* (pp. 239–278). Itaska, IL: F. E. Peacock.

Wolf, K. M., & Garett, K. (1978). Critical thinking: A review of its current status. *Improving Human Performance Quarterly, 7,* 244–255.

Wolk, A., & Henley, A. (1970). *The right to lie: A psychological guide to the uses of deceit in everyday life.* New York: Peter Hayden.

Wrightsman, L. S. (1988). *Personality development in adulthood.* Newbury Park, CA: Sage.

Yelsma, P. (1984). Marital communication, adjustment and perceptual differences between "happy" and "counseling" couples. *American Journal of Family Therapy, 12,* 26–36.

Young, R. E. (Ed.). (1980). *Fostering critical thinking.* San Francisco: Jossey-Bass.

AUTHOR INDEX

SUBJECT INDEX